Teacher Edition

SCIENCE
Fusion

fusion [FYOO • zhuhn] a combination of two
or more things that releases energy

HOLT McDOUGAL

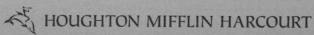

HOUGHTON MIFFLIN HARCOURT

Professional Development

Houghton Mifflin Harcourt and NSTA, the National Science Teacher's Association, have partnered to provide customized professional and development resources for teachers using *ScienceFusion*.

The Professional Development Resources in the NSTA Learning Center include:

—do-it-yourself resources, where you can study at your own pace.

—live and archived online seminars.

—journal articles, many of which include lesson plans.

—fee-based eBooks, eBook chapters, online short courses, symposia, and conferences.

Access to the NSTA Learning Center is provided in the *ScienceFusion* Online Resources.

Acknowledgments for Covers

Polar bear (bg) ©Mark Rodger-Snelson/Alamy; *false color x-rays on hand* (l) ©Lester Lefkowitz/Getty Images; *primate* (cl) ©Bruno Morandi/The Image Bank/Getty Images; *red cells* (cr) ©Todd Davidson/Getty Images; *fossils* (r) ©Yoshihi Tanaka/ amana Images/Getty Images.

Interior, digital screens: *giraffes* ©Corbis.

Printed in the U.S.A.

ISBN 978-0-547-59381-4

3 4 5 6 7 8 9 10 0914 20 19 18 17 16 15 14 13 12

4500379487   C D E F G

Contents in Brief

About the Program

Teaching Tools

Units at a Glance

Resources

Consulting Authors

Michael A. DiSpezio

Global Educator
North Falmouth, Massachusetts

Michael DiSpezio is a renaissance educator who moved from the research laboratory of a Nobel Prize winner to the K–12 science classroom. He has authored or coauthored numerous textbooks and written more than 25 trade books. For nearly a decade, he worked with the JASON Project under the auspices of the National Geographic Society, where he designed curriculum, wrote lessons, and hosted dozens of studio and location broadcasts.

Over the past two decades, he has developed supplementary material for organizations and shows that include PBS's *Scientific American Frontiers*, *Discover* magazine, and the Discovery Channel. He has extended his reach outside the United States and into topics of crucial importance today. To all his projects, he brings his extensive background in science and his expertise in classroom teaching at the elementary, middle, and high school levels.

Marjorie Frank

*Science Writer and
Content-Area Reading Specialist*
Brooklyn, New York

An educator and linguist by training, a writer and poet by nature, Marjorie Frank has authored and designed a generation of instructional materials in all subject areas, including past HMH Science programs. Her other credits include authoring science issues of an award-winning children's magazine; writing game-based digital assessments in math, reading, and language arts; and serving as instructional designer and coauthor of pioneering school-to-work software

for Classroom Inc., a nonprofit organization dedicated to improving reading and math skills for middle and high school learners. She wrote lyrics and music for *SCIENCE SONGS*, which was an American Library Association nominee for notable recording. In addition, she has served on the adjunct faculty of Hunter, Manhattan, and Brooklyn Colleges, teaching courses in science methods, literacy, and writing.

Michael R. Heithaus

Director, School of Environment and Society
Associate Professor, Department of Biological Sciences
Florida International University
North Miami, Florida

Mike Heithaus joined the Florida International University Biology Department in 2003. He has served as Director of the Marine Sciences Program and is now Director of the School of Environment and Society, which brings together the natural and social sciences and humanities to develop solutions to today's environmental challenges. While earning his doctorate, he began the research that grew into the Shark Bay Ecosystem Project in Western Australia, with which he still works. Back in the United States, he served as a Research Fellow with National Geographic, using remote imaging in his research and hosting a 13-part *Crittercam* television series on the National Geographic Channel. His current research centers on predator-prey interactions among vertebrates, such as tiger sharks, dolphins, dugongs, sea turtles, and cormorants.

Donna M. Ogle

Professor of Reading and Language
National-Louis University
Chicago, Illinois

Creator of the well-known KWL strategy, Donna Ogle has directed many staff development projects translating theory and research into school practice in middle and secondary schools throughout the United States. She is a past president of the International Reading Association and has served as a consultant on literacy projects worldwide. Her extensive international experience includes coordinating the Reading and Writing for Critical Thinking Project in Eastern Europe, developing an integrated curriculum for a USAID Afghan Education Project, and speaking and consulting on projects in several Latin American countries and in Asia. Her books include *Coming Together as Readers; Reading Comprehension: Strategies for Independent Learners; All Children Read;* and *Literacy for a Democratic Society*.

Program Reviewers

Content Reviewers

Paul D. Asimow, PhD
*Professor of Geology
and Geochemistry*
Division of Geological and Planetary Sciences
California Institute of Technology
Pasadena, CA

Laura K. Baumgartner, PhD
Postdoctoral Researcher
Molecular, Cellular, and Developmental Biology
University of Colorado
Boulder, CO

Eileen Cashman, PhD
Professor
Department of Environmental Resources Engineering
Humboldt State University
Arcata, CA

Hilary Clement Olson, PhD
Research Scientist Associate V
Institute for Geophysics, Jackson School of Geosciences
The University of Texas at Austin
Austin, TX

Joe W. Crim, PhD
Professor Emeritus
Department of Cellular Biology
The University of Georgia
Athens, GA

Elizabeth A. De Stasio, PhD
*Raymond H. Herzog Professor
of Science*
Professor of Biology
Department of Biology
Lawrence University
Appleton, WI

Dan Franck, PhD
Botany Education Consultant
Chatham, NY

Julia R. Greer, PhD
*Assistant Professor of Materials Science and
Mechanics*
Division of Engineering and Applied Science
California Institute of Technology
Pasadena, CA

John E. Hoover, PhD
Professor
Department of Biology
Millersville University
Millersville, PA

William H. Ingham, PhD
Professor (Emeritus)
Department of Physics and Astronomy
James Madison University
Harrisonburg, VA

Charles W. Johnson, PhD
*Chairman, Division of Natural Sciences,
Mathematics, and Physical Education*
Associate Professor of Physics
South Georgia College
Douglas, GA

Tatiana A. Krivosheev, PhD
Associate Professor of Physics
Department of Natural Sciences
Clayton State University
Morrow, GA

Joseph A. McClure, PhD
Associate Professor Emeritus
Department of Physics
Georgetown University
Washington, DC

Mark Moldwin, PhD
Professor of Space Sciences
Atmospheric, Oceanic, and Space Sciences
University of Michigan
Ann Arbor, MI

Russell Patrick, PhD
Professor of Physics
Department of Biology, Chemistry, and Physics
Southern Polytechnic State University
Marietta, GA

Patricia M. Pauley, PhD
Meteorologist, Data Assimilation Group
Naval Research Laboratory
Monterey, CA

Stephen F. Pavkovic, PhD
Professor Emeritus
Department of Chemistry
Loyola University of Chicago
Chicago, IL

L. Jeanne Perry, PhD
Director (Retired)
Protein Expression Technology Center
Institute for Genomics and Proteomics
University of California, Los Angeles
Los Angeles, CA

Kenneth H. Rubin, PhD
Professor
Department of Geology and Geophysics
University of Hawaii
Honolulu, HI

Brandon E. Schwab, PhD
Associate Professor
Department of Geology
Humboldt State University
Arcata, CA

Marllin L. Simon, Ph.D.
Associate Professor
Department of Physics
Auburn University
Auburn, AL

Larry Stookey, PE
Upper Iowa University
Wausau, WI

Kim Withers, PhD
Associate Research Scientist
Center for Coastal Studies
Texas A&M University-Corpus Christi
Corpus Christi, TX

Matthew A. Wood, PhD
Professor
Department of Physics & Space Sciences
Florida Institute of Technology
Melbourne, FL

Adam D. Woods, PhD
Associate Professor
Department of Geological Sciences
California State University, Fullerton
Fullerton, CA

Natalie Zayas, MS, EdD
Lecturer
Division of Science and Environmental Policy
California State University, Monterey Bay
Seaside, CA

Teacher Reviewers

Ann Barrette, MST
Whitman Middle School
Wauwatosa, WI

Barbara Brege
Crestwood Middle School
Kentwood, MI

Katherine Eaton Campbell, M Ed
Chicago Public Schools-Area 2 Office
Chicago, IL

Karen Cavalluzzi, M Ed, NBCT
Sunny Vale Middle School
Blue Springs, MO

Katie Demorest, MA Ed Tech
Marshall Middle School
Marshall, MI

Jennifer Eddy, M Ed
Lindale Middle School
Linthicum, MD

Tully Fenner
George Fox Middle School
Pasadena, MD

Dave Grabski, MS Ed
PJ Jacobs Junior High School
Stevens Point, WI

Amelia C. Holm, M Ed
McKinley Middle School
Kenosha, WI

Ben Hondorp
Creekside Middle School
Zeeland, MI

George E. Hunkele, M Ed
Harborside Middle School
Milford, CT

Jude Kesl
Science Teaching Specialist 6–8
Milwaukee Public Schools
Milwaukee, WI

Joe Kubasta, M Ed
Rockwood Valley Middle School
St. Louis, MO

Mary Larsen
Science Instructional Coach
Helena Public Schools
Helena, MT

Angie Larson
Bernard Campbell Middle School
Lee's Summit, MO

Christy Leier
Horizon Middle School
Moorhead, MN

Helen Mihm, NBCT
Crofton Middle School
Crofton, MDL

Jeff Moravec, Sr., MS Ed
Teaching Specialist
Milwaukee Public Schools
Milwaukee, WI

Nancy Kawecki Nega, MST, NBCT, PAESMT
Churchville Middle School
Elmhurst, IL

Mark E. Poggensee, MS Ed
Elkhorn Middle School
Elkhorn, WI

Sherry Rich
Bernard Campbell Middle School
Lee's Summit, MO

Mike Szydlowski, M Ed
Science Coordinator
Columbia Public Schools
Columbia, MO

Nichole Trzasko, M Ed
Clarkston Junior High School
Clarkston, MI

Heather Wares, M Ed
Traverse City West Middle School
Traverse City, MI

Power up with

SCIENCE Fusion

Print

The **Write-in Student Edition** teaches science content through constant **interaction** with the text.

Labs and Activities

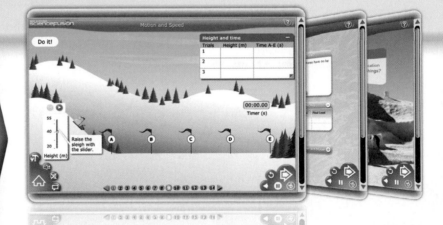

Motion, Forces, and Energy

Lab Manual

Digital

The parallel **Digital Curriculum** provides **e-learning digital lessons and virtual labs** for every print lesson of the program.

Energize your students through a multimodal blend of Print, Inquiry, and Digital experiences.

The **Hands-on Labs** and **Virtual Labs**

provide meaningful and exciting inquiry experiences.

Unit Assessment

Formative Assessment

Strategies RTI
Throughout TE

Lesson Reviews SE

Unit PreTest

Summative Assessment

Alternative Assessment
(1 per lesson) RTI

Lesson Quizzes

Unit Tests A and B

Unit Review RTI
(with answer remediation)

Practice Tests
(end of module)

Project-Based Assessment

🗒 *See the Assessment Guide for quizzes and tests.*

⊙ *Go Online to edit and create quizzes and tests.*

See RTI teacher support materials.

Print

The **Write-in Student Edition** teaches science content through constant **interaction** with the text.

Write-in Student Edition

360° of Inquiry

The *ScienceFusion* write-in student edition promotes a student-centered approach for

- **learning and applying inquiry skills in the student edition**

- **building STEM and 21st Century skills**

- **keeping digital natives engaged and interactive**

Research shows that an interactive text teaches students how to relate to content in a personal, meaningful way. They learn how to be attentive, energetic readers who reach a deep level of comprehension.

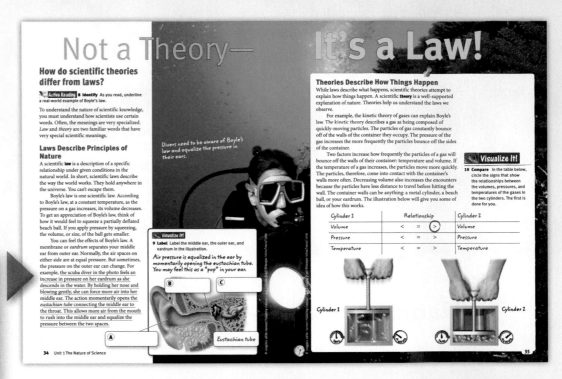

Big Ideas & Essential Questions

Each unit is designed to focus on a Big Idea and supporting lesson-level Essential Questions.

Connect Essential Questions

At the close of every unit, students build enduring understandings through synthesizing connections between different Essential Questions.

Active Reading

Annotation prompts and questions throughout the text teach students how to analyze and interact with content.

S.T.E.M.

STEM activities in every unit ask students to apply engineering and technology solutions in scenario-based learning situations.

Think Outside the Book

Students may wish to keep a Science Notebook to record illustrations and written work assignments. Blank pages at the end of each unit can also be used for this purpose.

Visualize It!

As concepts become more abstract, Visualize It! provides additional support for conceptual understanding.

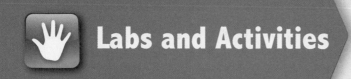

Labs and Activities

The **Hands-on Labs** and **Virtual Labs** provide meaningful and exciting inquiry experiences.

360° of Inquiry

Labs and Activities

S.T.E.M. Engineering & Technology

STEM activities in every unit focus on
- engineering and technology
- developing critical thinking and problem solving skills
- building inquiry, STEM, and 21st Century skills

Scenario-Based STEM Activity

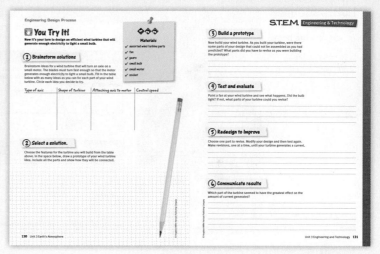

You Try It!

Hands-On and Virtual

Three levels—directed, guided, and independent—of labs and activities plus lesson level Virtual Labs give students wall-to-wall options for exploring science concepts and building inquiry skills.

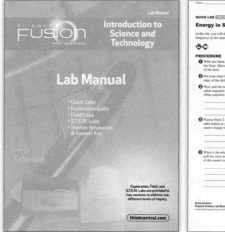

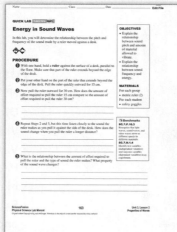

Hands-On Labs and Activities

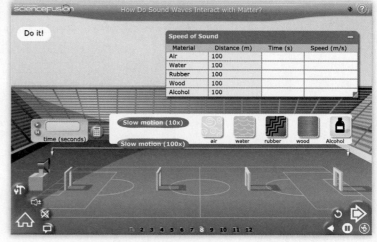

Virtual Lab

Digital Lessons and Virtual Labs

360° of Inquiry

Digital Lessons and Virtual Labs provide an e-Learning environment of interactivity, videos, simulations, animations, and assessment designed for the way digital natives learn. An online Student Edition provides students anytime access to their student book.

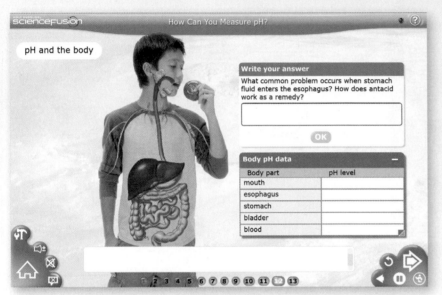

Digital Lessons

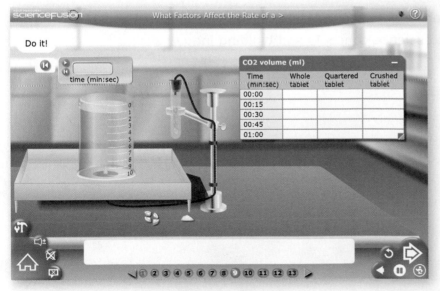

Virtual Labs

Online Student Edition

Video-Based Projects

Also available online:

- NSTA *SciLinks*
- Digital Lesson Progress Sheets
- Video-Based Projects
- Virtual Lab Datasheets
- People in Science Gallery
- Media Gallery
- Extra Support for Vocabulary and Concepts
- Leveled Readers

Classroom Management Integrated Assessment Options

The *ScienceFusion* assessment options give you maximum flexibility in assessing what your students know and what they can do. Both the print and digital paths include formative and summative assessment. See the **Assessment Guide** for a comprehensive overview of your assessment options.

Teacher Online Management Center

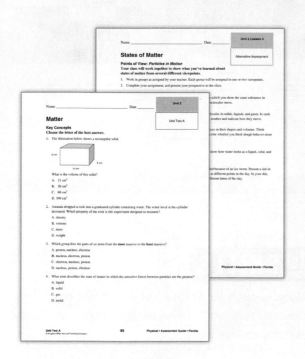

Print Assessment

The print **Assessment Guide** includes

- **Lesson Quizzes**
- **Unit Tests**
- **Unit Performance Assessments**

Online Assessment

The **Digital Assessment** includes

- **assignable leveled assessments for individuals**
- **customizable lesson quizzes and unit tests**
- **individual and whole class reporting**

Customizing Assessment for Your Classroom

Editable quizzes and tests are available in ExamView and online at ⊙ **thinkcentral.com.** You can customize a quiz or test by adding or deleting items, revising difficulty levels, changing formats, revising sequence, and editing items. Students can also take quizzes and tests directly online.

Choose Your Options

with two powerful teaching tools— a comprehensive
Teacher Edition and the **Teacher Online
Management Center.**

Classroom Management Teacher's Edition

Lesson level teaching support,
includes activities, probing
questions, misconception alerts,
differentiated instruction, and
interpreting visuals.

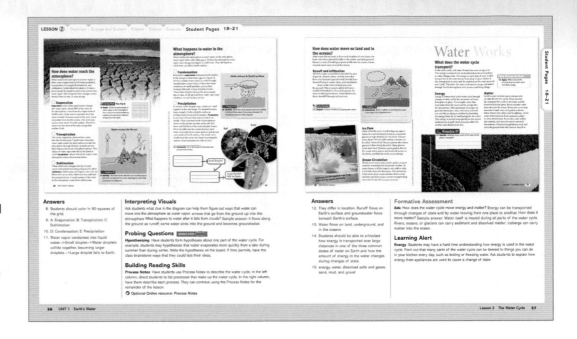

• Lessons organized around a
  5E lesson format

• Comprehensive support—print,
  digital, or hands-on—to match all
  teaching styles.

• Extension strategies for every
  lesson give teacher more tools to
  review and reinforce.

• Easy access to NSTA's e-professional development center,
  The Learning Center

• SciLinks provide students and teachers content-specific
  online support.

 **21st Century SKILLS**

Additional support for STEM activities focuses on
21st century skills and helping students master the multi-
dimensional abilities required of them in the 21st century.

 RTI ▶ Response to Intervention

Response to Intervention is a process for identifying and
supporting students who are not making expected progress
toward essential learning goals.

Probing Questions *Inquiry*

Lesson level questions and suggestions provide teachers
with options for getting students to think more deeply and
critically about a science concept.

 Professional Development

Unit and lesson level professional development focuses on
supporting teachers and building educator capacity in key
areas of academic achievement.

Learning Alert **MISCONCEPTION**

The Learning Alert section previews Inquiry Activities and
Lessons to gather and manage the materials needed for
each lesson.

Classroom Management
Online teaching and planning

ScienceFusion is a comprehensive, multimodal science program that provides all the digital tools teachers need to engage students in inquiry-based learning. *The Teacher Online Management Center,* at ⊙ **thinkcentral.com**, is designed to make it easier for teachers to access program resources to plan, teach, assess, and track.

▶ Program resources can be easily previewed in PDF format and downloaded for editing.

▶ Assign and schedule resources online, and they will appear in your students' inboxes.

▶ All quizzes and tests can be taken and automatically scored online.

▶ Easily monitor and track student progress.

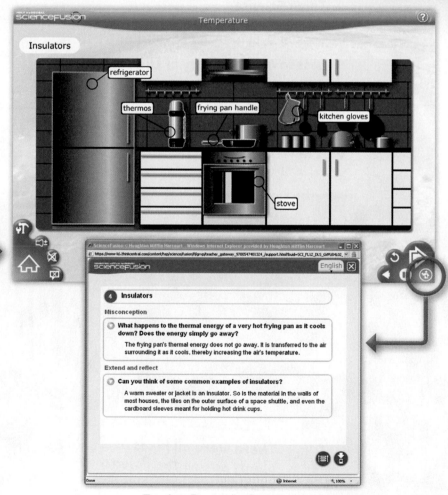

Teacher Resource Questions

Teaching with Technology Made Easy

ScienceFusion's 3,000+ animations, simulations, videos, & interactivities are organized to provide

▶ flexible options for delivering exciting and engaging digital lessons

▶ Teacher Resource Questions, for every lesson, to ensure that the important information is learned

▶ multimodal learning options that connect online learning to concepts learned from reading, writing, and hands-on inquiry

Student Edition Contents

Amber fossils form when small creatures become trapped in tree sap that hardens.

There were all kinds of plants during the Paleozoic era—all except flowering plants, that is, which hadn't developed yet.

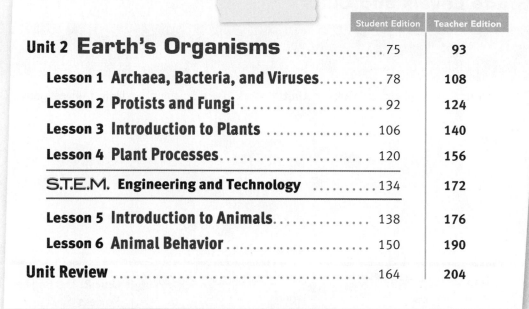

Back off! That's what male Anolis lizards mean when they puff out their colorful throat flaps.

It isn't a vegetable! Pangolins are animals. They use their long sticky tongues to gather ants and termites.

Assignments:
_____
_____
_____
_____
_____
_____
_____
_____
_____
_____
_____

Program Scope and Sequence

ScienceFusion is organized by five major strands of science. Each strand includes Big Ideas that flow throughout all grade levels and build in rigor as students move to higher grades.

ScienceFusion Grade Levels and Units

	GRADE K	GRADE 1	GRADE 2	GRADE 3
Nature of Science	**Unit 1** Doing Science	**Unit 1** How Scientists Work	**Unit 1** Work Like a Scientist	**Unit 1** Investigating Questions
STEM		**Unit 2** Technology All Around Us	**Unit 2** Technology and Our World	**Unit 2** The Engineering Process
Life Science	**Unit 2** Animals **Unit 3** Plants **Unit 4** Habitats	**Unit 3** Animals **Unit 4** Plants **Unit 5** Environments	**Unit 3** All About Animals **Unit 4** All About Plants **Unit 5** Environments for Living Things	**Unit 3** Plants and Animals **Unit 4** Ecosystems and Interactions

GRADE 4	GRADE 5	GRADES 6-8

Unit 1 Studying Science	**Unit 1** How Scientists Work	**Module K** Introduction to Science and Technology
		    Unit 1 The Nature of Science
		    Unit 2 Measurement and Data

Unit 2 The Engineering Process	**Unit 2** The Engineering Process	**Module K** Introduction to Science and Technology **Unit 3** Engineering, Technology, and Society

Unit 3 Plants and Animals
Unit 4 Energy and Ecosystems
	Unit 3 Cells to Body Systems
	Unit 4 Living Things Grow and Reproduce
	Unit 5 Ecosystems
	Unit 6 Energy and Ecosystems
		Module A Cells and Heredity
		    Unit 1 Cells
		    Unit 2 Reproduction and Heredity
		Module B The Diversity of Living Things
		    Unit 1 Life over Time
		    Unit 2 Earth's Organisms
		Module C The Human Body
		    Unit 1 Human Body Systems
		    Unit 2 Human Health
		Module D Ecology and the Environment
		    Unit 1 Interactions of Living Things
		    Unit 2 Earth's Biomes and Ecosystems
		    Unit 3 Earth's Resources
		    Unit 4 Human Impact on the Environment

ScienceFusion Grade Levels and Units

	GRADE K	GRADE 1	GRADE 2	GRADE 3
Earth Science	**Unit 5** Day and Night **Unit 6** Earth's Resources **Unit 7** Weather and the Seasons	**Unit 6** Earth's Resources **Unit 7** Weather and Seasons **Unit 8** Objects in the Sky	**Unit 6** Earth and Its Resources **Unit 7** All About Weather **Unit 8** The Solar System	**Unit 5** Changes to Earth's Surface **Unit 6** People and Resources **Unit 7** Water and Weather **Unit 8** Earth and Its Moon
Physical Science	**Unit 8** Matter **Unit 9** Energy **Unit 10** Motion	**Unit 9** All About Matter **Unit 10** Forces and Energy	**Unit 9** Changes in Matter **Unit 10** Energy and Magnets	**Unit 9** Matter **Unit 10** Simple and Compound Machines

GRADE 4	GRADE 5	GRADES 6-8
Unit 5 Weather	**Unit 7** Natural Resources	**Module E** The Dynamic Earth
Unit 6 Earth and Space	**Unit 8** Changes to Earth's Surface	**Unit 1** Earth's Surface
	Unit 9 The Rock Cycle	**Unit 2** Earth's History
	Unit 10 Fossils	**Unit 3** Minerals and Rocks
	Unit 11 Earth's Oceans	**Unit 4** The Restless Earth
	Unit 12 The Solar System and the Universe	**Module F** Earth's Water and Atmosphere
		Unit 1 Earth's Water
		Unit 2 Oceanography
		Unit 3 Earth's Atmosphere
		Unit 4 Weather and Climate
		Module G Space Science
		Unit 1 The Universe
		Unit 2 The Solar System
		Unit 3 The Earth-Moon-Sun System
		Unit 4 Exploring Space
Unit 7 Properties of Matter	**Unit 13** Matter	**Module H** Matter and Energy
Unit 8 Changes in Matter	**Unit 14** Light and Sound	**Unit 1** Matter
Unit 9 Energy	**Unit 15** Forces and Motion	**Unit 2** Energy
Unit 10 Electricity		**Unit 3** Atoms and the Periodic Table
Unit 11 Motion		**Unit 4** Interactions of Matter
		Unit 5 Solutions, Acids, and Bases
		Module I Motion, Forces, and Energy
		Unit 1 Motion and Forces
		Unit 2 Work, Energy, and Machines
		Unit 3 Electricity and Magnetism
		Module J Sound and Light
		Unit 1 Introduction to Waves
		Unit 2 Sound
		Unit 3 Light

![ScienceFusion icon] **ScienceFusion**

Video-Based Projects

🔘 **Available in Online Resources**

This video series, hosted by program authors Michael Heithaus and Michael DiSpezio, develops science learning through real-world science and engineering challenges.

Ecology

Leave your lab coat at home! Not all science research takes place in a lab. Host Michael Heithaus takes you around the globe to see ecology field research, including tagging sharks and tracking sea turtles. Students research, graph, and analyze results to complete the project worksheets.

Module	Video Title
A	Photosynthesis
B	Expedition Evolution Animal Behavior
D	A Trip Down Shark River The Producers of Florida Bay
E	Transforming Earth
I	Animals in Motion
J	Animals and Sound
K	Invaders in the Everglades Data from Space

S.T.E.M. Science, Technology, Engineering, and Math

Host Michael DiSpezio poses a series of design problems that challenge students' ingenuity. Each video follows the engineering process. Worksheets guide students through the process and help them document their results.

Module	Video Title
A	An Inside View**
C	Prosthetics Robotic Assist**
D	Got Water?
E	Seismic Monitoring
F	When the Wind Blows Tornado Warning
G	Soft Landing
H	Just Add Heat
I	Take the Long Way

** In partnership with Children's Hospital Of Boston

Enduring Understandings
Big Ideas, Essential Questions

It goes without saying that a primary goal for your students is to develop understandings of science concepts that endure well past the next test. The question is, what is the best way to achieve that goal?

by Marjorie Frank

Research and learning experts suggest that students learn most effectively through a constructivist approach in which they build concepts through active involvement in their own learning. While constructivism may lead to superior learning on a lesson-by-lesson basis, the approach does not address how to organize lessons into a program of instruction. Schema theory, from cognitive science, suggests that knowledge is organized into units and that information is stored in these units, much as files are stored in a digital or paper folder. Informed by our understanding of schema theory, we set about organizing *ScienceFusion*. We began by identifying the Big Ideas of science.

Big Ideas are generalizations—broad, powerful concepts that connect facts and events that may otherwise seem unrelated. Big Ideas are implicit understandings that help the world make sense. Big Ideas define the "folders," or units, of *ScienceFusion*. Each is a statement that articulates the overarching teaching and learning goals of a unit.

Essential Questions define the "files," or information, in a unit. Each Essential Question identifies the conceptual focus of a lesson that contributes to your students' growing understanding of the associated Big Idea. As such, Essential Questions give your students a sense of direction and purpose.

With *ScienceFusion*, our goal is to provide you with a tool that helps you help your students develop Enduring Understandings in science. Our strategy for achieving that goal has been to provide lesson plans with 5E-based learning experiences organized in a framework informed by schema theory.

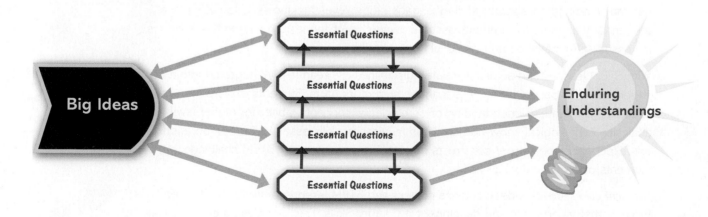

21st Century Skills/STEM

Skills Redefined

by Michael A. DiSpezio

Our world has changed. Globalization and the digital revolution have redefined the skill set that is essential for student success in the classroom and beyond. Known collectively as 21st Century Skills, these areas of competence and aptitude go beyond the three Rs of reading, writing, and arithmetic. 21st Century Skills incorporate a battery of high-level thinking skills and technological capabilities.

21st Century SKILLS A Sample List

Learning and Innovation Skills

- Creativity and Innovation
- Critical Thinking and Problem Solving
- Communication and Collaboration

Information, Media, and Technology Skills

- Information Literacy
- Media Literacy
- ICT (Information, Communications, and Technology) Literacy

Life and Career Skills

- Flexibility and Adaptability
- Initiative and Self-Direction
- Productivity and Accountability
- Leadership and Responsibility

S.T.E.M.

Curriculum that integrates Science, Technology, Engineering, and Mathematics

21st Century Skills are best taught in the context of the core subject areas. Science makes an ideal subject for integrating these important skills because it involves many skills, including inquiry, collaboration, and problem solving. An even deeper level of incorporating these skills can be found with Science, Technology, Engineering, and Mathematics (STEM) lessons and activities. Hands-on STEM lessons that provide students with engineering design challenges are ideal for developing Learning and Innovation Skills. Students develop creativity and innovation as they engineer novel solutions to posed problems. They communicate and collaborate as they engage higher-level thinking skills to help shape their inquiry experience. Students assume ownership of the learning. From this emerges increased self-motivation and personal accountability.

With STEM lessons and activities, related disciplines are seamlessly integrated into a rich experience that becomes far more than the sum of its parts. Students explore real-world scenarios using their understanding of core science concepts, ability for higher level analysis, technological know-how, and communication skills essential for collaboration. From this experience, the learner constructs not only a response to the STEM challenge, but the elements of 21st Century Skills.

ScienceFusion provides deep science content and STEM lessons, activities, and Video-Based Projects that incorporate and develop 21st Century Skills. This provides an effective learning landscape that will prepare students for success in the workplace—and in life.

Differentiated Instruction

Reaching All Learners

by Marjorie Frank

Your students learn in different ways, at different speeds, and through different means. Channeling the energy and richness of that diversity is part of the beauty of teaching. A classroom atmosphere that encourages academic risk-taking encourages learning. This is especially true in science, where learning involves making predictions (which could turn out to be inaccurate), offering explanations (which could turn out to be incomplete), and doing things (which could result in observable mistakes).

Like most people, students are more likely to take risks in a low-stress environment. Science, with its emphasis on exploring through hands-on activities and interactive reading, provides a natural vehicle for low-stress learning. Low stress, however, may mean different things to different people. For students with learning challenges, low stress may mean being encouraged to respond at the level they are able. Another factor in meeting the needs of diverse students is the instructional tools. Are they flexible? Inviting? *ScienceFusion* addresses the needs of diverse students at every step in the instructional process.

As You Plan

Select from these resources to meet individual needs.

- For each unit, the Differentiated Instruction page in the Teacher Edition identifies program resources specifically geared to diverse learners.

- Leveled activities in the Lesson Planning pages of the Teacher Edition provide additional learning opportunities for students with beginning, intermediate, or advanced proficiency.

- A bibliography contains notable trade books with in-depth information on content. Many of the books are recommendations of the National Science Teachers Association and the Children's Book Council.

- Online Resources: Alternative Assessment worksheets for each lesson provide varied strategies for learning content.

- Online Resources: Digital lessons, virtual labs, and video-based projects appeal to all students, especially struggling readers and visual learners.

- Student Edition with Audio is online as PDF files with audio readings for use with students who have vision impairments or learning difficulties.

- Student Edition reading strategies focus on vocabulary, concept development, and inquiry skills.

As You Teach

Take advantage of these point-of-use features.

- A mix of Directed Inquiry and Independent Inquiry prompts suitable for different kinds of learners

- Short-cut codes to specific interactive digital lessons

Take It Home

As you reach out to families, look for these school-home connections.

- Take It Home activities found at the beginning of many units in the Student Edition

- Additional Take It Home worksheets are available in the Online Resources

- School-Home Connection Letters for every unit, available online as files you can download and print as-is or customize

The 5E Model and Levels of Inquiry

How do students best learn science? Extensive research and data show that the most effective learning emerges from situations in which one builds understanding based upon personal experiences. Learning is not transmitted from instructor to passive receiver; instead, understanding is constructed through the experience.

by Michael A. DiSpezio

The 5E Model for Effective Science Lessons

In the 1960s, Robert Karplus and his colleagues developed a three-step instructional model that became known as the Learning Cycle. This model was expanded into what is today referred to as the 5E Model. To emulate the elements of how an actual scientist works, this model is broken down into five components for an effective lesson: Engage, Explore, Explain, Extend (or Elaborate), and Evaluate.

Engage—The engagement sets the scene for learning. It is a warm-up during which students are introduced to the learning experience. Prior knowledge is assessed and its analysis used to develop an effective plan to meet stated objectives. Typically, an essential question is then posed; the question leads the now motivated and engaged students into the exploration.

Explore—This is the stage where the students become actively involved in hands-on process. They communicate and collaborate to develop a strategy that addresses the posed problem. Emphasis is placed on inquiry and hands-on investigation. The hands-on experience may be highly prescribed or open-ended in nature.

Explain—Students answer the initial question by using their findings and information they may be reading about, discussing with classmates, or experiencing through digital media. Their experience and understanding of concepts, processes, and hands-on skills is strengthened at this point. New vocabulary may be introduced.

Extend (or Elaborate)—The explanation is now extended to other situations, questions, or problems. During this stage the learner more closely examines findings in terms of context and transferable application. In short, extension reveals the application and implication of the internalized explanation. Extension may involve connections to other curriculum areas.

Evaluate—Although evaluation is an ongoing process, this is the stage in which a final assessment is most often performed. The instructor evaluates lesson effectiveness by using a variety of formal and informal assessment tools to measure student performance.

The 5E lesson format is used in all the *ScienceFusion* Teacher Edition lessons.

Levels of Inquiry

It wasn't that long ago that science was taught mostly through demonstration and lecture. Today, however, most instructional strategies integrate an inquiry-based approach to learning science. This methodology is founded in higher-level thinking and facilitates the students' construction of understanding from experience. When offered opportunities to ask questions, design investigations, collect and analyze data, and communicate their findings, each student assumes the role of an active participant in shaping his or her own learning process.

The degree to which any activity engages the inquiry process is variable, from highly prescribed steps to a completely learner-generated design. Researchers have established three distinct levels of inquiry: directed (or structured) inquiry, guided inquiry, and independent (or open) inquiry. These levels are distinguished by the amount of guidance offered by the instructor.

DIRECTED inquiry

In this level of inquiry, the instructor poses a question or suggests an investigation, and students follow a prescribed set of instructions. The outcome may be unknown to the students, but it is known to the instructor. Students follow the structured outline to uncover an outcome that supports the construction of lesson concepts.

GUIDED inquiry

As in Directed Inquiry, the instructor poses to the students a question to investigate. While students are conducting the investigation, the instruction focuses on developing one or more inquiry skills. Focus may also be provided for students to learn to use methods or tools of science. In *ScienceFusion*, the Teacher Edition provides scaffolding for developing inquiry skills, science methods, or tools. Student pages accompany these lessons and provide prompts for writing hypotheses, recording data, and drawing conclusions.

INDEPENDENT inquiry

This is the most complex level of inquiry experience. A prompt is provided, but students must design their own investigation in response to the prompt. In some cases, students will write their own questions and then plan and perform scientific investigations that will answer those questions. This level of inquiry is often used for science fair projects. Independent Inquiry does not necessarily mean individual inquiry. Investigations can be conducted by individual students or by pairs or teams of students.

Response to Intervention

In a traditional model, assessment marks the end of an instructional cycle. Students work through a unit, take a test, and move on, regardless of their performance. However, current research suggests that assessment should be part of the instructional cycle, that it should be ongoing, and that it should be used to identify students needing intervention. This may sound like a tall order—who wants to give tests all the time?—but it may not be as difficult as it seems. In some ways, you are probably doing it already.

by Marjorie Frank

Assessment

Every student interaction has the potential to be an assessment. It all depends on how you perceive and use the interaction.

- Suppose you ask a question. You can just listen to your student's response, or you can assess it. Does the response indicate comprehension of the concept? If not, intervention may be needed.

- Suppose a student offers an explanation of a phenomenon depicted in a photo. You can assess the explanation. Does it show accurate factual knowledge? Does it reveal a misconception? If so, intervention may be needed.

- Suppose a student draws a diagram to illustrate a concept. You can assess the diagram. Is it accurate? If not, intervention may be needed.

As the examples indicate, assessing students' understandings can—and should—be an integral part of the instructional cycle and be used to make decisions about the next steps of instruction. For students making good progress, next steps might be exploring a related concept, a new lesson, or an additional challenge. For students who are not making adequate progress, intervention may be needed.

Assessment and intervention are tightly linked. Assessment leads to intervention—fresh approaches, different groupings, new materials—which, in turn, leads to assessment. Response to Intervention (RTI) gives shape and substance to this linkage.

RTI ▶ Response to Intervention

Response to Intervention is a process for identifying and supporting students who are not making expected progress toward essential learning goals.

RTI is a three-tiered approach based on an ongoing cycle of superior instruction, frequent monitoring of students' learning (assessments), and appropriate interventions. Students who are found not to be making expected progress in one Tier move to the next higher Tier, where they receive more intense instruction.

- **Tier I:** Students receive whole-class, core instruction.
- **Tier II:** Students work in small groups that supplement and reinforce core instruction.
- **Tier III:** Students receive individualized instruction.

How RTI and *ScienceFusion* Work

ScienceFusion provides many opportunities to assess students' understanding and many components appropriate for students in all Tiers.

TIER III Intensive Intervention

Individualized instruction, with options for auditory, visual, and second language learners. Special education is a possibility.

Differentiated Instruction Strategies

Online Student Edition

ScienceFusion Components

Online Student Edition lessons with audio recordings

Differentiated Instruction strategies in the Teacher Edition for every lesson

Appropriate for:
- Auditory learners

Appropriate for:
- Struggling readers
- Second-language learners

Students achieving at a lower level than their peers in Tier II

TIER II Strategic Intervention

Small Group Instruction in addition to core instruction

Leveled TE Activities

Alternative Assessment Worksheets

ScienceFusion Components

Leveled activities in the Lesson Planning pages of the Teacher Edition

Alternative Assessment Worksheets

Appropriate for:
- Struggling readers
- Visual learners
- Second-language learners
- Screening tools to assess students' responses to Tier II instruction

Students achieving at a lower level than their peers in Tier I

TIER I Core Classroom Instruction

With the help of extensive point-of-use strategies that support superior teaching, students receive whole-class instruction and engage productively in small-group work as appropriate.

Teacher Edition

Student Edition

Assessment Guide

ScienceFusion Components

Student Edition

Differentiated Instruction strategies in the TE for every lesson

Teacher Edition

Assessment Guide

Online Digital Curriculum

Appropriate for:
- Screening tools to assess students' responses to Tier I instruction
- Tier I intervention for students unable to complete the activity independently

Digital Curriculum

Active Reading

Reading is a complex process in which readers use their knowledge and experience to make meaning from text. Though rarely accompanied by obvious large-muscle movement, reading is very much an active endeavor.

by Marjorie Frank

Think back to your days as a college student when you pored over your textbooks to prepare for class or for an exam—or, more recently, concentrated on an article or book with information you wanted to remember.

▶ You probably paid close attention to the text.

▶ Perhaps you paused to ask yourself questions.

▶ You might have broken off temporarily to look up an important, but unfamiliar, word.

▶ You may have stopped to reread a challenging passage or to "catch up" if your mind wandered for a moment.

If you owned the reading material, you also may have used a pencil or marker to interact with the text right there on the page (or in a digital file).

In short, you were having a conversation with yourself about the text. You were engaged. You were thinking critically.

These are the characteristics of active readers. This is precisely the kind of reader you want your students to be, because research suggests that active reading enables readers to understand and remember more information.

Active Reading involves interacting with text cognitively, metacognitively, and quite literally. You can actually see active readers at work. They are not sitting quietly as they read; they're underlining, marking, boxing, bracketing, drawing arrows, numbering, and writing comments. Here is what they may be noting:

▶ key terms and main ideas

▶ connections between ideas

▶ questions they have, opinions, agreements, and disagreements

▶ important facts and details

▶ sequences of events

▶ words, such as *because, before,* and *but,* that signal connections between ideas

▶ problems/solutions

▶ definitions and examples

▶ characteristics

The very process of interacting actively with text helps keep readers focused, thinking, comprehending, and remembering. But interacting in this way means readers are marking up the text. This is exactly why *ScienceFusion* Student Editions are consumable. They are meant to be marked up.

Active Reading and *ScienceFusion*

ScienceFusion includes Active Reading prompts throughout the Student Editions. The prompts appear as part of the lesson opener and on most two-page spreads.

Students are often given an Active Reading prompt before reading a section or paragraph. These prompts ask students to underline certain words or number the steps in a process. Marking the text in this way is called *annotating*, and the students' marks are called *annotations*. Annotating the text can help students identify important concepts while reading. Other ways of annotating the text include placing an asterisk by vocabulary terms, marking unfamiliar or confusing terms and information with a question mark, and underlining main ideas. Students can even invent their own systems for annotating the text. An example of an annotation prompt is shown at right.

> **Active Reading** 5 **Identify** As you read, underline sources of energy for living things.

In addition, there are Active Reading questions throughout each lesson. These questions have write-on lines accompanying them, so students can answer right on the page. Students will be asked to **describe** what they've just read about, **apply** concepts, **compare** concepts, **summarize** processes, and **identify cause-and-effect** relationships. By answering these Active Reading questions while reading the text, students will be strengthening those and other critical thinking skills that are used so often in science.

> **Active Reading** 16 **Compare** What is the difference between the pulmonary and systemic circulations?

Students' Responses to Active Reading Prompts

Active Reading has benefits for you as well as for your students. You can use students' responses to Active Reading prompts and the other interactive prompts in *ScienceFusion* as ongoing assessments. A quick review of students' responses provides a great deal of information about their learning.

▶ Are students comprehending the text?

▶ How deeply do they understand the concepts developed?

▶ Did they get the main idea? the cause? the order in which things happen?

▶ Which part of a lesson needs more attention? for whom?

Answers to these questions are available in students' responses to Active Learning prompts throughout a lesson—long before you might see poor results on an end-of-lesson or end-of-unit assessment. If you are following Response to Intervention (RTI) protocols, these frequent and regular assessments, no matter how informal, are integral parts of an effective intervention program.

The Active Reading prompts in *ScienceFusion* help make everyone a winner.

Project-Based Learning

For a list of the *ScienceFusion* Video-Based Projects, see page xxii.

by
Michael R. Heithaus

When asked why I decided to become a biologist, the answer is pretty simple. I was inspired by spending almost every day outdoors, exploring under every rock, getting muddy in creeks and streams, and fishing in farm ponds, rivers, and—when I was really lucky—the oceans. Combine that with the spectacular stories of amazing animals and adventure that I saw on TV and I was hooked. As I've progressed in my career as a biologist, that same excitement and curiosity that I had as a ten-year-old looking for a salamander is still driving me.

But today's kids live in a very different world. Cable and satellite TV, Twitter, MP3 players, cell phones, and video games all compete with the outdoors for kids' time and attention. Education budget cuts, legal issues, and the pressures of standardized testing have also limited the opportunities for students to explore outdoors with their teachers.

How do we overcome these challenges so as to inspire kids' curiosity, help them connect with the natural world, and get them to engage in science and math? This is a critical issue. Not only do we need to ensure our national competitiveness and the conservation of our natural resources by training the next generation of scientists, we also need to ensure that every kid grows up to understand how scientists work and why their work is important.

To overcome these challenges, there is no question that we need to grab students' attention and get them to actively engage in the learning process. Research shows that students who are active and engaged participants in their learning have greater gains in concept and skills development than students who are passive in the classroom.

Project-based learning is one way to engage students. And when the stimulus for the project is exciting video content, engaged and active learning is almost guaranteed. Nothing captures a student's attention faster than exciting video. I have noticed that when my university students have video to accompany a lesson, they learn and retain the material better. It's no different for younger students! Videos need to do more than just "talk at" students to have a real impact. Videos need to engage students and require participation.

Teachers and students who use *ScienceFusion* video-based projects have noticed the following:

- The videos use captivating imagery, dynamic scientists, and cool stories to inspire kids to be curious about the world around them.
- Students connect to the projects by having the videos present interesting problems for them to solve.
- The videos engage students with projects woven into the story of the video so students are doing the work of real scientists!

The start-to-finish nature of the video projects, where students do background research and develop their own hypotheses, should lead to students' personal investment in solving the challenges that are presented. By seeing real scientists who are excellent role models gather data that they have to graph and interpret, students will not only learn the science standards being addressed, they will see that they can apply the scientific method to their lives. One day, they too could be a scientist!

Based on my experiences teaching in the university classroom, leading field trips for middle school students, and taking the first project-based videos into the classroom, project-based learning has considerable benefits. The video-based projects generate enthusiasm and curiosity. They also help students develop a deeper understanding of science content as well as how to go about a scientific investigation. If we inspire students to ask questions and seek answers for themselves, we will go a long way toward closing achievement gaps in science and math and facilitate the development of the next generation of scientists and scientifically literate citizens.

Developing Visual Literacy

Science teachers can build the bridges between students' general literacy and their scientific literacy by focusing attention on the particular kinds of reading strategies students need to be successful. One such strategy is that of knowing how to read and interpret the various visual displays used in science.

by Donna M. Ogle

Many young readers receive little instruction in reading charts, tables, diagrams, photographs, or illustrations in their language arts/reading classes. Science is where these skills can and must be developed. Science provides a meaningful context where students can learn to read visually presented forms of information and to create their own visual representations. Research studies have shown that students take longer to read science materials containing combinations of visual displays and narrative texts than they do to read narrative text alone. The process of reading the combination materials is slower and more difficult because the reader must relate the visual displays to the narrative text and build a meaning that is based on information from both.

We also know that students benefit when teachers take time to explain how each visual form is constructed and to guide students in the thinking needed to make sense of these forms. Even the seemingly simple act of interpreting a photograph needs to be taught to most students. Here are some ways to help students develop the ability to think more critically about what they view:

▶ Model for students how to look carefully at a photograph and list what they notice.

▶ Divide the photograph into quadrants and have students think more deeply about what the photographer has used as the focus of the image and what context is provided.

▶ Have students use language such as *zoom, close-up, foreground, background,* or *panorama views* to describe photographs.

The ability to interpret a photograph is clearly a part of the scientific skill of engaging in careful observation. This skill helps students when they are using print materials, observing nature, and making their own photographs of aspects of their experiments.

Attention to the other forms of visual displays frequently used in science is also important to students' learning of scientific concepts and processes. For example, students in grades 4 through 8 need to learn to interpret and then construct each of the types of graphs, from circle graphs and bar graphs to more complex line graphs.

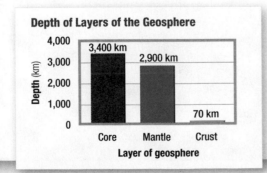

Depth of Layers of the Geosphere

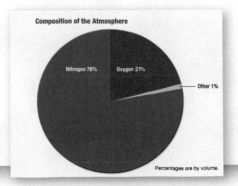

Composition of the Atmosphere

Students also need to be able to read diagrams and flow charts. Yet, in a recent study asking students to think aloud and point to how they visually scan tables and diagrams, we learned how inadequate many students were as readers of these visual forms. Because so much of the scientific information students will encounter is summarized in these visual formats, it is essential that students learn to interpret and construct visual displays.

A second aspect of interpreting visual displays is connecting the information in the visual formats with the narrative text information. Some students misinterpret what they see in visuals when even a few words differ between the text and the illustration. For example, in the excerpt below from a middle school Student Edition, the text says, "the arm of a human, the front leg of a cat, and the wing of a bat do not look alike . . . but they are similar in structure. "

The diagram labels (lower right) showing the bat wing and the cat's leg use *front limb*, not *wing* or *leg*. For students who struggle with English, the differing terms may cause confusion unless teachers show students how to use clues from later in the paragraph, where limb and wing/arm are connected, and how to connect this information to the two drawings. In some cases teachers have students draw lines showing where visual displays connect with the more extensive narrative text content. Developing students' awareness of how visual and narrative information support each other and yet provide different forms in which information can be shared is an important step in building scientific literacy.

Reading science requires students to use specific reading strategies. The more carefully science teachers across grade levels assess what students already know about reading scientific materials, the more easily they can focus instruction to build the scaffolds students need to gain independence and confidence in their reading and learning of science. Time spent explaining, modeling, and guiding students will yield the rewards of heightened student enjoyment, confidence, and engagement in the exciting world of scientific inquiry.

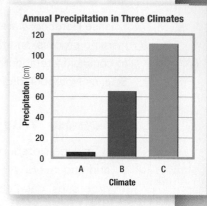

Annual Precipitation in Three Climates

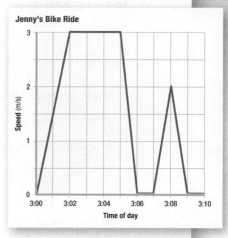

Jenny's Bike Ride

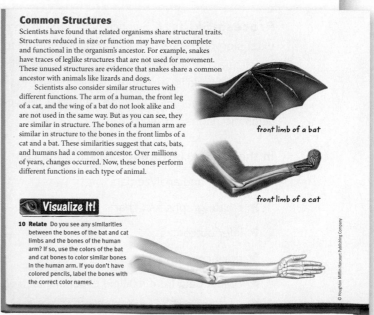

Common Structures

Scientists have found that related organisms share structural traits. Structures reduced in size or function may have been complete and functional in the organism's ancestor. For example, snakes have traces of leglike structures that are not used for movement. These unused structures are evidence that snakes share a common ancestor with animals like lizards and dogs.

Scientists also consider similar structures with different functions. The arm of a human, the front leg of a cat, and the wing of a bat do not look alike and are not used in the same way. But as you can see, they are similar in structure. The bones of a human arm are similar in structure to the bones in the front limbs of a cat and a bat. These similarities suggest that cats, bats, and humans had a common ancestor. Over millions of years, changes occurred. Now, these bones perform different functions in each type of animal.

front limb of a bat

front limb of a cat

Visualize It!

10 Relate Do you see any similarities between the bones of the bat and cat limbs and the bones of the human arm? If so, use the colors of the bat and cat bones to color similar bones in the human arm. If you don't have colored pencils, label the bones with the correct color names.

© Houghton Mifflin Harcourt Publishing Company

Science Notebooking

Science Notebooks are powerful classroom tools. They lead your students deep into the learning process, and they provide you with a window into that process as well as a means to communicate about it. Most middle-school students will have had some experience using a Science Notebook during their elementary years.

Notebook ▶ Why Use a Science Notebook?

A Science Notebook contains the writer's ideas, observations, and perceptions of events and endeavors. A Science Notebook also contains ideas and observations of scientific processes, data, conclusions, conjectures, and generalizations.

Inquiry Skills A Science Notebook is especially important when students do inquiry-based activities. It offers students a single place to record their observations, consider possibilities, and organize their thoughts. As such, it is a learner's version of the logs that professional scientists keep.

In their Science Notebooks, students can

▶ sketch their ideas and observations from experiments and field trips

▶ make predictions about what will happen in an experiment

▶ reflect on their work and the meaning they derived from experiments

▶ make inferences based on the data they have gathered

▶ propose additional experiments to test new hypotheses

▶ pose new questions based on the results of an activity or experiment

Process Skills A Science Notebook is an excellent extension of the textbook, allowing students to further practice and hone process skills. Students will not only apply these skills in relation to the specific science content they are learning, they will be gaining a deeper insight into scientific habits of mind.

In their Science Notebooks, students can

▶ record and analyze data

▶ create graphs and charts

▶ infer outcomes

▶ draw conclusions

▶ collect data from multiple experimental trials

▶ develop 21st Century organizational skills

A student's Science Notebook entry for a *ScienceFusion* Quick Lab
▼

Quick Lab: Balancing Act

Partner: Evan

Answers

2. Me: 12 adjustments
   Evan: 10 adjustments

3. No, I was not aware of my muscles making adjustments the first time. I think I didn't notice because I was concentrating more on just staying on one leg.

4. Yes, I was aware of my muscles making adjustments the second time. I think my muscles worked harder the second time because my leg was getting tired.

5. 12 times

6. Your body is always having to make adjustments to maintain a balanced internal environment. Most of these adjustments aren't even noticed by a person, just like I didn't notice my leg muscles adjusting during the first balancing test.

Notebook ▸ Science Notebooks and *ScienceFusion*

In many ways, the *ScienceFusion* worktexts are Science Notebooks in themselves. Students are encouraged to write answers directly in the text and to annotate the text for better understanding. However, a separate Science Notebook can still be an invaluable part of your student's learning experience with *ScienceFusion*. Student uses for a Science Notebook along with the worktext include:

▶ writing answers for the Unit Review

▶ writing responses to the Think Outside the Book features in each lesson

▶ planning for and writing answers to the Citizen Science feature in each unit

▶ working through answers before writing them in the worktext

▶ writing all answers if you choose not to have students work directly in the worktext

▶ taking notes on additional materials you present outside of the worktext

▶ making observations and recording data from Daily Demos and additional activities provided in the Teacher Edition

▶ collecting data and writing notes for labs performed from the Lab Manual

▶ making notes and writing answers for Digital Lessons and Virtual Labs

▶ collecting data and writing answers for the Project-Based Videos

Notebook ▸ The Benefits (for You and Your Students) of Science Notebooking

No doubt, it takes time and effort to help students set up and maintain Science Notebooks, not to mention the time it takes you to review them and provide meaningful feedback. The payoff is well worth it. Here's why:

Keeping a Science Notebook:

▶ leads each learner to engage with ideas

▶ engages students in writing—an active, thinking, analytical process

▶ causes students to organize their thinking

▶ provides students with multiple opportunities and modes to process new information

▶ makes learning experiences more personal

▶ provides students with a record of their own progress and accomplishments

▶ doubles as a study guide for formal assessments

▶ creates an additional vehicle for students to improve their reading and writing skills

As you and your students embrace Science Notebooking, you will surely find it to be an engaging, enriching, and very valuable endeavor.

Using the *ScienceFusion* Worktext

Research shows that an interactive text teaches students how to relate to content in a personal, meaningful way. They learn how to be attentive, energetic readers who reach a deep level of comprehension. Still, the worktext format may be new to you and your students. Below are some answers to questions—both pedagogical and practical—you may have about *ScienceFusion's* worktext format.

How does the worktext format help my students learn?

▶ In this format, your students will interact with the text and visuals on every page. This will teach them to read expertly, to think critically, and to communicate effectively—all skills that are crucial for success in the 21st century.

▶ The use of images and text on every page of the *ScienceFusion* worktext accommodates both visual and verbal learners. Students are engaged by the less formal, magazine-like presentation of the content.

▶ By the end of the school year, the worktexts become a record of the knowledge and skills your students learned in class. Students can use their books as a study guide to prepare for tests.

What are some features that make the *ScienceFusion* worktext different from a regular textbook?

Some of the special features of the *ScienceFusion* worktext include these prompts for writing directly in the worktext:

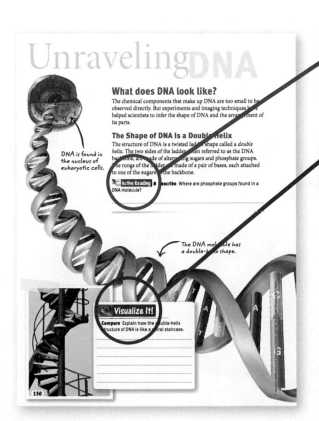

Active Reading

Annotation prompts and questions throughout the worktext teach students how to analyze and interact with content as they read.

Visualize It!

Questions and completion prompts that accompany images help develop visual literacy.

Engage Your Brain

Math problems, with on-page guidance, allow students to understand the relationships between math and science and to practice their math skills.

Do the Math

Interesting questions and activities on the lesson opener pages help prepare students for the lesson content.

Are my students really supposed to write directly in the book?

Yes! Write-on lines are provided for students to answer questions on-page, while the student is reading. Additional prompts are given for students to annotate the pages. You can even encourage your students to experiment with their own systems of annotation. More information can be found in "A How-To Manual for Active Reading" in the Look It Up! Section at the end of the Student Edition and Teacher Edition.

You might wish to encourage your students to write in the worktexts using pencils so that they can more easily revise their answers and notes as needed.

We will have to use the same set of worktexts for several years. How can students use the worktexts if they can't write in them?

Though *ScienceFusion* is set up in a worktext format, the books can still be used in a more traditional fashion. Simply tell your students that they cannot write in the textbooks but should instead use their Science Notebooks for taking notes and answering questions. (See the article titled "Science Notebooking" for more information about using Notebooks with *ScienceFusion*.)

How do I grade my students' answers in the worktext?

The pages in the worktext are conveniently perforated so that your students can turn in their work. Or you may wish for your students to leave the pages in the book, but turn in the books to you on a daily or weekly basis for you to grade them.

The Lesson Reviews and Unit Reviews are designed so students can turn in the pages but still keep their annotated pages for reference when moving on to the next lesson or unit or for review before a lesson or unit test.

- Tour the classroom while students are writing in their worktexts. Address any issues you see immediately or make note of items that need to be addressed with students later.

- Have students do 'self checks' and 'partner checks.' Choose a question in the worktext, and have all students check their responses. Or, have students trade their worktext with a partner to check each other's responses.

- Once a week, have students copy five questions and their responses from the worktext onto a sheet of notebook paper. You can review student answers to ensure they're using the worktext correctly without having students turn in worktext pages or the books themselves.

- Use a document camera to show students correct worktext answers.

- Every two weeks, review and grade one class's worth of student worktext answers per day. Or, grade a class's worktexts while the students are taking a test.

Pacing Guide

You have options for covering the lesson materials: you may choose to follow the digital path, the print path, or a combination of the two. Customize your Pacing Guide to plan print, inquiry, digital, and assessment mini-blocks based on your teaching style and classroom needs.

Pressed for Time? Follow the faster-paced compressed schedule.

	Total Days			Customize Your Pacing Guide			
	Traditional 1 = 45 min	Block 1 = 90 min	Compressed (T/B)	Print Path	Inquiry Labs & Activities	Digital Path	Review & Assess
UNIT 1 Life over Time							
Unit Project	3	1.5	3 (1.5)				
Lesson 1 Introduction to Living Things	4	2	3 (1.5)				
Lesson 2 Theory of Evolution by Natural Selection	5	2.5	4 (2)				
Lesson 3 Evidence of Evolution	4	2	3 (1.5)				
Lesson 4 The History of Life on Earth	5	2.5	4 (2)				
Lesson 5 Classification of Living Things	6	3	5 (2.5)				
Unit Review	2	1	1 (0.5)				
Total Days for Unit 1	29	14.5	23 (11.5)				
UNIT 2 Earth's Organisms							
Unit Project	3	1.5	3 (1.5)				
Lesson 1 Archaea, Bacteria, and Viruses	6	3	5 (2.5)				
Lesson 2 Protists and Fungi	6	3	5 (2.5)				
Lesson 3 Introduction to Plants	6	3	5 (2.5)				
Lesson 4 Plant Processes	6	3	5 (2.5)				
Lesson 5 Introduction to Animals	5	2.5	4 (2)				
Lesson 6 Animal Behavior	5	2.5	4 (2)				
Unit Review	2	1	1 (0.5)				
Total Days for Unit 2	39	19.5	32 (16)				

The Big Idea and Essential Questions

This Unit was designed to focus on this Big Idea and Essential Questions.

Big Idea **The types and characteristics of organisms change over time.**

Lesson	ESSENTIAL QUESTION	Student Mastery	 Professional Development	Lesson Overview
LESSON 1 Introduction to Living Things	**What are living things?**	To describe the necessities of life and the characteristics of living things	Content Refresher, TE p. 6	TE p. 14
LESSON 2 Theory of Evolution by Natural Selection	**What is the theory of evolution by natural selection?**	To describe the role of genetic and environmental factors in the theory of evolution by natural selection	Content Refresher, TE p. 7	TE p. 28
LESSON 3 Evidence of Evolution	**What evidence supports the theory of evolution?**	To describe the evidence that supports the theory of evolution by natural selection	Content Refresher, TE p. 8	TE p. 44
LESSON 4 The History of Life on Earth	**How has life on Earth changed over time?**	To describe evolution of life on Earth, using the geologic time scale	Content Refresher, TE p. 9	TE p. 58
LESSON 5 Classification of Living Things	**How are organisms classified?**	To describe how living things can be grouped by shared characteristics	Content Refresher, TE p. 10	TE p. 74

©Sinclair Stammers/Photo Researchers, Inc.

Professional Development **Science Background**

Use the key words at right to access

- Professional Development from **The NSTA Learning Center**
- **SciLinks** for additional online content appropriate for students and teachers

Key words

classification   extinction

evolution   natural selection

National Science Teachers Association

SCiLINKS®
THE WORLD'S A CLICK AWAY

Options for Instruction

Two parallel paths provide coverage of the Essential Questions, with a strong **Inquiry** strand woven into each. Follow the **Print Path,** the **Digital Path,** or your customized combination of print, digital, and inquiry.

	LESSON 1 Introduction to Living Things	LESSON 2 Theory of Evolution by Natural Selection	LESSON 3 Evidence of Evolution
Essential Questions	**What are living things?**	**What is the theory of evolution by natural selection?**	**What evidence supports the theory of evolution?**
Key Topics	• Characteristics of Living Things • Needs of Living Things	• Darwin's Observations • Natural Selection • Extinction and Environmental Change	• Fossil Evidence • Structural Evidence • Genetic Evidence • Embryological Evidence
Print Path	**Teacher Edition** pp. 14–27 **Student Edition** pp. 4–13	**Teacher Edition** pp. 28–41 **Student Edition** pp. 14–25	**Teacher Edition** pp. 44–57 **Student Edition** pp. 28–37
Inquiry Labs	**Lab Manual** **Quick Lab** Is a Clock Alive? **Quick Lab** The Needs of Producers, Consumers, and Decomposers	**Lab Manual** ☐ **Virtual Lab** Natural Selection **Exploration Lab** Environmental Change and Evolution	**Lab Manual** **Field Lab** Mystery Footprints **Quick Lab** Comparing Anatomy **Quick Lab** Genetic Evidence for Evolution
Digital Path	**Digital Path** TS673055	**Digital Path** TS673014	**Digital Path** TS673000

LESSON 4 This History of Life on Earth	**LESSON 5** Classification of Living Things	**UNIT 1** Unit Projects
How has life on Earth changed over time?	**How are organisms classified?**	**Citizen Science Project** Prehistoric Life Teacher's Edition p. 13 Student Edition pp. 2–3
• Fossil Record • Geologic Time Scale • The Precambrian and the Paleozoic • The Mesozoic and Cenozoic Eras	• Classification • Domains, Kingdoms, and Levels • Branching Diagrams and Dichotomous Keys	**Video-Based Projects** Expedition Evolution

		Unit Assessment
Teacher Edition pp. 58–71 **Student Edition** pp. 38–49	**Teacher Edition** pp. 74–89 **Student Edition** pp. 52–67	**Formative Assessment** **Strategies** `RTI` Throughout TE **Lesson Reviews** SE **Unit PreTest** **Summative Assessment** **Alternative Assessment** (1 per lesson) `RTI`
Lab Manual **Quick Lab** How do We Know What Happened When? **Quick Lab** Investigate Relative and Absolute Age	**Lab Manual** **Virtual Lab** Similarities in Animals **Exploration Lab** Developing Scientific Names	**Lesson Quizzes** **Unit Tests A and B** **Unit Review** `RTI` (with answer remediation) **Practice Tests** (end of module) **Project-Based Assessment** See the Assessment Guide for quizzes and tests.
Digital Path TS673208 	**Digital Path** TS663325 	Go Online to edit and create quizzes and tests. **Response to Intervention** See RTI teacher support materials on p. PD6.

Differentiated Instruction

English Language Proficiency

Strategies for **English Language Learners (ELL)** are provided for each lesson, under the Explain tabs.

LESSON 1 *Stimulus and Homeostasis*, TE p. 19

LESSON 2 *Evolution Terms*, TE p. 33

LESSON 3 *Picture Dictionary*, TE p. 49

LESSON 4 *Venn Diagram*, TE p. 63

LESSON 5 *Animal Books*, TE p. 79

Vocabulary strategies provided for all students can also be a particular help for ELL. Use different strategies for each lesson or choose one or two to use throughout the unit. Vocabulary strategies can be found under the Explain tab for each lesson (TE pp. 19, 33, 49, 63, and 79).

Leveled Inquiry

Inquiry labs, activities, probing questions, and daily demos provide a range of inquiry levels. Preview them under the Engage and Explore tabs starting on TE pp. 16, 30, 46, 60, and 76.

Levels of **Inquiry**

DIRECTED inquiry	**GUIDED** inquiry	**INDEPENDENT** inquiry
introduces inquiry skills within a structured framework.	develops inquiry skills within a supportive environment.	deepens inquiry skills with student-driven questions or procedures.

Each long lab has two inquiry options:

LESSON 2 **Exploration Lab** *Environmental Change and Evolution* Directed or Guided Inquiry

LESSON 3 **Field Lab** *Mystery Footprints* Directed or Guided Inquiry

LESSON 5 **Exploration Lab** *Developing Scientific Names* Directed or Guided Inquiry

Go Digital! **thinkcentral.com**

Digital Path

The Unit 1 Resource Gateway is your guide to all of the digital resources for this unit. To access the Gateway, visit thinkcentral.com.

Digital Interactive Lessons

Lesson 1 Introduction to Living Things TS673055

Lesson 2 The Theory of Evolution by Natural Selection TS673014

Lesson 3 Evidence of Evolution TS673000

Lesson 4 The History of Life on Earth TS673208

Lesson 5 Classification of Living Things TS663325

More Digital Resources

In addition to digital lessons, you will find the following digital resources for Unit 1:

Video-Based Project: Expedition Evolution (previewed on TE p. 13)

Virtual Labs: Natural Selection (previewed on TE p. 31) **Similarities in Animals** (previewed on TE p. 77)

RTI ▶ Response to Intervention

Response to Intervention (RTI) is a process for identifying and supporting students who are not making expected progress toward essential learning goals. The following *ScienceFusion* components can be used to provide strategic and intensive intervention.

Component	Location	Strategies and Benefits
STUDENT EDITION Active Reading prompts, Visualize It!, Think Outside the Book	**Throughout each lesson**	Student responses can be used as screening tools to assess whether intervention is needed.
TEACHER EDITION Formative Assessment, Probing Questions, Learning Alerts	**Throughout each lesson**	Opportunities are provided to assess and remediate student understanding of lesson concepts.
TEACHER EDITION Extend Science Concepts	**Reinforce and Review, TE pp. 20, 34, 50, 64, 80** **Going Further, TE pp. 20, 34, 50, 64, 80**	Additional activities allow students to reinforce and extend their understanding of lesson concepts.
TEACHER EDITION Evaluate Student Mastery	**Formative Assessment, TE pp. 21, 35, 51, 65, 81** **Alternative Assessment, TE pp. 21, 35, 51, 65, 81**	These assessments allow for greater flexibility in assessing students with differing physical, mental, and language abilities as well as varying learning and communication modes.
TEACHER EDITION Unit Review Remediation	**Unit Review, TE pp. 90–92**	Includes reference back to Lesson Planning pages for remediation activities and assignments.
INTERACTIVE DIGITAL LESSONS and VIRTUAL LABS	**thinkcentral.com** **Unit 1 Gateway** **Lesson 1 TS673055** **Lesson 2 TS673014** **Lesson 3 TS673000** **Lesson 4 TS673208** **Lesson 5 TS663325**	Lessons and labs make content accessible through simulations, animations, videos, audio, and integrated assessment. Useful for review and reteaching of lesson concepts.

Content Refresher

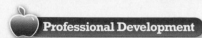
Professional Development

Introduction to Living Things
ESSENTIAL QUESTION
What are living things?

1. Characteristics of Living Things

Students will learn that all living things are made of cells, respond to change, reproduce, have DNA, use energy, and grow and develop.

Specialized cells have different structures and functions, but these structures and functions are similar in most organisms. For example, muscle cells in humans are similar to muscle cells in most mammals, such as horses.

Organisms reproduce asexually, sexually, or both. In asexual reproduction, a single parent produces offspring that are genetically identical to the parent. Methods of asexual reproduction include simple mitotic division (as in unicellular eukaryotic protists), budding (as in the multicellular animal hydra), and propagation from cuttings (as in Coleus plants). One advantage of asexual reproduction is the ability to reproduce without the assistance of another organism. One disadvantage of asexual reproduction is that the offspring are genetically identical to the parent, which can mean the offspring are less likely to survive a major environmental change.

During sexual reproduction, sex cells from two parents combine to form offspring that are similar to but not genetically identical to either parent. In some cases, a single organism may supply both sex cells. When this occurs in flowering plants, the process is called self-pollination. Sexual reproduction results in offspring that have a genome that is different from the parents. This can be an advantage, as more offspring are likely to be born with traits that help them to survive if the environment changes. However, sexual reproduction has disadvantages, too: it requires two parents and can result in fewer offspring than asexual reproduction.

All of the chemical reactions that take place within an organism make up the organism's metabolism. Metabolism encompasses thousands of chemical reactions, most of which occur along specific metabolic pathways. These pathways are controlled by enzymes, which speed up the rate of metabolic reactions. Metabolism is primarily concerned with the material and energy needs of the cell. Catabolic pathways, such as cellular respiration, result in the breakdown of molecules, often to release energy for use by the cell. Anabolic pathways, such as protein synthesis, consume energy to build molecules. The energy and materials released by catabolic pathways are used by the anabolic pathways. The form of energy involved in metabolic processes is chemical energy, and is sometimes called chemical potential energy. Chemical energy is stored in the bonds between the atoms in the molecules. When these bonds are broken, the chemical energy is converted to kinetic energy, and some of it is lost as heat.

2. Needs of Living Things

Students will learn that most living things need water, air, food, and a place to live.

The cells of all living organisms are made up mostly of water. Water plays an important role in metabolic reactions, both as a component of the medium in which these reactions take place and as a reactant. For example, water combines with carbon dioxide to produce carbohydrates during photosynthesis.

Air is a mixture of gases, including oxygen, nitrogen, and carbon dioxide, that enables organisms to perform vital life functions. Nearly all food chains on Earth depend on photosynthetic organisms. These organisms need carbon dioxide for photosynthesis. Without air, plants cannot produce the nutrients on which they and other organisms depend. In turn, most animals need the oxygen in air to break down food molecules for energy.

Food provides organisms with energy and the materials for building proteins and replacing or repairing cells. The materials in foods that are most important to organisms are carbohydrates, proteins, fats, vitamins, and minerals. Cells use carbohydrates to produce energy and to build proteins.

Teacher to Teacher

Sabine Laser
St. Cloud Middle School
St. Cloud, FL

Lesson 2 Theory of Evolution by Natural Selection   Students often have difficulty understanding natural selection unless they relate the concept to a familiar organism. For my students in Florida, I ask, "What would likely happen to a population of alligators if they were suddenly white instead of green?" Students recognize that the population might decrease fairly quickly, as alligators' green color is an adaptation that helps them survive in the current environment.

Lesson 2

Theory of Evolution by Natural Selection
ESSENTIAL QUESTION
What is the theory of evolution by natural selection?

1. Darwin's Observations

Students will learn how living things evolve.

English naturalist Charles Darwin (1809–1882) originated the theory of evolution by natural selection. In 1831, he began a voyage aboard the HMS *Beagle* to map the coastline of South America. On the trip, he explored the Galápagos Islands and collected specimens of the wildlife, including finches. Later, he observed that the beaks of the islands' finches differed slightly from island to island. Darwin concluded that the birds' beaks were likely modifications for different uses. Eventually, Darwin reasoned that these adaptations evolved from a population of common ancestors of today's finches (from the South American mainland). Scientists later confirmed that the birds' beaks were adaptations to different food sources on the various islands.

Darwin was influenced by existing ideas. These included naturalist Jean-Baptiste Lamarck's ideas about an organism's ability to adapt to its environment, geologist Charles Lyell's ideas related to uniformitarianism, and economist Thomas Malthus's ideas about population growth.

©William Leaman/Alamy Images

2. Natural Selection

Students will learn about the four processes that drive natural selection.

Darwin thought that the mechanism through which evolution occurs is natural selection. Natural selection is the process by which organisms that inherit advantageous traits tend to survive and reproduce more successfully than organisms that do not. Natural selection is comprised of four main parts:

- **Overproduction** Organisms produce more offspring than will survive to reproduce.
- **Genetic Variation** Individuals within a population have differences in traits, such as height and eye color.
- **Adaptation** Some inherited traits help organisms survive and reproduce in their environments.
- **Selection** Individuals with adaptations are more likely to outcompete less adapted individuals by increased survival and reproduction.

3. Extinction and Environmental Change

Students will learn about how species change over time.

Individuals with adaptations that are useful in a particular environment are more likely to survive and pass these traits to their offspring. After many generations, these adaptations become more common in the population.

Environmental change can prompt the extinction of a species if no members have adaptations that allow them to survive and reproduce in the changing environment. In some cases, however, extinctions occur due to natural disasters despite individuals' adaptations.

 COMMON MISCONCEPTIONS   **RTI**

THE "SELECTION" OF TRAITS Students may think that evolution results from an intent to change on the part of the species. Emphasize that natural selection is the process that results in evolutionary changes over many generations. The environmental

"selection" that occurs in this process is not a purposeful selecting of traits for survival in the environment.

This misconception is addressed in the Exploration Lab on p.31 and the Quick Lab Model Natural Selection on p. 39.

Content Refresher (continued)

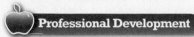 **Professional Development**

Evidence of Evolution

ESSENTIAL QUESTION
What evidence supports the theory of evolution?

1. Fossil Evidence

The fossil record is the history of life in the geologic past as preserved in fossils.

Sedimentary rocks hold important information about the history of life on Earth. Some ancient organisms that lived in or were buried by sediment were preserved as fossils when the sediment hardened into rock. Many organisms, such as dinosaurs, are only known to us because of fossil evidence. The process of fossilization preserves evidence of ancient life forms, and geologic interpretation of the enclosing sedimentary rock yields valuable information about the environments and relative time periods in which those ancient organisms lived. Fossils may be complete organisms or other evidence that the organism existed, such as footprints. Many fossils are impressions of hard parts only, because soft tissue usually decays before it has a chance to fossilize.

The fossil record organizes fossils by their estimated ages (based on data gathered through relative and radiometric dating) and physical similarities. Scientists use this knowledge and evidence in the fossil record to hypothesize the relationships between extinct and living organisms. The evolutionary history of a species, which tells the characteristics of the various species from which it descended, together with a species's genealogical relationship to every other species, is called its phylogeny. Diagrams called phylogenetic trees show which group of species evolved from a different group of species.

A transitional form between fish and four-legged land vertebrates may be this creature called *Tiktaalik roseae*.

2. Structural Evidence

Comparative anatomists study similarities and differences among organisms.

Anatomists have discovered significant similarities in the skeletal architecture and anatomical structures of vertebrates, from fish to humans. The most plausible explanation for this finding is that all vertebrates descended from a common ancestor. Studies of anatomical structures have led to the discovery of vestigial structures, structures that seem to serve little to no function for an organism but resemble structures with functional roles in related organisms. Vestigial structures are evidence that organisms have changed over time.

3. Genetic Evidence

Molecular biology has contributed much evidence in support of the theory of evolution.

Today, DNA sequencing allows scientists to compare the genetic codes of different organisms. Roundworms, for example, share close to 25% of their genes with humans. Scientists theorize that the greater the number of similarities between the DNA of any two species, the more recently that the two species shared a common ancestor. Scientists also compare the RNA, proteins, and other molecules of organisms to uncover molecular similarities.

4. Embryological Evidence

Embryos provide evidence of evolution.

Most scientists believe the development of embryos provides evidence for the evolutionary history of organisms. For example, at some time in their development, all vertebrate embryos have tail buds that become limbs, and pharyngeal pouches. The tail remains in most adult vertebrates, but only fish and immature amphibians retain pharyngeal pouches (which contain their gills). In other vertebrates, these pouches develop into the tissues that form the inner ear, sinuses, thymus gland, and other necessary organs. The more closely organisms share patterns of development, the more recently they have descended from a common ancestor.

The History of Life on Earth

ESSENTIAL QUESTION
How has life on Earth changed over time?

1. Fossil Record

Students will learn that scientists study the fossil record to understand the evolution of life on Earth.

Scientists study fossils dating as far back as 3.8 billion years for clues about what life on Earth was once like. After excavating these traces and imprints of ancient life, scientists use two different methods to date the fossils:

- Relative dating is used to estimate the relative age of a fossil by examining its position in layers of rock.
- Absolute dating is used to determine the age of a fossil in years through radiometric analysis of the rocks that surround it.

Along with chronicling life on Earth, the fossil record also depicts when, and sometimes how, species originate and then become extinct. Mass extinctions are also documented in the fossil record.

©Alamy Images

2. Geologic Time Scale

Students will learn that the geologic time scale is broken into units of time characterized by different conditions and ecosystems.

The geologic time scale breaks Earth's long natural history into units; from largest to smallest, these units are eons, eras, periods, and epochs. The four major divisions of the geologic time scale are Precambrian time, the Paleozoic era, the Mesozoic era, and the Cenozoic era. The geologic time scale is often presented as a vertical table that is read from the bottom up, mimicking how layers of sedimentary rock form, with the oldest layers on the bottom and the most recent at the top.

3. The Precambrian and the Paleozoic

Students will learn that life forms first appeared during Precambrian time and grew more complex during the Paleozoic.

Although Precambrian time covers about 80 percent of Earth's history, little is known about this first time period. Earth formed from dust and gas orbiting the sun, and then cooled down and developed a solid crust. Oceans formed from water vapor. The first life—single-celled prokaryotes—appeared in oceans at least 3.8 billion years ago.

More complex prokaryotes called *cyanobacteria* released oxygen into the atmosphere as a byproduct of photosynthesis. As atmospheric oxygen levels increased, so did the complexity of life, with the evolution of multicellular organisms. However, increased oxygen levels also led to the extinction of some organisms for which oxygen was toxic.

During the Paleozoic era, hard-shelled organisms and vertebrates evolved, including amphibians and reptiles. In this productive period, a rich assortment of plants and animals became established in terrestrial ecosystems. A mass extinction towards the end of the era resulted in the extinction of nearly 90 percent of marine species.

4. The Mesozoic and Cenozoic Eras

Students will learn that living things evolved, diversified, and colonized land during the Mesozoic and Cenozoic.

Life recovered during the Mesozoic era, and dinosaurs dominated Earth. In this "Age of Reptiles," the dinosaurs ruled, but birds and mammals also appeared, as did flowering plants. Another mass extinction at the end of the era, about 65 million years ago, wiped out the dinosaurs.

The demise of the dinosaurs provided an opportunity for the mammals to evolve and flourish, and they became an astonishingly diverse group. Primates and hominids appeared during the Cenozoic. Modern humans have evolved during the Holocene epoch of this era, the last 10,000 years.

Content Refresher (continued)

Lesson 5

Classification of Living Things

ESSENTIAL QUESTION
How are organisms classified?

1. Classification

Students will learn that organisms are classified by physical and genetic characteristics and have two-part names.

In the 1700s, Swedish scientist Carolus Linnaeus developed the classification system we use today. He gave each organism a two-part Latin name. The first part of the name refers to the genus, the second part to the species. For example, *Felis catus* is the scientific name for the domestic cat. If two species share similar characteristics but are unable to interbreed and produce fertile offspring, they are classified as different species but the same genus. The bobcat, or *Felis rufus,* shares the first part of its name with the domestic cat but not the second part.

2. Domains, Kingdoms, and Levels

Students will learn that all organisms fall into one of three domains, and eukaryotes one of four kingdoms.

The highest level of the classification system, domain, was created relatively recently. Before that, the highest level was kingdom. All prokaryotes were once put in the same kingdom, and it is easy to see why. Archaea and bacteria are alike in size and shape. Neither has a nucleus, and both have a circular chromosome. The distinctive features of archaea first became

apparent in the 1970s. Microbiologist and physicist Carl Woese began comparing the ribosomal RNA of prokaryotes. He discovered that some prokaryotes were very different from others. He eventually proposed the now widely accepted three-domain classification system. Prokaryotes are now classified into one of two domains, *Bacteria* or *Archaea.*

Eukaryotes belong to the domain *Eukarya.* They are further classified into one of four kingdoms, Protista, Fungi, Plantae, or Animalia. The kingdoms Plantae and Animalia were identified first. After microscopic organisms were discovered, they were placed into a third kingdom, Protista. Eventually a fourth kingdom, Fungi, was established.

Students will learn that there are eight levels for classifying organisms.

Besides genus and species, there are four other groupings in each kingdom. The genus *Felis* and three other genera of cats are grouped into larger units called families. Several families of similar organisms make up an order. Orders are grouped into classes. Mammals are an example of a class. Several classes are grouped into a phylum, which has a very large number of organisms. Phyla are grouped into kingdoms.

3. Branching Diagrams and Dichotomous Keys

Organisms are organized into groups.

A classification system identifies objects and gathers them into groups whose members are similar to one another. For example, the Dewey decimal classification system is used to organize books. In biological classification, objects with physical traits in common are often grouped together. Scientists also use biochemical characteristics such as DNA and RNA to identify related organisms.

 COMMON MISCONCEPTIONS **RTI**

CLASSIFICATION BY BEHAVIOR OR HABITAT Some students may think that organisms are classified by criteria such as an ability to fly, a superficial physical similarity such as coloration, or a similar habitat.

This misconception is addressed in the Discussion on p. 76 and in the Learning Alert on p. 83

©PhotoDisc/Getty Images

Teacher Notes

Advance Planning

These activities may take extended time or special conditions.

Unit 1

Video-Based Project Expedition Evolution, p. 12
multiple activities spanning several lessons

Project Prehistoric Life, p. 13
researching and creating timeline

Graphic Organizers and Vocabulary pp. 19, 20, 33, 34, 49, 50, 63, 64, 79, 80
ongoing with reading

Lesson 2

Quick Lab Analyzing Survival Adaptations, p. 31
aquarium containing live fish; species information sheets

Lesson 3

Daily Demo Observing Structural Similarities, p. 47
live animal; images or models of skeletons

Field Lab Mystery Footprints, p. 47
requires 90 min; may require outdoor observations

Quick Lab Comparing Anatomy, p. 47
pictures of animal anatomy

Lesson 5

Activity Classify Leaves, p. 76
various types of leaves

Daily Demo Growing Bread Mold, p. 77
follow-up observations after several days

Quick Lab Investigate Classifying Leaves, p. 77
leaves

Exploration Lab Developing Scientific Names, p. 77
chart of Latin and Greek terms

What Do You Think?

Have students think about what types of animals and plants may have lived in the area during prehistoric times.

Ask: Do you think this area looked the same in prehistoric times? How do you think it might have been different? **Sample answers:** It might have been underwater. It might have been grasslands.

Ask: Do you think dinosaurs lived in this area at one time? Explain. **Sample answer:** Yes, dinosaur fossils have been found here.

Ask: How can scientists find out what types of organisms lived here long ago? **Sample answer:** They can look at the fossils.

UNIT 1

Life over Time

Big Idea
The types and characteristics of organisms change over time.

Fossils provide valuable information about life over time. Some species, such as the ginkgo tree, have lived on Earth for millions of years.

What do you think?
Over Earth's history, life forms change as the environment changes. What kinds of organisms lived in your area during prehistoric times?

Modern ginkgo leaf

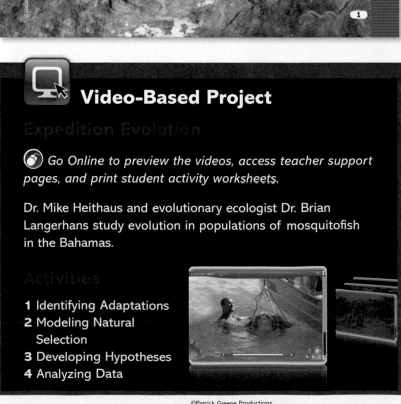

Video-Based Project

Expedition Evolution

Go Online to preview the videos, access teacher support pages, and print student activity worksheets.

Dr. Mike Heithaus and evolutionary ecologist Dr. Brian Langerhans study evolution in populations of mosquitofish in the Bahamas.

Activities

1 Identifying Adaptations
2 Modeling Natural Selection
3 Developing Hypotheses
4 Analyzing Data

©Patrick Greene Productions

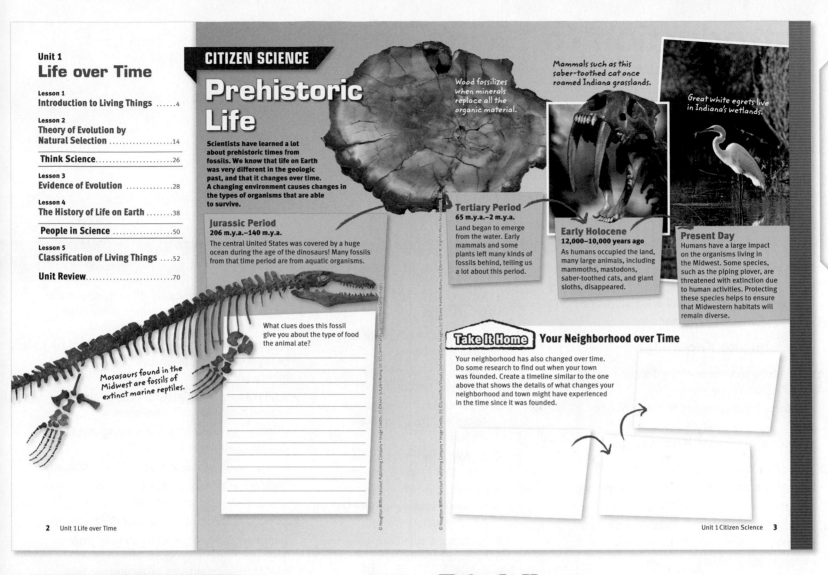

Unit 1
Life over Time

CITIZEN SCIENCE
Prehistoric Life

Scientists have learned a lot about prehistoric times from fossils. We know that life on Earth was very different in the geologic past, and that it changes over time. A changing environment causes changes in the types of organisms that are able to survive.

Wood fossilizes when minerals replace all the organic material.

Mammals such as this saber-toothed cat once roamed Indiana grasslands.

Great white egrets live in Indiana's wetlands.

Jurassic Period
206 m.y.a.–140 m.y.a.
The central United States was covered by a huge ocean during the age of the dinosaurs! Many fossils from that time period are from aquatic organisms.

Tertiary Period
65 m.y.a.–2 m.y.a.
Land began to emerge from the water. Early mammals and some plants left many kinds of fossils behind, telling us a lot about this period.

Early Holocene
12,000–10,000 years ago
As humans occupied the land, many large animals, including mammoths, mastodons, saber-toothed cats, and giant sloths, disappeared.

Present Day
Humans have a large impact on the organisms living in the Midwest. Some species, such as the piping plover, are threatened with extinction due to human activities. Protecting these species helps to ensure that Midwestern habitats will remain diverse.

What clues does this fossil give you about the type of food the animal ate?

Mosasaurs found in the Midwest are fossils of extinct marine reptiles.

Take It Home Your Neighborhood over Time

Your neighborhood has also changed over time. Do some research to find out when your town was founded. Create a timeline similar to the one above that shows the details of what changes your neighborhood and town might have experienced in the time since it was founded.

2   Unit 1 Life over Time

Unit 1 Citizen Science   3

CITIZEN SCIENCE

Unit Project Prehistoric Life

The strong jaw and large hooked teeth suggest that this was a meat eater.

To illustrate how environments have changed over time, lead a discussion about marine fossils being found in the same sediment as fossils of land animals in the central United States. Help students recognize that evidence of marine organisms and land animals in the same sediment supports the fact that the central United States changed from a marine environment to a terrestrial environment over time. Fossils of both types of organisms in the same sediment might suggest an intermediate period in which some parts of the central United States were still wet enough to support marine organisms but were near drier areas that could support land animals.

Take It Home

Students' timelines should include information on when their neighborhood, town, or city was founded and any historically significant changes that have occurred between then and now, such as major fires or other disasters, merging with other towns, a famous resident being born, and so on. Direct students to turn their timelines into illustrated posters. Invite volunteers to present their posters to the class.

🔊 *Optional Online rubric: Posters and Displays*

Introduction to Living Things

Essential Question What are living things?

 Professional Development

For more detailed information about the topics in this lesson, refer to the Content Refresher in the Unit Opener pages.

Opening Your Lesson

Begin the lesson by assessing students' prerequisite and prior knowledge.

Prerequisite Knowledge

- Understand some of the functions that living things perform
- Know several needs of living things

Accessing Prior Knowledge

Ask: Ask students to name some living things. Sample answers: students; plants; animals

Ask: What are some characteristics that all of these things share? These things need energy; they grow and move.

Customize Your Opening

- ☐ **Accessing Prior Knowledge,** above
- ☐ **Print Path** Engage Your Brain, SE p. 5
- ☐ **Print Path** Active Reading, SE p. 5
- ☐ **Digital Path** Lesson Opener

Key Topics/Learning Goals

Characteristics of Living Things

1 List characteristics that all living things share.
2 Explain why a cell is an important unit of life.
3 Describe how living things sense and respond to a stimulus.
4 Explain why homeostasis is important to living organisms.
5 Explain the difference between sexual reproduction and asexual reproduction.
6 Explain the role DNA plays in living organisms.
7 Explain how living things use energy.
8 Describe how living things grow and develop over time.

Needs of Living Things

1 List four things that most living things need to survive.
2 Explain how living things use nutrients.
3 Explain the differences among producers, consumers, and decomposers.

Supporting Concepts

- All living things are made of cells, sense and respond to change, reproduce, have DNA, use energy, and grow and develop.
- A cell is the smallest unit of life. Some organisms are made of only one cell, while others are made of many cells.
- A stimulus is anything that causes an organism to change its behavior.
- Homeostasis refers to maintaining stable internal conditions.
- Living things reproduce sexually or asexually.
- DNA is the genetic material that controls the structure and function of cells.
- Living things use energy to carry out activities.
- Over time, single-celled organisms grow larger, dividing to produce offspring. As multicellular organisms grow and develop, the number of cells in their bodies increases, and they get larger. Some living things go through different stages as they mature.

- Most living things require water, air, food, and a place to live.
- Living things use nutrients from food to fuel life processes.
- Producers make their own food. Most plants are producers. Consumers cannot make their own food and must consume, or eat, other organisms to get energy. Animals are consumers. Decomposers get energy by breaking down the nutrients in dead organisms or animal wastes. Fungi are decomposers.

Options for Instruction

Two parallel paths provide coverage of the Essential Questions, with a strong **Inquiry** strand woven into each.
Follow the **Print Path,** the **Digital Path,** or your customized combination of print, digital, and inquiry.

 Print Path
Teaching support for the Print Path appears with the Student Pages.

 Inquiry Labs and Activities

 **Digital Path**
Digital Path shortcut: TS673055

Share and Share Alike,
SE pp. 6–9
What characteristics do living things share?
- Living Things are Made of Cells
- Living Things Respond to their Environment
- Living Things Reproduce
- Living Things Use Energy
- Living Things Grow and Mature

Activity
Organisms React!

Quick Lab
Is a Clock Alive?

What Living Things Share
Slideshow

Living Things Reproduce
Interactive Images

Stayin' Alive, SE pp. 10–11
What do living things need to survive?
How do living things get food?

Activity
Make a Pamphlet

Daily Demo
Fire and Life

Quick Lab
The Needs of Producers, Consumers, and Decomposers

Four Things for Life
Interactive Images

Producers, Consumers, and Decomposers
Interactive Images

Options for Assessment

See the Evaluate page for options, including Formative Assessment, Summative Assessment, and Unit Review.

Engage and Explore

Activities and Discussion

Discussion *What Do We Share?*

Introducing Key Topics

 whole class

 10 min

 DIRECTED inquiry

Display a picture of a nature scene with several different types of plants and animals. Have students list the organisms in the scene. Then guide students to describe some of the ways the organisms are alike. Prompt students by asking what the organisms have in common. Discuss with students that all living things are made up of cells, sense and respond to change, reproduce, have DNA, use energy, and grow and develop.

Activity *Organisms React!*

Characteristics of Living Things

 individuals, then pairs

 15 min

 GUIDED inquiry

Think, Pair, Share Give students three minutes to write down as many examples  as they can that show how organisms respond to their environment. Remind students that homeostasis is a type of response; it refers to maintaining a stable internal environment. For example, when you get hot, your body sweats to cool down. After three minutes, have each student choose three examples from his or her list and discuss them with a partner. Each student should explain why he or she selected each example and tell how each organism is responding to its environment. Invite pairs to share an example with the class and discuss how and why they chose their examples.

Activity *Make a Pamphlet*

Engage

Needs of Living Things

 groups

 varies

 GUIDED inquiry

Direct students to collect images from magazines or the Internet and make a pamphlet that shows a living organism in its habitat. Encourage students to include images or illustrations that show the things organisms need to survive.

Take It Home *Pet Care*

Needs of Living Things

 adult-student pairs

 20 min

 GUIDED inquiry

Students work with an adult to write an animal-care booklet for a pet at home. The pair should pick an animal they have or might like to keep as a pet. Then the pair should list how they care for the pet or conduct research to find out how to care for it. The pair can use their list to write a booklet. Encourage the pair to include pictures and diagrams.

⊘ *Optional Online resource: student worksheet*

©Imagebroker/Alamy Images

Customize Your Labs

▧ *See the Lab Manual for lab datasheets.*

⊘ *Go Online for editable lab datasheets.*

Levels of **Inquiry** **DIRECTED** inquiry | **GUIDED** inquiry | **INDEPENDENT** inquiry

introduces inquiry skills within a structured framework. | develops inquiry skills within a supportive environment. | deepens inquiry skills with student-driven questions or procedures.

Labs and Demos

Daily Demo *Fire and Life*

Engage

Characteristics of Living Things

 whole class
 10 min
 GUIDED inquiry

PURPOSE **To demonstrate that some nonliving things can exhibit characteristics of living things**

MATERIALS

• **candle**
• **matches**

Demonstrate that some nonliving things can exhibit characteristics of living things. Show the class a burning candle. Ask students if they can think of similarities between the candle and a human. Then, discuss with students that both a human and a burning candle use oxygen and fuel (food and wax, respectively), and they both give off carbon dioxide and energy (in the form of heat). Next, elicit from students how a candle is different from a living thing. **Sample answer: A candle is not made up of cells, it cannot reproduce, it is not alive.**

Quick Lab *Is a Clock Alive?*

Characteristics of Living Things

 pairs
⏱ 15 min
inquiry **GUIDED** inquiry

Students will observe a clock, an object that shares some characteristics with a living thing, and determine whether it meets the criteria for a living organism.

See the Lab Manual or go Online for planning information.

Quick Lab *The Needs of Producers, Consumers, and Decomposers*

Needs of Living Things

 small groups
⏱ 30 min
inquiry **GUIDED** inquiry

Students are assigned a role (a producer, a consumer, or a decomposer) and must determine how they, as that organism, meet their needs for survival.

PURPOSE **To identify the needs of living things**

MATERIALS

• **paper**
• **scissors**
• **string**
• **tape**

After identifying needs, students create a web to visually represent how the organism meets those needs.

Activities and Discussion

☐ **Activity** Organisms React!
☐ **Activity** Make a Pamphlet
☐ **Take It Home** Pet Care
☐ **Discussion** What Do We Share?

Labs and Demos

☐ **Daily Demo** Fire and Life
☐ **Quick Lab** Is a Clock Alive?
☐ **Quick Lab** The Needs of Producers, Consumers, and Decomposers

Your Resources

_____

_____

_____

Explain Science Concepts

<table>
<tr><th></th><th>📄 Print Path</th><th>🖥 Digital Path</th></tr>
<tr><td>**Key Topics**</td><td></td><td></td></tr>
<tr>
<td>**Characteristics of Living Things**</td>
<td>

☐ **Share and Share Alike,** SE pp. 6–9
- Visualize It!, #5
- Visualize It!, #6
- Infer, #7
- Active Reading (Annotation strategy), #8
- Visualize It!, #9
- Describe, #10
- Visualize It!, #11

</td>
<td>

☐ **What Living Things Share**
Investigate the characteristics common to all living things.

☐ **Living Things Reproduce**
Study the difference between sexual and asexual reproduction.

</td>
</tr>
<tr>
<td>**Needs of Living Things**</td>
<td>

☐ **Stayin' Alive,** SE pp. 10–11
- Active Reading (Annotation strategy), #12
- Visualize It!, #13
- Visualize It!, #14

</td>
<td>

☐ **Four Things for Life**
Identify the four things that living things need to survive.

☐ **Producers, Consumers, and Decomposers**
Explore the worlds of producers, consumers, and decomposers.

</td>
</tr>
</table>

Differentiated Instruction

Basic *Looking at Consumers and Decomposers*

Needs of Living Things

 individuals or pairs

🕐 10 min

Many students understand written information more easily when they can tie it directly to their personal experiences. As you discuss consumers and decomposers, ask students to relate what they have seen animals eat. Then invite students to indicate whether the animals were consumers or decomposers. **Sample answer: A deer was eating shrubs in my backyard. The deer is a consumer.**

Advanced *How Much Alike?*

Characteristics of Living Things

 individuals

🕐 varies

Quick Research All living things have DNA, and students may be surprised at how much (or how little) of our DNA we have in common with other organisms. Have students find out the percentage by which DNA differs between parents and offspring in humans, between a human and a chimpanzee, between a human and a reptile, and between a human and a bacterium. Students should draw conclusions about why these differences exist. Have them share what they learned with the class.

ELL *Stimulus and Homeostasis*

Characteristics of Living Things

 individuals

🕐 10 min

Word Triangle Some students may have difficulty with the words *stimulus* and *homeostasis*. Define these words for students. (A stimulus is anything that an organism reacts to. Homeostasis is the ability to maintain internal body conditions.) Then have students make a Word Triangle for each word.

Lesson Vocabulary

cell	stimulus	homeostasis
sexual reproduction	asexual reproduction	DNA

Previewing Vocabulary

 whole class

🕐 10 min

Scientific vs. Common
- A *cell* refers to parts of larger things, such as rooms in a prison, the small spaces in a honeycomb, or the smaller area in a digital phone network. Relate this to the scientific meaning of the word.
- A *stimulus* is something that causes a reaction. A stimulus from the federal government might be money that helps revive a region. A stimulus in class might be something that makes you work harder. In science, a stimulus is something that makes an organism respond.

Reinforcing Vocabulary

 individuals

🕐 ongoing

Concentrating on Vocabulary Have students write each vocabulary term on an index card. Then, have students write the definition for each term on a second set of index cards. Have students turn over one card from each set, matching each term to its definition. When students find a match, have them pronounce the word and read the definition and example aloud.

Customize Your Core Lesson

Core Instruction
☐ **Print Path** choices
☐ **Digital Path** choices

Vocabulary
☐ **Previewing Vocabulary** Scientific vs. Common
☐ **Reinforcing** Concentrating on Vocabulary

Your Resources

Differentiated Instruction
☐ **Basic** Looking at Consumers and Decomposers
☐ **Advanced** How Much Alike?
☐ **ELL** Stimulus and Homeostasis

Extend Science Concepts

Reinforce and Review

Activity *Characteristics of Living Things*

Characteristics of Living Things

 whole class
🕐 30 min

Jigsaw Divide the class into six groups and assign each group a question from the list below. Each group will work together until they all become an expert in their area. Make sure groups stay together until all members can teach what they have learned to another group. After five to ten minutes, reassign groups. Each new group should contain one expert from each of the six groups.

1 Explain what a cell is and why a cell is important.

2 How do plants and animals sense and respond to a stimulus?

3 Define *homeostasis*. Tell why it is important to living things.

4 What is DNA? What job does it perform for living things?

5 Why do living things need energy? Describe four activities that require energy.

6 Tell how three different living things grow and develop. Include a unicellular organism, a multicellular organism, and an organism that has different body shapes during different stages of development, such as a frog.

Graphic Organizer

Needs of Living Things

 individuals
🕐 10 min

Mind Map After students have studied the lesson, encourage them to make a mind map with the following terms: needs of living things, food, water, air, and a place to live. Encourage students to include examples of how different living things, such as an elephant or a pine tree, obtain the things they need to survive.

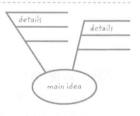

⊘ *Optional Online resource: Mind Map Support*

Going Further

Health Connection

Characteristics of Living Things

 individuals
🕐 ongoing

The Pancreas The pancreas helps the body maintain homeostasis by secreting insulin, a hormone that regulates blood sugar levels. Ask students to investigate the role of insulin. Invite them to share what they learn with the class through a multimedia or oral presentation.

Social Studies Connection

Needs of Living Things

 individuals or pairs
🕐 ongoing

Staple Crops Early hunter-gatherer societies required very large areas of land to sustain them. Eventually, humans developed farming techniques that made higher population densities possible. One strategy humans developed is planting staple crops that can be grown in large quantities. Staple crops vary around the world and include African millet and sorghum, European wheat and barley, American corn and squash, and Asian rice and soybeans. Have students choose a culture and research its staple crops. Then, have students research the advantages and disadvantages of these crops. Encourage students to report their findings to the class.

Customize Your Closing

▣ *See the Assessment Guide for quizzes and tests.*

⊘ *Go Online to edit and create quizzes and tests.*

Reinforce and Review

☐ **Activity** Characteristics of Living Things

☐ **Graphic Organizer** Mind Map

☐ **Print Path** Visual Summary, SE p. 12

☐ **Print Path** Lesson Review, SE p. 13

☐ **Digital Path** Lesson Closer

Evaluate Student Mastery

Formative Assessment

See the teacher support below the Student Pages for additional Formative Assessment questions.

Ask the following questions to assess student mastery of the material. **Ask:** What are characteristics that all living things share? All living things are made up of cells, sense and respond to change, reproduce, have DNA, use energy, and grow and develop. **Ask:** List four things that living things need to survive. Living things require water, air, food, and a place to live. **Ask:** How do living things use nutrients? Living things use nutrients from food to fuel life processes.

Reteach

Formative assessment may show that students need reinforcement for certain topics. The resources below are recommended for reteaching. If students were introduced to a topic through the Print path, you can also use the Digital Path to reteach, and vice versa.
🎧 *Can be assigned to individual students*

Characteristics of Living Things
Activity Make an Informational Pamphlet 🎧

Daily Demo Fire and Life

Quick Lab Is a Clock Alive? 🎧

Needs of Living Things
Activity Make a Pamphlet

Quick Lab Needs of Producers, Consumers, and Decomposers 🎧

Summative Assessment

Alternative Assessment
It's a Living (Thing)

🌐 *Online resources: student worksheet, optional rubrics*

Introduction to Living Things

Take Your Pick: *It's a Living (Thing)*

1. Work on your own or with a partner.
2. Choose items below for a total of 10 points. Check your choices.
3. Have your teacher approve your plan.
4. Submit or present your results.

2 Points

_____ **How Can You Tell?** Write about how you can tell that an apple tree is a living thing.

_____ **Growth and Development** Explain the difference between growth and development.

_____ **Name Three** Describe (using words or images) three things that your body does every day that require energy.

5 Points

_____ **Quiz Me!** Write a quiz that reviews the needs of living things. Your quiz should have at least 7 questions. Remember to include the answers.

_____ **Strange Creatures** Research an organism that takes in energy in an unusual way, such as the Venus Flytrap. Use this information to write a poem about this organism.

_____ **Hidden Worlds** Use the Internet to find pictures of microscopic, one-celled organisms. Sketch three of these organisms. Label each sketch with the organism's name. Write a descriptive paragraph about the different shapes you see.

_____ **Staying Warm** What do you do when you go outside and the air is cold? How do people use technology to improve their ability to maintain stable body temperatures?

8 Points

_____ **Alive or Not?** Design a computer presentation or a poster that shows three living things and three nonliving things. Write a paragraph next to each picture that explains the characteristics that identify each thing as either living or nonliving.

_____ **How Stimulating!** Read a short story. Find five examples of stimuli and responses in the story. Think about why the ability to respond to stimuli is important and write a paragraph about it, using examples from the short story to support your statements.

Going Further
☐ **Health Connection** The Pancreas
☐ **Social Studies Connection** Staple Crops

Formative Assessment
☐ **Strategies** Throughout TE
☐ **Lesson Review** SE

Summative Assessment
☐ **Alternative Assessment** It's a Living (Thing)
☐ **Lesson Quiz**
☐ **Unit Tests A and B**
☐ **Unit Review** SE End-of-Unit

Your Resources

_____   _____

_____   _____

Lesson ①

Introduction to Living Things

ESSENTIAL QUESTION

What are living things?

By the end of this lesson, you should be able to describe the necessities of life and the characteristics that all living things share.

Living things need energy to survive. This bluebird gets energy by eating insects like this dragonfly.

✋ **Lesson Labs**

Quick Labs
- Is a Clock Alive?
- The Needs of Producers, Consumers, and Decomposers

🧠 **Engage Your Brain**

1 Compare Both of these pictures show living things. How are these living things different?

2 List Many of the things that people need to stay alive are not found in space. List the things that the International Space Station must have to keep astronauts alive.

A

B

📖 **Active Reading**

3 Synthesize Many English words have their roots in other languages. Use the Greek words below to make an educated guess about the meaning of the word *homeostasis*.

Greek word	Meaning
hómoios	similar
stásis	standing still

Example sentence
On a hot day, your body sweats to maintain homeostasis.

homeostasis:

Vocabulary Terms
- cell
- DNA
- stimulus
- sexual reproduction
- homeostasis
- asexual reproduction

4 Identify This list contains the vocabulary terms you'll learn in this lesson. As you read, underline the definition of each term.

4   Unit 1 Life over Time

Lesson 1 Introduction to Living Things   5

Answers

Answers for 1–3 should represent students' current thoughts, even if incorrect.

1. Sample answer: Living thing B looks like it has more cells and structures than living thing A does.

2. Sample answer: The International Space Station must provide water, food, air for breathing, and energy to provide warmth.

3. Sample answer: Homeostasis describes stable conditions inside the body.

4. *See students' pages for annotations.*

Opening Your Lesson

Discuss student answers in response to #1 and #2 to assess their prerequisite knowledge and to estimate what they already know about living things.

Prerequisites Students should already understand some of the functions living things perform. Students should also know several needs of living things.

Learning Alert

Growing Crystals Some students may think that everything that grows is alive. To help students understand that growth is not the sole criteria that defines a living thing, make rock candy. Rock candy appears to grow, but when they compare the other characteristics of living things to that of the rock candy, they will conclude that the rock candy is not actually alive.

Share and Share Alike

What characteristics do living things share?

An amazing variety of living things exists on Earth. These living things may seem very different, but they are all alike in several ways. What does a dog have in common with a bacterium? What does a fish have in common with a mushroom? There are five characteristics that all living things share.

This is a microscopic view of cells in an onion root. An onion has many cells, so it is a multicellular organism.

Living Things Are Made of Cells

All living things are made of one or more cells. A **cell** is a membrane-covered structure that contains all of the materials necessary for life. Cells are the smallest unit of life, which means they are the smallest structures that can perform life functions. Most cells are so small they cannot be seen without a microscope. The membrane that surrounds a cell separates the cell's contents from its environment. Unicellular organisms are made up of only one cell. Multicellular organisms are made up of more than one cell. Some of these organisms have trillions of cells! Cells in a multicellular organism usually perform specialized functions.

Visualize It!

5 Categorize Identify each organism in the picture as unicellular or multicellular.

I'm an amoeba. I am:
☐ unicellular ☐ multicellular

I'm a cattail. I am:
☐ unicellular ☐ multicellular

I'm a turtle. I am:
☐ unicellular ☐ multicellular

Living Things Respond to Their Environment

All living things have the ability to sense change in their environment and to respond to that change. A change that affects the activity of an organism is called a **stimulus** (plural: stimuli). A stimulus can be gravity, light, sound, a chemical, hunger, or anything else that causes an organism to respond in some way. For example, when your pupils are exposed to light—a stimulus—they become smaller—a response.

Even though an organism's outside environment may change, conditions inside its body must stay relatively constant. Many chemical reactions keep an organism alive. These reactions can only happen when conditions are exactly right. An organism must maintain stable internal conditions to survive. The maintenance of a stable internal environment is called **homeostasis**. Your body maintains homeostasis by sweating when it gets hot and shivering when it gets cold. Each of these actions keeps the body at a stable internal temperature.

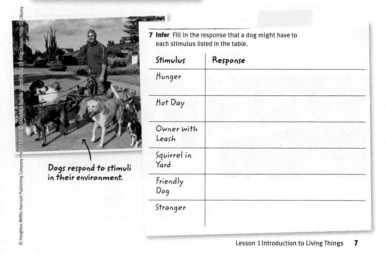

Visualize It!

6 Analyze Why are these sunflowers all facing in the same direction?

_____

_____

Dogs respond to stimuli in their environment.

7 Infer Fill in the response that a dog might have to each stimulus listed in the table.

Stimulus	Response
Hunger	
Hot Day	
Owner with Leash	
Squirrel in Yard	
Friendly Dog	
Stranger	

Lesson 1 Introduction to Living Things   **7**

Answers

5. amoeba: unicellular; cattail: multicellular; turtle: multicellular

6. The sunflowers are responding to light from the sun, which is a stimulus.

7. Sample answers: Hunger response: salivating, standing by a food dish; Hot Day response: panting; Owner with Leash response: wagging tail, jumping up and down; Squirrel in Yard response: barking and chasing squirrel; Friendly Dog response: wagging tail, sniffing; Stranger response: barking, growling.

Building Reading Skills

Paired Summarizing Have students work in pairs. Ask one student in each pair to read aloud the text under a heading while the other member of the pair takes notes. The pair should then discuss the notes to make sure that they both understand the material. Have students continue until they finish reading the entire section.

Probing Questions

Analyze Explain to students that multicellular organisms are more efficient than unicellular organisms. **Ask:** Using what you already know about multicellular animals, why do you think this is true? The cells of multicellular organisms are specialized to perform different functions and are therefore collectively more efficient than the single cell of unicellular organisms.

Living Things Reproduce

 **8 Identify** As you read, underline the ways in which organisms reproduce.

How does the world become filled with plants, animals, and other living things? Organisms make other organisms through the process of reproduction. When organisms reproduce, they pass copies of all or part of their DNA to their offspring. **DNA**, or deoxyribonucleic acid, is the genetic material that controls the structure and function of cells. DNA is found in the cells of all living things. Offspring share characteristics with their parents because they receive DNA from their parents.

Living things reproduce in one of two ways. Two parents produce offspring that share the characteristics of both parents through the process of **sexual reproduction**. Each offspring receives part of its DNA from each parent. Most animals and plants reproduce using sexual reproduction.

A single parent produces offspring that are identical to the parent through the process of **asexual reproduction**. Each offspring receives an exact copy of the parent's DNA. Most unicellular organisms and some plants and animals reproduce using asexual reproduction. Two methods of asexual reproduction are binary fission and budding. A unicellular organism splits into two parts during binary fission. During budding, a new organism grows on the parent organism until it is ready to separate.

A father pig is needed to produce piglets.

Visualize It!

9 Identify Use the check boxes to identify which offspring are identical to the parent or parents and which offspring are not identical.

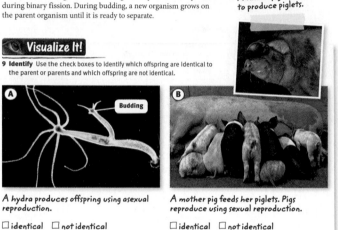

A Budding

A hydra produces offspring using asexual reproduction.

☐ identical ☐ not identical

A mother pig feeds her piglets. Pigs reproduce using sexual reproduction.

☐ identical ☐ not identical

8 Unit 1 Life over Time

Living Things Use Energy

Living things need energy to carry out the activities of life. Energy allows organisms to make or break down food, move materials into and out of cells, and build cells. Energy also allows organisms to move and interact with each other.

Where do living things get the energy they need for the activities of life? Plants convert energy from the sun into food. They store this food in their cells until they need to use it. Organisms that cannot make their own food must eat other organisms to gain energy. Some organisms eat plants. Others eat animals. Organisms such as fungi break down decaying material to gain energy.

10 Describe List three activities that you have done today that require energy.

_____
_____
_____

Living Things Grow and Mature

All living things grow during some period of their lives. When a unicellular organism grows, it gets larger and then divides, forming two cells. When a multicellular organism grows, the number of cells in its body increases, and the organism gets bigger.

Many living things don't just get larger as they grow. They also develop and change. Humans pass through different stages as they mature from childhood to adulthood. During these stages, the human body changes. Frogs and butterflies have body shapes that look completely different during different stages of development.

Visualize It!

11 Describe How does a frog grow and develop? Write a caption for each picture to describe each stage in a frog's life.

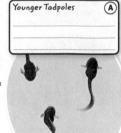

Younger Tadpoles **A**
_____
_____

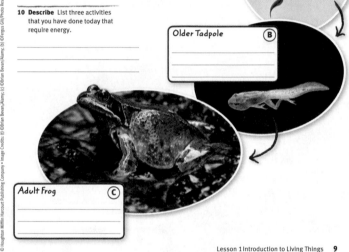

Older Tadpole **B**
_____
_____

Adult Frog **C**
_____
_____

Lesson 1 Introduction to Living Things 9

Answers

8. *See students' pages for annotations.*

9. A: identical; B: not identical

10. Student activities that require energy include walking, riding a bike, brushing their teeth, playing outside, etc.

11. Sample answers: A: Younger tadpoles have tails and can swim; B: An older tadpole develops legs and its tail gets shorter; C: An adult frog has four legs and no tail.

Interpreting Visuals

Identify Invite students to examine the figure of the hydra on this page. **Ask:** What structures will become new hydras? Sample answer: Two buds are forming near the base of the hydra. **Ask:** What other organisms reproduce asexually? Sample answer: Most unicellular organisms reproduce asexually. Then encourage students to identify other organisms that reproduce sexually.

Probing Questions

Drawing Conclusions Discuss with students how organisms obtain energy. Review how plants and animals acquire energy. **Ask:** How do organisms depend on one another for energy? Sample answer: Some animals obtain energy by eating other animals. Some animals obtain energy from eating plants.

Formative Assessment

Ask: What are the five characteristics of living things? Living things are made of cells; living things respond to their environment; living things reproduce; living things use energy; and living things grow and mature.

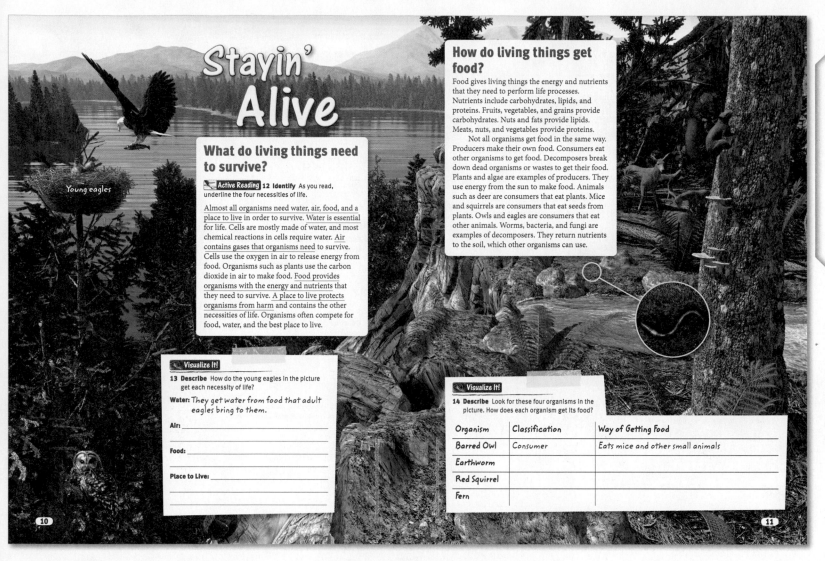

Stayin' Alive

Young eagles

What do living things need to survive?

Active Reading **12 Identify** As you read, underline the four necessities of life.

Almost all organisms need water, air, food, and a place to live in order to survive. Water is essential for life. Cells are mostly made of water, and most chemical reactions in cells require water. Air contains gases that organisms need to survive. Cells use the oxygen in air to release energy from food. Organisms such as plants use the carbon dioxide in air to make food. Food provides organisms with the energy and nutrients that they need to survive. A place to live protects organisms from harm and contains the other necessities of life. Organisms often compete for food, water, and the best place to live.

Visualize It!

13 Describe How do the young eagles in the picture get each necessity of life?

Water: They get water from food that adult eagles bring to them.

Air: _____

Food: _____

Place to Live: _____

How do living things get food?

Food gives living things the energy and nutrients that they need to perform life processes. Nutrients include carbohydrates, lipids, and proteins. Fruits, vegetables, and grains provide carbohydrates. Nuts and fats provide lipids. Meats, nuts, and vegetables provide proteins.

Not all organisms get food in the same way. Producers make their own food. Consumers eat other organisms to get food. Decomposers break down dead organisms or wastes to get their food. Plants and algae are examples of producers. They use energy from the sun to make food. Animals such as deer are consumers that eat plants. Mice and squirrels are consumers that eat seeds from plants. Owls and eagles are consumers that eat other animals. Worms, bacteria, and fungi are examples of decomposers. They return nutrients to the soil, which other organisms can use.

Visualize It!

14 Describe Look for these four organisms in the picture. How does each organism get its food?

Organism	Classification	Way of Getting Food
Barred Owl	Consumer	Eats mice and other small animals
Earthworm		
Red Squirrel		
Fern		

10

11

Answers

12. *See students' pages for annotations.*

13. Sample answer: Air: Young eagles breathe air; Food: Adult eagles bring food like fish to the young eagles; Place to Live: Adult eagles build a nest high in a tree to protect young eagles from animals that could harm them.

14. Sample answers: Earthworm/ Decomposer/Breaks down dead material; Red squirrel/Consumer/Eats seeds from plants; Fern/Producer/Makes food using photosynthesis

Building Math Skills

Explain to students that most cells in the human body are about 70% water. **Ask:** What would the mass of a 40-kg person be if there were no water in his body? Sample answer for a 40-kg person: 40 kg × 0.7 = 28 kg. The person's mass without water would be 40 kg − 28 kg = 12 kg.

Probing Questions

Inferring Discuss with students how the cells of organisms need gases, such as oxygen, to release the energy contained in food. **Ask:** Could life, as we know it, exist on Earth if air contained only oxygen? Sample answer: No, some organisms, such as green plants, algae, and some bacteria, need carbon dioxide. These organisms would not survive with only oxygen.

Formative Assessment

Ask: What are the needs of living things? water, air, food, and a place to live

Visual Summary

To complete this summary, circle the correct word. Then use the key below to check your answers. You can use this page to review the main concepts of the lesson.

Introduction to Living Things

All living things are made of cells that contain DNA. Living things use energy, grow and develop, and reproduce. They also respond to changes in their environment.

15 Sunlight is an example of (a) homeostasis / stimulus.

16 Binary fission is an example of asexual / sexual reproduction.

Almost all living things need water, air, food, and a place to live.

17 Plants are producers / consumers.

18 Decomposers return organisms / nutrients to the environment.

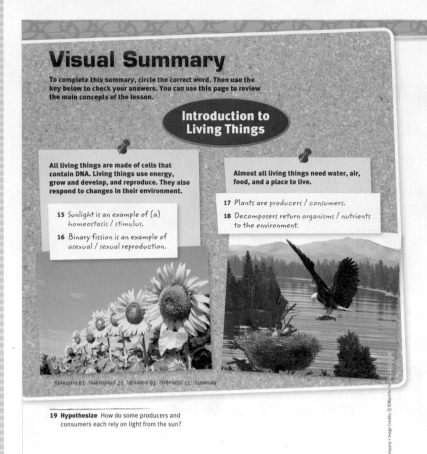

Answers: 15 stimulus; 16 asexual; 17 producers; 18 nutrients

19 Hypothesize How do some producers and consumers each rely on light from the sun?

Lesson Review

Vocabulary

In your own words, define the following terms.

1 homeostasis

2 asexual reproduction

3 cell

Key Concepts

4 Explain What is the relationship between a stimulus and a response?

5 Describe What happens to DNA during sexual reproduction?

6 Contrast What are the differences between producers, consumers, and decomposers?

Critical Thinking

Use the pictures to answer the questions below.

7 Describe What is happening to the birds in the picture above?

8 Explain How do nutrients and energy allow the changes shown in the picture to happen?

9 Compare How is a fish similar to an oak tree?

10 Making Inferences Could life as we know it exist on Earth if air contained only oxygen? Explain.

Visual Summary Answers

15. stimulus

16. asexual

17. producers

18. nutrients

19. Sample answer: Producers need light from the sun to produce food. Many consumers eat producers to get energy.

Lesson Review Answers

1. Homeostasis means maintaining stable internal conditions.

2. In asexual reproduction, one parent makes an identical copy of itself.

3. Each cell contains all the materials needed to live. It is covered in a membrane and contains DNA.

4. A stimulus is anything that causes a response in an organism.

5. Part of each parent's DNA is passed to offspring during sexual reproduction.

6. Producers make their own food. Consumers must eat other organisms to get energy. Decomposers break down dead organisms to get energy.

7. The birds are growing and developing into adults.

8. Nutrients and energy allow cells to divide, which allows the birds to grow and develop.

9. A fish and an oak tree are both made of cells that contain DNA. They both use energy, reproduce, and grow and develop. They also both sense and respond to their environment.

10. No, life as we know it could not exist with only oxygen because plants and other producers need carbon dioxide to produce food.

Theory of Evolution by Natural Selection

Essential Question What is the theory of evolution by natural selection?

 Professional Development

For more detailed information about the topics in this lesson, refer to the Content Refresher in the Unit Opener pages.

Opening Your Lesson

Begin the lesson by assessing students' prerequisite and prior knowledge.

Prerequisite Knowledge

- Basic knowledge of environments and species
- Basic knowledge of cells, heredity, and living things

Accessing Prior Knowledge

To gauge what students already know about evolution by natural selection, have students evaluate the correctness of these statements:

1 Charles Darwin was the first person to have ideas about how species change.

2 Organisms that inherit advantageous traits tend to survive and reproduce more successfully than other organisms.

3 Evolution and natural selection are the same.

Customize Your Opening

- ☐ **Accessing Prior Knowledge,** above
- ☐ **Print Path** Engage Your Brain, SE p. 15
- ☐ **Print Path** Active Reading, SE p. 15
- ☐ **Digital Path** Lesson Opener

Key Topics/Learning Goals	Supporting Concepts
Darwin's Observations 1 Define *evolution*. 2 Describe Darwin's observations. 3 Define *species, population, variation, adaptation*, and *artificial selection*.	• Evolution is the process by which populations gradually change over time. • Darwin observed differences among species of finches in the Galápagos Islands. • A species is a group of organisms that mate to produce fertile offspring. A population is all of the individuals of a species in an area at a given time. • Genetic variation refers to the differences in inherited traits of individuals in a population. • Adaptation refers to the inherited characteristics that help organisms survive and reproduce. • Artificial selection is breeding for certain traits.
Natural Selection 1 Define *natural selection*. 2 Describe the four parts of natural selection. 3 Explain how descendants may become genetically different from their ancestors.	• Natural selection is the process by which organisms that are better adapted to their environment survive and reproduce more than less-well-adapted organisms do. • The four parts of natural selection are overproduction (species produce more offspring than will survive), genetic variation, adaptation, and selection (those with adaptations are most likely to survive and reproduce in a given environment). • Over many generations, small genetic differences can add up and make descendants differ from their ancestors.
Extinction and Environmental Change 1 Define *extinction*. 2 Describe how environmental change can affect a species.	• Extinction occurs when all of the members of a species have died. • Environmental change can prompt extinction if no individuals have traits that help them thrive in the changed environment.

Options for Instruction

Two parallel paths provide coverage of the Essential Questions, with a strong **Inquiry** strand woven into each. Follow the **Print Path,** the **Digital Path,** or your customized combination of print, digital, and inquiry.

 Print Path
Teaching support for the Print Path appears with the Student Pages.

 Inquiry Labs and Activities

 Digital Path
Digital Path shortcut: TS673014

Darwin's Voyage, SE pp. 16–17
What did Darwin observe?
• Differences among Species

Darwin's Homework,
SE pp. 18–19
What other ideas influenced Darwin?
• Organisms Pass Traits on to Offspring
• Organisms Acquire Traits
• Earth Changes over Time
• A Struggle for Survival Exists

Quick Lab
The Opposable Thumb

Daily Demo
Modeling Bird Beaks

Activity
Artificial Selection

Darwin's Discoveries
Interactive Graphics

Natural Selection, SE pp. 20–21
What are the four parts of natural selection?
• Overproduction
• Genetic Variation
• Selection
• Adaptation

Well-Adapted, SE p. 22
How do species change over time?
• Over Generations, Adaptations...
• Genetic Differences Add Up

Virtual Lab
Natural Selection

Quick Lab
Model Natural Selection

Activity
Natural Selection Game

Natural Selection
Interactive Images

Populations and Individuals
Slideshow

Artificial Selection
Video

Well-Adapted, SE p. 23
What happens to species as the environment changes?
• Adaptations Can Allow a Species...
• Some Species May Become Extinct

Exploration Lab
Environmental Change and Evolution

Quick Lab
Analyzing Survival Adaptations

Genetics and the Environment
Graphic Sequence

Well-Adapted
Interactive Graphics

Options for Assessment

See the Evaluate page for options, including Formative Assessment, Summative Assessment, and Unit Review.

Engage and Explore

Activities and Discussion

Discussion *Cat Traits*

Introducing Key Topics

 whole class
🕐 10 min
(Inquiry) **GUIDED** inquiry

Students may be familiar with variations in cat traits. Guide students to brainstorm cat traits, such as fur color, length of fur, ear shape, and face shape that are determined by the genes. Then have them catalog all the cat traits they can think of. **Ask:** What do you conclude about cat variation? Sample answers: There are many different traits within a population. Some traits are more common than others.

Activity *Artificial Selection*

Charles Darwin's Observations

 individuals, pairs, whole class
🕐 varied
(Inquiry) **DIRECTED** inquiry

Think, Pair, Share Assign each individual a particular type of dog breed, and ask the student to research the breed and find a picture. Students should write down as much as they can about that breed's characteristics. Then have pairs of students discuss each other's dog breed and consider why people might have wanted dogs to have those traits. Conclude the activity by inviting groups to share their ideas about their breed traits with the class.

⊙ *Optional Online resource: Think, Pair, Share support*

Labs and Demos

Daily Demo *Modeling Bird Beaks*

 Engage

Charles Darwin's Observations

 whole class
🕐 10 min
(Inquiry) **DIRECTED** inquiry

Use this demo after you have discussed Darwin's observations.

PURPOSE **To show how differently shaped beaks are adapted for different purposes**

MATERIALS

- clothespins, toothpicks, straws, spoons, plastic scoops, tweezers, or other implements
- soda crackers, raisins, sunflower seeds, uncooked shell macaroni, hay or grass, water (to simulate nectar), or other small food items
- plates, paper
- cup

1 Explain that the utensils represent types of bird beaks, and the cup represents a bird's stomach.
2 Place one type of food on each plate.
3 Demonstrate how each type of beak is adapted to pick up and break open (if needed) certain types of food.
4 **Analyzing Ask:** Which beak type works better for each type of food? Sample answers: Tweezers were adapted to breaking open the sunflower seeds. Toothpicks were good for spearing the raisins. Straws worked better for sipping nectar.
5 **Relating Ask:** How might the type of beak a bird has affect its diet? Sample answer: Beaks are shaped differently, and this determines what a bird is likely to eat.

Variation If materials are available, this demo can also be done as a student activity.

Customize Your Labs

 See the Lab Manual for lab datasheets.

 Go Online for editable lab datasheets.

Exploration Lab *Environmental Change and Evolution*

Extinction and Environmental Change

👥 small groups
🕐 45 min
Inquiry **DIRECTED or GUIDED** inquiry

Students will model ways that natural variation in a population affects the survival of that population if the environment changes.

PURPOSE **To explore how natural variation in a population affects the survival of that population**

MATERIALS

- aluminum foil
- cotton balls or batting
- feathers, different sizes
- felt or cloth
- plastic wrap
- marbles, small foam spheres, or other objects to represent organisms

Quick Lab *Analyzing Survival Adaptations*

Natural Selection

👥 individuals
🕐 20 min
Inquiry **GUIDED** inquiry

Students will analyze the survival advantages offered by various adaptations when comparing and contrasting two fish species.

PURPOSE **To explore the adaptations that help fish survive in different habitats**

MATERIALS

- aquarium containing live fish
- colored pencils or markers
- habitat information of aquarium fish
- paper, blank

Quick Lab *Model Natural Selection*

Natural Selection

👥 pairs
🕐 15 min
Inquiry **DIRECTED** inquiry

Students will use provided materials to model natural selection.

PURPOSE **To observe how traits can affect the success of an organism in a particular environment**

MATERIALS

- white cloth, approximately 20 x 20 cm
- 25 miniature marshmallows, same color
- 25 miniature marshmallows, white

Quick Lab *The Opposable Thumb*

PURPOSE **To explore how the opposable thumb helps perform everyday tasks**

See the Lab Manual or go Online for planning information.

 Virtual Lab *Natural Selection*

Natural Selection

👥 flexible
🕐 45 min
Inquiry **GUIDED** inquiry

Students will simulate the process of natural selection.

PURPOSE **To observe the process of natural selection**

Activities and Discussion

- ☐ **Discussion** Cat Traits
- ☐ **Activity** Artificial Selection

Labs and Demos

- ☐ **Daily Demo** Modeling Bird Beaks

- ☐ **Exploration Lab** Environmental...
- ☐ **Quick Lab** Analyzing Survival...
- ☐ **Quick Lab** Model Natural Selection
- ☐ **Quick Lab** The Opposable Thumb
- ☐ **Virtual Lab** Natural Selection

Your Resources

_____

_____

_____

Explain Science Concepts

	📖 Print Path	💻 Digital Path
Key Topics		

Darwin's Observations

☐ **Darwin's Voyage,** SE pp. 16–17
- Think Outside the Book, #5
- Visualize It!, #6

☐ **Darwin's Homework,** SE pp. 18–19
- List, #7
- Active Reading (Annotation strategy), #8
- Apply, #9
- Visualize It!, #10

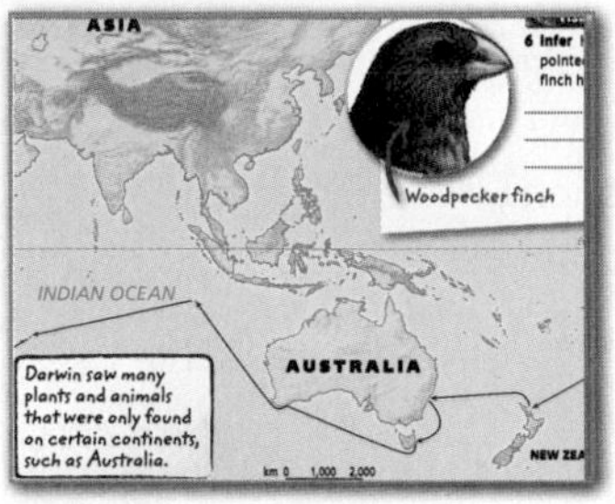

☐ **Darwin's Discoveries**
Learn about the discoveries made by Charles Darwin as a result of his voyage on the HMS *Beagle*.

Natural Selection

☐ **Natural Selection,** SE pp. 20–21
- Infer, #11
- Summarize, #12
- Explain, #13

☐ **Well-Adapted,** SE p. 22
- Active Reading (Annotation strategy), #14
- Visualize It!, #15

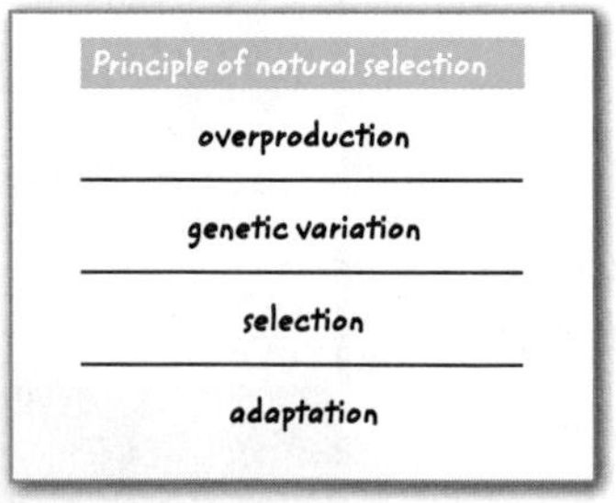

☐ **Natural Selection**
Learn about the process and four principles of natural selection.

☐ **Artificial Selection**
Learn how Charles Darwin used artificial selection experiments to test his ideas on natural selection.

☐ **Populations and Individuals**
Explore the concept of evolution.

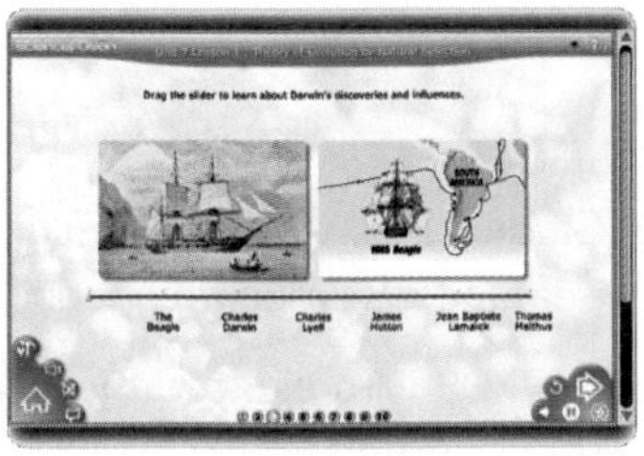

Extinction and Environmental Change

☐ **Well-Adapted,** SE p. 23
- Visualize It!, #16–17

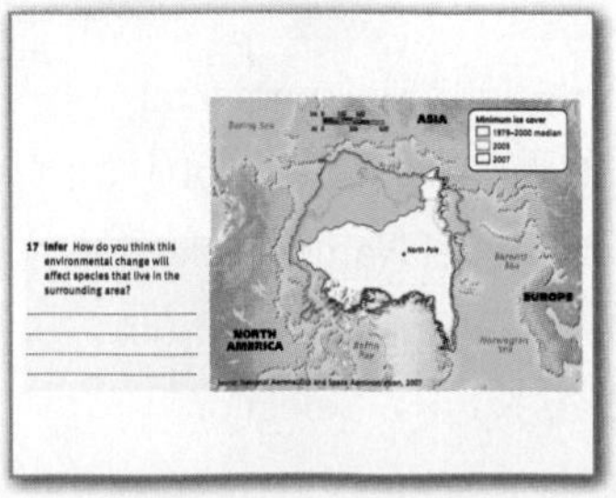

☐ **Genetics and Environment**
Examine the impact of genetics and the environment on adaptation and survival.

☐ **Well-Adapted**
Explore the relationships of adaptation, natural selection, and extinction.

Differentiated Instruction

Basic *Important Adaptations*

Natural Selection　 individuals　🕐 20 min

After students have learned why adaptations are important for survival, ask them to think of a species of animal and the adaptations it possesses. Have students make a sketch of their chosen animal and label the sketch to identify its adaptations to life in its environment. Have students write a caption for their sketch to explain how each adaptation they highlighted helps the animal to survive in its environment.

Basic *The Voyage of the* Beagle

Charles Darwin's Observations　 small groups　🕐 varied

Skit Have students write and perform a skit in which they imagine that they have been transported back in time and have signed up to help Charles Darwin explore the Galápagos Islands. Have students role-play collecting specimens and making observations.

Advanced *Darwin's Findings*

Synthesizing Key Topics　individuals or pairs　🕐 varied

Quick Research In addition to Galápagos Island finches, Darwin cataloged tortoises and other organisms. Have student pairs conduct research to learn more about what Darwin discovered from his voyage on the *Beagle*. Ask them to prepare a short report addressing the following: *What are two different types of organisms Darwin studied after his voyage to the Galápagos Islands? What did he learn about the different species of these organisms? How did this research support his theory of evolution by natural selection?*

ELL *Evolution Terms*

Synthesizing Key Topics　 individuals or pairs　🕐 20 min

Have students create a glossary of evolution terms that contains labeled pictures. English-language learners and students who are comfortable with drawings can team up with students who prefer words.

Lesson Vocabulary

evolution	variation	adaptation
artificial selection	natural selection	extinction
mutation		

Previewing Vocabulary

👥 whole class　🕐 5 min

Suffixes Knowing suffixes can help students determine the meanings of unfamiliar words. A suffix is a word part attached to the end of a base word or root that alters the meaning of that base word or root. Share the meaning and function of the following suffixes:
• **-tion** "state or quality of"; forms nouns from verbs
• **-al** "of, relating to, or characterized by"; forms adjectives from nouns

🔘 *Optional Online resource: Suffixes support*

Reinforcing Vocabulary

👥 individuals　🕐 ongoing

Magnet Word Have students develop Magnet Word diagrams for each vocabulary term in the lesson.

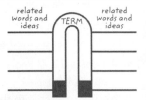

🔘 *Optional Online resource: Magnet Word support*

Customize Your Core Lesson

Core Instruction
☐ **Print Path** choices
☐ **Digital Path** choices

Vocabulary
☐ **Previewing Vocabulary** Suffixes
☐ **Reinforcing Vocabulary** Magnet Word

Your Resources

_____

_____

Differentiated Instruction
☐ Basic Important Adaptations
☐ Basic The Voyage of the *Beagle*
☐ Advanced Darwin's Findings
☐ ELL Evolution Terms

Extend Science Concepts

Reinforce and Review

Activity *Natural Selection Game*

Natural Selection

flexible

10–15 min

Four Corners Pick four corners of the classroom to represent the four parts of natural selection: overproduction, variation, selection, and adaptation. Read the following descriptions to students. After each one, ask individual students, pairs, or small groups to go to the corner they think the description corresponds to. Give each student in the correct corner a point. You can continue the game with additional examples provided by student volunteers.

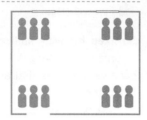

1 Some rabbits in a population can run very fast. Other rabbits in the same population run slower. The slower rabbits are more likely to be eaten by predators. **selection**

2 One species of clam lives on a certain beach. Some of the clams of this species have a pinkish shell, and some have a grayish shell. **variation**

3 A mother chipmunk has a litter of five pups. Only two of the pups survive to adulthood and reproduce. **overproduction**

4 A population of mostly dark-colored deer mice moves into an area that has light, sandy soil. Light-colored deer mice in the population blend in better with the sandy soil, helping them avoid predators. Over many generations, the population changes to have mostly light-colored deer mice. **adaptation**

Variation Assign the terms 1, 2, 3, and 4, and have students use mini white boards at their seats to give their responses.

Graphic Organizer

Natural Selection

individuals

15 min

Main Idea Web After students have studied the lesson, ask them to create a main idea web with the following main idea: *Darwin thought that most evolution happens by the natural selection of beneficial traits.*

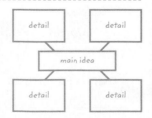

⊙ *Optional Online resource: Main Idea Web support*

Going Further

Social Studies Connection

Charles Darwin's Observations

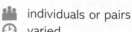
individuals or pairs

varied

Posters Today, the Galápagos Islands are a UNESCO World Heritage site and are largely protected. Have students research the islands. Encourage them to learn about the islands' location, geography, climate, wildlife, and human population. Then direct each group to create a poster to display their findings. Posters may focus on one aspect of the islands or may include a number of fun facts. Have students illustrate the posters with drawings of the islands and indigenous wildlife.

⊙ *Optional Online rubric: Posters and Displays*

Earth Science Connection

Synthesizing Key Topics

individuals

varied

Quick Research Geologist Charles Lyell proposed the theory that the geological findings of the present represent the accumulation of very small geologic changes that have occurred over a long period of time. Darwin related concepts from this theory to help support his theory of natural selection. Have students research how Earth is thought to have formed and the ways in which scientists judge its age. Direct students to write a short report on the topic.

⊙ *Optional Online rubric: Written Pieces*

Customize Your Closing

🗒 *See the Assessment Guide for quizzes and tests.*

⊙ *Go Online to edit and create quizzes and tests.*

Reinforce and Review

☐ **Activity** Natural Selection Game

☐ **Graphic Organizer** Main Idea Web

☐ **Print Path** Visual Summary, SE p. 24

☐ **Digital Path** Lesson Closer

Evaluate Student Mastery

Formative Assessment

See the teacher support below the Student Pages for additional Formative Assessment questions.

Ask: What are some ways that organisms from this lesson are adapted to survive or reproduce in their environments? Sample answer: The cheetah's coloring helps it to blend in with its surroundings, which helps it avoid being seen by prey. The long tongue of the butterfly helps it reach nectar deep inside flowers. The red throat pouch of the male frigate bird helps it attract mates.

Reteach

Formative assessment may show that students need reinforcement for certain topics. The resources below are recommended for reteaching. If students were introduced to a topic through the Print Path, you can also use the Digital Path to reteach, and vice versa.
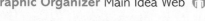 *Can be assigned to individual students*

Charles Darwin's Observations
Quick Lab The Opposable Thumb 🎧
Basic Important Adaptations 🎧

Natural Selection
Virtual Lab Natural Selection 🎧
Graphic Organizer Main Idea Web 🎧

Extinction and Environmental Change
Quick Lab Analyzing Survival Adaptations

Summative Assessment

Alternative Assessment
Evolving Activities

💿 *Online resources: student worksheet, optional rubrics*

Theory of Evolution by Natural Selection

Climb the Pyramid: *Evolving Activities*
Climb the pyramid to show what you've learned about Darwin's observations and the theory of evolution by natural selection.

1. Work on your own, with a partner, or with a small group.

2. Choose one item from each layer of the pyramid. Check your choices.

3. Have your teacher approve your plan.

4. Submit or present your results.

__ Scientific Dialogue
Work with a group to write a dialogue in which Jean Baptiste Lamarck, Charles Lyell, Thomas Malthus, and Charles Darwin discuss and compare their theories. Perform your dialogue for the class.

__ Evolution Quiz
Write a quiz that could be used to test knowledge of natural selection. Have classmates try your quiz and give you feedback. Remember to write an answer key for the quiz.

__ Evolution Story
Write a fictional story about several generations of any type of organism during an environmental change. Stories may feature extinction.

__ Darwin's Journal
Imagine you are Charles Darwin. Write two or three journal entries about your discoveries and the ideas they inspired.

__ Book Cover
Design a cover for Charles Darwin's book about his theory of evolution, *The Origin of Species*. The cover should have an image on the front appropriate to the subject matter. Text on the back should summarize Darwin's theory in as few words as possible.

__ Galápagos Comic
Draw a comic strip that illustrates Darwin's discoveries during his voyage on the HMS *Beagle*. Be creative, but include factual details about what Darwin did and what he discovered on the islands.

Going Further
☐ Social Studies Connection
☐ Earth Science Connection

Formative Assessment
☐ **Strategies** Throughout TE
☐ **Lesson Review** SE

Summative Assessment
☐ **Alternative Assessment** Evolving Activities
☐ **Lesson Quiz**
☐ **Unit Tests A and B**
☐ **Unit Review** SE End-of-Unit

Your Resources

_____   _____

_____   _____

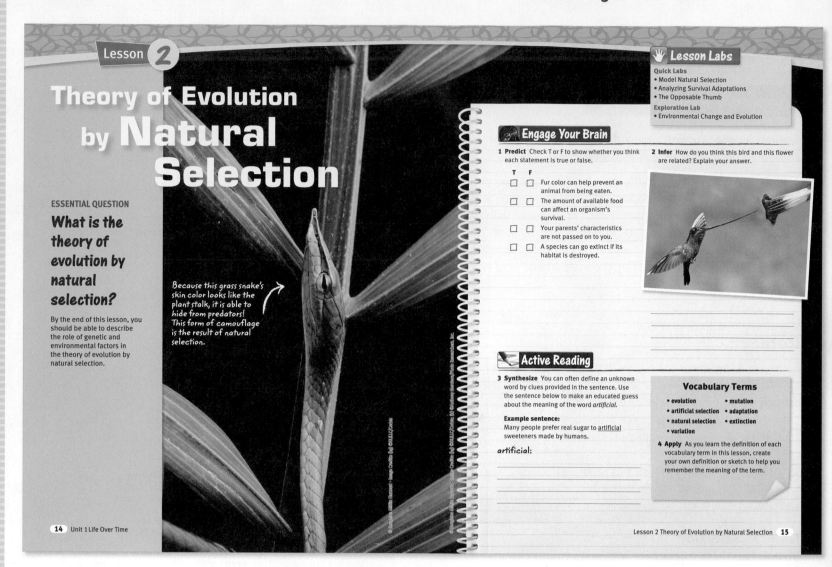

Answers

Answers for 1–3 should represent students' current thoughts, even if incorrect.

1. T, T, F, T

2. Sample answer: I think that the bird gets nectar from the flower because the long flower fits the bird's long beak. The red color may be attractive to the bird.

3. Sample answer: Artificial means something that is not real or not natural.

4. Students should define or sketch each vocabulary term in the lesson.

Opening Your Lesson

Discuss student responses to items 1 and 2 to assess students' prerequisite knowledge and to estimate what they already know about the theory of evolution by natural selection.

Prerequisites Students should already know that a species is a group of living things that can breed with one another to produce offspring that can breed as well; that a fossil is the imprint or the hardened remains of a plant or animal that lived long ago; and that an environment is everything that surrounds a living thing.

Learning Alert

Everyday Definitions In everyday speech, the word *theory* is often used to refer to a guess or an opinion. A scientific theory, however, is subject to a much higher level of investigation. A scientific theory is a system of ideas that explains many related observations and is supported by a large body of evidence. A theory is never described as proven or true; however, it may become firmly established by the evidence supporting it. As students read, have them pay close attention to the evidence Darwin used to support his theory of evolution by natural selection.

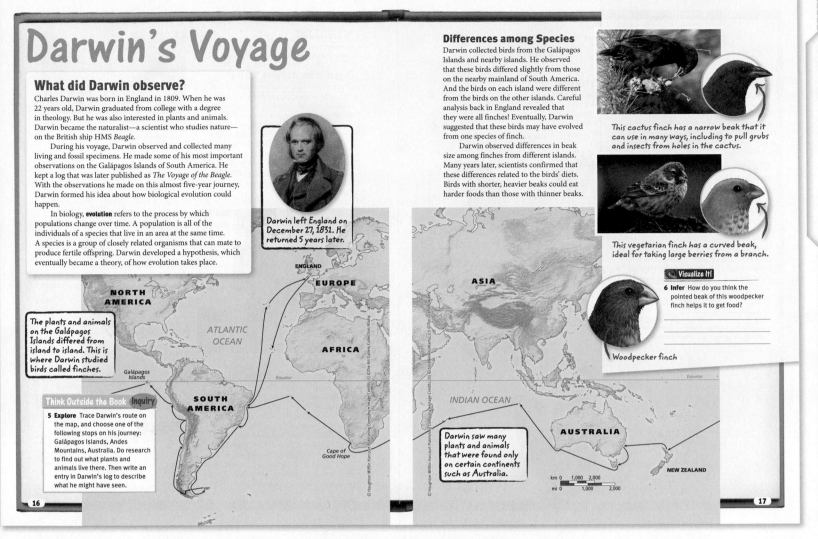

Darwin's Voyage

What did Darwin observe?

Charles Darwin was born in England in 1809. When he was 22 years old, Darwin graduated from college with a degree in theology. But he was also interested in plants and animals. Darwin became the naturalist—a scientist who studies nature—on the British ship HMS *Beagle.*

During his voyage, Darwin observed and collected many living and fossil specimens. He made some of his most important observations on the Galápagos Islands of South America. He kept a log that was later published as *The Voyage of the Beagle.* With the observations he made on this almost five-year journey, Darwin formed his idea about how biological evolution could happen.

In biology, **evolution** refers to the process by which populations change over time. A population is all of the individuals of a species that live in an area at the same time. A species is a group of closely related organisms that can mate to produce fertile offspring. Darwin developed a hypothesis, which eventually became a theory, of how evolution takes place.

Darwin left England on December 27, 1831. He returned 5 years later.

The plants and animals on the Galápagos Islands differed from island to island. This is where Darwin studied birds called finches.

Think Outside the Book Inquiry

5 Explore Trace Darwin's route on the map, and choose one of the following stops on his journey: Galápagos Islands, Andes Mountains, Australia. Do research to find out what plants and animals live there. Then write an entry in Darwin's log to describe what he might have seen.

NORTH AMERICA
ENGLAND
EUROPE
ASIA
ATLANTIC OCEAN
AFRICA
Galápagos Islands
Equator
SOUTH AMERICA
INDIAN OCEAN
Cape of Good Hope
AUSTRALIA

Darwin saw many plants and animals that were found only on certain continents such as Australia.

km 0   1,000   2,000
mi 0   1,000   2,000
NEW ZEALAND

Differences among Species

Darwin collected birds from the Galápagos Islands and nearby islands. He observed that these birds differed slightly from those on the nearby mainland of South America. And the birds on each island were different from the birds on the other islands. Careful analysis back in England revealed that they were all finches! Eventually, Darwin suggested that these birds may have evolved from one species of finch.

Darwin observed differences in beak size among finches from different islands. Many years later, scientists confirmed that these differences related to the birds' diets. Birds with shorter, heavier beaks could eat harder foods than those with thinner beaks.

This cactus finch has a narrow beak that it can use in many ways, including to pull grubs and insects from holes in the cactus.

This vegetarian finch has a curved beak, ideal for taking large berries from a branch.

Visualize It!

6 Infer How do you think the pointed beak of this woodpecker finch helps it to get food?

Woodpecker finch

Answers

5. Student answers should be written as entries in Darwin's log, and should include information about living things in the destination chosen.

6. Sample answer: It might help the bird peck into wood to find insects.

Building Reading Skills

Context Clues: Examples Remind students that a word's context, or the other words and sentences around it, can be clues to the word's meaning. Have students use examples in context to figure out the meaning of the word *specimen*. Sample answer: an individual, item, or part that is representative of a group

🌐 *Optional Online resource: Context Clues: Examples support*

Probing Questions   DIRECTED Inquiry

Drawing Conclusions Why do you think Darwin labeled the finch specimens with information about the islands on which he observed them? Sample answers: so he could keep track of where each specimen came from; so he could identify differences between birds on different islands How might having a shorter, heavier beak allow a bird to eat harder foods than a bird that has a longer, thinner beak? Sample answer: A short, heavy beak would probably be strong enough to break apart hard foods. A longer, thinner beak might not be able to break apart food that was too hard. **Prompt:** Which would more easily break open a large nut, such as a walnut: a heavy pair of pliers or a lightweight pair of tweezers?

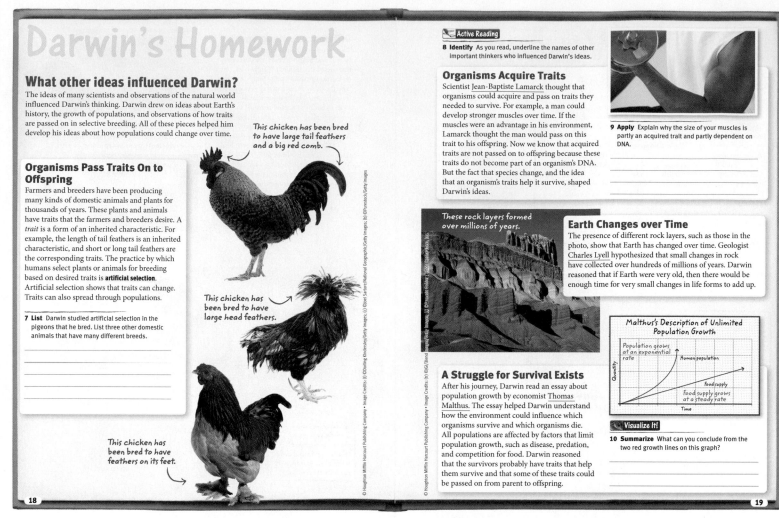

Darwin's Homework

What other ideas influenced Darwin?

The ideas of many scientists and observations of the natural world influenced Darwin's thinking. Darwin drew on ideas about Earth's history, the growth of populations, and observations of how traits are passed on in selective breeding. All of these pieces helped him develop his ideas about how populations could change over time.

This chicken has been bred to have large tail feathers and a big red comb.

Organisms Pass Traits On to Offspring

Farmers and breeders have been producing many kinds of domestic animals and plants for thousands of years. These plants and animals have traits that the farmers and breeders desire. A *trait* is a form of an inherited characteristic. For example, the length of tail feathers is an inherited characteristic, and short or long tail feathers are the corresponding traits. The practice by which humans select plants or animals for breeding based on desired traits is **artificial selection**. Artificial selection shows that traits can change. Traits can also spread through populations.

7 List Darwin studied artificial selection in the pigeons that he bred. List three other domestic animals that have many different breeds.

This chicken has been bred to have large head feathers.

This chicken has been bred to have feathers on its feet.

Active Reading

8 Identify As you read, underline the names of other important thinkers who influenced Darwin's ideas.

Organisms Acquire Traits

Scientist Jean-Baptiste Lamarck thought that organisms could acquire and pass on traits they needed to survive. For example, a man could develop stronger muscles over time. If the muscles were an advantage in his environment, Lamarck thought the man would pass on this trait to his offspring. Now we know that acquired traits are not passed on to offspring because these traits do not become part of an organism's DNA. But the fact that species change, and the idea that an organism's traits help it survive, shaped Darwin's ideas.

9 Apply Explain why the size of your muscles is partly an acquired trait and partly dependent on DNA.

These rock layers formed over millions of years.

Earth Changes over Time

The presence of different rock layers, such as those in the photo, show that Earth has changed over time. Geologist Charles Lyell hypothesized that small changes in rock have collected over hundreds of millions of years. Darwin reasoned that if Earth were very old, then there would be enough time for very small changes in life forms to add up.

A Struggle for Survival Exists

After his journey, Darwin read an essay about population growth by economist Thomas Malthus. The essay helped Darwin understand how the environment could influence which organisms survive and which organisms die. All populations are affected by factors that limit population growth, such as disease, predation, and competition for food. Darwin reasoned that the survivors probably have traits that help them survive and that some of these traits could be passed on from parent to offspring.

Malthus's Description of Unlimited Population Growth

Population grows at an exponential rate — *Human population* — *Food supply grows at a steady rate*

Visualize It!

10 Summarize What can you conclude from the two red growth lines on this graph?

18 · 19

Answers

7. Sample answers: dogs; chickens; pigs

8. *See students' pages for annotations.*

9. Although DNA affects a person's body shape and size, a person's activities will determine the size of the person's muscles.

10. The human population size increases faster than the food supply.

Probing Questions GUIDED Inquiry

Applying Dogs have been bred by people for thousands of years. What are some physical and behavioral traits of dogs? Sample answers: physical traits—black or brown fur, long or short fur, long or short snout, short or tall stature; behavioral traits—hunting/retrieving ability, having docile or aggressive temperament, level of intelligence
Prompt: Think about corresponding characteristics for each trait.

Comparing How does an inherited characteristic differ from an acquired characteristic? Give some examples. Sample answer: An inherited characteristic is passed on from parents to offspring; for example, eye color. An acquired characteristic is developed during an organism's lifetime; for example, a scar.

Formative Assessment

Ask: How did the ideas of Jean-Baptiste Lamarck, Charles Lyell, and Thomas Malthus influence Darwin's thinking? Sample answer: Lamarck influenced Darwin to think about how an organism's traits could help it survive, and that an organism can change over time. Lyell presented evidence that Earth was hundreds of millions of years old. Darwin reasoned that this would provide the time needed for populations to slowly change. Malthus's essay helped Darwin understand how competition for resources could affect populations and their survival.

Natural Selection

What are the four parts of natural selection?

Darwin proposed that most evolution happens through the natural selection of advantageous traits. **Natural selection** is the process by which organisms that inherit advantageous traits tend to reproduce more successfully than other organisms do.

Overproduction

When a plant or animal reproduces, it usually makes more offspring than the environment can support. For example, a female jaguar may have up to four pups at a time. Only some of them will survive to adulthood, and a smaller number of them will successfully reproduce.

11 Infer A fish may have hundreds of offspring at a time, and only a small number will survive. Which characteristics of fish might allow them to survive?

_____

_____

Not all of these jaguar cubs will survive long enough to reproduce.

Genetic Variation

Variation exists in the jaw sizes of these two jaguars. This variation will be passed on to the next generation.

Within a species there are naturally occurring differences, or **variations**, in traits. For example, in the two jaguar skulls to the left, one jaw is larger than the other. This difference results from a difference in the genetic material of the jaguars. Genetic variations can be passed on from parent to offspring. An important source of variation is a **mutation**, or change in genetic material.

As each new generation is produced, genetic variation may be introduced into a population. The more genetic variation in a population, the more likely it is that some individuals might have traits that will be advantageous if the environment changes. Also, genetic variation can lead to diversity of organisms as a population adapts to changing environments.

Selection

Individuals try to get the resources they need to survive. These resources include food, water, space and, in most cases, mates for reproduction. About 11,000 years ago, jaguars faced a shortage of food because the climate changed and many prey species died out. A genetic variation in jaw size then became important for survival. Jaguars with larger jaws could eat hard-shelled reptiles when other prey were hard to find.

Darwin reasoned that individuals with a particular trait, such as a large jaw, are more likely to survive long enough to reproduce. As a result, the trait is "selected" for, becoming more common in the next generation of offspring.

12 Summarize How did large jaws and teeth become typical traits of jaguars?

_____

_____

A larger jaw makes it easier for this jaguar to eat hard-shelled turtles.

Adaptation

An inherited trait that helps an organism survive and reproduce in its environment is an **adaptation**. Adaptation is the selection of naturally occurring trait variations in populations. Jaguars with larger jaws were able to survive and reproduce when food was hard to find. As natural selection continues, adaptations grow more common in the population with each new generation. Over time, the population becomes better adapted to the environment.

Large jaw size is one adaptation of jaguars.

13 Explain In the table below, explain how each part of natural selection works.

Principle of natural selection	How it works
overproduction	
genetic variation	
selection	
adaptation	

© Houghton Mifflin Harcourt Publishing Company

Answers

11. Sample answers: ability to swim fast; ability to eat a variety of food; ability to blend in with the surroundings

12. Jaguars with large jaws and teeth survived and reproduced more than other jaguars, so these traits became more common.

13. overproduction: Organisms have more offspring than can survive; genetic variation: Offspring have slight differences in their traits; selection: Some traits increase the chances that an organism will survive; adaptation: Over time, a trait that helps survival will become more common.

Learning Alert 🚧 MISCONCEPTION 🚧

The "Selection" of Traits Students may think that species evolve purposefully in order to satisfy a new need. The environmental selection that occurs as part of natural selection is the result of differential reproductive success of organisms with particular collections of traits in their current environment. As an example, ask students to consider the process of natural selection that led salmon to have a slightly curved tail. The curve in their tails allows salmon to swim faster and, thus, avoid being eaten by predators. Because of this greater ability to avoid predators, individuals with the curved tail tended to survive and reproduce more often than those without curved tails. The curved-tail salmon passed on this beneficial trait to their offspring. Over time, most salmon evolved to have a curve in their tails.

Probing Questions DIRECTED Inquiry

Inferring When a mutation in an organism's DNA makes it more likely to survive than other members of the group, that mutation gets passed along. Animals with that mutation survive longer and reproduce more. **Ask:** What do you think happens if a genetic mutation occurs that is not advantageous to the animal? Sample answers: Nothing happens if the trait has neither an advantage or a disadvantage. The trait will still be passed along at the same rate as other traits. If the trait makes an animal less likely to survive, it won't be passed along as often, and may eventually become absent in the population.

Well-adapted

How do species change over time?

In order for a population to change, some individuals have to be different from other members of the population. Mutations are one of the main sources of genetic variation. Offspring sometimes inherit a gene that has a slight mutation, or change, from the gene the parent has. Mutations can be harmful, helpful, or have no effect. Beneficial mutations help individuals survive and reproduce.

Over Generations, Adaptations Become More Common

Active Reading 14 **Identify** Underline examples of adaptations.

Adaptations are inherited traits that help organisms survive and reproduce. Some adaptations, such as a duck's webbed feet, are internal or external structures. Other adaptations are inherited behaviors that help an organism find food, protect itself, or reproduce. At first, an adaptation is rare in a population. Imagine a bird population in which some birds have short beaks. If more birds with shorter beaks survive and reproduce than birds with longer beaks, more birds in the next generation will probably have short beaks. The number of individuals with the adaptation would continue to increase.

Visualize It!

15 Write a caption to describe how this butterfly's long mouth part helps it to survive.

_____
_____
_____

The male frigate bird uses his red throat pouch to attract a female, which could lead to reproduction.

Genetic Differences Add Up

Parents and offspring often have small differences in genetic material. Over many generations, the small differences can add up so that organisms alive now are often very different from their ancestors. As a result, there is great diversity among organisms. For example, the antibiotic penicillin was able to kill many types of bacteria in the 1950s. Today, some of those species of bacteria are now completely resistant to penicillin. The genetic makeup of these bacterial populations has changed. New fossil discoveries and new information about genes add to scientists' understanding of natural selection and evolution.

What happens to species as the environment changes?

Certain environments favor certain traits. Consider a snake population with either brown- or green-colored snakes. In a forest that has many dead leaves on the ground, brown snakes will blend in better than green snakes will. But in an area with more grass, the green snakes may be better at hiding from predators. Changes in environmental conditions can affect the survival of organisms with a particular trait. Environmental changes can also lead to diversity of organisms by increasing the number of species.

Dinosaurs went extinct 65 million years ago.

Adaptations Can Allow a Species to Survive

All organisms have traits that allow them to survive in specific environments. For example, plants have xylem tissue that carries water up from the roots to the rest of the plant.

If the environment changes, a species is more likely to survive if it has genetic variation. For example, imagine a species of grass in which some plants need less water than others. If the environment became drier, many grass plants would die, but the plants that needed less water might survive. These plants might eventually become a new species if they cannot reproduce with the plants that needed more water.

Some Species May Become Extinct

If no individuals have traits that help them to survive and reproduce in the changed environment, a species will become extinct. **Extinction** occurs when all members of a species have died. Greater competition, new predators, and the loss of habitat are examples of environmental changes that can lead to extinction. Some extinctions are caused by natural disasters. Because a natural disaster can destroy resources quickly, organisms may die no matter what adaptations they have. The fossil record shows that many species have become extinct in the history of life on Earth.

Visualize It!

Environmental change has affected the environmental conditions near the North Pole.

16 **Summarize** How has ice cover near the North Pole changed in the last few decades?

_____
_____

17 **Infer** How do you think this environmental change will affect species that live in the surrounding area?

_____
_____
_____
_____
_____

Source: National Aeronautics and Space Administration, 2007

22 | 23

Answers

14. *See students' pages for annotations.*

15. Sample answer: This butterfly uses its long mouth part to reach the nectar deep within flowers.

16. It has decreased substantially.

17. Sample answer: Organisms with adaptations that allow them to survive in the new conditions will survive and reproduce. These adaptations will become more common. Some species may become extinct.

Learning Alert

Physical and Behavioral Adaptations You may wish to provide students with additional examples of physical and behavioral adaptations. Physical adaptations include frogs' webbed feet, elephants' trunks, and whales' fins. Behavioral adaptations include instincts such as nest-building and migration in some birds and hibernation in woodchucks, bats, and certain other animals. Note that plants also have adaptations, such as roses' protective thorns and the hard shells of coconuts.

Formative Assessment

Provide students with a list of the following: *rocks, pond, alligator, mud, heart, grass, tail, sand,* and *sense of smell.* **Ask:** Which of these are environmental factors that might influence the traits present in a population of organisms? rocks; pond; alligator; mud; grass; sand

Ask: Arctic foxes live in cold arctic regions. In the snowy and icy winter, their fur is white. When the weather is warmer in the spring and summer and the snow melts, their fur changes to brown or gray. How might this adaptation help arctic foxes survive in their environment? Sample answer: This adaptation helps the arctic fox blend in with its environment all year. This trait helps it hide from predators.

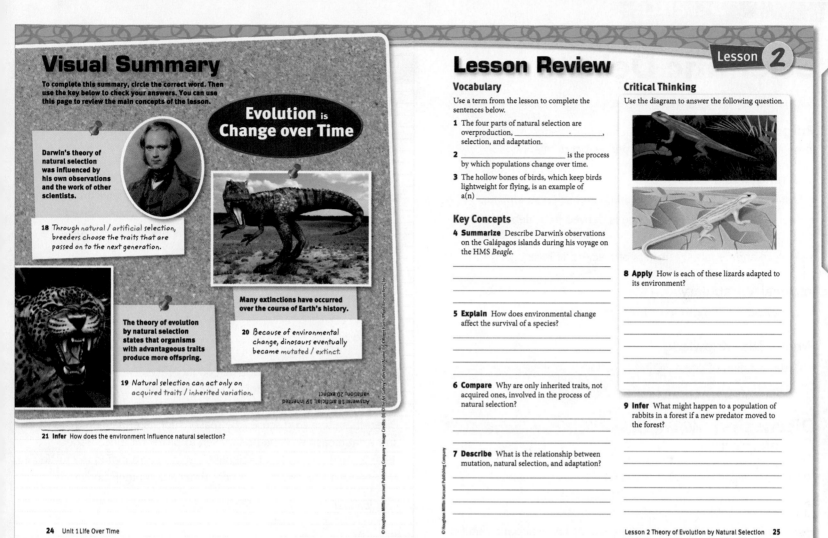

Visual Summary

To complete this summary, circle the correct word. Then use the key below to check your answers. You can use this page to review the main concepts of the lesson.

Evolution is Change over Time

Darwin's theory of natural selection was influenced by his own observations and the work of other scientists.

18 Through natural / artificial selection, breeders choose the traits that are passed on to the next generation.

Many extinctions have occurred over the course of Earth's history.

20 Because of environmental change, dinosaurs eventually became mutated / extinct.

The theory of evolution by natural selection states that organisms with advantageous traits produce more offspring.

19 Natural selection can act only on acquired traits / inherited variation.

Answers: 18 artificial; 19 inherited variation; 20 extinct

21 Infer How does the environment influence natural selection?

24   Unit 1 Life Over Time

Lesson Review

Vocabulary

Use a term from the lesson to complete the sentences below.

1 The four parts of natural selection are overproduction, _____, selection, and adaptation.

2 _____ is the process by which populations change over time.

3 The hollow bones of birds, which keep birds lightweight for flying, is an example of a(n) _____

Key Concepts

4 Summarize Describe Darwin's observations on the Galápagos islands during his voyage on the HMS *Beagle*.

_____

_____

_____

5 Explain How does environmental change affect the survival of a species?

_____

_____

_____

6 Compare Why are only inherited traits, not acquired ones, involved in the process of natural selection?

_____

_____

_____

7 Describe What is the relationship between mutation, natural selection, and adaptation?

_____

_____

_____

Critical Thinking

Use the diagram to answer the following question.

8 Apply How is each of these lizards adapted to its environment?

_____

_____

_____

_____

9 Infer What might happen to a population of rabbits in a forest if a new predator moved to the forest?

_____

_____

_____

_____

Lesson 2 Theory of Evolution by Natural Selection   25

Visual Summary Answers

18. artificial
19. inherited variation
20. extinct
21. Sample answer: Different traits are advantageous, depending on the environment.

Lesson Review Answers

1. genetic variation
2. Evolution
3. adaptation
4. Darwin saw variations in finches that lived on neighboring islands. Finches on different islands had different types of beaks.
5. It can lead to the extinction of a species unless variations allow for adaptation.
6. Acquired traits are not passed on to offspring.
7. Mutations are a main source of variation. Some mutations are beneficial. The resulting adaptations will become more common through natural selection.

8. The lizard's body color blends in with the surroundings. This helps it hide from predators.
9. Rabbits with advantageous traits, such as the ability to run very fast, could survive, and the rabbit population could change over time. Or the rabbits might not survive.

 Think Science

Scientific Debate

Purpose To understand how scientific knowledge is gained through scientific debate and independent confirmation

Learning Goals
- Distinguish between experimentation and scientific debate.
- Explain how scientific knowledge is derived from debate and independent confirmation.
- Analyze and debate the results of a scientific investigation.

Informal Vocabulary
factor, experimental group, control group, bias

Prerequisite Knowledge
- Understanding of scientific investigations

Discussion *Where Scientific Knowledge Comes From*

 whole class   15 min

Inquiry GUIDED inquiry

Have students think about what they already know about scientific knowledge. **Ask:** If you wanted to know more about sea turtles, do you think you would learn more by conducting an experiment or by discussing sea turtles with a turtle expert? Why? Sample answer: I would learn more from an expert because an experiment would probably only tell me one thing, but an expert could tell me many things. **Ask:** Could you learn about sea turtles by listening to two experts who disagree with each other? Explain. Sample answer: Yes, I would learn about the turtles, and I would also learn about areas of controversy. Then I could evaluate the evidence for myself to form my own opinion.

 Optional Online rubric: Class Discussion

Basic *Debate It*

 small groups   🕐 25 min

Role Playing Students should use the information in the tutorial to answer the questions about the passage. Then have small groups take the role of scientists and conservationists. Direct each group to conduct a scientific debate about the best ways to protect Barbour's map turtles.

Advanced *Barbour's Map Turtle*

 individuals   🕐 30 min

Quick Research Have students conduct research to learn more about the Barbour's map turtle. Encourage them to find out more about the turtle's physical characteristics, behavior, and habitat. Direct them to also discover the reasons for its endangered status and what measures have been taken to protect it. Encourage them to note any areas of scientific debate surrounding the turtle. Have students write a brief report summarizing their findings.

 Optional Online rubric: Written Pieces

ELL *Draw a Fossil*

👥 individuals   🕐 10 min

Have students look at the fossil shown on these pages and think about and draw what other fossils might look like. Have them think about these questions before they begin: What might a fossil of a flying animal look like? What might a fossil of a fish look like? What might a fossil of a plant-eater look like? A meat eater? Encourage students to draw fossils of several different types of organisms.

Variation Provide students with images of fossils and have them draw what they think the original organism might have looked like.

Customize Your Feature

☐ **Discussion** Where Scientific Knowledge Comes From

☐ **Basic** Debate It

☐ **Advanced** Barbour's Map Turtle

☐ **ELL** Draw a Fossil

Scientific Debate

Not all scientific knowledge is gained through experimentation. It is also the result of a great deal of debate and confirmation.

Tutorial

As you prepare for a debate, look for information from the following sources.

Controlled Experiments Consider the following points when planning or examining the results of a controlled experiment.

- Only one factor should be tested at a time. A factor is anything in the experiment that can influence the outcome.
- Samples are divided into experimental group(s) and a control group. All of the factors of the experimental group(s) and the control group are the same except for one variable.
- A variable is a factor that can be changed. If there are multiple variables, only one variable should be changed at a time.

Independent Studies The results of a different group may provide stronger support for your argument than your own results. And using someone else's results helps to avoid the claim that your results are biased. Bias is the tendency to think about something from only one point of view. The claim of bias can be used to argue against your point.

Comparison with Similar Objects or Events If you cannot gather data from an experiment to help support your position, finding a similar object or event might help. The better your example is understood, the stronger your argument will be.

Read the passage below and answer the questions.

Many people want to protect endangered species but do not agree on the best methods to use. Incubating, or heating eggs to ensure hatching, is commonly used with bird eggs. It was logical to apply the same technique to turtle eggs. The Barbour's map turtle is found in Florida, Georgia, and Alabama. To help more turtles hatch, people would gather eggs and incubate them. However, debate really began when mostly female turtles hatched. Were efforts to help the turtles really harming them? Scientists learned that incubating eggs at 25°C (77°F) produces males and at 30°C (86°F) produces females. As a result, conservation programs have stopped artificially heating the eggs.

1 What is the variable described in the article about Barbour's map turtles?

2 Write a list of factors that were likely kept the same between the sample groups described in the article.

3 What argument could people have used who first suggested incubating the turtle eggs?

You Try It!

Fossils from the Burgess Shale Formation in Canada include many strange creatures that lived over 500 million years ago. The fossils are special because the soft parts of the creatures were preserved. Examine the fossil of the creature *Marrella* and the reconstruction of what it might have looked like.

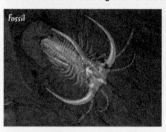
Fossil

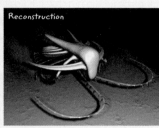
Reconstruction

1 Recognizing Relationships Find four features on the reconstruction that you can also identify in the fossil. Write a brief description of each feature.

2 Applying Concepts *Marrella* is extinct. How do you think *Marrella* behaved when it was alive? What did it eat? How did it move? On what do you base your argument?

3 Communicating Ideas Share your description with a classmate. Discuss and debate your positions. Complete the table to show the points on which you agree and disagree.

Agree	Disagree

Take It Home

Research more about the creatures of the Burgess Shale Formation. Find at least one other fossil creature and its reconstruction. What do you think the creature was like?

Answers

1. Students should point out and briefly describe the four features of the reconstruction that they can also see in the fossil.

2. Students should make predictions about how they think the creature behaved, what it ate, and how it moved, based on their interpretation of the uses of the features they see in the reconstruction and fossil.

3. Students should have a list in their table of points in which they agreed and disagreed with a classmate, having discussed and debated with a classmate.

Take It Home

The Burgess Shale Formation contains organisms from the Cambrian Period of 545 to 525 million years ago. Organisms found in the formation include trilobites, algae, worms, and sea anemones. When describing what they think the creature they chose was like, encourage students to make their own observations rather than relying solely on descriptions accompanying the fossil and its reconstruction.

Evidence of Evolution

Essential Question What evidence supports the theory of evolution?

 Professional Development

For more detailed information about the topics in this lesson, refer to the Content Refresher in the Unit Opener pages.

Opening Your Lesson

Begin the lesson by assessing students' prerequisite and prior knowledge.

Prerequisite Knowledge

- Theory of evolution by natural selection
- Extinction

Accessing Prior Knowledge

Ask: What evidence did the finches Darwin observed on the Galápagos Islands provide for the theory of evolution by natural selection? Sample answer: Darwin thought the differences in the beak shapes of the finches were related to the birds' diets. He concluded that, over time, the finches on different islands had evolved to be better adapted to eating the food sources on their islands.

Customize Your Opening

☐ **Accessing Prior Knowledge,** above

☐ **Print Path** Engage Your Brain, SE p. 29

☐ **Print Path** Active Reading, SE p. 29

☐ **Digital Path** Lesson Opener

Key Topics/Learning Goals

Fossil Evidence

1 Identify different types of fossils.
2 Describe how fossils form.
3 Describe the fossil record.
4 Describe how scientists use fossil evidence to determine relationships between organisms.

Structural Evidence

1 Define *common ancestor*.
2 Describe how unused body structures are evidence for evolution.
3 Describe how similar body structures with different functions are evidence for evolution.

Genetic Evidence

1 Describe how genetic evidence supports evolution.

Embryological Evidence

1 Describe how similarities in developmental patterns provide evidence of evolution.

Supporting Concepts

- Fossils are the remains or traces of once-living organisms.
- Cast fossils form when an organism is covered by sediment; as time passes, more sediment is layered over the organism. Over time, minerals seep into the organism and replace the organism with stone.
- The fossil record is the history of life in the geologic past as preserved in fossils; older fossils are in lower rock layers.

- A common ancestor is the most recent species from which two different species evolved.
- An unused body structure in an organism is a structure now reduced in size or function that may have been complete and functional in the organism's ancestors.
- Shared body structures suggest that organisms had a common ancestor.

- The more similar the DNA is between two species, the more closely related the species are likely to be.

- If organisms share patterns of development, it is likely that they also share a common ancestor.

Options for Instruction

Two parallel paths provide coverage of the Essential Questions, with a strong **Inquiry** strand woven into each. Follow the **Print Path,** the **Digital Path,** or your customized combination of print, digital, and inquiry.

 Print Path
Teaching support for the Print Path appears with the Student Pages.

 Inquiry Labs and Activities

 Digital Path
Digital Path shortcut: TS673000

Fossil Hunt, SE pp. 30–31
How do fossils form?
• Many Fossils Form in Sedimentary Rock
How do fossils show change over time?

Field Lab
Mystery Footprints

Activity
Tar Pit Fossils

Solid as a Rock!
Interactive Image

The Fossil Record
Diagram

The Fossil Record in Action
Interactive Image

More Clues. . . , SE p. 32
What other evidence supports evolution?
• Common Structures

Quick Lab
Comparing Anatomy

Daily Demo
Observing Structural Similarities

Activity
What's That For?

Is That All?
Interactive Image

Structural Similarities
Diagram

More Clues. . . , SE p. 33
• Similar DNA

Quick Lab
Genetic Evidence for Evolution

Is That All?
Interactive Image

More Clues. . . , SE p. 33
• Developmental Similarities

Is That All?
Interactive Image

Options for Assessment

See the Evaluate page for options, including Formative Assessment, Summative Assessment, and Unit Review.

Engage and Explore

Activities and Discussion

Take It Home *Similar Structures*

Engage

Introducing Key Topics

 adult-student pairs
🕐 30 min
GUIDED inquiry

Students should work with an adult to observe organisms seen during a neighborhood walk, within a home, on a web site, or in books or videos. The pair should note the features of different organisms and sketch them if possible. They should then discuss physical similarities between and among the organisms and how these similarities may be evidence of common ancestry.

 Optional Online resource: student worksheet

Discussion *Archaeopteryx*

Engage

Fossil Evidence

 whole class
🕐 15 min

Discussion Fossils of an ancient creature known as *Archaeopteryx* provide evidence of evolution. *Archaeopteryx* was contemporary with many dinosaurs. Fossils show it was similar to dinosaurs and their reptile descendants in having a long tail and in the shape and features of its skull, including that it had teeth and no bill. It also shares some features with modern birds, including feathers, a wishbone, reduced fingers, and wings. Have students discuss how *Archaeopteryx* provides evidence of common ancestry between birds and reptiles.

Probing Question *Snake Legs*

Embryological Evidence

 small group
🕐 20 min
DIRECTED inquiry

Interpreting Tell students that as embryos, some species of snakes have little buds that look as if they would develop into hind legs. These disappear later in development. Ask students what they think this evidence tells about snakes' ancestors.

Activity *What's That For?*

Engage

Structural Evidence

 small groups
🕐 30 min
GUIDED inquiry

Jigsaw Have small groups each research an unused body structure of a particular organism. Possible choices include the wings of flightless birds, the eyes of blind fish or certain cave-dwelling animals, and the dewclaws of some dog breeds.  Direct students to learn about the structure's current form as well as any evidence of its form and function in the organism's ancestors. Once groups have become "experts" on their unused body structure, rearrange the class into new groups. Have the mixed groups each create an informational poster about one or two of the body structures that the original groups researched. Have groups share their posters with the class and discuss what they learned.

Probing Questions *Cetacean Similarities*

Synthesizing Key Topics

 individuals
🕐 20 min
GUIDED inquiry

Inferring Whales and dolphins are both cetaceans that share a recent common ancestry. Have students infer what similarities scientists would find between whales and dolphins and what these similarities might show about their common ancestry. You may wish to show photographs of whales and dolphins, both living and skeletal, for reference. You may also wish to allow students to perform research to check their ideas.

DIRECTED inquiry variation Work with students to consider what fossil, structural, genetic, and embryological evidence they would expect scientists to find that would support the idea that whales and dolphins evolved from a common ancestor.

Levels of Inquiry

DIRECTED inquiry	**GUIDED** inquiry	**INDEPENDENT** inquiry
introduces inquiry skills within a structured framework.	develops inquiry skills within a supportive environment.	deepens inquiry skills with student-driven questions or procedures.

Labs and Demos

Daily Demo *Observing Structural Similarities*

Engage

Structural Evidence

- whole class
- 15 min
- **GUIDED** inquiry

PURPOSE **To explore the similarities and differences in form and function between shared skeletal structures**

MATERIALS

- live animal that shares limb skeletal structures with humans, such as a cat, lizard, or frog
- images or models of the human skeleton and the skeleton of the animal

1 Have students observe the movements of your arm and the forelimb of the animal and compare the shared skeletal structures.

2 Students should draw what they observe and analyze how similar structures function differently. Then they should share their observations with the class.

Quick Lab *Genetic Evidence for Evolution*

PURPOSE **To use similarities and differences in DNA sequences to determine the evolutionary relationships between several organisms**

See the Lab Manual or go Online for planning information.

Quick Lab *Comparing Anatomy*

PURPOSE **To compare the anatomy of several vertebrate animals**

See the Lab Manual or go Online for planning information.

Field Lab *Mystery Footprints*

Fossil Evidence

- small groups
- 90 min
- **DIRECTED or GUIDED** inquiry

Students investigate a set of mystery footprints and study their own footprints in order to infer information about the person or persons who made the mystery prints.

PURPOSE **To describe features of unknown people based on their footprints**

MATERIALS

- box or poster board, at least 1 m²
- meterstick
- paper, blank
- ruler, metric
- sand, slightly damp
- scale, bathroom
- lab apron
- safety goggles

Customize Your Labs

 See the Lab Manual for lab datasheets.

 Go Online for editable lab datasheets.

Activities and Discussions

- ☐ **Take It Home** Similar Structures
- ☐ **Discussion** *Archaeopteryx*
- ☐ **Probing Question** Snake Legs
- ☐ **Activity** What's That For?
- ☐ **Probing Questions** Cetacean Similarities

Labs and Demos

- ☐ **Daily Demo** Observing Structural Similarities
- ☐ **Quick Lab** Genetic Evidence for Evolution
- ☐ **Quick Lab** Comparing Anatomy
- ☐ **Field Lab** Mystery Footprints

Your Resources

Explain Science Concepts

	Print Path	Digital Path
Key Topics		

Fossil Evidence

Print Path

☐ **Fossil Hunt,** SE pp. 30–31
- Examine, #5
- Active Reading (Annotation strategy), #6
- Visualize It!, #7–8

A transitional form between fish and four-legged land vertebrates may be this creature called *Tiktaalik roseae*.

Digital Path

☐ **Solid as a Rock!**
Examine how the fossil record supports the theory of evolution.

☐ **The Fossil Record in Action**
Use fossils and structural evidence to determine relationships between species.

Structural Evidence

Print Path

☐ **More Clues. . . ,** SE p. 32
- Active Reading, #9
- Visualize It!, #10

Digital Path

☐ **Structural Similarities**
Compare the skeletal structures of animals that have a common ancestor.

Genetic Evidence

Print Path

☐ **More Clues. . . ,** SE p. 33
- Visualize It!, #11

Cytochrome C Comparison	
Organism	Number of amino acid differences from human cytochrome c
Chimpanzee	0
Rhesus monkey	1
Whale	10
Turtle	15
Bullfrog	18
Lamprey	20

Digital Path

☐ **Is That All?**
Examine structural, genetic, and embryological evidence for evolution.

Embryological Evidence

Print Path

☐ **More Clues. . . ,** SE pp. 33–35
- Visualize It!, #11–13
- Analyze, #14

Digital Path

☐ **Is That All?**
Examine structural, genetic, and embryological evidence for evolution.

Basic *Organism Relationships*

Synthesizing Key Topics	pairs
	🕐 15 min

Provide students with images of living or extinct organisms. Have pairs examine the images and discuss how the organisms might be related to one another based on their physical features. Then tell pairs to arrange in a diagram all or some of the organisms they studied. The diagram should illustrate the perceived relationships among the organisms, with organisms that seem more closely related closer together than those that seem more distantly related. Check students' work and discuss their decisions. Explain that similar physical features sometimes, but not always, represent relatedness of organisms.

Advanced *Ancestors and Relatives*

Synthesizing Key Topics	individuals
	30 min

Quick Research Have students conduct research on a living organism of their choice. Ask them to prepare a short report addressing one or more of the following: *What organisms from the fossil record is this organism related to? Does the organism share any common ancestors with other living organisms? What evidence—fossil, skeletal, embryonic, or genetic—supports the relationships among the organisms?*

ELL *Picture Dictionary*

Synthesizing Key Topics	pairs or small groups
	25 min

Layered Book Fold Struggling or EL learners may have difficulty with complex terms in the lesson such as *molecular biology* and *common ancestor*. Define these terms for students and provide cognates when possible  *(molecular biology: la biología molecular, common ancestor: ancestro/antepasado común).* Then have pairs make a layered book fold to develop a picture dictionary for the terms. Explain that their drawings can either directly illustrate the terms or provide examples or other mnemonic devices.

fossil　　　　　**fossil record**

Previewing Vocabulary

whole class	🕐 15 min

Word Meanings Share the following to help students remember terms:

- **record** is an account or information or facts or information or data about a particular subject that is collected and preserved from the Latin *antecedere*, meaning "precede, go before."

Reinforcing Vocabulary

individuals	🕐 ongoing

Frame Game Have students draw a rectangle with a smaller rectangle inside it, and add lines connecting the outer corners of the rectangles to form four sections. Students place the term in the center of the frame. Then they decide which information to frame with the term in the outer sections. They can use examples, a definition, descriptions, parts, sentences that use the term, or pictures.

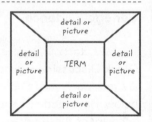

 Optional Online resource: Frame Game support

Customize Your Core Lesson

Core Instruction

- ☐ **Print Path** choices
- ☐ **Digital Path** choices

Vocabulary

- ☐ **Previewing Vocabulary** Word Meanings
- ☐ **Reinforcing Vocabulary** Frame Game

Your Resources

Differentiated Instruction

- ☐ **Basic** Organism Relationships
- ☐ **Advanced** Ancestors and Relatives
- ☐ **ELL** Picture Dictionary

_____

_____

Extend Science Concepts

Activity *Tar Pit Fossils*

Fossil Evidence

 small groups
🕐 45 min

Modeling The La Brea Tar Pits in Los Angeles, California, are a rich source of fossil evidence for evolution. Have groups research one type of fossil found in the tar pits and learn about that organism's closest living relative. Have them make clay models showing the similarities and differences between the extinct and living organisms. Groups can then present and explain their models to the class.

Discussion *Hemoglobin*

Genetic Evidence

👥 whole class
🕐 15 min

Quick Discussion Hemoglobin is a protein in vertebrates. Proteins are molecules made up of units called *amino acids*. Share the chart below. Have students explain what these data reveal about the ancestry of these organisms:

Species	Amino acid differences from human hemoglobin protein
Gorilla	1
Rhesus monkey	8
Mouse	27
Chicken	45
Frog	67
Lamprey	125

Graphic Organizer

Synthesizing Key Topics

👥 individual
🕐 ongoing

Idea Wheel Have students make an idea wheel with four sections. Have them write "Evidence For Evolution" at the center and label the outside sections "Fossil Evidence," "Structural Evidence," "Genetic Evidence," and "Embryological Evidence." Then direct them to add details related to each category.

Fine Arts Connection

Fossil Evidence

👥 small groups or whole class
🕐 30 min

Research and Discuss The role of a scientific illustrator is to create accurate pictures of organisms and things that scientists study. In the case of long-extinct species, such as dinosaurs, artists must sometimes hypothesize about what an organism looked like. Have students look for and compare several examples of illustrations of a specific extinct organism (*Iguanadon* is a good choice). Ask them to try to identify ways in which artistic interpretation is used. For comparison, show students examples of similar illustrations from one hundred years ago, when much less was known about many fossil organisms.

Earth Science Connection

Synthesizing Key Topics

👥 individual
🕐 varied

Quick Research The fossil record not only provides evidence of how species have changed over time, it also provides evidence of how Earth's environments have changed. For example, fossils of ocean organisms have been found far from any body of salt water. Have students research the fossil record to learn more about what it shows about how Earth's environments have changed over time. Ask them to share their findings with the class in posters or in a computer presentation.

🖰 *Optional Online rubrics: Posters and Displays; Multimedia Presentations*

Customize Your Closing

📖 *See the Assessment Guide for quizzes and tests.*

🖰 *Go Online to edit and create quizzes and tests.*

Reinforce and Review

☐ **Activity** Tar Pit Fossils

☐ **Discussion** Hemoglobin

☐ **Graphic Organizer** Idea Wheel

☐ **Print Path** Visual Summary, SE p. 36

☐ **Digital Path** Lesson Closer

Evaluate Student Mastery

Formative Assessment

See the teacher support below the Student Pages for additional Formative Assessment questions.

Ask: Suppose scientists discover fossil evidence of a recent common ancestor of two living species they did not previously believe were closely related. What other evidence could scientists collect to verify the relationship between the species? **Sample answer:** Scientists could look at the anatomy of the two species to see if similar structures suggest a close relationship. They could compare samples of the species' DNA or other molecules. If there are many similarities between the molecules, the species probably did share a common ancestor. They could also study the embryos to look for similarities in their development.

Reteach

Formative assessment may show that students need reinforcement for certain topics. The resources below are recommended for reteaching. If students were introduced to a topic through the Print Path, you can also use the Digital Path to reteach, and vice versa.

🎧 *Can be assigned to individual students*

Fossil Evidence
Activity Tar Pit Fossils 🎧

Structural Evidence
Daily Demo Observing Structural Similarities

Genetic Evidence
Quick Lab Genetic Evidence for Evolution 🎧

Embryological Evidence
Probing Question Snake Legs 🎧

Summative Assessment

Alternative Assessment
Prove It!

⊘ *Online resources: student worksheet, optional rubrics*

Evidence of Evolution

Tic-Tac-Toe: *Prove It!*
Imagine you are on a research team that is studying two species believed to share a common ancestor.

1. Work on your own, with a partner, or with a small group.

2. Choose three quick activities from the game. Check the boxes you plan to complete. They must form a straight line in any direction.

3. Have your teacher approve your plan.

4. Do each activity, and turn in your results.

__ Into the Past	__ It's in the Bones	__ Silence Doubts
Write a poem about the common ancestor of the two species. Include details about how the form of the common ancestor is similar to and different from its descendants.	Draw and label a body part, such as a leg or leaf, from each of the two species that displays a shared body structure. You may wish to color-code the parts, such as bones, to indicate corresponding structures.	Write a persuasive letter to another scientist who thinks the two species are too different to be related. Use evidence to convince the scientist of your team's findings.
__ Eureka!	__ Breaking News	__ Frozen in Time
Imagine your team has just made an important discovery. You have found evidence that the two species share a common ancestor. Discuss your findings and what they might mean.	Write a newspaper article that outlines your team's findings for an everyday audience. The article should explain all the evidence that points to the two species sharing a common ancestor.	Build a model of a fossil dig site. The model should depict layers of rock, one of which includes a fossil of the common ancestor of the two species.
__ Scientific Conference	__ Evolution Song	__ Interesting Developments
Give a multimedia presentation to share your findings at a scientific conference. Your presentation should include genetic evidence that the two species share a common ancestor.	Write and perform a song about the two species and their common ancestor. Include details about the structural evidence for a common ancestor.	Make an illustration that depicts embryological similarities between the two species. Label common structures and write a caption explaining the illustration.

Going Further

☐ **Fine Arts Connection**

☐ **Earth Science Connection**

Formative Assessment

☐ **Strategies** Throughout TE

☐ **Lesson Review** SE

Summative Assessment

☐ **Alternative Assessment** Prove It!

☐ **Lesson Quiz**

☐ **Unit Tests A and B**

☐ **Unit Review** SE End-of-Unit

Your Resources

_____   _____

_____   _____

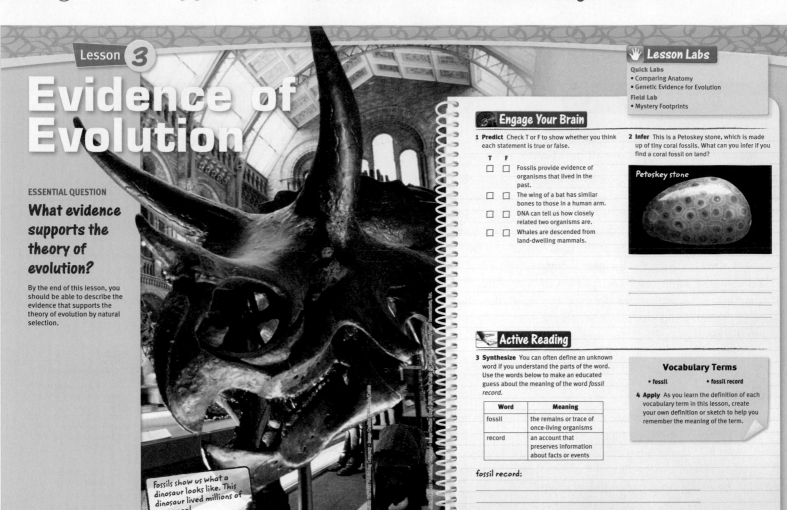

Lesson ③

Evidence of Evolution

ESSENTIAL QUESTION

What evidence supports the theory of evolution?

By the end of this lesson, you should be able to describe the evidence that supports the theory of evolution by natural selection.

Fossils show us what a dinosaur looks like. This dinosaur lived millions of years ago!

28 Unit 1 Life over Time

Lesson Labs

Quick Labs
• Comparing Anatomy
• Genetic Evidence for Evolution

Field Lab
• Mystery Footprints

Engage Your Brain

1 Predict Check T or F to show whether you think each statement is true or false.

T F

☐ ☐ Fossils provide evidence of organisms that lived in the past.

☐ ☐ The wing of a bat has similar bones to those in a human arm.

☐ ☐ DNA can tell us how closely related two organisms are.

☐ ☐ Whales are descended from land-dwelling mammals.

2 Infer This is a Petoskey stone, which is made up of tiny coral fossils. What can you infer if you find a coral fossil on land?

Petoskey stone

_____

_____

_____

_____

Active Reading

3 Synthesize You can often define an unknown word if you understand the parts of the word. Use the words below to make an educated guess about the meaning of the word *fossil record*.

Word	Meaning
fossil	the remains or trace of once-living organisms
record	an account that preserves information about facts or events

Vocabulary Terms
• fossil   • fossil record

4 Apply As you learn the definition of each vocabulary term in this lesson, create your own definition or sketch to help you remember the meaning of the term.

fossil record: _____

_____

_____

Lesson 3 Evidence of Evolution 29

Answers

1. T; T; T; T

2. Sample answer: There was once a sea where the fossil was found.

3. Sample answer: A fossil record is an account of the remains of living organisms.

4. Students should define or sketch each vocabulary term in the lesson.

Opening Your Lesson

Discuss the image of the dinosaur in the museum. **Prompt:** Think about why scientists study dinosaurs.

Accessing Prior Knowledge Students probably already have some knowledge of fossils. Tell them that now they will learn about how fossils provide evidence for the theory of evolution. Have students begin a KWL chart to record what they know and want to learn about fossils and evolution. As they study the lesson, have them fill in what they learn.

🌐 *Optional Online resource: KWL support*

Prerequisites Students should already know the theory of evolution by natural selection and its component parts: overproduction, variation, selection, and adaptation. They should also know that many species that once lived on Earth are now extinct.

Learning Alert

Comparing Evidence Anatomical similarities between organisms are perhaps the most readily understandable evidence for evolution. However, beginning in the 1980s, breakthroughs in the study of DNA and other molecules have provided what scientists believe to be more precise indicators of the evolutionary relationships among organisms than anatomy can provide.

Fossil Hunt

How do fossils form?

Evidence that organisms have changed over time can be found in amber, ice, or sedimentary rock. Sedimentary rock is formed when particles of sand or soil are deposited in horizontal layers. Often this occurs as mud or silt hardens. After one rock layer forms, newer rock layers form on top of it. So, older layers are found below or underneath younger rock layers. The most basic principle of dating such rocks and the remains of organisms inside is "the deeper it is, the older it is."

This flying dinosaur is an example of a cast fossil.

tusks   eye

Because this woolly mammoth was frozen in ice, its skin and hair were preserved.

Amber fossils form when small creatures are trapped in tree sap and the sap hardens.

5 Examine What features of the organism are preserved in amber?

_____

_____

_____

Many Fossils Form in Sedimentary Rock

Rock layers preserve evidence of organisms that were once alive. The remains or imprints of once-living organisms are called **fossils**. Fossils commonly form when a dead organism is covered by a layer of sediment or mud. Over time, more sediment settles on top of the organism. Minerals in the sediment may seep into the organism and replace the body's material with minerals that harden over time. This process produces a cast fossil. Many familiar fossils are casts of hard parts, such as shells and bones. If the organism rots away completely after being covered, it may leave an imprint of itself in the rock. Despite all of the fossils that have been found, it is rare for an organism to become a fossil. Most often, the dead organism is recycled back into the biological world by scavengers, decomposers, or the process of weathering.

Active Reading

6 Identify As you read, underline the steps that describe how a cast fossil forms.

How do fossils show change over time?

All of the fossils that have been discovered make up the **fossil record**. The fossil record provides evidence about the order in which species have existed through time, and how they have changed over time. By examining the fossil record, scientists can learn about the history of life on Earth.

Despite all the fossils that have been found, there are gaps in the fossil record. These gaps represent chunks of geologic time for which a fossil has not been discovered. Also, the transition between two groups of organisms may not be well understood. Fossils that help fill in these gaps are *transitional fossils*. The illustration on the right is based on a transitional fossil.

Fossils found in newer layers of Earth's crust tend to have physical or molecular similarities to present-day organisms. These similarities indicate that the fossilized organisms were close relatives of the present-day organisms. Fossils from older layers are less similar to present-day organisms than fossils from newer layers are. Most older fossils are of earlier life-forms such as dinosaurs, which don't exist anymore.

Visualize It!

A transitional form between fish and four-legged land vertebrates may be this creature called Tiktaalik roseae.

7 Identify Describe the environment in which this organism lives.

_____

_____

8 Infer How is this organism like both a fish and a four-legged vertebrate, such as an amphibian?

_____

_____

_____

30 | 31

Answers

5. The amber preserves all of an organism's features, even soft body parts and wings.

6. *See students' pages for annotations.*

7. This organism lives on the edge of a body of water, and possibly on both water and land.

8. Sample answer: The organism has a tail and fins like a fish, but lives above water like a four-legged vertebrate.

Learning Alert

Sediment The particles from which sedimentary rock forms are called *sediment*. Sediment is small rock and mineral pieces that have broken down from larger rock over time. The terms *sand*, *silt*, and *clay* refer to sediment of different sizes. Sediment is a main component of all soil.

Interpreting Visuals

Have students examine the fossilized organisms in the photographs and consider what present-day organisms they may be related to. Sample answers: Pterosaur—winged dinosaur—related to birds; mammoth related to elephants; *Tiktaalik roseae* related to fish and crocodiles.

Formative Assessment

Ask: How can scientists tell, based on rock layers, which fossils are younger and which are older? Older layers lay below or underneath younger rock layers, so fossils in deeper rock layers are older than fossils in rock layers above them. **Ask:** Why are fossils in older rock layers less similar to present-day organisms than fossils in younger layers? Sample answer: Fossils in lower rock layers are not as closely related to present-day organisms.

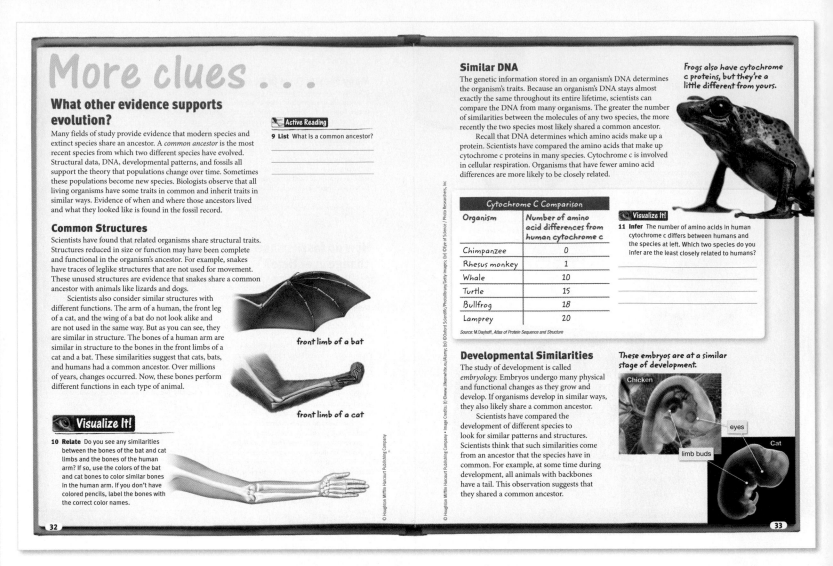

More clues . . .

What other evidence supports evolution?

Many fields of study provide evidence that modern species and extinct species share an ancestor. A *common ancestor* is the most recent species from which two different species have evolved. Structural data, DNA, developmental patterns, and fossils all support the theory that populations change over time. Sometimes these populations become new species. Biologists observe that all living organisms have some traits in common and inherit traits in similar ways. Evidence of when and where those ancestors lived and what they looked like is found in the fossil record.

Common Structures

Scientists have found that related organisms share structural traits. Structures reduced in size or function may have been complete and functional in the organism's ancestor. For example, snakes have traces of leglike structures that are not used for movement. These unused structures are evidence that snakes share a common ancestor with animals like lizards and dogs.

Scientists also consider similar structures with different functions. The arm of a human, the front leg of a cat, and the wing of a bat do not look alike and are not used in the same way. But as you can see, they are similar in structure. The bones of a human arm are similar in structure to the bones in the front limbs of a cat and a bat. These similarities suggest that cats, bats, and humans had a common ancestor. Over millions of years, changes occurred. Now, these bones perform different functions in each type of animal.

front limb of a bat

front limb of a cat

👁 Visualize It!

10 Relate Do you see any similarities between the bones of the bat and cat limbs and the bones of the human arm? If so, use the colors of the bat and cat bones to color similar bones in the human arm. If you don't have colored pencils, label the bones with the correct color names.

📖 Active Reading

9 List What is a common ancestor?

Similar DNA

The genetic information stored in an organism's DNA determines the organism's traits. Because an organism's DNA stays almost exactly the same throughout its entire lifetime, scientists can compare the DNA from many organisms. The greater the number of similarities between the molecules of any two species, the more recently the two species most likely shared a common ancestor.

Recall that DNA determines which amino acids make up a protein. Scientists have compared the amino acids that make up cytochrome c proteins in many species. Cytochrome c is involved in cellular respiration. Organisms that have fewer amino acid differences are more likely to be closely related.

Cytochrome C Comparison	
Organism	Number of amino acid differences from human cytochrome c
Chimpanzee	0
Rhesus monkey	1
Whale	10
Turtle	15
Bullfrog	18
Lamprey	20

Source: M.Dayhoff, *Atlas of Protein Sequence and Structure*

Frogs also have cytochrome c proteins, but they're a little different from yours.

👁 Visualize It!

11 Infer The number of amino acids in human cytochrome c differs between humans and the species at left. Which two species do you infer are the least closely related to humans?

Developmental Similarities

The study of development is called *embryology*. Embryos undergo many physical and functional changes as they grow and develop. If organisms develop in similar ways, they also likely share a common ancestor.

Scientists have compared the development of different species to look for similar patterns and structures. Scientists think that such similarities come from an ancestor that the species have in common. For example, at some time during development, all animals with backbones have a tail. This observation suggests that they shared a common ancestor.

These embryos are at a similar stage of development.

Chicken — eyes — limb buds — Cat

32 | 33

Answers

9. A common ancestor is the most recent species from which two different species evolved.

10. The bones in the human arm should match in color or in color name to the bones in the cat arm/bat wing. Colors or color names to be used are yellow, dark green, teal, purple, and orange.

11. Out of the species listed, bullfrog and lamprey are the least closely related to humans, because their cytochrome c molecules differ the most from human cytochrome c.

Building Reading Skills

Student Vocabulary Strategy Students may be unfamiliar with words in the text such as *developmental* and *molecular*. Have students preview the reading to identify words with which they are unfamiliar. They should then record each word in their notebooks, use a dictionary to find and write its definition, and then write a sentence using the word.

Learning Alert

Homologies vs. Analogies Just because two organisms share similar structures does not mean that they share common ancestry. Structures that are similar due to common ancestry are called *homologies* or *homologous structures*. Similar structures that did not develop through common ancestry are called *analogies* or *analogous structures*. Analogies often come about because two species faced similar environmental pressures and evolved similarly to adapt to these pressures.

Formative Assessment

Ask: The leg of a frog and the wing of a bird serve very different purposes, but the bones in their limbs are similar in structure. What does this suggest about frogs and birds? They had a common ancestor.

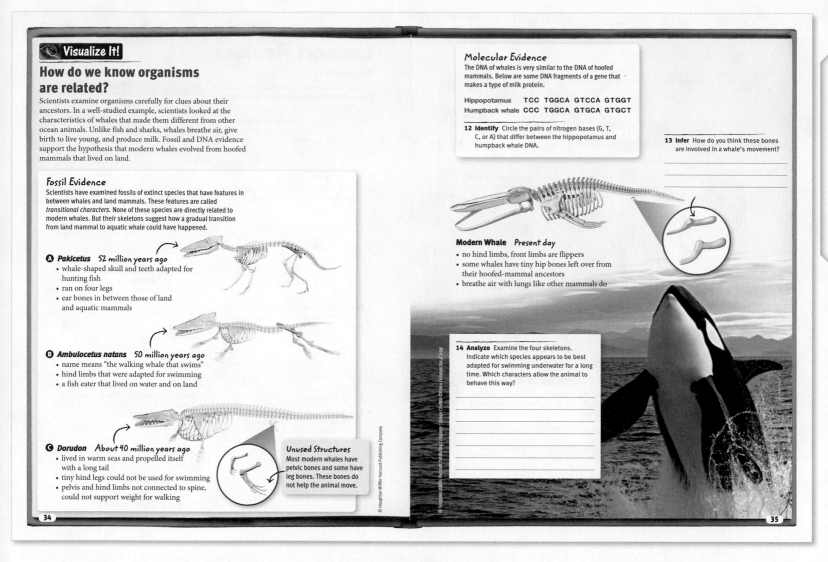

Visualize It!

How do we know organisms are related?

Scientists examine organisms carefully for clues about their ancestors. In a well-studied example, scientists looked at the characteristics of whales that made them different from other ocean animals. Unlike fish and sharks, whales breathe air, give birth to live young, and produce milk. Fossil and DNA evidence support the hypothesis that modern whales evolved from hoofed mammals that lived on land.

Fossil Evidence

Scientists have examined fossils of extinct species that have features in between whales and land mammals. These features are called *transitional characters*. None of these species are directly related to modern whales. But their skeletons suggest how a gradual transition from land mammal to aquatic whale could have happened.

A *Pakicetus* 52 million years ago
- whale-shaped skull and teeth adapted for hunting fish
- ran on four legs
- ear bones in between those of land and aquatic mammals

B *Ambulocetus natans* 50 million years ago
- name means "the walking whale that swims"
- hind limbs that were adapted for swimming
- a fish eater that lived on water and on land

C *Dorudon* About 40 million years ago
- lived in warm seas and propelled itself with a long tail
- tiny hind legs could not be used for swimming
- pelvis and hind limbs not connected to spine, could not support weight for walking

Unused Structures
Most modern whales have pelvic bones and some have leg bones. These bones do not help the animal move.

Molecular Evidence

The DNA of whales is very similar to the DNA of hoofed mammals. Below are some DNA fragments of a gene that makes a type of milk protein.

Hippopotamus   TCC TGGCA GTCCA GTGGT
Humpback whale CCC TGGCA GTGCA GTGCT

12 Identify Circle the pairs of nitrogen bases (G, T, C, or A) that differ between the hippopotamus and humpback whale DNA.

13 Infer How do you think these bones are involved in a whale's movement?

Modern Whale   Present day
- no hind limbs, front limbs are flippers
- some whales have tiny hip bones left over from their hoofed-mammal ancestors
- breathe air with lungs like other mammals do

14 Analyze Examine the four skeletons. Indicate which species appears to be best adapted for swimming underwater for a long time. Which characters allow the animal to behave this way?

34

35

Answers

12. Students should circle the following differences between the hippopotamus/humpback whale DNA sequences: T/C, C/G, G/C.

13. Sample answer: These tiny bones are not involved in the whale's movement at all.

14. Sample answer: The modern whale appears to be best adapted for swimming long distances under water because it has fins to swim fast and can breathe underwater for a long time.

Learning Alert

Whale Hip Bones The tiny hip bones present in modern-day whales are not used for locomotion. They do, however, play a role in whale reproduction.

Interpreting Visuals

Ask: Besides pelvic and leg bones, what similarities do you see between the skeletons of modern whales and the skeletons of whale ancestors? Sample answer: similar skulls, similar rib cages

Probing Questions   GUIDED Inquiry

Analyzing The tail of *Pakicetus* was small. A modern whale, however, has a very long tail. Why might whales have evolved to have very long tails? Explain. **Prompt:** Think about natural selection. Sample answer: *Pakicetus* was a land animal; whales live in water and use their tails to swim. Having a longer tail with flukes helps whales move through the water more efficiently. When whales' ancestors moved from land to life in water, individuals with longer tails could likely swim better. This would aid in finding food and escaping predators, which helped them survive and reproduce. Over many generations through natural selection, whales evolved to have long tails.

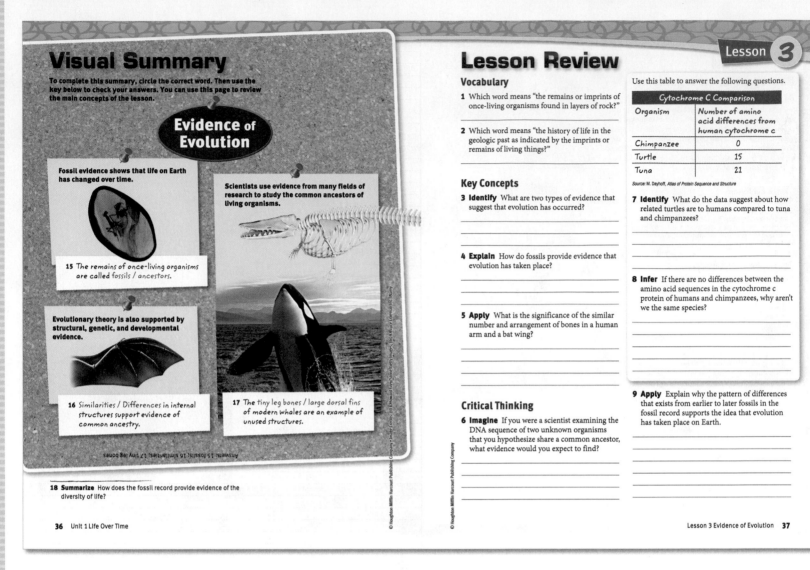

Visual Summary Answers

15. fossils
16. Similarities
17. tiny leg bones
18. The fossil record is a history of the organisms that existed in the geologic past, as preserved in fossils.

Lesson Review Answers

1. fossil
2. fossil record
3. Accept fossil evidence, anatomical evidence, molecular evidence, or developmental evidence.
4. Fossil evidence shows that organisms have changed over time.
5. It suggests that a human and a bat shared a common ancestor.
6. Sample answer: I would expect to find either common structures, common embryological evidence, common DNA, or unused structures in common.
7. The data suggest that turtles are more related to humans than tuna, but not as closely related as chimpanzees.
8. Cytochrome c is just one protein that is being compared. There are many others in which we would find differences between our species and the chimpanzee.
9. In the fossil record, later fossils are more similar to modern organisms than early fossils. This suggests that change has occurred over time.

The History of Life on Earth

Essential Question How has life on Earth changed over time?

Professional Development

For more detailed information about the topics in this lesson, refer to the Content Refresher in the Unit Opener pages.

Opening Your Lesson

Begin the lesson by assessing students' prerequisite and prior knowledge.

Prerequisite Knowledge

- A general understanding of the basic requirements for life to exist on Earth
- A basic knowledge of the theory of evolution by natural selection

Accessing Prior Knowledge

Invite students to make a Tri-Fold KWL chart to access prior knowledge about the history of life on Earth. Have students put what they know in the first column and what they want to know in the second column. After they have finished the lesson, they can complete the third column with what they learned.

⊙ *Online resource: Tri-Fold FoldNote support*

Customize Your Opening

- ☐ **Accessing Prior Knowledge,** above
- ☐ **Print Path** Engage Your Brain, SE p. 39
- ☐ **Print Path** Active Reading, SE p. 39
- ☐ **Digital Path** Lesson Opener

Key Topics/Learning Goals	Supporting Concepts
Fossil Record 1 Understand how scientists use fossils to gauge how long Earth had life. 2 Tell how to date a fossil. 3 Describe how the fossil record records extinctions and mass extinctions.	• Fossils of bacteria place the origin of life on Earth at about 3.8 billion years ago. • Fossils are dated by relative dating, which determines age by comparing two fossils, and absolute dating, which estimates the time at which a fossil formed. • The presence of a species and the number of fossils in the fossil record give clues to extinctions and mass extinctions
Geologic Time Scale 1 Describe the four major divisions of the geologic time scale. 2 Understand that divisions in the geologic time scale are based on mass extinction events.	• The geologic time scale divides Earth's history into manageable parts. The largest division is the eon. Eons are divided into eras. Eras are further divided into periods. • The four major divisions of the geologic time scale are Precambrian time, the Paleozoic era, the Mesozoic era, and the Cenozoic era. • The major divisions in the geologic time scale correspond to mass extinctions.
The Precambrian and the Paleozoic 1 Describe the changes that occurred to life during Precambrian time and the Paleozoic era.	• Single-celled, ocean-dwelling organisms dominated the Precambrian. • Prokaryotes capable of photosynthesis evolved and increased the amount of oxygen on Earth. This allowed for the evolution of new species that need oxygen to live. • During the Paleozoic, living things colonized the land. Insects and vertebrates evolved.
The Mesozoic and Cenozoic Eras 1 Describe the changes that occurred to life during the Mesozoic and Cenozoic eras.	• During the Mesozoic, dinosaurs evolved and the mammals and birds appeared. • The Cenozoic era is the current era. During this era, primates, including humans, evolved.

Options for Instruction

Two parallel paths provide coverage of the Essential Questions, with a strong **Inquiry** strand woven into each. Follow the **Print Path,** the **Digital Path,** or your customized combination of print, digital, and inquiry.

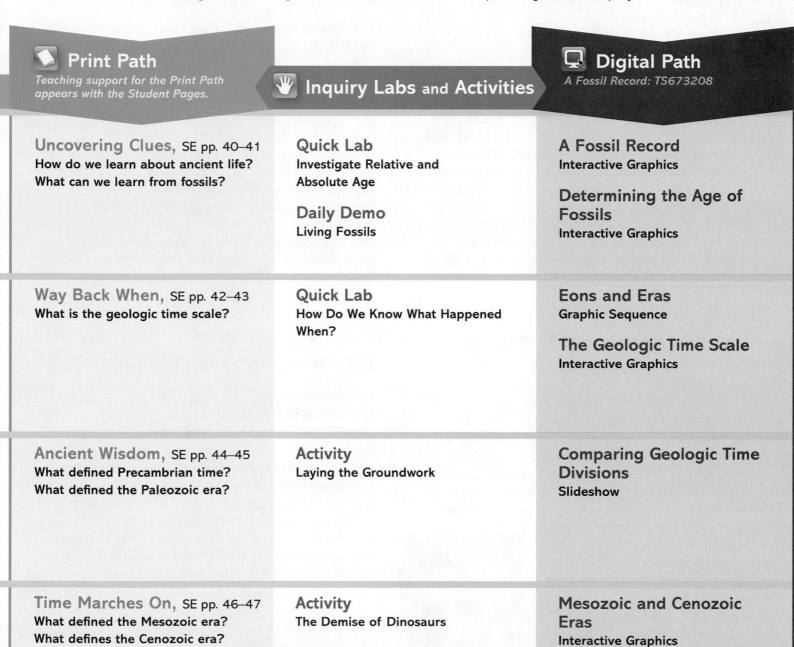

Print Path
Teaching support for the Print Path appears with the Student Pages.

Inquiry Labs and Activities

Digital Path
A Fossil Record: TS673208

Uncovering Clues, SE pp. 40–41
How do we learn about ancient life?
What can we learn from fossils?

Quick Lab
Investigate Relative and Absolute Age

Daily Demo
Living Fossils

A Fossil Record
Interactive Graphics

Determining the Age of Fossils
Interactive Graphics

Way Back When, SE pp. 42–43
What is the geologic time scale?

Quick Lab
How Do We Know What Happened When?

Eons and Eras
Graphic Sequence

The Geologic Time Scale
Interactive Graphics

Ancient Wisdom, SE pp. 44–45
What defined Precambrian time?
What defined the Paleozoic era?

Activity
Laying the Groundwork

Comparing Geologic Time Divisions
Slideshow

Time Marches On, SE pp. 46–47
What defined the Mesozoic era?
What defines the Cenozoic era?

Activity
The Demise of Dinosaurs

Mesozoic and Cenozoic Eras
Interactive Graphics

Options for Assessment

See the Evaluate page for options, including Formative Assessment, Summative Assessment, and Unit Review.

Engage and Explore

Activities and Discussion

Probing Question *Fossil Sequences*

Engage

Fossil Record

 individuals
 10 min
 GUIDED inquiry

Analyzing Explain to students that more than 200 years ago, a man named William Smith discovered that fossils occur in a particular sequence. Older rock layers lie below younger rock layers; and older rocks contain older fossils, while younger rocks contain fossils of more recent organisms. Based on Smith's discovery, scientists can infer that certain types of fossils should never be found together in the same rock layer. For example, *a Tyrannosaurus rex* fossil should never be found in the same rock layer as a woolly mammoth fossil. Ask students to write a short paragraph explaining why this is true. *T. rex* and the woolly mammoth lived during different geologic eras. Therefore, their fossils should be located in different rock layers.

Activity *The Demise of Dinosaurs*

**The Mesozoic
and Cenozoic Eras**

 whole class
 15 min
 DIRECTED inquiry

Think, Pair, Share Tell students that there are many theories about why dinosaurs became extinct at the end of the Mesozoic era. Some believe that a giant meteorite hit Earth, setting off a deadly chain of events: dust and smoke blocked out sunlight, killling all the plants, which caused plant-eaters to perish, followed by the meat-eating dinosaurs. Other scientists believe that dinosaurs died before the meteorite hit Earth, perhaps from disease, starvation, or suffocation from volcanic ash. Have students research about the various theories, and then pair up and discuss their ideas. Ask for volunteers to share their own ideas with the class.

Activity *Laying the Groundwork*

**The Precambrian and
the Paleozoic**

 whole class
 15 min
 DIRECTED inquiry

Ranking Ladder Review with students that plants, fungi, and air-breathing animals colonized land during the Paleozoic era. Tell them that several changes took place during Precambrian time that helped make this colonization of land possible. Have students rank the following Precambrian events in order they occurred: multicellular organisms evolved; cyanobacteria released oxygen into the air; many organisms became extinct; oxygen formed an ozone layer in the upper atmosphere. **Ask:** Which events were most necessary for the colonization of land? Encourage students to debate the ranking order. Prompt them to support their ideas with details from the text.

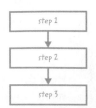

Take It Home *Extinct in America*

**The Mesozoic
and Cenozoic Eras**

 adult-student pairs
 30–40 min
 INDEPENDENT inquiry

With an adult, students research a prehistoric animal of North America that went extinct. Pairs record where and when the animal lived, why it might have gone extinct, its habitat, a description of the animal including what modern animal it resembled, and what fossils reveal about the animal's behavior and diet. After researching, pairs should design a trading card with the animal's image on the front and pertinent information on the back. Encourage students to circulate their trading cards with classmates.

Customize Your Labs

 See the Lab Manual for lab datasheets.

 Go Online for editable lab datasheets.

Levels of  **Inquiry**

DIRECTED inquiry	**GUIDED** inquiry	**INDEPENDENT** inquiry
introduces inquiry skills within a structured framework.	develops inquiry skills within a supportive environment.	deepens inquiry skills with student-driven questions or procedures.

Labs and Demos

Daily Demo *Living Fossils*

Engage

Fossil Record

 whole class
🕐 20 min
inquiry **GUIDED** inquiry

PURPOSE **To explore the horseshoe crab, an ancient creature that predates most species on Earth and offers insights into evolution**

MATERIALS

• **Model or photographs of a horseshoe crab**

1 Show students a model or photographs of a horseshoe crab. Explain that this prehistoric creature is not a true crab; it is more closely related to spiders and scorpions than it is to other crabs. This species evolved 100 million years before dinosaurs and has changed little over the last 350 million years.

2 **Compare and Contrast** Have students compare and contrast the anatomy of a horseshoe crab with similar creatures such as a spider, a true crab, and a beetle. Point out the horseshoe crab's armored shell, spike tail, compound eyes, gills, and six pairs of legs.

3 **Analyzing** Explain that the horseshoe crab is often called a living fossil because it has survived and remained the same for millions of years. **Ask:** Why do you think horseshoe crabs have survived while thousands of other species have become extinct? Sample answers: The horseshoe crab's hard shell protects its soft body. It is well adapted to its ocean habitat.

Quick Lab *How Do We Know What Happened When?*

Geologic Time Scale

 pairs
🕐 30 min
inquiry **GUIDED** inquiry

Students use personal life histories to distinguish between the implications of major and minor events when creating a timeline.

PURPOSE **To explore how index fossils can be used to create an evidence-based geologic timeline**

MATERIALS

• **index cards**
• **string**
• **tape**

Quick Lab *Investigate Relative and Absolute Age*

Fossil Record

 small groups
🕐 20 min
inquiry **GUIDED** inquiry

Students use a model to better understand relative age and absolute age.

PURPOSE **To investigate relative dating and absolute age**

MATERIALS

• **5 or more newspapers with different dates**
• **2 pencils**

Activities and Discussion

☐ **Probing Questions** Fossil Sequences

☐ **Activity** Laying the Groundwork

☐ **Activity** The Demise of Dinosaurs

☐ **Take It Home** Extinct in America

Labs and Demos

☐ **Daily Demo** Living Fossils

☐ **Quick Lab** How Do We Know What Happened When?

☐ **Quick Lab** Investigate Relative and Absolute Age

Your Resources

_____

_____

_____

Explain Science Concepts

Key Topics	📄 Print Path	💻 Digital Path
Fossil Record	☐ **Uncovering Clues,** SE pp. 40–41 • Visualize It!, #5 • Visualize It!, #6 • Visualize It!, #7 • Active Reading (Annotation strategy), #8 **Visualize It!** **7 Describe** What changes do you see in the limb structure of the three animals above?	☐ **A Fossil Record** Explore how fossils tell about Earth's past. ☐ **Determining the Age of Fossils** Study relative and absolute dating.
Geologic Time Scale	☐ **Way Back When,** SE pp. 42–43 • Active Reading (annotation strategy), #9 • Visualize It!, #10 • Visualize It!, #11 **Active Reading** **9 Identify** Underline one reason why it is hard for scientists to study the early history of Earth.	☐ **Eons and Eras** Investigate the geologic time scale. ☐ **The Geologic Time Scale** Explore the structure of the geologic time scale.
The Precambrian and Paleozoic	☐ **Ancient Wisdom,** SE pp. 44–45 • Summarize, #12 • Think Outside the Book, #13 • Visualize It!, #14 **12 Summarize** How are cyanobacteria related to increases in oxygen in the atmosphere?	☐ **Comparing Geologic Time Divisions** Investigate the Precambrian and Paleozoic.
The Mesozoic and Cenozoic Eras	☐ **Time Marches On,** SE pp. 46–47 • Active Reading (Annotation strategy), #15 • Summarize, #16 • Hypothesize, #17 **Active Reading** **15 Identify** As you read, underline the names of animals that lived in the Mesozoic era.	☐ **Mesozoic and Cenozoic Eras** Examine the Mesozoic and Cenozoic.

Differentiated Instruction

Basic *An Epic Mural*

Geologic Time Scale small groups
 varies

Students will better understand the division of geologic time if they can see the differences between the periods or eras covered in this lesson. Separate students into groups of four. Give each group a large piece of butcher paper. Assign each student one of the time periods discussed in the lesson (Precambrian, Paleozoic, Mesozoic, or Cenozoic). Have students create a scene from the time period they have been assigned. They should include descriptions of Earth environments that existed, and drawings of living things. Invite groups to tell the class about their work.

Advanced *Fins and Limbs*

The Precambrian and Paleozoic individuals
 varies

During the Paleozoic era, animals colonized the land. Encourage students to research the changes that had to occur in animals' limbs to accommodate the different physical requirements that life on land imposes on an organism, as opposed to what limbs must be able to do in an aquatic environment. Encourage students to build models contrasting the leg of an early amphibian, such as *Paracyclotosaurus*, and the flipper of a lobe-finned fish, such as *Panderichthys*. Students should not make the mistake of assuming that the amphibian is a direct descendant of the fish.

ELL *Venn Diagram*

Fossil Record individuals or pairs
 10 min

Have students, individually or in pairs, make a Venn diagram comparing relative dating and absolute dating of fossils. They should draw two overlapping circles, one for each item they are comparing. In the overlapping section, students should list the characteristics that are shared by both types of dating. In the outer sections, they should list the characteristics that are peculiar to each item. Ask students to write a summary that describes the information in the Venn diagram.

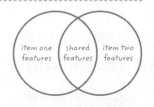

Lesson Vocabulary

fossils	**fossil record**
extinction	**geologic time scale**

Previewing Vocabulary

 whole class   15 min

Word Origins Share the following to help students remember terms:
- **Fossil** comes from the Latin word *fossilis,* which means "dug up."
- **Extinction** comes from the Latin word *extinctionem,* which means "to extinguish or wipe out." *Extinctionem* originally referred to fires and lights, and later to debts and people. In 1784, the word was first used to refer to species.

Reinforcing Vocabulary

 individuals   ongoing

Four Square To help students remember the different terms introduced in the lesson, have them draw a 2-by-2 matrix with a circle at the center. Students place a term in the circle and then fill in the surrounding cells with the types of information shown.

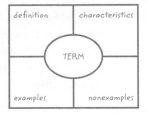

Customize Your Core Lesson

Core Instruction
☐ **Print Path** choices
☐ **Digital Path** choices

Vocabulary
☐ **Previewing Vocabulary** Word Origins
☐ **Reinforcing Vocabulary** Four Square

Your Resources

Differentiated Instruction
☐ **Basic** An Epic Mural
☐ **Advanced** Fins and Limbs
☐ **ELL** Venn Diagram

Extend Science Concepts

Reinforce and Review

Activity

Synthesizing Key Topics

 whole class
🕐 20 min

Inside/Outside Circles Help students review vocabulary and other key terms by following these steps:

1. After students have read the lesson, give each an index card with a word from the text on one side and a definition on the other. The words can be vocabulary terms or other key terms such as *absolute dating, relative dating, mass extinction, Precambrian, Paleozoic, Mesozoic,* or *Cenozoic.*

2. Students pair up and form two circles. One partner is in an inside circle; the other is in an outside circle. The students in the inside circle face out, and the students in the outside circle face in.

3. Each student in the inside circle asks his or her partner the definition of the term on the index card. The partner answers. If the answer is incorrect, the student in the inside circle teaches the other student the correct definition. Repeat this step with the outside-circle students asking the definitions.

4. Have each student on the outside circle rotate one person to the right. He or she faces a new partner and gets a new term to define. Students rotate after each pair of words and definitions.

FoldNote

Synthesizing Key Topics

 individuals
🕐 30 min

Layered Book FoldNote Have students create a Layered Book FoldNote that includes a page for each of the following: Fossil Record; Geologic Time Scale; Precambrian Time; and Paleozoic, Mesozoic, and Cenozoic Eras. Students should label each page and include a description and illustration (where appropriate) for that topic. Encourage students to also include key concepts from the text.

Going Further

Real World Connection

The Mesozoic and Cenozoic Eras

 pairs or small groups
🕐 25 min

Dinosaur Provincial Park Field Trip About 75 million years ago, dinosaurs lived along the banks of the Red Deer River in Alberta, Canada. Fossils from 60 species of dinosaurs have been discovered in this region, which is now a United Nations World Heritage Site. Have interested students write a letter to a local business requesting funding for a school field trip to Dinosaur Provincial Park. Students' letters should explain how the trip will enhance their studies in science and social studies.

Earth Science Connection

Fossil Record

 pairs
🕐 45 min

Map The huge plants that grew in forests during the Paleozoic era later became coal. Ask students to research the locations of the world's coal deposits and mark them on a world map. Most of the known coal reserves are in Australia, China, Germany, Poland, Great Britain, India, Russia, South Africa, the United States, and Canada. Also ask students to create an illustrated summary of the process by which coal forms from dead plants buried underground.

Customize Your Closing

🔹 *See the Assessment Guide for quizzes and tests.*

🔸 *Go Online to edit and create quizzes and tests.*

Reinforce and Review

- ☐ **Activity** Inside/Outside Circles
- ☐ **FoldNote** Layered Book FoldNote
- ☐ **Print Path** Visual Summary, SE p. 48
- ☐ **Digital Path** Lesson Closer

Evaluate Student Mastery

Formative Assessment

See the teacher support below the Student Pages for additional Formative Assessment questions.

Ask the following questions to assess student mastery of the material: **Ask:** Why do scientists study the fossil record so carefully? The fossil record helps scientists learn how species have changed over millions of years and how and when some species went extinct. **Ask:** How are fossils fundamental to the geologic time scale? Fossils provide important clues to help scientists determine what happened during different time intervals. **Ask:** What significant event occurred at the end of the Paleozoic era? a mass extinction

Reteach

Formative assessment may show that students need reinforcement for certain topics. The resources below are recommended for reteaching. If students were introduced to a topic through the Print path, you can also use the Digital Path to reteach, or vice versa.

🎧 *Can be assigned to individual students*

Fossil Record
Quick Lab Investigate Relative and Absolute Age

Geologic Time Scale
Quick Lab How Do We Know What Happened When?

The Precambrian and the Paleozoic
Activity Laying the Groundwork

The Mesozoic and Cenozoic Eras
Activity The Demise of Dinosaurs

Summative Assessment

Alternative Assessment
Partner with a Paleontologist

🌐 *Online resources: student worksheet, optional rubric*

The History of Life on Earth

Tic-Tac-Toe: *Partner with a Paleontologist*
You have been selected to join scientists at a remote site where fossils of dinosaurs and other organisms have been discovered.

1. Work on your own, with a partner, or with a small group.

2. Choose three quick activities from the game. Check the boxes you plan to complete. They must form a straight line in any direction.

3. Have your teacher approve your plan.

4. Do each activity, and turn in your results.

__ Terrestrial Thing	__ Timeless Tree Sap	__ Dinosaur Debate
You discovered a fossil of an unnamed animal that lived on land. Sketch the creature; give it a name; and draw a close-up detail of one adaptation that allowed this animal to survive on land.	Write a text message to a scientist about an insect you found embedded in amber. What questions would you ask about the remains of this ancient winged creature?	A group of students is debating whether birds are "living dinosaurs." Write a persuasive paragraph that states your position on the topic.
__ The Ediacarians	__ Soft Bodied	__ Diorama Design
Organisms called Ediacarians were among the first multicellular life-forms to evolve in Precambrian time. Research the Ediacarians and create a pamphlet that summarizes what is known about them and what remains unknown.	The Burgess Shale fossils are traces of soft-bodied animals, and give science a rare glimpse into the past. Research these unusual organisms and choose one. Prepare a poster or a multimedia presentation about the organism.	Make a diorama representing the Precambrian, Paleozoic, Mesozoic, or Cenozoic. Include at least three different life forms common in the chosen time period. Use a box with a cover and other art materials.
__ Paleozoic Poster	__ Trilobite Traits	__ Pre-Penguin Journal
Research possible causes of the Permian mass extinction, when 90 percent of Earth's marine species became extinct. Then design a poster spotlighting a natural disaster that may have contributed to the mass extinction.	Design an exhibit of trilobites, hard-shelled animals that lived in Earth's oceans for 300 million years. With more than 20,000 trilobite species to consider, which interesting facts will your exhibit spotlight about this diverse group of extinct animals?	Some ancient animals resemble a jigsaw puzzle of various parts. Write a journal entry describing a toothed bird that swam through the seas instead of flying through the air.

Going Further
☐ **Real World Connection**
☐ **Earth Science Connection**

Formative Assessment
☐ **Strategies** Throughout TE
☐ **Lesson Review** SE

Summative Assessment
☐ **Alternative Assessment** Partner with a Paleontologist
☐ **Lesson Quiz**
☐ **Unit Tests A and B**
☐ **Unit Review** SE End-of-Unit

Your Resources

Lesson ④

The History of Life on Earth

ESSENTIAL QUESTION

How has life on Earth changed over time?

By the end of this lesson, you should be able to describe the evolution of life on Earth over time, using the geologic time scale.

Trilobites like this one lived on Earth about 400 million years ago. This fossil preserved great detail of the trilobite's body parts.

Lesson Labs

Quick Labs
• How Do We Know What Happened When?
• Investigate Relative and Absolute Age

Engage Your Brain

1 Predict Check T or F to show whether you think each statement is true or false.

T F

☐ ☐ A mass extinction occurs when a large number of species go extinct during a relatively short amount of time.

☐ ☐ The largest division of the geologic time scale is the era.

☐ ☐ We currently live in the Cenozoic era.

☐ ☐ Fossils show that the first living things were very tiny.

2 Draw Imagine you find a fossil of a fish. Which parts of the fish could you see in the fossil? Draw what you think you would see below.

Active Reading

3 Apply Use context clues to write your own definition for the words *fossil record* and *extinction*.

Example sentence
Scientists develop hypotheses about Earth's history based on observable changes in the <u>fossil record</u>.

fossil record:

_____

Example sentence
Endangered species are protected by law in an effort to preserve them from <u>extinction</u>.

extinction:

_____

Vocabulary Terms
• fossil   • extinction
• fossil record   • geologic time scale

4 Identify As you read, place a question mark next to any words that you don't understand. When you finish reading the lesson, go back and review the text that you marked. If the information is still confusing, consult a classmate or a teacher.

Answers

Answers for 1–3 should represent students' current thoughts, even if incorrect.

1. T; F; T; T

2. Students should draw a fish. A fossil is likely to show the hard parts of an animal, such as the bones.

3. Sample answer: The fossil record is all of the fossils found worldwide that tell the story of Earth's history. Extinction is the death of all members of a species.

4. Students' annotations will vary.

Opening Your Lesson

Discuss students' answers to item 1 to assess what they already know about the key topics.

Prerequisites Students should already have some understanding of basic requirements for living things to survive on Earth and should be aware that all species developed from earlier forms of life. In this lesson, they will apply this understanding to describe the evolution of life on Earth in the context of the geologic time scale.

Learning Alert

Difficult Concept While Earth's 4.6-billion-year history has been broken into more manageable divisions (eons, eras, periods, and epochs), students might be overwhelmed by the concept of geologic time. A useful analogy is to compress Earth's history into a single year. This condensed calendar would start with New Year's Day—when Earth and the solar system were formed—and end with New Year's Eve—when humans appeared on the scene around 11:35 PM. Create a wall chart using calendar pages and fill in corresponding dates for major events in Earth's time scale.

Uncovering Clues

How do we learn about ancient life?

Paleontologists look for clues to understand what happened in the past. These scientists use fossils to reconstruct the history of life. A **fossil** is a trace or imprint of a living thing that is preserved by geological processes. Fossils of single-celled organisms date as far back as 3.8 billion years.

What can we learn from fossils?

All of the fossils that have been discovered worldwide make up the **fossil record**. By examining the fossil record, scientists can identify when different species lived and died. There are two ways to describe the ages of fossils. *Relative dating* determines whether a fossil formed before or after another fossil. When an organism is trapped in mud or sediment, the resulting fossil becomes part of that sedimentary layer of rock. In rock layers that are not disturbed, newer fossils are found in layers of rock that are above older fossils. *Absolute dating* estimates the age of a fossil in years. Estimations are based on information from radioactive elements in certain rocks near the fossil.

Visualize It!

The abbreviation Ma stands for mega annum. A mega annum is equal to 1 million years. Ma is often used to indicate "million years ago."

5 Infer What does relative dating tell you about fossil A?

6 Solve What does absolute dating tell you about fossil A?

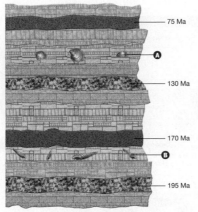

75 Ma
Ⓐ
130 Ma
170 Ma
Ⓑ
195 Ma

© Houghton Mifflin Harcourt Publishing Company

40 Unit 1 Life Over Time

---

385 Ma   365 Ma
Eusthenopteron   Tiktaalik   Ichthyostega

Fossils (names of the species shown above) indicate changes in limb structure as adaptations allowed movement on land.

How Life Forms Have Changed over Time

The fossil record gives evidence of many of the different organisms that have lived during Earth's long history. Each fossil gives information about a single organism. But the overall fossil record helps us understand larger patterns of change.

Over many generations, populations change. These changes can be preserved in fossils. For example, fossils show the gradual change in limb structure, over many millions of years, of animals such as the ones shown in the drawing above.

Some species are present in the fossil record for a relatively short period of time. Other species have survived for long time spans without much change. The hard-plated horseshoe crab, for example, has changed little over the last 350 million years.

When Extinctions Occurred

An **extinction** happens when every individual of a species dies. A mass extinction occurs when a large number of species go extinct during a relatively short amount of time. Gradual environmental changes can cause mass extinctions. Catastrophic events, such as the impact of an asteroid, can also cause mass extinctions.

Extinctions and mass extinctions are documented in the fossil record. Fossils that were common in certain rock layers may decrease in frequency and eventually disappear altogether. Based on evidence in the fossil record, scientists form hypotheses about how and when species went extinct.

Visualize It!

7 Describe What changes do you see in the limb structure of the three animals above?

Active Reading

8 Describe How can the extinction of an organism be inferred from evidence in the fossil record?

© Houghton Mifflin Harcourt Publishing Company

Lesson 4 The History of Life on Earth 41

Answers

5. Organism A lived more recently than organism B.

6. Organism A lived between 75 and 130 million years ago.

7. Sample answer: The earliest animal has fewer bones at the end of its limb. Over time, the number of bones increased, and the limb became more suitable for land travel.

8. Sample answer: Fossils of that organism are no longer present in the fossil record.

Interpreting Visuals

Have students examine the visual of fossil layers illustrating aspects of relative dating and absolute dating. **Ask:** Why are rock layers near Earth's surface generally younger than the rock layers below them? The sediments that form rock layers are deposited one layer at a time. Each new layer is usually deposited on top of older layers. **Ask:** Suppose the rock layers in an area had been overturned by an earthquake. Would the relative dating method still be accurate? Why or why not? No. If the order of the rock layers has changed, then newer fossils might not be found above older fossils.

Building Reading Skills

Student Vocabulary Students may be familiar with the noun *relative,* used to describe a family member. But many students may be unfamiliar with the adjective *relative,* as used in the term *relative dating.* Have students analyze the meaning of the adjective *relative* by completing a Student Vocabulary worksheet. Make sure all students understand that the adjective *relative* indicates that a comparison is being made. Then, discuss examples of everyday uses of the word. **Ask:** How could I describe the relative height of a building? You could compare the height of the building to the height of surrounding buildings.

🌐 *Online resource: Student Vocabulary support*

Way Back When

What is the geologic time scale?

9 Identify Underline one reason why it is hard for scientists to study the early history of Earth.

After a fossil is dated, a paleontologist can place the fossil in chronological order with other fossils. This ordering allows scientists to hypothesize about relationships between species and how organisms changed over time. To keep track of Earth's long history, scientists have developed the geologic time scale. The **geologic time scale** is the standard method used to divide Earth's long 4.6-billion-year natural history into manageable parts.

Paleontologists adjust and add details to the geologic time scale when new evidence is found. The early history of Earth has been poorly understood, because fossils from this time span are rare. As new evidence about early life on Earth accumulates, scientists may need to organize Earth's early history into smaller segments of time.

Visualize It!

10 Identify When did the Paleozoic era begin and end?

A Tool to Organize Earth's History

Boundaries between geologic time intervals correspond to significant changes in Earth's history. Some major boundaries are defined by mass extinctions or significant changes in the number of species. Other boundaries are defined by major changes in Earth's surface or climate.

The largest divisions of the geologic time scale are eons. Eons are divided into eras. Eras are characterized by the type of organism that dominated Earth at the time. Each era began with a change in the type of organism that was most dominant. Eras are further divided into periods, and periods are divided into epochs.

The four major divisions that make up the history of life on Earth are Precambrian time, the Paleozoic era, the Mesozoic era, and the Cenozoic era. Precambrian time is made up of the first three eons of Earth's history.

Geologic Time Up Until Today

Earth formed

- Precambrian time
- Paleozoic era
- Mesozoic era
- Cenozoic era

A circle graph can be used to illustrate the divisions of geologic time. As you can see above, most of Earth's past is Precambrian time. Today's era, the Cenozoic era, makes up just a very small percentage of Earth's history.

Visualize It!

11 List Which three periods make up the Mesozoic era?

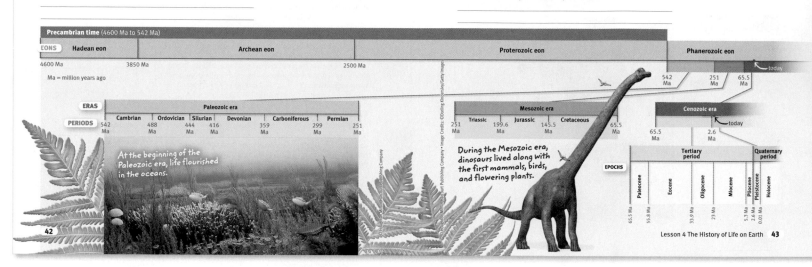

Precambrian time (4600 Ma to 542 Ma)

EONS | Hadean eon | Archean eon | Proterozoic eon | Phanerozoic eon

4600 Ma | 3850 Ma | 2500 Ma | today

Ma = million years ago

542 Ma | 251 Ma | 65.5 Ma

ERAS Paleozoic era | Mesozoic era | Cenozoic era

PERIODS 542 Ma | Cambrian | Ordovician | Silurian | Devonian | Carboniferous | Permian | 251 Ma

488 Ma | 444 Ma | 416 Ma | 359 Ma | 299 Ma

251 Ma | Triassic | Jurassic | Cretaceous | 65.5 Ma

199.6 Ma | 145.5 Ma

65.5 Ma | 2.6 Ma | today

At the beginning of the Paleozoic era, life flourished in the oceans.

During the Mesozoic era, dinosaurs lived along with the first mammals, birds, and flowering plants.

Tertiary period | Quaternary period

EPOCHS Paleocene | Eocene | Oligocene | Miocene | Pliocene | Pleistocene | Holocene

65.5 Ma | 55.8 Ma | 33.9 Ma | 23 Ma | 5.3 Ma | 2.6 Ma | 0.01 Ma

42

Lesson 4 The History of Life on Earth **43**

Answers

9. *See students' pages for annotations.*

10. It began 542 million years ago and ended 251 million years ago.

11. Triassic, Jurassic, and Cretaceous

Interpreting Visuals

Guide students as they interpret the visual of the geologic time scale. Remind them that the geologic time scale divides Earth's history into blocks of time, and that each block may be subdivided into smaller blocks. **Ask:** How are colors used in the visual to help us understand the divisions of time? Eons, eras, periods, and epochs are each represented by a different color. **Ask:** What color is used to represent epochs? yellow **Ask:** Why are lines used to connect some blocks in the visual with other blocks? These lines indicate when a division of time is being further subdivided. **Ask:** What epoch are we living in today? the Holocene Ask a volunteer to explain how he or she arrived at that answer.

Probing Questions GUIDED Inquiry

Inferring Of the time periods shown in the Geologic Time graphic, which period do you think we've learned the most about through the fossil record? Explain. Sample answer: I think we know the most about the Cenozoic era. That's the most recent era, and fossils from that era should be plentiful and relatively easy to find.

Ancient Wisdom

What defined Precambrian time?

Precambrian time started 4.6 billion years ago, when Earth formed, and ended about 542 million years ago. Life began during this time. *Prokaryotes*—single-celled organisms without a nucleus—were the dominant life form. They lived in the ocean. The earliest prokaryotes lived without oxygen.

Life Began to Evolve and Oxygen Increased

Fossil evidence suggests that prokaryotes called *cyanobacteria* appeared over 3 billion years ago. Cyanobacteria use sunlight to make their own food. This process releases oxygen. Before cyanobacteria appeared, Earth's atmosphere did not contain oxygen. Over time, oxygen built up in the ocean and air. Eventually, the oxygen also formed *ozone*, a gas layer in the upper atmosphere. Ozone absorbs harmful radiation from the sun. Before ozone formed, life existed only in the oceans and underground.

Multicellular Organisms Evolved

Increased oxygen allowed for the evolution of new species that used oxygen to live. The fossil record shows that after about 1 billion years, new types of organisms evolved. These organisms were larger and more complex than prokaryotes. Called *eukaryotes*, these organisms have cells with a nucleus and other complex structures. Later, eukaryotic organisms evolved that were multicellular, or made up of more than one cell.

Mass Extinctions Occurred

Increased oxygen was followed by the evolution of some organisms, but the extinction of others. For some organisms, oxygen is toxic. Many of these organisms became extinct. Less is known about Precambrian life than life in more recent time intervals, because microscopic organisms did not preserve well in the fossil record.

44 Unit 1 Life Over Time

12 Summarize How are cyanobacteria related to increases in oxygen in the atmosphere?

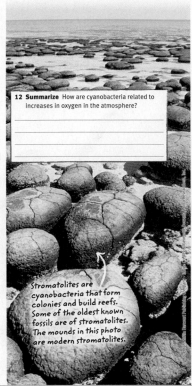

Stromatolites are cyanobacteria that form colonies and build reefs. Some of the oldest known fossils are of stromatolites. The mounds in this photo are modern stromatolites.

What defined the Paleozoic era?

The word *Paleozoic* comes from Greek words that mean "ancient life." When scientists first named this era, they thought it was the time span in which life began.

The Paleozoic era began about 542 million years ago and ended about 251 million years ago. Rocks from this era are rich in fossils of animals such as sponges, corals, snails, and trilobites. Fish, the earliest animals with backbones, appeared during this era, as did sharks.

Think Outside the Book Inquiry

13 Compose Select one of the organisms that lived during the Paleozoic era and find out more about it. Make a poster with information about the organism.

Life Moved onto Land

Plants, fungi, and air-breathing animals colonized land during the Paleozoic era. Land dwellers had adaptations that allowed them to survive in a drier environment. All major plant groups except flowering plants appeared. Crawling insects were among the first animals to live on land, followed by large salamander-like animals. By the end of the era, forests of giant ferns covered much of Earth, and reptiles and winged insects appeared.

A Mass Extinction Occurred

The Permian mass extinction took place at the end of the Paleozoic era. It is the largest known mass extinction. By 251 million years ago, as many as 96% of marine species had become extinct. The mass extinction wiped out entire groups of marine organisms such as trilobites. Oceans were completely changed. Many other species of animals and plants also became extinct. However, this opened up new habitats to those organisms that survived.

Visualize It!

14 Describe Based on this drawing, describe the landscape that existed during the Carboniferous period of the Paleozoic era.

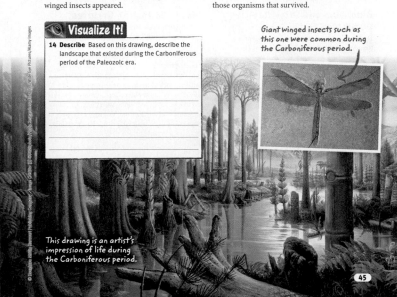

Giant winged insects such as this one were common during the Carboniferous period.

This drawing is an artist's impression of life during the Carboniferous period.

45

Answers

12. Sample answer: Cyanobacteria release oxygen into the atmosphere as a byproduct of using sunlight to make their own food (photosynthesis).

13. Student output should demonstrate that they have researched one of the plants or animals that lived during the Paleozoic era. They may draw and describe the organism's size and shape, its place in the food chain, and where it lived.

14. Sample answer: The landscape was very marshy. There were lots of tall plants that looked like trees and ferns.

Formative Assessment

Ask: Why do scientists know relatively little about Precambrian life forms? Sample answer: Most Precambrian organisms were microscopic and did not preserve well in the fossil record. **Ask:** Why do scientists know more about the development of life during the Paleozoic era? Rocks from the Paleozoic era are rich in fossils.

Probing Questions GUIDED Inquiry

Relating Concepts What change that happened during Precambrian time made it possible for life forms to colonize land during the Paleozoic era? Cyanobacteria released oxygen into the air, which led to the formation of the ozone layer. Ozone in the upper atmosphere protects living things from the sun's harmful radiation.

Analyzing Plants colonized land during the Paleozoic era. What effect do you think plants had on the makeup of Earth's atmosphere? (Hint: Think about ways in which plants are similar to cyanobacteria.) As plants spread across Earth's surface, the amount of oxygen and ozone in Earth's atmosphere probably increased. This is because plants release oxygen in the same way that cyanobacteria do.

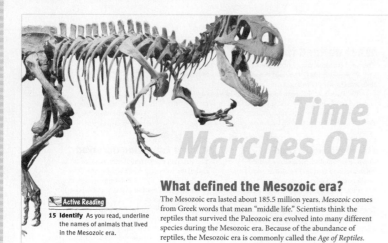

Time Marches On

Active Reading

15 Identify As you read, underline the names of animals that lived in the Mesozoic era.

What defined the Mesozoic era?

The Mesozoic era lasted about 185.5 million years. *Mesozoic* comes from Greek words that mean "middle life." Scientists think the reptiles that survived the Paleozoic era evolved into many different species during the Mesozoic era. Because of the abundance of reptiles, the Mesozoic era is commonly called the *Age of Reptiles.*

Dinosaurs and Other Reptiles Dominated Earth

Dinosaurs are the most well-known reptiles that evolved during the Mesozoic era. They dominated Earth for about 150 million years. A great variety of dinosaurs lived on Earth, and giant marine lizards swam in the ocean. The first birds and mammals also appeared. The most important plants during the early part of the Mesozoic era were conifers, or cone-bearing plants, which formed large forests. Flowering plants appeared later in the Mesozoic era.

A Mass Extinction Occurred

Why did dinosaurs and many other species become extinct at the end of the Mesozoic era? Different hypotheses are debated. Evidence shows that an asteroid hit Earth around this time. A main hypothesis is that this asteroid caused giant dust clouds and worldwide fires. With sunlight blocked by dust, many plants would have died. Without plants, plant-eating dinosaurs also would have died, along with the meat-eating dinosaurs that ate the other dinosaurs. In total, about two-thirds of all land species went extinct.

16 Summarize Make a cause-and-effect chart to explain the chain of events that, according to a main hypothesis, resulted in a mass extinction at the end of the Mesozoic era.

[ ] → [ ] → [ ]

46 Unit 1 Life Over Time

What defines the Cenozoic era?

The Cenozoic era began about 65 million years ago and continues today. *Cenozoic* comes from Greek words that mean "recent life." More is known about the Cenozoic era than about previous eras, because the fossils are closer to Earth's surface and easier to find.

Birds, Mammals, and Flowering Plants Dominate Earth

We currently live in the Cenozoic era. Mammals have dominated the Cenozoic the way reptiles dominated the Mesozoic. Early Cenozoic mammals were small, but larger mammals appeared later. Humans appeared during this era. The climate has changed many times during the Cenozoic. During ice ages, many organisms migrated toward the equator. Other organisms adapted to the cold or became extinct.

Primates evolved during the Cenozoic era.

Primates Evolved

Primates are a group of mammals that includes humans, apes, and monkeys. Primates' eyes are located at the front of the skull. Most primates have five flexible digits, one of which is an opposable thumb.

The ancestors of primates were probably nocturnal, mouse-like mammals that lived in trees. The first primates did not exist until after dinosaurs died out. Millions of years later, primates that had larger brains appeared.

17 Hypothesize How might the mass extinction that occurred at the end of the Mesozoic era relate to the dominance of mammals in the Cenozoic era?

The Cenozoic era has been dominated by mammals. Woolly mammoths were well-adapted to surviving in a cold climate.

47

Answers

15. *See students' pages for annotations.*

16. Sample answer: (Box 1) A large asteroid hit Earth, causing a lot of dust and fires. (Box 2) The dust and smoke from fires blocked a lot of sunlight. (Box 3) Insufficient sunlight caused many plants to die. Then animals further up the food chain died, too.

17. Sample answer: The mass extinction of many dinosaurs and other reptile species opened up new habitats and feeding opportunities for mammals. The mammals were able to flourish in this environment.

Using Annotations

Text Structure: Cause-and-Effect Chain Making a Cause-and-Effect Chain is an effective way for students to analyze how one step in a process or sequence can lead to another step. Remind students that a *cause* is an action or event that makes something else happen; an *effect* is what happens because of a certain action or event. After students complete the chart, have them exchange charts with a partner. Ask students to review their partner's chart to make sure that the boxes list events in the proper sequence.

⊙ *Optional Online resource: Cause-and-Effect Chain support*

Probing Questions   GUIDED Inquiry

Analyzing How was the woolly mammoth equipped to survive during the last ice age? The woolly mammoth had long, dark fur to keep it warm.

Formative Assessment

Ask: What kind of event happened at the end of both the Paleozoic and Mesozoic eras? a mass extinction **Ask:** What does *Cenozoic* mean? "recent life"

Visual Summary

To complete this summary, circle the correct word. Then, use the key below to check your answers. You can use this page to review the main concepts of the lesson.

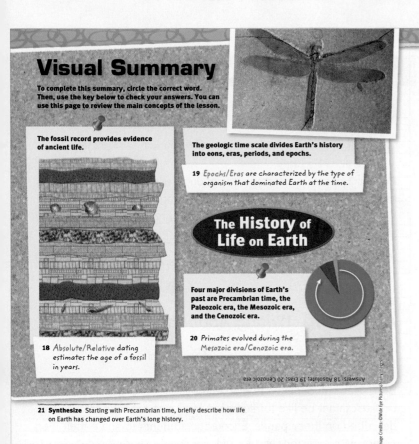

The fossil record provides evidence of ancient life.

The geologic time scale divides Earth's history into eons, eras, periods, and epochs.

19 *Epochs/Eras are characterized by the type of organism that dominated Earth at the time.*

The History of Life on Earth

Four major divisions of Earth's past are Precambrian time, the Paleozoic era, the Mesozoic era, and the Cenozoic era.

20 *Primates evolved during the Mesozoic era/Cenozoic era.*

18 *Absolute/Relative dating estimates the age of a fossil in years.*

Answers: 18 Absolute; 19 Eras; 20 Cenozoic era

21 Synthesize Starting with Precambrian time, briefly describe how life on Earth has changed over Earth's long history.

48   Unit 1 Life over Time

© Houghton Mifflin Harcourt Publishing Company • Image Credits: ©Wide Eye Pictures/Alamy Images

---

Lesson Review

Vocabulary

Draw a line to connect the following terms to their definitions.

1 fossil

2 geologic time scale

3 fossil record

4 extinction

A all of the fossils that have been discovered worldwide

B death of every member of a species

C trace or remains of an organism that lived long ago

D division of Earth's history into manageable parts

Key Concepts

5 List What four major divisions make up the history of life on Earth in the geologic time scale?

6 Explain What is one distinguishing feature of each of the four major divisions listed in your previous answer?

Critical Thinking

7 Contrast How do the atmospheric conditions near the beginning of Precambrian time contrast with the atmospheric conditions that are present now? Which organism is largely responsible for this change?

Use this drawing to answer the following question.

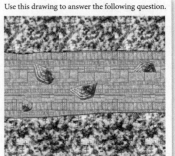

8 Explain The fossils shown are of a marine organism. In which of the three rock layers would you expect to find fossils of an organism that went extinct before the marine organism evolved? Explain your answer.

© Houghton Mifflin Harcourt Publishing Company

Lesson 4 The History of Life on Earth   49

Visual Summary Answers

18. Absolute

19. Eras

20. Cenozoic era

21. Student output should include a synthesis of the overall changes of life on Earth, starting with the microscopic organisms that lived in Precambrian time.

Lesson Review Answers

1. C

2. D

3. A

4. B

5. Precambrian time, the Paleozoic era, the Mesozoic era, and the Cenozoic era

6. Sample answer: Single-celled prokaryotes dominated Earth during Precambrian time. Plants, fungi, and air-breathing animals colonized land during the Paleozoic era. Dinosaurs dominated Earth during the Mesozoic era. Mammals have dominated Earth during the Cenozoic era.

7. Sample answer: The atmosphere has a much greater percentage of oxygen now than it did before; cyanobacteria.

8. Fossils of an organism that went extinct before this organism evolved would be found only in the very bottom rock layer, beneath the fossil shown, because that rock layer is older and formed first.

People in Science

Erica Bree Rosenblum: Evolutionary Biologist

Differentiated Instruction

Purpose To learn about the work of Erica Bree Rosenblum and what some biologists do

Basic *Frogs*

👥 pairs   🕐 30 min

Learning Goals

- Describe some different types of work done by evolutionary biologists.
- Understand a primary cause of recent declines in amphibian populations.

Poster Have pairs of students conduct research to find out more about why frogs are endangered. Encourage students to make a poster with captions that highlights their findings. Have students share their posters with the class.

💿 *Optional Online rubric: Posters and Displays*

Informal Vocabulary

evolutionary biologist, biological diversity, adaptive evolution, extinction, amphibian, fungus

Advanced *Writing About a Profession*

👥 individuals   🕐 30 min

Prerequisite Knowledge

- Understanding of evolution by natural selection
- Knowledge of evidence of evolution

Blog Have students write blog entries that describe what a day or week might be like for someone in one of the four professions described on these pages. Encourage students to share their blog entries with a partner and to add any new ideas that result from the discussion.

Activity *Which Job Is Best for Me?*

👥 individuals   🕐 10 min

🔵 **GUIDED** inquiry

ELL *Biologists*

👥 pairs   🕐 10 min

Ranking Ladder Have students use a ranking ladder to rank the four jobs featured on the student pages. Have them put the job they would most like to do at the top of their ladder and the job they would least like to do at the bottom of their ladder. Beneath the ladder, have students describe why they think they are best suited for the job at the top of their ladder.

most important

least important

Have pairs use a sunshine outline to show what an evolutionary biologist does. Have students write the words *Evolutionary Biologist* in the center circle. Around the circle, have students write what Dr. Rosenblum does. Students may want to take turns reading sentences in the feature aloud. After each sentence, have students think about whether the sentence described anything that an evolutionary biologist does.

what? *when?* *who?* *how?* *where?* *why?*

Customize Your Feature

- ☐ **Activity** Which Job Is Best for Me?
- ☐ **Basic** Frogs
- ☐ **Advanced** Writing About a Profession
- ☐ **ELL** Biologists
- ☐ **Social Studies Connection**
- ☐ **Job Board**

People in Science

Dr. Erica Bree Rosenblum

EVOLUTIONARY BIOLOGIST

Think about watching a little frog hop around. Now, imagine a world of children who have neither seen nor heard of a frog, except in very old videos. It is true that the world's amphibian population is declining. But thanks to scientists such as Dr. Erica Bree Rosenblum, frogs will likely be part of the world for kids in future generations.

Dr. Rosenblum does research in the areas of biological diversity and adaptive evolution at the University of Idaho. Her research includes studying both the emergence of new species and the extinction of existing species. In the case of frogs, her work will hopefully prevent their extinction.

A fungus known as Bd (*Batrachochytrium dendrobatidis*) is killing many amphibians, including frogs. Since the 1980s, amphibians have declined about 70%, and this fungus is partially responsible for the decline. Dr. Rosenblum and her colleagues are studying frogs' responses to the Bd fungus under certain conditions. With continued effort, these researchers may be able to help amphibians survive this widespread fungal infection.

Frogs range in size from about one inch long to one foot long.

Social Studies Connection

Find ten different countries that report amphibian declines due to the Bd fungus. On a world map, shade in the countries you find. Share your map with classmates to get an idea of the widespread nature of the amphibian decline.

JOB BOARD

Vet Technician

What You'll Do: Assist veterinarians in taking care of the health of animals.

Where You Might Work: In a veterinary clinic, animal humane society, pet hospital, or zoo.

Education: A veterinarian technician license is preferred.

Other Job Requirements: You should have compassion for animals and an ability to perform a variety of tasks, including surgical assistance, laundry and exam-room cleaning, animal feeding, and dog walking.

Student Research Assistant

What You'll Do: Assist in molecular/genome research under the supervision of university faculty by recording and inputting data into the computer.

Where You Might Work: In a lab within a university building on your college campus.

Education: You must be a student within a science-based degree program at the university.

Other Job Requirements: You should be willing to work odd hours with short notice, have attention to detail, excellent data-entry skills, and an ability to follow directions carefully.

Wildlife Photographer

What You'll Do: Take photos of wildlife in their natural habitat.

Where You Might Work: For a publishing company, advertising agency, magazine, or as a freelance photographer. If you work as a freelancer, you would have to secure contracts with companies in order to be paid for your work.

Education: No degree is required; however, having an associate's or bachelor's degree in photojournalism would make it easier to get a job as a wildlife photographer. With or without a degree, you will need a portfolio of your work to take to interviews.

50   51   Unit 1 People in Science

Social Studies Connection

As an extension of the activity, encourage interested students to make a booklet with names and images of different species of frogs. Underneath each frog species, have students identify the countries or regions where the species is found and tell whether or not it is endangered. Provide time for students to share their booklets with the class.

Job Board

Have students create a Booklet FoldNote. Then invite students to begin compiling a Job Booklet that describes science professions they find interesting. In their booklet, have students list any of the professions on this page or professions from earlier lessons. As they continue to read, have them add new professions to their booklet whenever they find one that they might like to do one day.

🌐 *Online resource: Booklet FoldNote support*

Classification of Living Things

Essential Question How are organisms classified?

 Professional Development

For more detailed information about the topics in this lesson, refer to the Content Refresher in the Unit Opener pages.

Opening Your Lesson

Begin the lesson by assessing students' prerequisite and prior knowledge.

Prerequisite Knowledge

- The characteristics of living things
- Cell structure and function
- Definitions of prokaryotes and eukaryotes

Accessing Prior Knowledge

Ask: What are some of the characteristics common to all living things? organization, ability to develop and grow, ability to respond to the environment, ability to reproduce

Ask: How are prokaryotic and eukaryotic cells alike and different? Both have cell membranes and cytoplasm. Eukaryotic cells have their DNA in a nucleus, whereas prokaryotic cells have no nucleus.

Customize Your Opening

☐ **Accessing Prior Knowledge,** above
☐ **Print Path** Engage Your Brain, SE p. 53
☐ **Print Path** Active Reading, SE p. 53
☐ **Digital Path** Lesson Opener

Key Topics/Learning Goals	Supporting Concepts
Classification 1 Identify why and how scientists classify living things. 2 Identify Carolus Linnaeus's contribution to classification. 3 Describe the parts of a scientific name. 4 Define *taxonomy*.	• Classification helps scientists figure out what characteristics define living things and how living things are related to each other. • Physical and chemical characteristics help identify relationships among species. • Carolus Linnaeus simplified the naming of living things by giving them a two-part name. • A scientific name consists of a genus name and a species name. • Taxonomy is the science of describing, classifying, and naming living things.
Domains, Kingdoms, and Levels 1 List and compare the three domains of living things. 2 List and compare the four kingdoms of domain Eukarya. 3 List the eight levels of classification.	• The domains of living things are Bacteria, Archaea, and Eukarya. Bacteria and archaea are unicellular prokaryotes. Some archaea live in harsh climates. Domain Eukarya consists of eukaryotes, which can be unicellular or multicellular. • Protista, Fungi, Plantae, and Animalia are the eukaryotic kingdoms. Protists are single-celled, or simple, multicellular. Most fungi and plants are multicellular. Animals are complex multicellular organisms. • The levels of classification: domain, kingdom, phylum, class, order, family, genus, species.
Branching Diagrams and Dichotomous Keys 1 Describe branching diagrams and dichotomous keys.	• Branching diagrams show relationships among species with shared characteristics. A dichotomous key uses a series of paired statements to identify organisms.

Options for Instruction

Two parallel paths provide coverage of the Essential Questions, with a strong **Inquiry** strand woven into each.
Follow the **Print Path,** the **Digital Path,** or your customized combination of print, digital, and inquiry.

 Print Path
Teaching support for the Print Path appears with the Student Pages.

 Inquiry Labs and Activities

 Digital Path
Digital Path shortcut: TS663325

Sorting Things Out!,
SE pp. 54–55
Why do we classify living things?
How do scientists know living things are related?
• Physical and Chemical Characteristics

What's in a Name?, SE p. 56
How are living things named?
• Scientific Names

Exploration Lab
Developing Scientific Names

Quick Lab
Investigate Classifying Leaves

Virtual Lab
Similarities in Animals

Why We Classify
Interactive Image

Levels of Classification
Interactive Image

What's in a Name?, SE p. 57
What are the levels of classification?

Triple Play, SE pp. 58–59
What are the three domains?
• Bacteria; Archaea; Eukarya

My Kingdom for a Eukaryote!, SE pp. 60–62
What are the kingdoms in Eukarya?
• Protista; Fungi; Plantae; Animalia
How classification systems change.

Daily Demo
Growing Bread Mold

Activity
Mystery Objects

Domains and Kingdoms
Interactive Image

My Kingdom for a Eukaryote!, SE p. 62
Branching diagrams

Keys to Success, SE pp. 64–65
How can organisms be identified?
• Dichotomous Keys

Quick Lab
Using a Dichotomous Key

Activity
What's In a Name?

Branching Diagrams
Diagram

Using a Dichotomous Key
Interactive Image

Options for Assessment

See the Evaluate page for options, including Formative Assessment, Summative Assessment, and Unit Review.

Engage and Explore

Activities and Discussion

Activity *Mystery Objects*

Engage

Introducing Key Topics

 whole class or small groups
 10 min
 GUIDED inquiry

Have one student think of a secret object. The student should then tell the class one characteristic (shape, color, size, type, and so on) of that object. The rest of the class guesses the object's identity. Each time someone guesses incorrectly, another characteristic of the object should be given. Record the characteristics and guesses as you go. When the secret object is identified, begin again with a different student picking a different secret object. Afterwards the class can discuss how this activity relates to naming organisms.

Discussion *Earthworms and Caterpillars*

Classification

 whole class
10 min

Earthworms and caterpillars share many characteristics. Both animals have long, skinny bodies that are divided into segments. However, an earthworm moves underground, has no legs or eyes, and can regrow lost segments. A caterpillar crawls above ground and is just one part of a butterfly's life cycle. Have students explain why they would classify these animals together or separately.

Take It Home *Neighborhood Walk*

Branching Diagrams and Dichotomous Keys

 adult-student pairs
30 min
 GUIDED inquiry

Students should work with an adult to observe three organisms seen on a neighborhood walk. First, students take a photograph of or sketch the organism. Next they make a list of its physical traits and behaviors. Students should then use a dichotomous key from a field guide or the Internet to identify the organism.

Optional Online resource: student worksheet

Probing Question *What Is a "Felis?"*

Classification

 whole class
 10 min
 GUIDED inquiry

Comparing Write the following names on the board: *Felis catus*, *Felis onca*, and *Felis concolor*. Tell students that *Felis catus* is the scientific name for the domestic house cat. Explain to students that all three animals listed belong to the genus *Felis*, which means they share many of the same characteristics. Ask students what they think *felis* means and what they can determine about the other two organisms based on their understanding of the word *felis*. Show students pictures of a *Felis onca* (jaguar) and a *Felis concolor* (known as puma, cougar, or mountain lion). Have students list the similarities among all three animals.

Activity *Classify Writing Tools*

Engage

Classification

 small groups
 20 min
 GUIDED inquiry

Provide or collect from students as many different writing and drawing tools, such as pens and markers, as you can. Then, have each group decide which traits they will use to classify them. They can use size, length, color, ink or pencil, or anything else that they observe. Then each group will sort their writing and drawing tools into several groups, based on the characteristics chosen. Next, have each group write down their classification scheme. Prompt students to compare classification schemes.

Customize Your Labs

 See the Lab Manual for lab datasheets.

 Go Online for editable lab datasheets.

Levels of

DIRECTED inquiry	GUIDED inquiry	INDEPENDENT inquiry
introduces inquiry skills within a structured framework.	develops inquiry skills within a supportive environment.	deepens inquiry skills with student-driven questions or procedures.

Labs and Demos

Daily Demo *Growing Bread Mold*

Domains, Kingdoms, and Levels

 whole class

 10 min and 10 min at a later date for observation

 DIRECTED inquiry

PURPOSE **To observe a eukaryote from the kingdom Fungi**

MATERIALS

- bread
- dropper
- microscope, PC
- microscope slide, slip cover
- resealable plastic bags
- tweezers or forceps

1 Grow bread molds by placing slices of bread in resealable plastic bags and placing them in a warm place for several days.

2 Use tweezers or forceps to collect a small amount of mold. Place this on the slide, then use the dropper to add a small drop of water. Place the slip cover on top of the slide.

3 Use a PC microscope to observe the molds. Have students sketch their observations.

3 **Analyzing** Have students compare characteristics of the molds.

Quick Lab *Using a Dichotomous Key*

Branching Diagrams and Dichotomous

 individuals

 10 min

DIRECTED inquiry

Students use a dichotomous key to identify an organism.

PURPOSE **To use a dichotomous key to identify an organism**

MATERIALS

- pencil

Quick Lab *Investigate Classifying Leaves*

PURPOSE **To develop a classification system for tree leaves**

See the Lab Manual or go Online for planning information.

Exploration Lab *Developing Scientific Names*

Classification

 individuals

 45 min

DIRECTED or GUIDED inquiry

Students will practice using Greek and Latin word roots to develop two-part scientific names for imaginary organisms.

PURPOSE **To create scientific names to describe fictional organisms**

MATERIALS

- chart of Latin and Greek terms
- paper, 2 sheets

Virtual Lab *Similarities in Animals*

Engage

Classification

 flexible

45 min

GUIDED inquiry

Students identify homologous structures among a variety of animals.

PURPOSE **To study homologous structures**

Activities and Discussion

- [ ] **Activity** Mystery Objects
- [ ] **Discussion** Earthworms/Caterpillars
- [ ] **Take It Home** Neighborhood Walk
- [ ] **Probing Question** What Is a *"Felis?"*
- [ ] **Activity** Classify Writing Tools

Labs and Demos

- [ ] **Daily Demo** Growing Bread Mold
- [ ] **Quick Lab** Using a Dichotomous Key
- [ ] **Quick Lab** Classifying Leaves
- [ ] **Exploration Lab** Developing Scientific Names
- [ ] **Virtual Lab** Similarities in Animals

Your Resources

Explain Science Concepts

Key Topics	📖 Print Path	💻 Digital Path

📖 Print Path

💻 Digital Path

Classification

☐ **Sorting Things Out!,** SE pp. 54–55
- Visualize It!, #5
- Summarize, #6
- List, #7

☐ **What's in a Name?,** SE p. 56
- Apply, #8

☐ **Why We Classify**
Learn about taxonomy and the contributions made by Carolus Linnaeus to classification.

☐ **Levels of Classification**
Explore the different levels of classification.

Domains, Kingdoms, and Levels

☐ **What's in a Name?,** SE p. 57
- Active Reading (Annotation strategy), #9
- Visualize It!, #10

☐ **Triple Play,** SE pp. 58–59
- Active Reading (Annotation strategy), #11
- Visualize It!, #12
- Compare, #13

☐ **My Kingdom for a Eukaryote!,**
SE pp. 60–62
- Compare, #14
- Active Reading, #15
- Classify, 16
- Active Reading, #17

It may look like a pinecone, but the pangolin is actually an animal from Africa. It is in Domain Eukarya.

☐ **Domains and Kingdoms**
Explore the three domains of living things and the four kingdoms in Domain Eukarya.

Branching Diagrams and Dichotomous Keys

☐ **My Kingdom for a Eukaryote!,** SE p. 62
- Visualize It!, #18

☐ **Keys to Success,** SE pp. 64–65
- Apply, #22
- Visualize It!, #23
- Think Outside the Book, #24

Ferns

☐ **Branching Diagrams**
Learn how scientists construct and use branching diagrams.

☐ **Using a Dichotomous Key**
Learn how to read and use a dichotomous key.

Differentiated Instruction

Basic *Button Classification*

Classification

 individuals or pairs
🕐 20 min

Have struggling or ELL students complete this classification activity. Provide students with a selection of buttons in various sizes, shapes, and colors. Have students create a classification system for the buttons. Ask students to explain their choices. You can further simplify the activity by using a deck of playing cards. Have students examine the variety of ways in which they might sort these cards (by suits, by colors, by numbers, by pictures versus numbers).

Advanced *Make a Dichotomous Key*

Branching Diagrams and Dichotomous Keys

 individuals or pairs
🕐 20 min

Make a Key Have students devise a dichotomous key that could help identify a piece of fruit such as a banana, orange, strawberry, blueberry, peach, or apple. Students should construct a key similar to the ones shown on the student pages. Have students compare keys to see if there are any similarities in the pairs of questions. Challenge interested students to create a computer program that works as a dichotomous key.

ELL *Animal Books*

Classification

 individuals or pairs
🕐 20 min

Animal Book Give each student a ten-page blank book. Have students write the name in English of one animal on each page. Under the name they should draw a picture of the animal. Then have students who speak a language other than English at home give the names for the pictured animals in their home language. Discuss how many variations there are for each name. Interested students may want to use research materials to add the scientific name for each animal.

You can extend this activity by making a chart with pictures or drawings of different animals, and invite the entire class to write the names of the animals in languages they may know or speak at home under the pictures. Point out how the many different names underscore the need for a universal classification system.

Lesson Vocabulary

species	Bacteria	Protista	Plantae
genus	Archaea	Fungi	Animalia
domain	Eukarya		

Previewing Vocabulary

 whole class
🕐 15 min

Word Origins Share the following to help students remember terms:
- **Genus** comes from the Latin *genus*, which means "race; stock."
- **Species** comes from the Latin *speciés*, which means "a form."
- **Bacteria** comes from the Greek *baktron*, which means "stick or rod" because the first observed bacteria were rod-shaped.
- **Fungi** comes from the Latin *fungus*, which means "mushroom."

Reinforcing Vocabulary

👥 individuals
🕐 ongoing

Four Square Have students draw a 2-by-2 matrix with a circle at the center. Students place a term in the circle and then fill in the surrounding cells with the types of information shown.

🌐 *Optional Online resource: Four Square Diagram support*

Customize Your Core Lesson

Core Instruction
☐ Print Path choices
☐ Digital Path choices

Vocabulary
☐ Previewing Vocabulary Word Origins
☐ Reinforcing Vocabulary Four Square

Your Resources

Differentiated Instruction
☐ Basic Button Classification
☐ Advanced Make a Dichotomous Key
☐ ELL Animal Books

Extend Science Concepts

Reinforce and Review

Activity *What's in a Name?*

Synthesizing Key Topics small groups
🕐 25 min

Inside/Outside Circles Give each student an index card with one of the questions listed below written on it. Students write their answers on the back of the index cards. Check that the students' answers are correct, and have students fix any incorrect answers. Next, have students pair up and form two circles. One partner is in an inside circle facing out, and the other is in an outside circle facing in. Each student in the inside circle asks his or her partner the question on the index card. If the answer the partner gives is incorrect, the student in the inside circle teaches the other student the correct answer. Repeat this step with the outside circle student asking the questions. Next, each student on the outside circle rotates one person to the right. He or she faces a new partner and gets a new question. Students rotate after each pair of questions. Use the questions listed below, or write your own.

1. Why do we classify living things?
2. How do scientists know living things are related?
3. How are living things named?
4. What are the eight levels of classification?
5. Name the three domains. What are the characteristics of living things in each domain?
6. Name the four kingdoms in Eukarya. What are the characteristics of living things in each kingdom?
7. How do classification systems change?
8. How are classification relationships illustrated?

Graphic Organizer

Domains, Kingdoms, and Levels individuals
🕐 ongoing

Mind Map After students have studied the lesson, ask them to create a Mind Map with the following terms: *genus, species, domain, Bacteria, Archaea, Eukarya, kingdom, Protista, Fungi, Plantae,* and *Animalia.*

🕐 *Optional Online resource: Mind Map support*

Going Further

Social Studies Connection

Domains, Kingdoms, and Levels individuals
🕐 varied

Poster Yeast is a fungus. Yeast used in baking is related to wild fungi living in the air around us. Strains of native yeasts vary regionally. For example, sourdough from San Francisco has its characteristic taste because bakers there use a yeast that is common in the air around that city. Not all breads require yeast. Many cultures have flat breads, such as tortillas from Mexico. Have students research other region-specific organisms that are used in the preparation of foods such as breads. Have them create a poster showing the region where the organism can be found, what foods it is used to produce, and the genus and species name of the organism.

Earth Science Connection

Classification individuals
🕐 varied

Classify Minerals One of the ways that geologists classify minerals is by observing physical characteristics. Physical characteristics that geologists look for include luster, hardness, fluorescence, and magnetism. Encourage interested students to research mineral classification and gather a group of rocks to classify. Have them relate classifying minerals to living things.

Customize Your Closing

🗂 *See the Assessment Guide for quizzes and tests.*

⏲ *Go Online to edit and create quizzes and tests.*

Reinforce and Review

☐ **Activity** What's in a Name?
☐ **Graphic Organizer** Mind Map
☐ **Print Path** Visual Summary, SE p. 66
☐ **Print Path** Lesson Review, SE p. 67
☐ **Digital Path** Lesson Closer

Evaluate Student Mastery

Formative Assessment

See the teacher support below the Student Pages for additional Formative Assessment questions.

Ask: Why do people sort living things into groups? Sorting things into groups helps people organize information so that it is easy to understand. **Ask:** How are living things sorted? by physical and chemical characteristics **Ask:** What are the three domains of living things? Bacteria, Archaea, Eukarya **Ask:** What are the kingdoms in Eukarya? Protista, Fungi, Plantae, Animalia

Reteach

Formative assessment may show that students need reinforcement for certain topics. The resources below are recommended for reteaching. If students were introduced to a topic through the Print Path, you can also use the Digital Path to reteach, and vice versa.

🎧 *Can be assigned to individual students*

Classification
Discussion Earthworms and Caterpillars

Activity Classify Writing Tools

Exploration Lab Developing Scientific Names 🎧

Domains, Kingdoms, and Levels
Daily Demo Growing Bread Mold

Branching Diagrams and Dichotomous Keys
Take It Home Neighborhood Walk

Quick Lab Using a Dichotomous Key 🎧

Summative Assessment

Alternative Assessment
Classifying

⊘ *Online resources: student worksheet, optional rubrics*

Classification of Living Things

Take Your Pick: *Classifying*

1. Work on your own, with a partner, or with a small group.
2. Choose items below for a total of 10 points. Check your choices.
3. Have your teacher approve your plan.
4. Submit or present your results.

2 Points

_____ **Make a List** Brainstorm a list of five different methods of organization. For example, you can list the way books are organized in a library, or groceries are organized at a supermarket.

_____ **Use a Cladogram** Cladograms are diagrams that show evolutionary relationships among groups of organisms. Find an example of a cladogram and use it to explain how the various organisms in the diagram are related.

5 Points

_____ **Plant Collection** Collect small samples or pictures of five different types of plants. Attach each to a separate piece of paper. Label each plant with its common and scientific names.

_____ **New Species** Write a descriptive paragraph about an imaginary new organism that you have discovered. How would you classify the organism, or what research would you do in order to classify the organism? What else would you want to research about the organism?

_____ **Design a Poster** Design and make a colorful poster that shows the three domains and the four kingdoms in the domain Eukarya that scientists use to classify living things.

_____ **Assign Scientific Names** Pick ten objects. Select or invent up to three genus names, and give each object a genus name. You may only use three genus names. Give each object a species name. Use a dictionary, thesaurus, or encyclopedia to help you find descriptive or meaningful words to use in your names.

8 Points

_____ **Investigate Protists** Protists are a diverse group of eukaryotic organisms. Historically they have been grouped together in one kingdom; however, that is changing. Research why some scientists want to classify protists into different groups. Prepare a short report on your findings to share with the class.

_____ **Create a Dichotomous Key** Choose four objects, such as pliers, a wrench, a socket wrench, and tongs, that you tend to confuse. List some of the similarities and differences among the objects. Use this information to create a dichotomous key that can be used to tell your objects apart.

Going Further
☐ **Social Studies Connection**

☐ **Earth Science Connection**

☐ **Print Path** Why It Matters, SE p. 63

Formative Assessment
☐ **Strategies** Throughout TE

☐ **Lesson Review** SE

Summative Assessment
☐ **Alternative Assessment** Classifying

☐ **Lesson Quiz**

☐ **Unit Tests A and B**

☐ **Unit Review** SE End-of-Unit

Your Resources

_____

_____

_____

_____

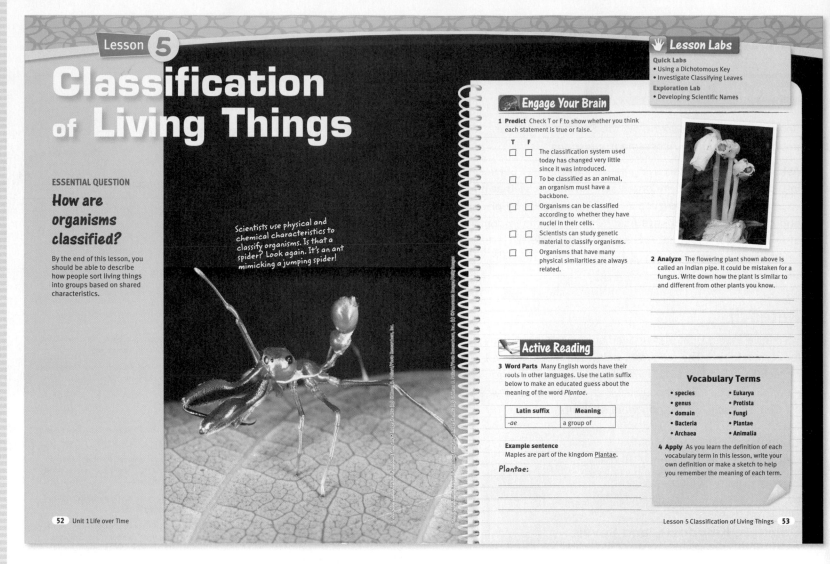

Answers

Answers for 1–3 should represent students' current thoughts, even if incorrect.

1. F; F; T; T; F

2. Sample answer: The plant does not have green leaves surrounding its stem. It has petals like other plants.

3. Sample answer: a group of plants

4. Students should define or sketch each vocabulary term in the lesson.

Opening Your Lesson

Discuss student answers to item 2 to assess students' prerequisite knowledge and to estimate what they already know about the key topics.

Preconceptions Students may think that an organism's behavior, such as swimming, and its habitat, such as a pond, are the criteria for its classification.

Prerequisites Students should recognize the characteristics of living things and understand how cell structure is related to its function. Students should also know that prokaryotes are a group of organisms that lack a cell nucleus and that most of these organisms are unicellular. Eukaryotes are organisms with cells that contain a nucleus. All species of plants and animals are eukaryotes.

Learning Alert

Classifying Living Things Some students may still have difficulty classifying examples of living and nonliving things. Students may classify items such as fire, milk, clouds, cars, and energy as living. Occasionally students will erroneously classify trees as nonliving.

Sorting Things Out!

Why do we classify living things?

There are millions of living things on Earth. How do scientists keep all of these living things organized? Scientists *classify* living things based on characteristics that living things share. Classification helps scientists answer questions such as:

- How many kinds of living things are there?
- What characteristics define each kind of living thing?
- What are the relationships among living things?

Sharks have fins and gills.

Dolphins also have fins, but not gills.

🔍 Visualize It!

5 Analyze The photos show two organisms. In the table, place a check mark in the box for each characteristic that the organisms have.

Yellow pansy butterfly

American goldfinch

	Wings	Antennae	Beak	Feathers
Yellow pansy butterfly				
American goldfinch				

6 Summarize What characteristics do yellow pansy butterflies have in common with American goldfinches? How do they differ?

_____
_____
_____

How do scientists know living things are related?

If two organisms look similar, are they related? To classify organisms, scientists compare physical characteristics. For example, they may look at size or bone structure. Scientists also compare the chemical characteristics of living things.

Physical Characteristics

How are chickens similar to dinosaurs? If you compare dinosaur fossils and chicken skeletons, you will see that chickens and dinosaurs share many physical characteristics. Scientists look at physical characteristics, such as skeletal structure. They also study how organisms develop from an egg to an adult. For example, animals with similar skeletons and development may be related.

Chemical Characteristics

Scientists can identify the relationships among organisms by studying genetic material such as DNA and RNA. They study mutations and genetic similarities to find relationships among organisms. Organisms that have very similar gene sequences or have the same mutations are likely related. Other chemicals, such as proteins and hormones, can also be studied to learn how organisms are related.

The two pandas below share habitats and diets. They look alike, but they have different DNA.

Red panda

The red panda is a closer relative to a raccoon than it is to a giant panda.

Giant panda

Raccoon

Spectacled bear

The giant panda is a closer relative to a spectacled bear than it is to a red panda.

7 List How does DNA lead scientists to better classify organisms?

_____
_____
_____
_____
_____

Answers

5. Students should fill in the table with the following check marks: Yellow pansy butterfly: wings, antennae; American goldfinch: wings, beak, feathers

6. The butterfly and goldfinch are both animals, and they both have yellow and black coloration and wings. They are different kinds of animals and have different body parts and coverings.

7. DNA indicates characteristics that may not be visible to scientists. It is also more objective than an observation. A red panda looks a bit like a giant panda, but its DNA indicates that they are not as similar as they look.

Probing Questions

Examining What are some benefits of a classification system? Sample answer: It allows people to organize a lot of items or data so that they are easy to find or understand. **Prompt:** Think about why librarians classify books in a library.

Learning Alert 🚧 MISCONCEPTION 🚧

Classification by Behavior or Habitat Some students may think that organisms are classified by criteria such as the ability to fly or having a similar habitat. To correct this, point out that some animals may share several common traits but are not grouped together scientifically. For example, the yellow pansy butterfly and the American goldfinch are both yellow and can fly. However, they are not grouped together as yellow flying animals. Ask students to study the photographs of other animals in this lesson and make a chart comparing the traits of some of these organisms. Assess by asking students to present charts and explain why organisms with similar traits should or should not be grouped together scientifically. Make sure students understand that organisms with similar appearance, behavior, or habitat are not necessarily biologically similar or related.

What's in a Name?

How are living things named?

Early scientists used names as long as 12 words to identify living things, and they also used common names. So, classification was confusing. In the 1700s, a scientist named Carolus Linnaeus (KAR•uh•luhs lih•NEE•uhs) simplified the naming of living things. He gave each kind of living thing a two-part *scientific name*.

Scientific Names

Each species has its own scientific name. A **species** (SPEE•sheez) is a group of organisms that are very closely related. They can mate and produce fertile offspring. Consider the scientific name for a mountain lion: *Puma concolor*. The first part, *Puma*, is the genus name. A **genus** (JEE•nuhs; plural, *genera*) includes similar species. The second part, *concolor*, is the specific, or species, name. No other species is named *Puma concolor*.

A scientific name always includes the genus name followed by the specific name. The first letter of the genus name is capitalized, and the first letter of the specific name is lowercase. The entire scientific name is written either in italics or underlined.

HELLO my name is
Carolus Linnaeus

The A.K.A. Files

Some living things have many common names. Scientific names prevent confusion when people discuss organisms.

Scientific name:
Puma concolor

Scientific name:
Acer rubrum

Common names:
Mountain lion
Puma
Cougar
Panther

Common names:
Red maple
Swamp maple
Soft maple

8 Apply In the scientific names above, circle the genus name and underline the specific name.

Active Reading

9 Identify As you read, underline the levels of classification.

What are the levels of classification?

Linnaeus's ideas became the basis for modern taxonomy (tak•SAHN•uh•mee). *Taxonomy* is the science of describing, classifying, and naming living things. At first, many scientists sorted organisms into two groups: plants and animals. But numerous organisms did not fit into either group.

Today, scientists use an eight-level system to classify living things. Each level gets more specific. Therefore, it contains fewer kinds of living things than the level above it. Living things in the lower levels are more closely related to each other than they are to organisms in the higher levels. From most general to more specific, the levels of classification are domain, kingdom, phylum (plural, *phyla*), class, order, family, genus, and species.

Classifying Organisms

Domain **Domain Eukarya** includes all protists, fungi, plants, and animals.

Kingdom **Kingdom Animalia** includes all animals.

Phylum Animals in **Phylum Chordata** have a hollow nerve cord in their backs. Some have a backbone.

Class Animals in **Class Mammalia**, or mammals, have a backbone and nurse their young.

Order Animals in **Order Carnivora** are mammals that have special teeth for tearing meat.

Family Animals in **Family Felidae** are cats. They are carnivores that have retractable claws.

Genus Animals in **Genus** *Felis* are cats that cannot roar. They can only purr.

Species The species *Felis domesticus*, or the house cat, has unique traits that other members of genus *Felis* do not have.

From domain to species, each level of classification contains a smaller group of organisms.

Visualize It!

10 Apply What is true about the number of organisms as they are classified closer to the species level?

Answers

8. *See students' pages for annotations.*

9. *See students' pages for annotations.*

10. There are fewer organisms in the level of classification.

Probing Questions

Analyzing Why do people need a universal system of naming organisms? Sample answer: Having a universal naming system allows people speaking different languages to refer to all organisms in the same way.

Interpreting Visuals

Have students look at the picture of the mountain lion and the red maple on this page. Ask them the different common names for the mountain lion. Then ask students to name the different common names for the maple. Ask students to discuss how scientific names help avoid confusion. Scientists can be sure that they are all referring to the same organism.

Formative Assessment

Explain how scientific names are determined. **Ask:** What are the two parts of a scientific name? genus and specific name (also called "species descriptor") What is the difference between these two parts? A genus is a group of species that has similar characteristics. One or more species make up a genus. Then follow up by asking students to name the eight levels used to classify living things. domain, kingdom, phylum, class, order, family, genus, species

Triple Play

11 Identify As you read, underline the first mention of the three domains of life.

What are the three domains?

Once, kingdoms were the highest level of classification. Scientists used a six-kingdom system. But scientists noticed that organisms in two of the kingdoms differed greatly from organisms in the other four kingdoms. So scientists added a new classification level: domains. A **domain** represents the largest differences among organisms. The three domains are Bacteria (bak•TIR•ee•uh), Archaea (ar•KEE•uh), and Eukarya (yoo•KAIR•ee•uh).

Bacteria

All bacteria belong to Domain Bacteria. Domain **Bacteria** is made up of prokaryotes that usually have a cell wall and reproduce by cell division. *Prokaryotes* are single-cell organisms that lack a nucleus in their cells. Bacteria live in almost any environment—soil, water, and even inside the human body!

Archaea

Domain **Archaea** is also made up of prokaryotes. They differ from bacteria in their genetics and in the makeup of their cell walls. Archaea live in harsh environments, such as hot springs and thermal vents, where other organisms could not survive. Some archaea are found in the open ocean and soil.

Bacteria from the genus Streptomyces are commonly found in soil.

Archaea from the genus Sulfolobus are found in hot springs.

Eukarya

What do algae, mushrooms, trees, and humans have in common? All of these organisms are *eukaryotes*. Eukaryotes are made up of cells that have a nucleus and membrane-bound organelles. The cells of eukaryotes are more complex than the cells of prokaryotes. For this reason, the cells of eukaryotes are usually larger than the cells of prokaryotes. Some eukaryotes, such as many protists and some fungi, are single-celled. Many eukaryotes are multicellular organisms. Some protists and many fungi, plants, and animals are multicellular eukaryotes. Domain **Eukarya** is made up of all eukaryotes.

It may look like a pinecone, but the pangolin is actually an animal from Africa. It is in Domain Eukarya.

Visualize It!

12 Identify Fill in the blanks with the missing labels.

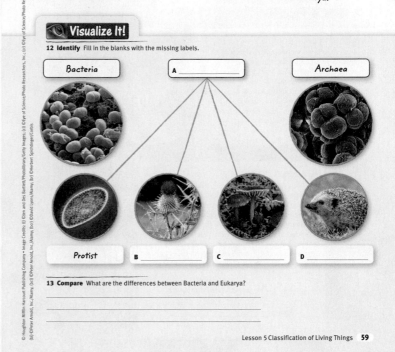

Bacteria   A _____   Archaea

Protist   B _____   C _____   D _____

13 Compare What are the differences between Bacteria and Eukarya?

_____
_____
_____

Answers

11. *See students' pages for annotations.*

12. A: Eukarya; B: Plants; C: Fungi; D: Animals

13. Bacteria are single-celled, have cell walls, and reproduce by cell division. They do not have a nucleus. Eukarya may be multicellular and have cell membranes instead of walls. They contain a nucleus, and have larger and more complex cells.

Interpreting Visuals

To help students understand the differences between the three domains, have them use the photographs, text, and *Visualize It!* activity on this page. Ask students which two domains are made up of organisms with prokaryotic cells. Bacteria and Archaea Then focus students' attention on the kingdoms. How many kingdoms are in the domain Bacteria? one What is it? Bacteria How many kingdoms are in the domain Archaea? one What is it? Archaea Which domain is made up of organisms with eukaryotic cells? Eukarya How many kingdoms are in the domain Eukarya? four What are they? Protista, Fungi, Plantae, and Animalia

Learning Alert

Confusing Levels of Classification Students might confuse the differences among domains, kingdoms, and the other levels of classification. Call attention to the chart and point out that kingdoms are a subgroup of the three domains. Each kingdom is then further divided into six more levels of organization.

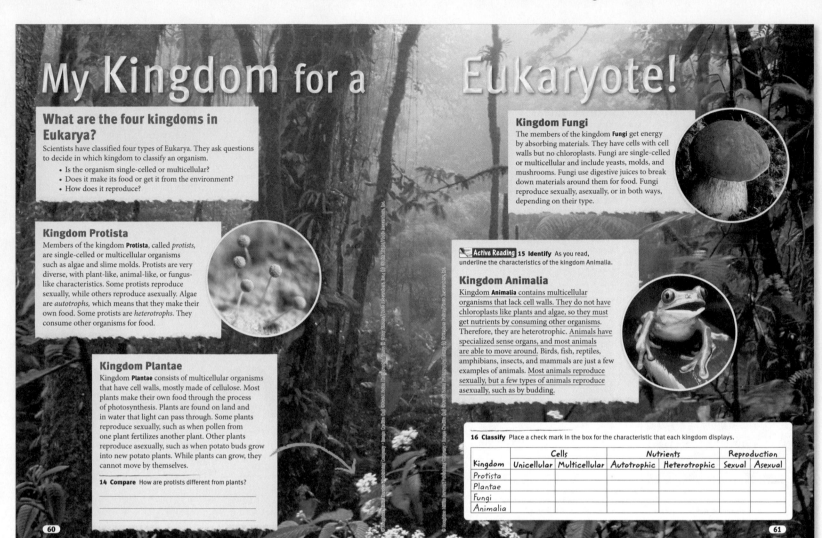

My Kingdom for a   Eukaryote!

What are the four kingdoms in Eukarya?

Scientists have classified four types of Eukarya. They ask questions to decide in which kingdom to classify an organism.

- Is the organism single-celled or multicellular?
- Does it make its food or get it from the environment?
- How does it reproduce?

Kingdom Protista

Members of the kingdom **Protista**, called *protists*, are single-celled or multicellular organisms such as algae and slime molds. Protists are very diverse, with plant-like, animal-like, or fungus-like characteristics. Some protists reproduce sexually, while others reproduce asexually. Algae are *autotrophs*, which means that they make their own food. Some protists are *heterotrophs*. They consume other organisms for food.

Kingdom Plantae

Kingdom **Plantae** consists of multicellular organisms that have cell walls, mostly made of cellulose. Most plants make their own food through the process of photosynthesis. Plants are found on land and in water that light can pass through. Some plants reproduce sexually, such as when pollen from one plant fertilizes another plant. Other plants reproduce asexually, such as when potato buds grow into new potato plants. While plants can grow, they cannot move by themselves.

14 Compare How are protists different from plants?

_____
_____
_____

Kingdom Fungi

The members of the kingdom **Fungi** get energy by absorbing materials. They have cells with cell walls but no chloroplasts. Fungi are single-celled or multicellular and include yeasts, molds, and mushrooms. Fungi use digestive juices to break down materials around them for food. Fungi reproduce sexually, asexually, or in both ways, depending on their type.

Active Reading **15 Identify** As you read, underline the characteristics of the kingdom Animalia.

Kingdom Animalia

Kingdom **Animalia** contains multicellular organisms that lack cell walls. They do not have chloroplasts like plants and algae, so they must get nutrients by consuming other organisms. Therefore, they are heterotrophic. Animals have specialized sense organs, and most animals are able to move around. Birds, fish, reptiles, amphibians, insects, and mammals are just a few examples of animals. Most animals reproduce sexually, but a few types of animals reproduce asexually, such as by budding.

16 Classify Place a check mark in the box for the characteristic that each kingdom displays.

Kingdom	Cells		Nutrients		Reproduction	
	Unicellular	Multicellular	Autotrophic	Heterotrophic	Sexual	Asexual
Protista						
Plantae						
Fungi						
Animalia						

60   61

Answers

14. Protists may be single-celled or multicellular, while plants are always multicellular. Protists either make their own food or eat other organisms. Almost all plants make their own food.

15. *See students' pages for annotations.*

16. Students should fill in the table with the following check marks: Protista: All boxes are checked; Plantae: Unicellular, Multicellular, Autotrophic, Sexual, Asexual; Fungi: Unicellular, Multicellular, Sexual, Asexual; Animalia: Multicellular, Heterotrophic, Sexual, Asexual

Probing Questions

Comparing What are two things that all of the organisms on the pages have in common? All these animals belong to the kingdom Eukarya and have eukaryotic cells.

Inferring Does scientific knowledge stay the same? How do you know? Scientific knowledge does not stay the same. Scientists are always learning new information. This new information has led to changes such as those that occurred in the classification system.

Learning Alert

Only Mammals or Vertebrates are Animals Students may think that only mammals or vertebrates are animals and that animals do not include organisms such as fish, amphibians, reptiles, or invertebrates. Many students will limit their classification of animals to land mammals. Students might also have difficulty classifying an organism as both a bird and an animal. To correct this, encourage students to list the characteristics that set the animal kingdom apart from the other three Eukarya kingdoms. Then, ask them to list as many examples of animals as they can.

How do classification systems change over time?

Millions of organisms have been identified, but millions have yet to be named. Many new organisms fit into the existing system. However, scientists often find organisms that don't fit. Not only do scientists identify new species, but sometimes these species do not fit into existing genera or phyla. In fact, many scientists argue that protists are so different from one another that they should be classified into several kingdoms instead of one. Classification continues to change as scientists learn more about living things.

How do branching diagrams show classification relationships?

How do you organize your closet? What about your books? People organize things in many different ways. Linnaeus' two-name system worked for scientists long ago, but the system does not represent what we know about living things today. Scientists use different tools to organize information about classification.

Scientists often use a type of branching diagram called a *cladogram* (KLAD•uh•gram). A cladogram shows relationships among species. Organisms are grouped according to common characteristics. Usually these characteristics are listed along a line. Branches of organisms extend from this line. Organisms on branches above each characteristic have the characteristic. Organisms on branches below lack the characteristic.

Active Reading

17 Predict How might the classification of protists change in the future?

Visualize It!

18 Apply How can you use the branching diagram to tell which plants produce seeds?

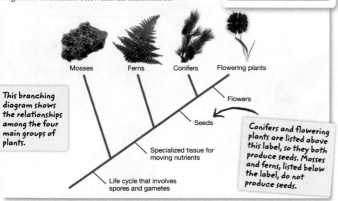

Mosses   Ferns   Conifers   Flowering plants

This branching diagram shows the relationships among the four main groups of plants.

Flowers

Seeds

Conifers and flowering plants are listed above this label, so they both produce seeds. Mosses and ferns, listed below the label, do not produce seeds.

Specialized tissue for moving nutrients

Life cycle that involves spores and gametes

62   Unit 1 Life over Time

© Houghton Mifflin Harcourt Publishing Company

Why It Matters

WEIRD SCIENCE

A Class by Themselves

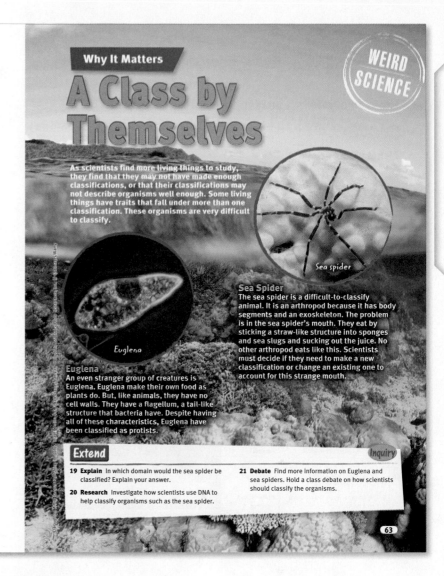

As scientists find more living things to study, they find that they may not have made enough classifications, or that their classifications may not describe organisms well enough. Some living things have traits that fall under more than one classification. These organisms are very difficult to classify.

Sea spider

Euglena

Euglena
An even stranger group of creatures is Euglena. Euglena make their own food as plants do. But, like animals, they have no cell walls. They have a flagellum, a tail-like structure that bacteria have. Despite having all of these characteristics, Euglena have been classified as protists.

Sea Spider
The sea spider is a difficult-to-classify animal. It is an arthropod because it has body segments and an exoskeleton. The problem is in the sea spider's mouth. They eat by sticking a straw-like structure into sponges and sea slugs and sucking out the juice. No other arthropod eats like this. Scientists must decide if they need to make a new classification or change an existing one to account for this strange mouth.

Extend   **Inquiry**

19 Explain In which domain would the sea spider be classified? Explain your answer.

20 Research Investigate how scientists use DNA to help classify organisms such as the sea spider.

21 Debate Find more information on Euglena and sea spiders. Hold a class debate on how scientists should classify the organisms.

63

Answers

17. Sample answer: Protists may need to be classified in several kingdoms instead of just one.

18. All of the plants to the right of the line marked "seeds" produce seeds. This means flowering plants and conifers produce seeds.

19. A sea spider would be in the domain Eukarya, because it is an animal.

20. Student output should demonstrate knowledge of how DNA is used to classify organisms.

21. Student output should demonstrate knowledge of the characteristics used to classify Euglena and sea spiders.

Learning Alert

Cladograms Originally, scientists based cladograms, or branching diagrams, completely on observable characteristics in an organism. Today, however, scientists are using information gathered from DNA and RNA sequencing more and more. Ideally, both observable characteristics and molecular information should be used to generate a cladogram. To generate an actual cladogram, scientists usually use a complex computer program because there is so much data to be analyzed.

Why it Matters

Sea Spiders Sea spiders can be found almost anywhere in the world, and that means that there are many species of sea spider—in fact, there are over 1,300 known species. Sea spiders can be as small as a millimeter and as big as 90 centimeters long. Antarctica is home to many species of sea spiders. One type of sea spider in Antarctica has an extra body segment—this extra segment means it has five pairs of legs instead of four.

Keys to Success

How can organisms be identified?

Imagine walking through the woods. You see an animal sitting on a rock. It has fur, whiskers, and a large, flat tail. How can you find out what kind of animal it is? You can use a dichotomous key.

Dichotomous Keys

A *dichotomous key* (dy•KAHT•uh•muhs KEE) uses a series of paired statements to identify organisms. Each pair of statements is numbered. When identifying an organism, read each pair of statements. Then choose the statement that best describes the organism. Either the chosen statement identifies the organism, or you will be directed to another pair of statements. By working through the key, you can eventually identify the organism.

22 Apply Use the dichotomous key below to identify the animals shown in the photographs.

Dichotomous Key to Six Mammals in the Eastern United States

1	A	The mammal has no hair on its tail.	Go to step 2
	B	The mammal has hair on its tail.	Go to step 3
2	A	The mammal has a very short naked tail.	Eastern mole
	B	The mammal has a long naked tail.	Go to step 4
3	A	The mammal has a black mask.	Raccoon
	B	The mammal does not have a black mask.	Go to step 5
4	A	The mammal has a flat, paddle-shaped tail.	Beaver
	B	The mammal has a round, skinny tail.	Possum
5	A	The mammal has a long furry tail that is black on the tip.	Long-tailed weasel
	B	The mammal has a long tail that has little fur.	White-footed mouse

A _____

B _____

64 Unit 1 Life over Time

Visualize It!

23 Apply Some dichotomous keys are set up as diagrams instead of tables. Work through the key below to identify the unknown plant.

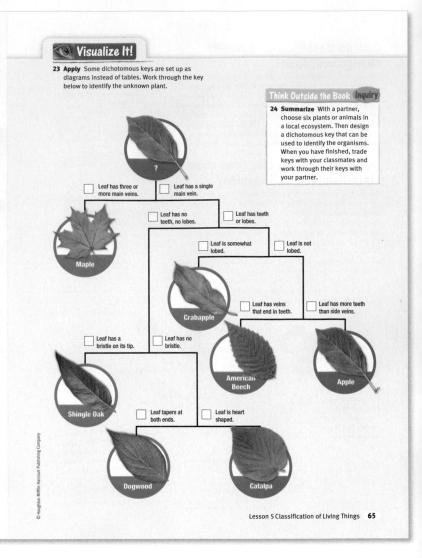

Leaf has three or more main veins. / Leaf has a single main vein.

Leaf has no teeth, no lobes. / Leaf has teeth or lobes.

Maple

Leaf is somewhat lobed. / Leaf is not lobed.

Crabapple

Leaf has veins that end in teeth. / Leaf has more teeth than side veins.

Leaf has a bristle on its tip. / Leaf has no bristle.

American Beech

Apple

Shingle Oak

Leaf tapers at both ends. / Leaf is heart shaped.

Dogwood

Catalpa

Think Outside the Book Inquiry

24 Summarize With a partner, choose six plants or animals in a local ecosystem. Then design a dichotomous key that can be used to identify the organisms. When you have finished, trade keys with your classmates and work through their keys with your partner.

Lesson 5 Classification of Living Things 65

Answers

22. A: beaver; B: long-tailed weasel
23. *See students' pages for annotations.*
24. Student output should demonstrate knowledge of how dichotomous keys are set up.

Formative Assessment

Have students discuss the six kingdoms of living organisms. **Ask:** Which kingdoms include single-celled organisms? Protista, Fungi, Archaea, and Bacteria **Ask:** How would a dichotomous key help you to identify an organism? The key asks a series of questions with only two possible answers. After all of the questions have been answered, the genus and species of the organism should be identified.

For greater depth, encourage students to practice using dichotomous keys, like the ones on this page, to identify different organisms.

Interpreting Visuals

To help students interpret the dichotomous key of an unknown leaf, ask them to identify how many choices are given for each characteristic. two Which characteristics in the key are used to identify the species of leaf? number of veins; whether or not it has teeth; whether or not it is lobed; whether or not it has a bristle tip; whether or not it is heart-shaped Which characteristics help you identify the unknown plant? It is single veined; it has teeth; it is not lobed; it has more teeth than side veins.

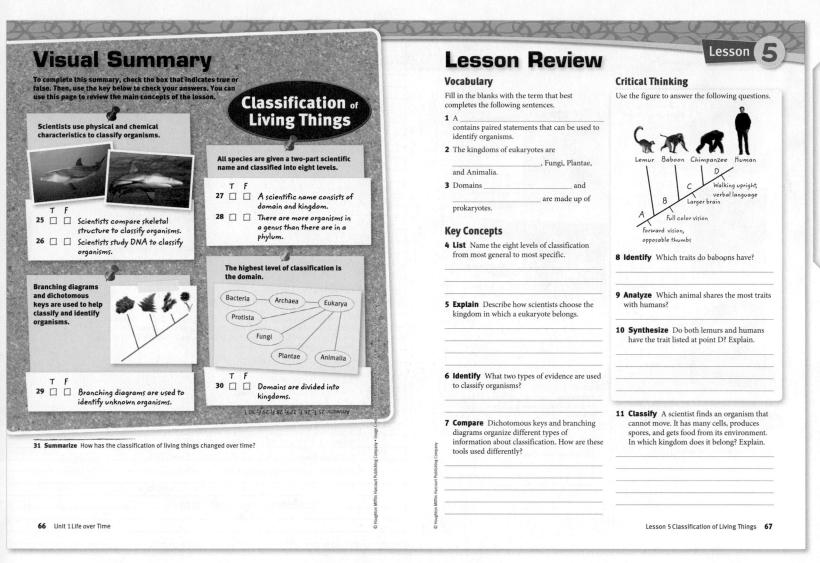

Visual Summary

To complete this summary, check the box that indicates true or false. Then, use the key below to check your answers. You can use this page to review the main concepts of the lesson.

Classification of Living Things

Scientists use physical and chemical characteristics to classify organisms.

T F
25 ☐ ☐ Scientists compare skeletal structure to classify organisms.
26 ☐ ☐ Scientists study DNA to classify organisms.

All species are given a two-part scientific name and classified into eight levels.

T F
27 ☐ ☐ A scientific name consists of domain and kingdom.
28 ☐ ☐ There are more organisms in a genus than there are in a phylum.

Branching diagrams and dichotomous keys are used to help classify and identify organisms.

T F
29 ☐ ☐ Branching diagrams are used to identify unknown organisms.

The highest level of classification is the domain.

Bacteria — Archaea — Eukarya
Protista
Fungi
Plantae — Animalia

T F
30 ☐ ☐ Domains are divided into kingdoms.

Answers: 25 T, 26 T, 27 F, 28 F, 29 F, 30 T

31 Summarize How has the classification of living things changed over time?

66 Unit 1 Life over Time

Lesson Review

Vocabulary

Fill in the blanks with the term that best completes the following sentences.

1 A _____ contains paired statements that can be used to identify organisms.

2 The kingdoms of eukaryotes are _____, Fungi, Plantae, and Animalia.

3 Domains _____ and _____ are made up of prokaryotes.

Key Concepts

4 List Name the eight levels of classification from most general to most specific.

5 Explain Describe how scientists choose the kingdom in which a eukaryote belongs.

6 Identify What two types of evidence are used to classify organisms?

7 Compare Dichotomous keys and branching diagrams organize different types of information about classification. How are these tools used differently?

Critical Thinking

Use the figure to answer the following questions.

Lemur Baboon Chimpanzee Human
Walking upright; verbal language
Larger brain
Full color vision
Forward vision, opposable thumbs

8 Identify Which traits do baboons have?

9 Analyze Which animal shares the most traits with humans?

10 Synthesize Do both lemurs and humans have the trait listed at point D? Explain.

11 Classify A scientist finds an organism that cannot move. It has many cells, produces spores, and gets food from its environment. In which kingdom does it belong? Explain.

Lesson 5 Classification of Living Things 67

Visual Summary Answers

25. T
26. T
27. F
28. F
29. F
30. T
31. Sample answer: Scientists can now classify living things according to DNA. In the past, scientists could only look at physical characteristics.

Lesson Review Answers

1. dichotomous key
2. Protista
3. Bacteria; Archaea
4. domain, kingdom, phylum, class, order, family, genus, and species
5. Scientists ask questions, such as: Is the organism unicellular or multicellular, autotrophic or heterotrophic? How does the organism reproduce?
6. physical characteristics and chemical characteristics
7. Sample answer: Dichotomous keys are used to identify unknown organisms. Branching diagrams are used to describe the characteristics that different organisms share.
8. forward vision, opposable thumbs, and full color vision
9. chimpanzees
10. No, they do not both have the trait. Only humans have the trait. Lemurs are listed on a branch to the left of the trait, so they do not have it.
11. Sample answer: The organism belongs in Kingdom Fungi. Fungi can be multicellular. Most cannot move, and they get food by releasing digestive juices into their environment.

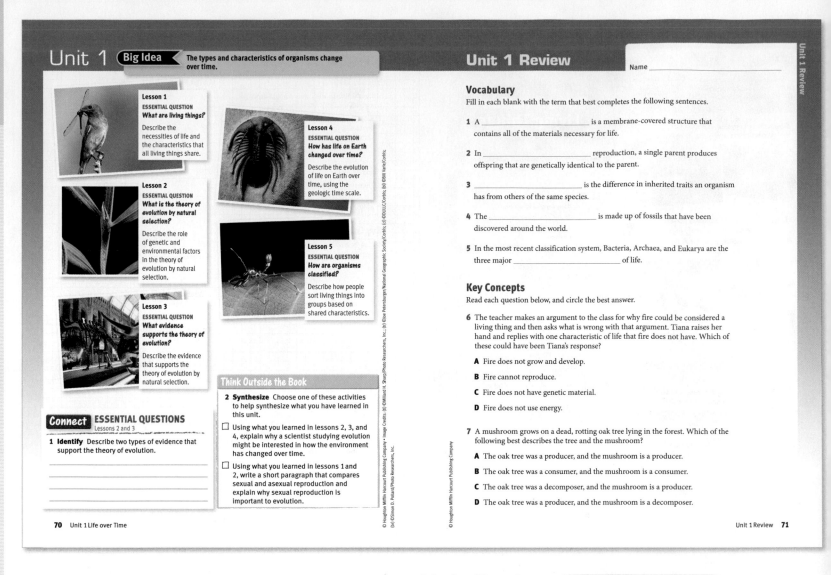

Unit 1 (Big Idea) The types and characteristics of organisms change over time.

Unit 1 Review

Name _____

Vocabulary

Fill in each blank with the term that best completes the following sentences.

1. A _____ is a membrane-covered structure that contains all of the materials necessary for life.

2. In _____ reproduction, a single parent produces offspring that are genetically identical to the parent.

3. _____ is the difference in inherited traits an organism has from others of the same species.

4. The _____ is made up of fossils that have been discovered around the world.

5. In the most recent classification system, Bacteria, Archaea, and Eukarya are the three major _____ of life.

Key Concepts

Read each question below, and circle the best answer.

6. The teacher makes an argument to the class for why fire could be considered a living thing and then asks what is wrong with that argument. Tiana raises her hand and replies with one characteristic of life that fire does not have. Which of these could have been Tiana's response?

   A Fire does not grow and develop.

   B Fire cannot reproduce.

   C Fire does not have genetic material.

   D Fire does not use energy.

7. A mushroom grows on a dead, rotting oak tree lying in the forest. Which of the following best describes the tree and the mushroom?

   A The oak tree was a producer, and the mushroom is a producer.

   B The oak tree was a consumer, and the mushroom is a consumer.

   C The oak tree was a decomposer, and the mushroom is a producer.

   D The oak tree was a producer, and the mushroom is a decomposer.

Lesson 1
ESSENTIAL QUESTION
What are living things?
Describe the necessities of life and the characteristics that all living things share.

Lesson 2
ESSENTIAL QUESTION
What is the theory of evolution by natural selection?
Describe the role of genetic and environmental factors in the theory of evolution by natural selection.

Lesson 3
ESSENTIAL QUESTION
What evidence supports the theory of evolution?
Describe the evidence that supports the theory of evolution by natural selection.

Lesson 4
ESSENTIAL QUESTION
How has life on Earth changed over time?
Describe the evolution of life on Earth over time, using the geologic time scale.

Lesson 5
ESSENTIAL QUESTION
How are organisms classified?
Describe how people sort living things into groups based on shared characteristics.

Think Outside the Book

2 **Synthesize** Choose one of these activities to help synthesize what you have learned in this unit.

☐ Using what you learned in lessons 2, 3, and 4, explain why a scientist studying evolution might be interested in how the environment has changed over time.

☐ Using what you learned in lessons 1 and 2, write a short paragraph that compares sexual and asexual reproduction and explain why sexual reproduction is important to evolution.

Connect ESSENTIAL QUESTIONS
Lessons 2 and 3

1 **Identify** Describe two types of evidence that support the theory of evolution.

_____

_____

_____

Unit Summary Answers

1. The fossil record and developmental similarities in organisms that share a common ancestor are two types of evidence that support evolution.

2. Option 1: Sample answer: Knowing how the environment has changed over time could help a scientist understand the environment that a particular species once inhabited and what traits might have increased its chances of survival in that environment.

   Option 2: In sexual reproduction, two parents produce offspring that will share characteristics of both parents. In asexual reproduction, a single parent produces offspring that are identical to the parent. Sexual reproduction allows for genetic variation within a species. High genetic variation is important for the survival of species because individuals might have traits that will be advantageous if the environment changes.

Unit Review (Response to Intervention)

A Quick Grading Chart follows the Answers. See the Assessment Guide for more detail about correct and incorrect answer choices. Refer back to the Lesson Planning pages for activities and assignments that can be used as remediation for students who answer questions incorrectly.

Answers

1. cell The answer is cell because a cell is the basic unit of life. (Lesson 1)

2. asexual The answer is asexual reproduction because this type of reproduction does not result in offspring with a combination of genes from two genetically different parents. (Lesson 1)

3. Variation Differences in traits are called variation and are one of the things that must exist to allow evolution to occur. (Lesson 3)

Unit 1 Review continued

Name_____

8 Darwin's theory of natural selection consists of four important parts. Which of these correctly lists the four essential parts of natural selection?

A living space, adaptation, selection, and hunting

B overproduction, genetic variation, selection, and adaptation

C selection, extinction, underproduction, and competition

D asexual reproduction, genetic variation, selection, and adaptation

9 Charles Darwin studied the finches of the Galápagos Islands and found that their beaks vary in shape and size.

Darwin found that the finches that ate mostly insects had long, narrow beaks. Finches that ate mostly seeds had shorter, broad beaks to crush seeds. Which statement below best describes how natural selection resulted in the four types of finches shown above?

A The residents of the Galápagos Islands selectively bred together finches having the traits that they wanted them to have.

B The narrow-beaked finches came first and evolved into the broad-beaked finches through a series of natural mutations.

C The broad-beaked finches wore down their beaks digging for insects and passed these narrower beaks on to their offspring.

D Over time, the finches that were born with beaks better suited to the available food supply in their habitats survived and reproduced.

10 Which of these describes a likely reason why a species would become extinct after a major environmental change?

A There are not enough members of the species born with a trait necessary to survive in the new environment.

B The environmental changes mean fewer predators are around.

C The change in the environment opens new resources with less competition.

D There are more homes for the species in the changed environment.

11 Which of the following provides structural evidence for evolution?

A A fossil from the Mesozoic era shows an extinct animal similar to a modern animal.

B A comparison of similar bones in the legs of a human, a dog, and a bat.

C A genetic analysis of two animals shows similar sequences of DNA.

D The embryos of two animals look similar at similar stages.

12 The pictures below show four types of sea organisms.

1   2   3   4

Which of these would you most expect to be true if these organisms were classified by their physical characteristics only?

A Organisms 1 and 3 would be in the same species.

B Organisms 2 and 4 would be in the same genus.

C Organisms 1 and 3 would be more closely related than organisms 2 and 4.

D Organisms 2 and 4 would be more closely related than organisms 1 and 3.

13 Which of the following happened in Precambrian time?

A Life began to evolve on Earth.

B The first mammals appeared.

C A mass extinction wiped out most dinosaurs.

D Life on Earth began to move from water to land.

Answers *(continued)*

4. **fossil record** The fossil record is made up of the many fossils that have been discovered over time in many different places. The fossil record extends the history of life into the distant geologic past. (Lesson 3)

5. **domains** Bacteria, Archaea, and Eukarya are the three domains of living things in the domain system of classification. (Lesson 5)

6. **Answer C is correct** because fire does not have genetic material, so it is not a living thing. (Lesson 1)

7. **Answer D is correct** because a plant like an oak tree makes food for itself, so it is a producer. A mushroom is a fungus, which gets energy by breaking down dead organisms, so it is a decomposer. (Lesson 1)

8. **Answer B is correct** because all four of these must exist for natural selection to occur. (Lesson 2)

9. **Answer D is correct** because natural selection says those with beneficial adaptations will survive and reproduce more successfully. (Lesson 2)

10. **Answer A is correct** because this describes the key reason for extinction due to environmental change. (Lesson 2)

11. **Answer B is correct** because *structural evidence* refers to corresponding structures in related animals. (Lesson 3)

12. **Answer C is correct** because these two types of fish are closer in physical appearance than are the octopus and jellyfish. (Lesson 3)

13. **Answer A is correct** because life did first evolve on Earth in Precambrian time. (Lesson 4)

14. **Key Elements:**

   • Order: Orectolobiformes

   • Domain: Eukarya; Kingdom: Animalia (Lesson 5)

Unit 1 Review continued

Critical Thinking

Answer the following questions in the space provided.

14 The dichotomous key below helps identify the order of some sharks.

Orders of Sharks

Use the diagram to determine the order to which this shark belongs. Then name its domain and kingdom.

Order: _____

Domain: _____   Kingdom: _____

15 Describe how the changes that happened during the first division of the geologic time scale affected the evolution of organisms on Earth.

_____
_____
_____
_____

Connect ESSENTIAL QUESTIONS
Lessons 2, 3, 4, and 5

Answer the following question in the space provided.

16 Explain why mass extinctions occur and why they often mark divisions of geologic time.

_____
_____
_____
_____

74 Unit 1 Life over Time

© Houghton Mifflin Harcourt Publishing Company

Quick Grading Chart

Use the chart below for quick test grading. The lesson correlations can help you target reteaching for missed items.

Item	Answer	Cognitive Complexity	Lesson
1.	—	Low	1
2.	—	Low	1
3.	—	Low	3
4.	—	Low	3
5.	—	Low	5
6.	C	Moderate	1
7.	D	Moderate	1
8.	B	Moderate	2
9.	D	High	2
10.	A	Moderate	2
11.	B	Moderate	3
12.	C	Moderate	3
13.	A	Moderate	4
14.	—	High	5
15.	—	Low	4
16.	—	High	4

Cognitive Complexity refers to the demand on thinking associated with an item, and may vary with the answer choices, the number of steps required to arrive at an answer, and other factors, but not the ability level of the student.

Answers *(continued)*

15. Key Elements:

Life first evolved during Precambrian time. The first organisms that evolved thrived in an environment without oxygen. Then a new group of organisms evolved that released large amounts of oxygen into the environment, which changed the oceans and the atmosphere. This led to the mass extinction of those organisms to which oxygen was toxic. The buildup of oxygen also led to the success of organisms that are dependent on oxygen. (Lesson 4)

16. Key Elements:

Mass extinctions are usually the result of some major change in the environment, such as an asteroid impact on Earth. Such changes cause species that are not adapted to the new environment to go extinct. Mass extinctions usually change the classes of organisms dominant on Earth. The change in prevalent species after mass extinctions makes these events a natural, logical division for eras. (Lesson 4)

UNIT 2 Earth's Organisms

The Big Idea and Essential Questions

This Unit was designed to focus on this Big Idea and Essential Questions.

Big Idea Organisms can be characterized by their structures, by the ways they grow and reproduce, and by the ways they interact with their environment.

Lesson	ESSENTIAL QUESTION	Student Mastery	PD Professional Development	Lesson Overview
LESSON 1 Archaea, Bacteria, and Viruses	**What are microorganisms?**	To describe the characteristics of archaea, bacteria, and viruses and explain how they reproduce or replicate	Content Refresher, TE p. 100	TE p. 108
LESSON 2 Protists and Fungi	**What are protists and fungi?**	To describe the characteristics of protists and fungi, and explain how they grow and reproduce	Content Refresher, TE p. 101	TE p. 124
LESSON 3 Introduction to Plants	**What are plants?**	To list the characteristics of plants and explain plant classification	Content Refresher, TE p. 102	TE p. 140
LESSON 4 Plant Processes	**How do plants stay alive?**	To describe the processes through which plants obtain energy, reproduce, and respond to their environments	Content Refresher, TE p. 103	TE p. 156
LESSON 5 Introduction to Animals	**What are animals?**	To explain the characteristics of animals and describe some different kinds of animals	Content Refresher, TE p. 104	TE p. 176
LESSON 6 Animal Behavior	**What are some different animal behaviors?**	To describe some behaviors that help animals survive and reproduce	Content Refresher, TE p. 105	TE p. 190

©Marcel Maierhofer/imagebroker/Alamy Images

 **Professional Development** **Science Background**

Use the key words at right to access

- Professional Development from **The NSTA Learning Center**
- **SciLinks** for additional online content appropriate for students and teachers

Keywords

animals   plants
bacteria   viruses
fungi

National Science Teachers Association

SCILINKS
THE WORLD'S A CLICK AWAY

Options for Instruction

Two parallel paths provide coverage of the Essential Questions, with a strong **Inquiry** strand woven into each. Follow the **Print Path,** the **Digital Path,** or your customized combination of print, digital, and inquiry.

	LESSON 1 Archaea, Bacteria, and Viruses	**LESSON 2** Protists and Fungi	**LESSON 3** Introduction to Plants
Essential Questions	**What are microorganisms?**	**What are protists and fungi?**	**What are plants?**
Key Topics	• Characteristics of Archaea and Bacteria • How Archaea and Bacteria Reproduce • Characteristics of Viruses • How Viruses Replicate	• Characteristics of Protists • Reproduction and Diversity in Protists • Characteristics of Fungi • Reproduction and Diversity in Fungi	• Characteristics of Plants • Structures and Functions of Plants • Classification of Plants
Print Path	**Teacher Edition** pp. 108–123 **Student Edition** pp. 78–91	**Teacher Edition** pp. 124–139 **Student Edition** pp. 92–105	**Teacher Edition** pp. 140–155 **Student Edition** pp. 106–119
Inquiry Labs	**Lab Manual** **Field Lab** Culturing Bacteria from the Environment **Quick Lab** Modeling Viral Replication **Quick Lab** Observing Bacteria	**Lab Manual** **Exploration Lab** Survey of Reproduction in Protists and Fungi **Quick Lab** What Do Protists Look Like?	**Lab Manual** **Quick Lab** Investigating Flower Parts **Quick Lab** Observing Transport
Digital Path	**Digital Path** TS673065 	**Digital Path** TS673068 	**Digital Path** TS663354

LESSON 4 Plant Processes	LESSON 5 Introduction to Animals	LESSONS 6 and UNIT 2 Unit Projects
How do plants stay alive?	**What are animals?**	*See the next page*
• Plants and Energy • Plant Reproduction • Plant Responses	• Animal Characteristics • Animal Diversity • Invertebrates • Vertebrates	

Teacher Edition pp. 156–171	Teacher Edition pp. 176–189	**Unit Assessment** *See the next page*
Student Edition pp. 120–133	Student Edition pp. 138–149	

Lab Manual Virtual Lab What Affects Photosynthesis Rate? **Exploration Lab** Fertilization in Angiosperms	Lab Manual **Quick Lab** Form and Motion **Quick Lab** Characteristics of Animals	

Digital Path TS663364	**Digital Path** TS663424

Options for Instruction

Two parallel paths provide coverage of the Essential Questions, with a strong **Inquiry** strand woven into each. Follow the **Print Path,** the **Digital Path,** or your customized combination of print, digital, and inquiry.

	LESSON 6 Animal Behavior	**UNIT 2** Unit Projects
Essential Questions	**What are some different animal behaviors?**	Citizen Science Project Native and Nonnative Species Teacher Edition p. 107 Student Edition pp. 76–77
Key Topics	• Animal Behavior • Survival Behaviors • Reproductive and Seasonal Behaviors • Social Behaviors	Animal Behavior

Print Path

Teacher Edition pp. 190–203

Student Edition pp. 150–161

Unit Assessment

Formative Assessment

Strategies **RTI**
Throughout TE

Lesson Reviews SE

Unit PreTest

Summative Assessment

Alternative Assessment
(1 per lesson) **RTI**

Lesson Quizzes

Unit Tests A and B

Unit Review **RTI**
(with answer remediation)

Practice Tests
(end of module)

Project-Based Assessment

📓 *See the Assessment Guide for quizzes and tests.*

🖱 *Go Online to edit and create quizzes and tests.*

Response to Intervention

See RTI teacher support materials on p. PD6.

Inquiry Labs

Lab Manual

📱 **Virtual Lab**
Animal Migration

Quick Lab At a Snail's Pace

Quick Lab Modeling Predator-Prey Scenarios

Digital Path

Digital Path
TS663436

Teacher Notes

Differentiated Instruction

English Language Proficiency

Strategies for **English Language Learners (ELL)** are provided for each lesson, under the Explain tabs.

LESSON 1 *Bacteria and Virus Terms,* TE p. 113

LESSON 2 *Protist Posters,* TE p. 129

LESSON 3 *Roots, Stems, or Leaves,* TE p. 145

LESSON 4 *Plant Process Pictures,* TE p. 161

LESSON 5 *Vertebrate Body Coverings,* TE p. 181

LESSON 6 *Body Language,* TE p. 195

Vocabulary strategies provided for all students can also be a particular help for ELL. Use different strategies for each lesson or choose one or two to use throughout the unit. Vocabulary strategies can be found under the Explain tab for each lesson (TE pp. 113, 129, 145, 161, 181, and 195).

Leveled Inquiry

Inquiry labs, activities, probing questions, and daily demos provide a range of inquiry levels. Preview them under the Engage and Explore tabs starting on TE pp. 110, 126, 142, 158, 178, and 192.

 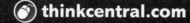

Levels of **Inquiry**

DIRECTED inquiry	**GUIDED** inquiry	**INDEPENDENT** inquiry
introduces inquiry skills within a structured framework.	develops inquiry skills within a supportive environment.	deepens inquiry skills with student-driven questions or procedures.

Each long lab has two inquiry options:

LESSON 1 **Field Lab** *Culturing Bacteria from the Environment Directed or Guided Inquiry*

LESSON 2 **Exploration Lab** *Survey of Reproduction in Protists and Fungi Guided or Independent Inquiry*

LESSON 4 **Exploration Lab** *Fertilization in Angiosperms Directed or Guided Inquiry*

🖥 Go Digital! ⊚ thinkcentral.com

Digital Path

The Unit 2 Resource Gateway is your guide to all of the digital resources for this unit. To access the Gateway, visit thinkcentral.com.

Digital Interactive Lessons

Lesson 1 Archaea, Bacteria, and Viruses TS673065

Lesson 2 Protists and Fungi TS673068

Lesson 3 Introduction to Plants TS663354

Lesson 4 Plant Processes TS663364

Lesson 5 Introduction to Animals T663424

Lesson 6 Animal Behavior TS663436

More Digital Resources

In addition to digital lessons, you will find the following digital resources for Unit 2:

Video-Based Project: Animal Behavior (previewed on TE p. 107)

Virtual Labs: What Affects Photosynthesis Rate? (previewed on TE p. 159) Animal Migration (previewed on TE p. 193)

©Patrick Greene Productions

RTI ▶ Response to Intervention

Response to Intervention (RTI) is a process for identifying and supporting students who are not making expected progress toward essential learning goals. The following *ScienceFusion* components can be used to provide strategic and intensive intervention.

Component	Location	Strategies and Benefits
STUDENT EDITION Active Reading prompts, Visualize It!, Think Outside the Book	**Throughout each lesson**	Student responses can be used as screening tools to assess whether intervention is needed.
TEACHER EDITION Formative Assessment, Probing Questions, Learning Alerts	**Throughout each lesson**	Opportunities are provided to assess and remediate student understanding of lesson concepts.
TEACHER EDITION Extend Science Concepts	**Reinforce and Review, TE pp. 114, 130, 146, 162, 182, 196** **Going Further, TE pp. 114, 130, 146, 162, 182, 196**	Additional activities allow students to reinforce and extend their understanding of lesson concepts.
TEACHER EDITION Evaluate Student Mastery	**Formative Assessment, TE pp. 115, 131, 147, 163, 183, 197** **Alternative Assessment, TE pp. 115, 131, 147, 163, 183, 197**	These assessments allow for greater flexibility in assessing students with differing physical, mental, and language abilities as well as varying learning and communication modes.
TEACHER EDITION Unit Review Remediation	**Unit Review, TE pp. 204–207**	Includes reference back to Lesson Planning pages for remediation activities and assignments.
INTERACTIVE DIGITAL LESSONS and VIRTUAL LABS	**thinkcentral.com** **Unit 2 Gateway** **Lesson 1 TS673065** **Lesson 2 TS673068** **Lesson 3 TS663354** **Lesson 4 TS663364** **Lesson 5 TS663424** **Lesson 6 TS663436**	Lessons and labs make content accessible through simulations, animations, videos, audio, and integrated assessment. Useful for review and reteaching of lesson concepts.

Content Refresher

Professional Development

Archaea, Bacteria, and Viruses

ESSENTIAL QUESTION
What are microorganisms?

1. Characteristics of Archaea and Bacteria

Students will learn about the characteristics of archaea and bacteria.

Prokaryotes are organisms that do not have a nucleus or membrane-bound organelles. Almost all are single-celled. Prokaryotes can be subdivided into two Domains—Archaea and Bacteria.

Almost all archaea have cell walls. Their walls and many of their chemicals are distinct from those of bacteria. Archaea contain molecules that are not found in any other organisms. Archaea also contain molecules that are very similar to some found in eukaryotic cells. This leads scientists to believe that ancient archaea may have given rise to the first eukaryotes. Archaea were once thought to live only in extreme environments. Recent research has shown them to be found everywhere. However, archaea are noteworthy for their ability to live where almost nothing else can, including hot springs, deep-sea vents, and salt lakes.

Most prokaryotes are bacteria. Found everywhere on Earth, bacteria have DNA, proteins, a cell membrane, and a rigid outer wall that gives them the shape of a rod, spiral, or sphere. These shapes have scientific names that are often reflected in the species of the bacteria. The rod shaped bacteria, or bacillus, include *Bacillus anthracis*, which causes anthrax. The sphere shaped bacteria, called coccus, include *Staphylococcus aureus*, which causes staph infections. The spiral shaped bacteria, called spirillum, include the genus *Spirillum,* as well as many other genera such as *Borrelia burgdorferi*, the bacterium that causes Lyme disease. Some bacteria survive harsh conditions by encasing their genetic material and ribosomes in a thick-walled protective coat called an endospore. Many endospores can survive in hot, cold, and very dry places. *Clostridium botulinum,* the bacteria that causes food poisoning in canned foods, is one example of bacteria that produce endospores.

2. How Archaea and Bacteria Reproduce

Students will learn how archaea and bacteria reproduce.

Both bacteria and archaea reproduce by binary fission. Some bacteria can divide every 10 minutes. Binary fission is a form of asexual reproduction in single-celled organisms in which one cell divides into two cells of the same size. During binary fission, the DNA is copied to form two loops that bind to different places inside the cell membrane. As the cell's membrane grows, the loops of DNA separate. Finally, when the cell is approximately twice its original size, the membrane pinches inward and separates the two cells. Each new cell has one copy of the parent cell's DNA.

Bacteria can exchange genetic material before dividing. When two bacteria join in conjugation, a plasmid (a short loop of DNA containing fewer genes than a chromosome) is transferred from one bacterium to another. The bacterium that receives the plasmid has new genes that may be useful. Bacteria can also take up DNA strands from their environment.

3. Characteristics of Viruses

Students will learn about the parts of a virus.

A virus is a microscopic particle, made of a nucleic acid (RNA or DNA) and a protein coat, that enters a cell, replicates, and often destroys the cell. Viruses are smaller than the smallest bacteria. Viruses are not considered living because they lack properties of living things. Viruses do not eat and release energy from food. They do not maintain homeostasis. Viruses do not respond to stimuli such as light or touch. Viruses cannot reproduce on their own.

4. How Viruses Replicate

Students will learn how viruses replicate.

In order to replicate, a virus must enter a host cell or insert its genetic material into a host cell. The virus's DNA causes the cell to produce virus proteins. New viruses are made within the cell. Often, the cell bursts and the new virus particles are released. This process is called the *lytic cycle.*

Lesson 5 Introduction to Animals   To introduce animal classification, collect 20–25 various animal photos from magazines. Cut out a small region of each animal (beak, paw, tail) and glue it on a 5 × 7 note card. Number the cards, and create a handout with hints that students can use to determine the species and class of each animal. Laminate your deck of cards for years of reuse. Encourage students to make a few of their own cards.

Lesson 2

Protists and Fungi

ESSENTIAL QUESTION
What are protists and fungi?

1. Characteristics of Protists

Students will learn about the characteristics of protists.

The kingdom Protista is a very diverse group of organisms that may be reclassified into multiple kingdoms as more is learned about the relationships between protists and other organisms. Protists are eukaryotic, meaning they have a nucleus and membrane-bound organelles. Animals, plants, and fungi are thought to have evolved from protist ancestors.

All protists thrive in moist habitats, and most are single-celled. Some move using hairlike cilia or whiplike flagella. Amoebas and amoeboid protists move by extending their cell membrane and flowing into the extended pseudopod, or "false foot." Some protists, including types of seaweed, are multicellular. Other protists are colonial.

2. Reproduction and Diversity in Protists

Students will learn how protists reproduce and describe different types of protists.

Most protists can reproduce asexually. Methods include binary fission (the splitting of a single-celled protist into two identical cells) and fragmentation (a new protist arising from a piece of the parent's body). In asexual reproduction, offspring are genetically identical to the parent.

Many protists can also reproduce sexually. In sexual reproduction, each parent produces haploid (1*n*) sex cells called *gametes*. Two gametes unite to form the new organism. Some protists reproduce both sexually and asexually in a process called alternation of generations.

Protists can be grouped based on how they obtain energy. Animal-like protists obtain nutrients and energy by consuming other organisms. Plant-like protists use photosynthesis to

make their own food. Fungus-like protists absorb nutrients from their surroundings, including from dead organisms, and reproduce with structures called spores.

2. Characteristics of Fungi

Students will learn about the characteristics of fungi.

The kingdom Fungi is made up of organisms that absorb nutrients from their surroundings. Fungi secrete digestive enzymes and then absorb the nutrients into their cells. Many fungi are decomposers, so they get their energy by breaking down dead organic matter and absorbing it into their bodies. Other fungi are parasites, so they get energy through their attachment to living organisms. Most fungi are multicellular, but some, including yeasts, are single-celled.

Fungal cells generally form threadlike hyphae that join together to form a network called the *mycelium*. The mycelium acts like a plant's roots to take in water and nutrients.

4. Reproduction and Diversity in Fungi

Students will learn how fungi reproduce and describe different types of fungi.

Fungi can reproduce asexually either through the growth of hyphae or by producing spores. They reproduce sexually when hyphae from two fungi join together.

Fungi are classified into several groups based on their sexual reproductive structures. Zygote fungi reproduce sexually by producing zygotes inside a tough capsule called a *zygospore*. Most molds belong to the zygote fungi. Sac fungi include yeasts, mildews, morels, and cup fungi. Sac fungi produce spores inside microscopic sac-like structures. Club fungi include mushrooms and brackets. Club fungi produce spores inside microscopic structures which look like clubs.

Some fungi form mutualistic relationships in which the fungus and a partner live in close contact. A mycorrhiza is a mutualistic symbiosis between a fungus and a plant's roots. A lichen is a partnership between a fungus and a cyanobacterium or alga. In both relationships, the fungus gains nutrients from its partner and in return provides nitrogen and minerals.

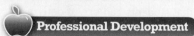

Content Refresher (continued)

Professional Development

Lesson 3

Introduction to Plants

ESSENTIAL QUESTION
What are plants?

1. Characteristics of Plants

Students will learn about the characteristics of plants.

To be classified as a plant, an organism must have certain characteristics. Plants are multicellular eukaryotes. Plant cells have walls made of cellulose. They have large central vacuoles, which are membrane-bound organelles that store water. They also have chloroplasts. Chloroplasts are organelles that contain chlorophyll. Chlorophyll is a green pigment that captures energy from sunlight and gives plants their green color. Plants carry out photosynthesis, in which energy from sunlight is captured and used to produce glucose from carbon dioxide and water. All plants, except a few parasitic plants, are producers. Plant life cycles have two stages. During one stage, the sporophyte stage, plants reproduce asexually by spores. During the other stage, the gametophyte stage, plants reproduce sexually by fusion of gametes.

2. Structure and Function in Plants

Students will learn about structures that make up the body systems of plants.

The two main groups of plants are vascular plants, those that have a vascular system, and nonvascular plants, those without a vascular system. A vascular system is a system of tube-like tissues that transport water and nutrients from one part of an organism to another. Nonvascular plants depend on diffusion to move water and nutrients. As a result, these plants tend to be small. Vascular plants can grow much larger because they are able to transport water and nutrients more efficiently.

Vascular plants have two body systems: the root system and the shoot system. Roots make up a plant's root system. Stems and leaves make up a plant's shoot system. Roots anchor plants in the soil and supply plants with water and minerals.

Stems support the plant and allow it to grow upright. Vascular tissue found in the stems transports water and minerals from the roots up to the leaves and transports glucose from the leaves to the roots. Leaves are usually the site of photosynthesis. Chloroplasts in leaf cells capture the sun's energy to power photosynthesis.

3. Classification of Plants

Students will learn about plant reproduction, the parts of a flower, and the major groups of plants.

All nonvascular plants, and some vascular plants, are seedless. Seedless plants disperse by spores. Spores develop into male and female gametophytes that produce sperm and eggs. Seedless plants depend on water to allow their sperm to swim to fertilize eggs. The fertilized eggs develop into new sporophytes. Seedless nonvascular plants include mosses, liverworts, and hornworts. Vascular seedless plants include ferns, whisk ferns, horsetails, and club mosses.

Most vascular plants produce seeds. A seed is a plant embryo inside a protective coating. The embryo can remain inside the seed until conditions are right for growth. All seed plants produce pollen. Pollen is a structure that contains the male gametophyte. Pollen is carried from the male reproductive structure to the female reproductive structure. There, the male gametophyte grows and produces sperm within the female reproductive structure. This eliminates the need for sperm to swim to fertilize an egg.

Seed plants are classified by whether or not their seeds are enclosed in fruit. A gymnosperm is a seed plant whose seeds are not enclosed by fruit. Some gymnosperms produce woody structures called cones that protect the plant's seeds. Ginkgoes, cycads, and conifers are examples of gymnosperms. An angiosperm is a flowering seed plant that produces seeds within a fruit. A flower is the reproductive structure of an angiosperm. It has specialized leaves called sepals and petals. A stamen is the male reproductive structure, and a pistil is the female reproductive structure. Pollen is produced at the tip of the stamen. A seed develops within the ovary at the base of the pistil.

(l) ©Corbis/(r) ©HMH

Plant Processes

ESSENTIAL QUESTION

How do plants stay alive?

1. Plants and Energy

Students will learn that plants obtain, store, and release energy though the processes of photosynthesis and cellular respiration.

Plants are autotrophs, which means they convert energy from sunlight into chemical energy in a process called photosynthesis. During photosynthesis, plants use energy from sunlight to convert carbon dioxide and water into glucose and oxygen. The process of photosynthesis can be summarized by the following equation:

$$6CO_2 + 6H_2O \xrightarrow{\text{light energy}} C_6H_{12}O_6 + 6O_2$$

The energy plants store in glucose can then be used to power cell processes. In order for this energy to be used, it must be converted to ATP (adenosine triphosphate). During cellular respiration, glucose is broken down, and the chemical energy stored in the bonds of the glucose is used to generate about 38 molecules of ATP. The process of cellular respiration can be summarized by the following equation:

$$C_6H_{12}O_6 + 6O_2 \longrightarrow 6CO_2 + 6H_2O + \text{energy}$$

The energy stored in the phosphate bonds of ATP is used by both plants and animals to power cell processes.

2. Plant Reproduction

Students will learn that plants have a two-part life cycle, and that seed plants and seedless plants have differences in reproduction.

Plants undergo "alteration of generations." This two-part life cycle includes two distinct phases: the haploid gametophyte (with a single set of chromosomes) and the diploid sporophyte (with two sets of chromosomes, one from each gamete). As in algae, alternation of generations includes a diploid sporophyte that produces haploid spores by meiosis. The spores develop into a haploid gametophyte. The gametophyte produces haploid gametes by mitosis. The gametes fuse, develop into a diploid sporophyte, and the cycle begins again. In mosses, liverworts, and other seedless nonvascular plants, the gametophyte phase is the dominant phase. In most plant groups, such as conifers and flowering plants, the sporophyte phase is the dominant phase.

In flowering plants, the flower contains the reproductive structures. Both male and female gametophytes are produced in flowers. Pollination is the process by which the male gametophyte is transferred to the female reproductive structures. After pollination, fertilization can occur and a seed develops. Seeds are dispersed by wind, water, or animals.

3. Plant Responses

Students will learn that plants respond to both internal and external stimuli.

Plants respond to internal and external stimuli in order to maintain homeostasis (a stable set of internal conditions). For example, plants respond to changing water levels by controlling the opening and closing of stomata. Tropism is a general term used to describe plant growth in response to a stimulus. For example, in phototropism, plants grow toward light. In gravitropism, plant roots grow downward in response to gravity. Thigmotropism is growth in response to touch.

Plants also respond to seasonal changes, such as changes in day length. In many plants, flowering is controlled by the length of nights (darkness). This reaction, called photoperiodism, ensures that plants flower when environmental conditions are optimal for that particular species.

Length of day, change in temperatures, and other seasonal changes can trigger dormancy in plants. This response to external stimuli helps plants survive winters by conserving energy. Plants emerge from dormancy when conditions are more favorable.

Content Refresher (continued)

Professional Development

Lesson 5

Introduction to Animals

ESSENTIAL QUESTION
What are animals?

1. Animal Characteristics

Students will learn six characteristics that most animals share.

Animals share many unique characteristics that separate them from organisms in other kingdoms. All animals are multicellular. Most animals reproduce sexually, though some, such as a variety of invertebrates, reproduce asexually. Animals are eukaryotic and have specialized structures to perform a variety of functions, including movement. The process by which cells specialize is known as differentiation. As animals develop, their cells differentiate; this process gives rise to specialized cells that can form tissues, organs, and organ systems. Animals are consumers, and therefore must consume other organisms to get energy. They also maintain their own body temperature within a specific range. Temperature regulation can occur by chemical reactions in the body or, as in some reptiles, relying on the environment.

2. Animal Diversity

Students will learn that animals are the most physically diverse kingdom of organisms.

Animals can be grouped as invertebrates and vertebrates. Most of the animals on Earth are invertebrates, which have no backbone and no bones. Many have a hard, external covering called an exoskeleton. Vertebrates have a backbone, which is part of an endoskeleton, or internal skeleton made of bone and cartilage that provides support. Animals vary in size, shape, body coverings, body plan, and where they live.

3. Invertebrates

Students will learn about characteristics of invertebrates.

Over 95% of the animals on Earth are invertebrates, which belong to one of the phyla described below.

- Porifera have specialized cells but no tissues. They live on the ocean floor and feed by filtering water.
- Cnidaria have two body forms—polyp (cylindrical tubes with upward-facing tentacles) and medusa (umbrella-shapes with mouth and tentacles on the underside).
- Ctenophora have comb-like rows of cilia on their bodies that are used to move. They only live in marine environments.
- Platyhelminthes includes flatworms, which are thin, flattened worms with simple tissues and sensory organs.
- Mollusca includes soft-bodied aquatic animals that usually have a protective outer shell, such as snails and clams.
- Annelida includes segmented worms, such as earthworms.
- Nematoda are small, round worms; many are parasitic.
- Arthropoda includes animals with an exoskeleton and jointed appendages. Lobsters, spiders, and insects are arthopods.
- Echinoderms have an internal skeleton, a water vascular system for movement, and a complete digestive system.

4. Vertebrates

Students will learn about characteristics of vertebrates.

All vertebrates belong to the phylum Chordata. Chordates have a notochord, a hollow nerve tube, pharyngeal slits, and a tail at some point in development. Not all chordates are vertebrates. Tunicates and lancelets are invertebrate chordates; they have all four traits of chordates, but they do not have a backbone.

All vertebrates have an endoskeleton, a braincase, vertebrae, and bones. Vertebrates include fish, amphibians, reptiles, birds, and mammals. Fish, such as sharks, live underwater. Amphibians, such as frogs, have four limbs and can live both on land and in water. Reptiles, such as lizards, live on land, are covered with scales or plates, and lay eggs. Birds, such as penguins, have hollow bones, wings, and feathers. Mammals, such as whales and humans, share four characteristics: hair, mammary glands, a middle ear with three bones, and a jaw.

©James Gritz/Photodisc/GettyImages

Animal Behavior

ESSENTIAL QUESTION
What are some different animal behaviors?

1. Animal Behavior

Students will learn that behaviors are responses to stimuli.

Animal behaviors are actions taken by animals in response to a stimulus or the environment. A stimulus may be internal or external. Internal stimuli occur within an animal's body, such as feeling hungry or tired. External stimuli occur within an animal's environment, such as the sound of a predator nearby. Behaviors develop as innate or learned. Innate behaviors are inherited behaviors that do not depend on the environment or experience. They include reflexes and even complex skills like a newborn elephant knowing how to stand and walk at birth. Learned behaviors must be acquired with experience and observing other animals, such as learning to hunt.

2. Survival Behaviors

Students will learn that animals exhibit survival behaviors.

Survival behaviors include finding food, maintaining a territory, and defensive skills. Territories are marked and defended in different ways to secure the area for mating, food, and shelter for offspring.

©Digital Vision/Getty Images

3. Reproductive and Seasonal Behaviors

Students will learn that animals exhibit certain behaviors to aid in reproduction and to survive seasonal changes.

The reproduction process begins with courtship behaviors and for some animals ends with parenting behaviors. Courtship refers to behaviors that help an animal find a mate. Typically the male performs specific behaviors, such as building a nest or performing special movements, to get the attention of the female. Parenting behaviors refer to behaviors used to raise the young, such as teaching them to hunt or forage for food. Not all animals exhibit parenting behaviors.

Surviving seasonal changes is a challenge for many animals. Some animals may either hibernate or estivate. These are periods of decreased activity and lowered body temperature. Hibernation occurs in winter. Estivation occurs during hot, dry conditions. Some animals migrate, or move to other areas to avoid harsh climate conditions for certain times of the year. Daily cycles, or circadian rhythms, and seasonal cycles are controlled by a natural internal control, or biological clock.

4. Social Behaviors

Students will learn that animals have social behaviors.

Animals of the same species may have a set of interactions that define their social behavior. Some animals live in groups. The advantage of this is protection from predators and in finding food. The disadvantage is competition within the group for food or mates, and the spreading of disease. Social hierarchy refers to groups that exhibit clear dominant individual(s). Individuals can fight to move up. In set social structures, positions are defined at birth and do not change.

  COMMON MISCONCEPTIONS **RTI**

COMMON MISCONCEPTIONS Students may think that hibernation is the same thing as sleeping. Hibernation is not sleeping; it is simply a period of decreased activity and lowered body temperature, allowing the animal to conserve energy during winter months.

This misconception is addressed in the Learning Alert on p. 201.

Advance Planning

These activities may take extended time or special conditions.

What Do You Think?

Encourage students to consider how living organisms are alike and different.

Ask: What do all living things have in common? Sample answers: They use energy; they grow; they reproduce.

Ask: Is a dog more like an oak tree or a cow? Explain. Sample answer: A dog is more like a cow; they have similar body structures, and they both move around and eat food for energy.

UNIT 2
Earth's Organisms

Big Idea
Organisms can be characterized by their structures, by the ways they grow and reproduce, and by the ways they interact with their environment.

Webbed feet allow flamingos to stand in the soft mud of their shallow water environment.

What do you think?

Organisms have many different characteristics that help them survive in their environment. Humans and birds are both animals that use two legs and two feet to move. How else are they alike? Different?

Human feet allow for walking and running easily on solid ground.

75

 Video-Based Project

Animal Behavior

 *Go Online to preview the videos, access teacher support pages, and print student activity worksheets.*

Dr. Mike Heithaus and colleagues explore the interaction between dolphins and sharks as dolphins balance their need for food with the need to stay safe.

Activities

1 Dolphin Food
2 Dolphin Foraging Habitats
3 Do Dolphins Give up Foraging Opportunities to Avoid Sharks?

©Patrick Greene Productions

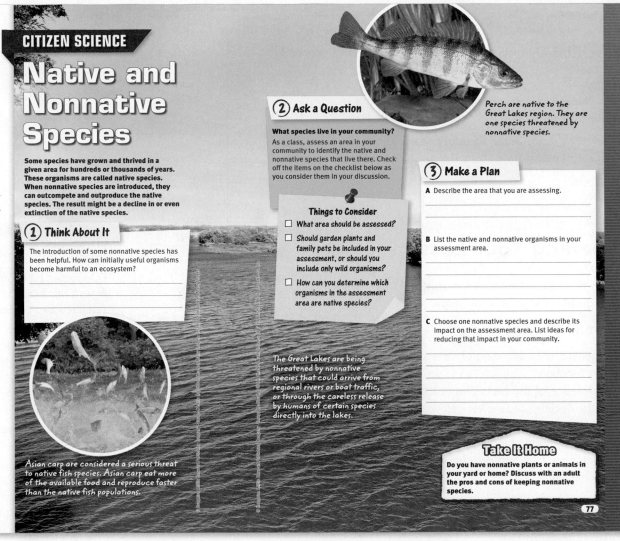

Unit 2
Earth's Organisms

CITIZEN SCIENCE
Native and Nonnative Species

Some species have grown and thrived in a given area for hundreds or thousands of years. These organisms are called native species. When nonnative species are introduced, they can outcompete and outproduce the native species. The result might be a decline in or even extinction of the native species.

① Think About It

The introduction of some nonnative species has been helpful. How can initially useful organisms become harmful to an ecosystem?

Asian carp are considered a serious threat to native fish species. Asian carp eat more of the available food and reproduce faster than the native fish populations.

② Ask a Question

What species live in your community?
As a class, assess an area in your community to identify the native and nonnative species that live there. Check off the items on the checklist below as you consider them in your discussion.

Things to Consider

☐ What area should be assessed?

☐ Should garden plants and family pets be included in your assessment, or should you include only wild organisms?

☐ How can you determine which organisms in the assessment area are native species?

Perch are native to the Great Lakes region. They are one species threatened by nonnative species.

The Great Lakes are being threatened by nonnative species that could arrive from regional rivers or boat traffic, or through the careless release by humans of certain species directly into the lakes.

③ Make a Plan

A Describe the area that you are assessing.

B List the native and nonnative organisms in your assessment area.

C Choose one nonnative species and describe its impact on the assessment area. List ideas for reducing that impact in your community.

Take It Home

Do you have nonnative plants or animals in your yard or home? Discuss with an adult the pros and cons of keeping nonnative species.

76 Unit 2 Earth's Organisms

77

CITIZEN SCIENCE

Unit Project Native and Nonnative Species

1. Think About It

If students struggle, ask them to identify resources that all organisms need, such as water, space, and food. Then encourage them to consider what might happen if a nonnative species reproduced faster than native species. How might this affect the native species competing for the same resources?

2. Ask a Question

Encourage students to brainstorm or research a list of some of the organisms that can be found in their community. Ask students whether they think these organisms have been there since before humans arrived or if they think these organisms were introduced by humans at a later point.

3. Make a Plan

A. Students should delineate the area that they are including in their assessment.

B. Have students separate their lists into two parts: native species and nonnative species. Remind students that a native species is one that was not introduced by humans.

C. Allow students time to use library resources or the Internet to research the impact of nonnative species and strategies for reducing negative impacts.

Take It Home

Ask students to provide a note from an adult confirming that the student discussed the topic with him or her. Ask students to share some of the ideas that resulted from brainstorming with adults.

🔘 *Optional Online rubric: Class Discussion*

Archaea, Bacteria, and Viruses

Essential Question What are microorganisms?

 Professional Development

For more detailed information about the topics in this lesson, refer to the Content Refresher in the Unit Opener pages.

Opening Your Lesson

Begin the lesson by assessing students' prerequisite and prior knowledge.

Prerequisite Knowledge

- A general understanding of cells and how they function
- Knowledge of the parts of a cell, such as the nucleus, organelles, cell walls, cell membranes, and so on
- A general understanding of the differences between prokaryotes and eukaryotes

Accessing Prior Knowledge

Invite students to make a double-door Foldnote to compare the characteristics of prokaryotes and eukaryotes.

Customize Your Opening

- ☐ **Accessing Prior Knowledge,** above
- ☐ **Print Path** Engage Your Brain, SE p. 79
- ☐ **Print Path** Active Reading, SE p. 79
- ☐ **Digital Path** Lesson Opener

Key Topics/Learning Goals	Supporting Concepts
Characteristics of Archaea and Bacteria 1 Recall the characteristics of prokaryotes and eukaryotes. 2 Describe the characteristics of archaea. 3 Describe the characteristics of bacteria.	• Eukaryotes have one or more cells, which have a nucleus and organelles; prokaryotes (archaea and bacteria) are usually single-celled and have no nucleus. • Archaea have some unique molecules; they are found everywhere on Earth, including extreme environments, such as salt lakes. • Bacteria have DNA, proteins, a cell membrane, and a strong outer wall.
How Archaea and Bacteria Reproduce 1 Explain how bacteria reproduce.	• Bacteria reproduce by binary fission. • Sometimes bacteria can exchange genetic material before dividing; conjugation occurs when two cells join to recombine nuclear material and then undergo binary fission. • Bacteria can also take up DNA strands from their environment. • Some bacteria form endospores around DNA and ribosomes to survive harsh conditions.
Characteristics of Viruses 1 Name the parts of a virus.	• A virus is a nonliving, infectious particle made of nucleic acid and a protein coat. It can invade and destroy a cell. • The genetic material of viruses can be DNA or RNA.
How Viruses Replicate 1 Explain how viruses replicate.	• Viruses cannot replicate on their own. • Viruses enter or insert their genetic material into a host cell. • The lytic cycle is a method of viral reproduction that destroys a host cell and releases new viruses.

Options for Instruction

Two parallel paths provide coverage of the Essential Questions, with a strong **Inquiry** strand woven into each.
Follow the **Print Path,** the **Digital Path,** or your customized combination of print, digital, and inquiry.

 Print Path
Teaching support for the Print Path appears with the Student Pages.

 Inquiry Labs and Activities

Digital Path
Digital Path shortcut: TC673065

Print Path	Inquiry Labs and Activities	Digital Path
Sized Extra-Small, SE pp. 80–81 What is a prokaryote? What ... characteristics of archaea? **Beautiful Bacteria,** SE pp. 82–83 What ... characteristics of bacteria?	**Activity** Bacteria Q & A **Daily Demo** All in a Drop of Water **Quick Lab** Observing Bacteria	**Archaea** Slideshow **Sized Extra-Small** Interactive Images
Split Personality, SE pp. 84–85 How do bacteria reproduce? How do bacteria exchange DNA?	**Activity** Bacteria and Viruses **Field Lab** Culturing Bacteria from the Environment	**Binary Fission** Video **Conjugation** Graphic Sequence
Alive or Not Alive? SE p. 86 What are some characteristics of viruses? Are viruses living?	**Activity** Bacteria and Viruses	**Viruses** Interactive Images
A Gift for the Host . . . , SE pp. 88–89 How do viruses replicate?	**Quick Lab** Modeling Viral Replication	**Viral Replication** Interactive Images

Options for Assessment

*See the Evaluate page for options, including Formative Assessment,
Summative Assessment, and Unit Review.*

Engage and Explore

Activities and Discussion

Activity *Bacteria Q & A*

Engage

Characteristics of Archaea and Bacteria

 whole class
 10 min
 GUIDED inquiry

Have students work in small groups to brainstorm questions and answers about bacteria and their characteristics. The questions should be based on material they find in the text. Then, have groups quiz each other with their questions. The group that answers the most questions can win a small prize, such as a night without homework.

Discussion *Cells*

Introducing Key Topics

 whole class
 10 min
 GUIDED inquiry

Invite students to tell you what they know about cells. Sample answers: Cells are the smallest unit of living things. Some organisms have one cell. Others have many cells. **Ask:** What does a cell do? Sample answers: Cells take in nutrients, convert nutrients into energy, carry out specific functions, and reproduce. **Ask:** What are the simplest cells? Prokaryotes, which are one-celled organisms that do not have a nucleus. Invite students to share other things they know about cells. Write ideas on the board.

Activity *Bacteria and Viruses*

Introducing Key Topics

 individuals or pairs
 ongoing
 GUIDED inquiry

Have students work together to make a Venn diagram that compares characteristics of bacteria and viruses. (For a challenge, they can add a third circle about Archaea.)

item one features | shared features | item two features

©Corbis

Underneath the diagram, have students list questions they have about bacteria and viruses. Encourage students to look for the answers to their questions as they work through the lesson. When students are finished, list some of the ideas and questions on the board. Discuss some student ideas about bacteria and viruses.

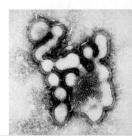

Take It Home *Bacteria and Food Safety*

Characteristics of Archaea and Bacteria

 adult-student pairs
 ongoing
 GUIDED inquiry

Students and adults work together to examine their home to see what they do to keep food safe from harmful bacteria. Pairs can look in the refrigerator, freezer, and cupboards to list how different types of foods are stored. Then they can categorize foods by whether they need to be kept frozen, refrigerated, or kept at room temperature. For example, meat should be refrigerated, or frozen if not used within day or so; it cannot be stored in a cupboard.

Customize Your Labs

 See the Lab Manual for lab datasheets.

 Go Online for editable lab datasheets.

Levels of  Inquiry

DIRECTED inquiry introduces inquiry skills within a structured framework.

GUIDED inquiry develops inquiry skills within a supportive environment.

INDEPENDENT inquiry deepens inquiry skills with student-driven questions or procedures.

Labs and Demos

Daily Demo *All in a Drop of Water*

Engage

Characteristics of Archaea and Bacteria

 whole class
 10 min
 GUIDED inquiry

PURPOSE **To show bacteria in water supplies**

MATERIALS **Water samples from the tap, a local pond, and a mud puddle; a microscope and slides; a projector to display the microscope images**

1 Show students the water samples and describe where you got them.

2 Invite students to predict which samples will have the most bacteria and why.

3 Put a drop of tap water on a microscope slide. Project the image so the class can see it. Have students describe what they see.

4 Follow the same procedure for the other two water samples. **Observing** Which water samples had the most bacteria? Which water would you most like to drink and why? The tap water should have the fewest bacteria while the pond water might have the most.

Quick Lab *Modeling Viral Replication*

How Viruses Replicate

 whole class
 15 min
 DIRECTED inquiry

PURPOSE **To model the lytic cycle**

See the Lab Manual or go Online for planning information.

Field Lab *Culturing Bacteria from the Environment*

How Archaea and Bacteria Reproduce

 individuals
 two 45-min periods
 DIRECTED and GUIDED inquiry

PURPOSE **To grow and observe colonies of bacteria**

MATERIALS

- gloves
- hand lens
- permanent marker
- petri dish with sterile agar
- swab
- goggles

In this lab, students will prepare cultures of bacteria using agar plates, identify places where bacteria live, and distinguish bacterial colonies from other micro-organism colonies. First, they will make predictions about the single-celled organisms found in the environment around them. Students will probably find that both bacterial and fungal colonies grow on their agar plates; they can distinguish the two because bacterial colonies tend to have shiny surfaces, while fungi colonies do not.

Caution: Be sure students use care in handling and disposing of the microorganisms in the lab and wash their hands thoroughly.

Quick Lab *Observing Bacteria*

Characteristics of Archaea and Bacteria

 small groups
15 min
DIRECTED inquiry

PURPOSE **To observe bacteria and classify them based on shape**

See the Lab Manual or go Online for planning information.

Activities and Discussion

- [ ] **Activity** Bacteria Q & A
- [ ] **Discussion** Cells
- [ ] **Activity** Bacteria and Viruses
- [ ] **Take It Home** Bacteria and Food Safety

Labs and Demos

- [ ] **Daily Demo** All in a Drop of Water
- [ ] **Field Lab** Culturing Bacteria from the Environment
- [ ] **Quick Lab** Observing Bacteria
- [ ] **Quick Lab** Modeling Viral Replication

Your Resources

_____

_____

Explain Science Concepts

Key Topics	📖 Print Path	🖥 Digital Path
Characteristics of Archaea and Bacteria	☐ **Sized Extra-Small,** SE pp. 80–81 • Active Reading (Annotation strategy), #5 • Visualize It!, #6 • Active Reading (Annotation strategy), #7 • Explain, #8 ☐ **Beautiful Bacteria,** SE pp. 82–83 • Visualize It!, #9 • Active Reading, #10 • Visualize It!, #11 **Visualize It!** **9 Illustrate** Draw an example of each of the three bacteria shapes described above.	☐ **Archaea** Explore archaea, including their characteristics and environments. ☐ **What are bacteria?** Investigate bacteria and their characteristics.
How Archaea and Bacteria Reproduce	☐ **Split Personality,** SE pp. 84–85 • Active Reading (Annotation strategy), #12 • Do the Math, #13 • Visualize It!, #14 **Visualize It!** **14 Diagram** Fill in the missing labels in this flow chart to complete the description of conjugation.	☐ **Binary Fission** Observe binary fission. ☐ **Conjugation** Contrast binary fission and conjugation.
Characteristics of Viruses	☐ **Alive or Not Alive?** SE p. 86 • Active Reading, #15 **Active Reading 15 Identify** List three reasons viruses are not living things.	☐ **Viruses** Find out more about viruses, including why scientists don't consider them to be alive.
How Viruses Replicate	☐ **A Gift for the Host . . . ,** SE pp. 88–89 • Explain, #19 • Visualize It!, #20 • Think Outside the Book, #21 **Think Outside the Book** Inquiry **21 Apply** With a classmate, discuss why some scientists say that viruses replicate instead of reproduce.	☐ **Viral Replication** Discover the importance of hosts.

Differentiated Instruction

Basic *Bacteria Poster*

Characteristics of Archaea and Bacteria

 pairs
 20 min

Invite students, individually or in pairs, to make posters showing places where bacteria can be found. Encourage students to use their imaginations and to think about some of the things bacteria do, such as causing disease, breaking down dead matter, producing food, and so on. Encourage students to label their posters. When students have finished, display the posters.

Advanced *Diagramming the Lytic Cycle*

How Viruses Replicate

 individuals
15 min

Invite students to make a diagram or flow chart that shows the steps of the lytic cycle. Students can make the diagram or flow chart either by hand or on a computer. Encourage students to label each step clearly, so that someone who knows nothing about the lytic cycle could understand the process after looking at the diagram or flow chart. When they have finished, invite students to share their diagrams with the class.

ELL *Bacteria and Virus Terms*

Synthesizing Key Topics

 pairs
10 min

Word Triangles Have pairs of students make Word Triangle graphic organizers for vocabulary terms. Pairs should choose a difficult term from this lesson and write the term and its definition in the bottom section. In the middle section, have them work together to write a sentence in which the term is used correctly. In the top section, have them draw a small picture to illustrate and help them remember the term.

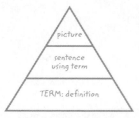

Lesson Vocabulary

Archaea	Bacteria	binary fission
virus	host	

Previewing Vocabulary

 whole class
10 min

Word Origins Remind students that thinking about the meaning of word parts can help them decipher a new word.

- **Archaea** comes from the Latin word *archaeo-*, which means "ancient."
- **Bacteria** comes from the Greek word *bacter*, meaning "rod" or "staff," and some bacteria are shaped like rods.
- **Binary fission** comes from *bi-*, which means "two," and *fissus*, which means "to split."
- **Virus** comes from the Latin word *virus*, which means "poison."

Reinforcing Vocabulary

 individuals
ongoing

Frame Game To help students remember the vocabulary terms, have them complete a Frame Game graphic organizer.

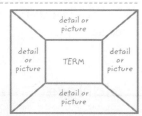

Customize Your Core Lesson

Core Instruction

☐ **Print Path** choices
☐ **Digital Path** choices

Vocabulary

☐ **Previewing Vocabulary** Word Origins
☐ **Reinforcing Vocabulary** Frame Game

Your Resources

Differentiated Instruction

☐ **Basic** Bacteria Poster
☐ **Advanced** Diagramming the Lytic Cycle
☐ **ELL** Bacteria and Virus Terms

Extend Science Concepts

Reinforce and Review

Activity *Inside/Outside Circles*

Synthesizing Key Topics    whole class
⏱ 25 min

Inside/Outside Circles After students have
read the lesson, give each an index card with a
question from the text. Have students write their
answer on the back of the index card. Check to
make sure the answers are correct. Have students
adjust incorrect answers.

Have students pair up and form two circles. One
partner is in an inside circle, facing out; the other is in an outside
circle, facing in. The student in the inside circle asks his or her partner
the question on the index card. The partner answers. If the answer
is incorrect, the student in the inside circle teaches the other student
the correct answer. Then, the outside-circle student asks his or her
question.

When done, have each student on the outside circle rotate one
person to the right, repeating the process with a new partner.
Students rotate after each pair of questions until all questions have
been answered.

FoldNote

Synthesizing Key Topics   👤 individuals
⏱ 15 min

Two-Panel Flip Chart After students have
studied the lesson, have them make a two-
panel flip chart to compare characteristics
of bacteria and viruses, including how they
reproduce or replicate.

 *Optional Online resource: Two-Panel
Flip Chart support*

Going Further

Real World Connection

**Characteristics of
Viruses**   👥 individuals
⏱ 20 min

Have interested students conduct research to find out more
about flu pandemics or epidemics. Some students may want to
take a historical approach to learn about flu pandemics of the
past. Others may want to research what can be done to prevent
flu pandemics in the future. Encourage students to describe the
results of their research.

Speech Connection

**How Archaea and
Bacteria Reproduce**   👤 individual
⏱ 20 min

Binary Fission Invite interested students to imagine they are a
sports announcer giving the play-by-play during binary fission.
Encourage students to use their voices for dramatic effect and
to use sequence words such as *first, second, then, next,* and *last.*
Students may record their play-by-play if desired.

Customize Your Closing

📔 *See the Assessment
Guide for quizzes
and tests.*

⏱ *Go Online to edit
and create quizzes
and tests.*

Reinforce and Review

☐ **Activity** Inside/Outside Circles

☐ **FoldNote** Two-Panel Flip Chart

☐ **Print Path** Visual Summary,
SE p. 90

☐ **Digital Path** Lesson Closer

Evaluate Student Mastery

Formative Assessment

See the teacher support below the Student Pages for additional Formative Assessment questions.

Ask: What are some characteristics of bacteria? They are single-celled, live everywhere, and are often shaped like rods, spheres, or spirals. **Ask:** How do bacteria reproduce? They divide in a process called binary fission, sometimes exchanging genetic material first through conjugation. **Ask:** What are some characteristics of viruses? They are microscopic, not living, and have different shapes. **Ask:** How do viruses replicate? One method is a process called the lytic cycle, in which a virus attaches to a host cell, and the host cell replicates the virus's DNA.

Reteach

Formative assessment may show that students need reinforcement for certain topics. The resources below are recommended for reteaching. If students were introduced to a topic through the Print Path, you can also use the Digital Path to reteach, and vice versa.

🎧 *Can be assigned to individual students*

Characteristics of Archaea and Bacteria
Quick Lab Observing Bacteria 🎧

How Archaea and Bacteria Reproduce
Field Lab Culturing Bacteria from the Environment 🎧

Characteristics of Viruses
Activity Bacteria and Viruses 🎧

How Viruses Replicate
Quick Lab Modeling Viral Replication

Summative Assessment

Alternative Assessment
Bacteria and Viruses

🌐 *Online resources: student worksheet, optional rubric*

Archaea, Bacteria, and Viruses

Points of View: *Bacteria and Viruses*
Your class will work together to show what you've learned about bacteria and viruses from several different viewpoints.

1. Work in groups as assigned by your teacher. Each group will be assigned to one or two viewpoints.

2. Complete your assignment, and present your perspective to the class.

 Vocabulary Define *binary fission* and *conjugation* in your own words. Then read a textbook definition. Finally, write three sentences for each term that describes the sequence of events that occurs during each process.

 Illustrations Draw diagrams or illustrations to show how bacteria reproduce or viruses replicate.

 Observations Look at slides of bacteria under a microscope. Describe the shape of each type of bacteria that you observe. List any other observations that you make. In complete sentences, tell the ways in which the various bacteria are alike and different.

 Calculations Find the names and sizes of several kinds of bacteria and viruses. Using your data, on average, how much bigger are bacteria than viruses?

 Details Provide details that explain how the 1918 flu was different from other strains of the flu. Then explain whether you think this type of flu pandemic could ever occur again, and give reasons to support your answer.

 Models Use clay or other materials to make models of several bacteria and viruses. Add labels to your models.

Going Further
- ☐ **Real World Connection**
- ☐ **Speech Connection**
- ☐ **Print Path** Why It Matters, SE p. 87

Your Resources

Formative Assessment
- ☐ **Strategies** Throughout TE
- ☐ **Lesson Review** SE

Summative Assessment
- ☐ **Alternative Assessment** *Bacteria and Viruses*
- ☐ **Lesson Quiz**
- ☐ **Unit Tests A and B**
- ☐ **Unit Review** SE End-of-Unit

Lesson ①

Archaea, Bacteria, and Viruses

ESSENTIAL QUESTION

What are micro-organisms?

By the end of this lesson, you should be able to describe the characteristics of archaea, bacteria, and viruses, and explain how they reproduce or replicate.

Crystals of salt ring the edge of this salt lake in China. The lake is red because it is full of archaea, tiny microorganisms. The red-pigmented archaea in this lake are adapted to live in very salty environments.

78 Unit 2 Earth's Organisms

Lesson Labs

Quick Labs
• Observing Bacteria
• Modeling Viral Replication

Field Lab
• Culturing Bacteria from the Environment

Engage Your Brain

1 Predict Check T or F to show whether you think each statement is true or false.

T F
☐ ☐ Some bacteria are helpful.
☐ ☐ Viruses are living things.
☐ ☐ A single bacterium can produce many offspring at one time.

2 Predict Using the photo on the right and what you know of bacteria, how do you think bacteria and archaea are similar?

_____
_____
_____

This organism is a member of the domain Archaea. It is a halophile, which means "salt lover." It lives in extremely salty environments like the one shown to the left.

Active Reading

3 Apply Many scientific words, such as *host*, also have everyday meanings. Use context clues to write your own definition for each meaning of the word *host*.

Example sentence
The host greeted the guests as they arrived at her house for the party.

host: _____
_____

Example sentence
A virus takes over a host cell and causes it to make new viruses.

host: _____
_____

Vocabulary Terms

• Bacteria   • virus
• Archaea   • host
• binary fission

4 Identify This list contains the vocabulary terms you'll learn in this lesson. As you read, circle the definition of each term.

Lesson 1 Archaea, Bacteria, and Viruses 79

Answers

Answers for 1–3 should represent students' current thoughts, even if incorrect.

1. True, False, False

2. Sample answer: They are both single celled, they are both microscopic, and they both lack a nucleus.

3. Sample answers: first "host": somebody who organizes an event; second "host": an organism that becomes infected

4. Students' annotations will vary.

Opening Your Lesson

Discuss students' answers to item 1 to assess their understanding of the characteristics of bacteria and viruses.

Prerequisites Students should already have some understanding of cells, DNA, and RNA. They should know what proteins are, what a nucleus is, what organelles are, and have a general understanding of how bacteria and viruses can cause disease.

Learning Alert

Difficult Concept Students may need to be reminded that some living organisms, such as archaea and bacteria, have only one cell, and that other particles, like viruses, are not even as large as one cell. Archaea, bacteria, and viruses are too small to see with the naked eye.

Learning Alert

Classification Scientists are constantly debating how best to classify living things, including bacteria and archaea. In the past, scientists considered archaea to be part of the kingdom Bacteria. Now, scientists agree that they belong in separate groups. Archaea and bacteria are classified as domains in a three domain system. Provide interested students with additional opportunities to find out about taxonomy and how taxonomists work.

SIZED Extra-Small

What is a prokaryote?

5 Identify As you read, underline characteristics of prokaryotes.

All living things fit into one of two major groups: prokaryote or eukaryote (yoo•KAIR•ee•oht). Eukaryotes are made up of one or many cells that each have a nucleus enclosed by a membrane. Prokaryotes do not have a nucleus or membrane-bound organelles and almost all are single-celled. Prokaryotes are so small we can only see them with a microscope, so they are called *microorganisms*. Prokaryotes are divided into two domains. **Bacteria** is a domain of prokaryotes that usually have a cell wall and that usually reproduce by cell division. **Archaea** (ar•KEE•uh) is a domain of prokaryotes that are genetically very different from bacteria and that have unique chemicals in their cell walls. Although they are very small, prokaryotes can get energy and reproduce, and many can move. A handful of soil may contain trillions of prokaryotes!

Visualize It!

6 On the lines below, describe the characteristics of prokaryotic cells and eukaryotic cells.

Prokaryotic Cell

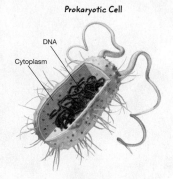

Cytoplasm
DNA

Eukaryotic Cell

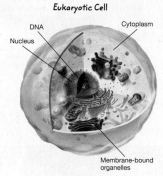

DNA
Nucleus
Cytoplasm
Membrane-bound organelles

What are some characteristics of archaea?

Active Reading 7 Identify As you read, underline unusual places where archaea can live.

Archaea are organisms that have many unique molecular traits. Like bacteria, archaea are prokaryotes. But the cell walls of archaea are chemically different from those of bacteria. Some of the molecules in archaea are similar to the molecules in eukaryotes. Some of the molecules in archaea are not found in any other living things.

Archaea often live where nothing else can. Scientists have found them in the hot springs at Yellowstone National Park. They can live in extremely acidic and extremely salty habitats. They flourish near deep-sea vents where no light reaches, and they can use sulfur to convert energy. Archaea have even been found living 8 km below the Earth's surface! It was once thought that archaea only lived in extreme environments. But recent research has shown that archaea are everywhere!

8 Explain What evidence suggests that archaea are more closely related to eukaryotes than bacteria are?

Some archaea can live in hot springs that reach near boiling temperatures.

Some archaea can live in deep-sea vents where there is no oxygen.

Answers

5. *See students' pages for annotations.*

6. Sample answer: Prokaryote: no nucleus, no membrane-bound organelles, has cytoplasm and DNA; eukaryote: cells have a nucleus, membrane-bound organelles, cytoplasm, and DNA.

7. *See students' pages for annotations.*

8. Sample answer: Archaea have molecules that are similar to the molecules in eukaryotes.

Building Reading Skills

Supporting Main Ideas To help students understand the relationships between bacteria, archaea, and eukaryotes, draw a two-column chart on the board. Label the columns *Prokaryotes* and *Eukaryotes*. Beneath *Prokaryotes,* write *Bacteria* and *Archaea*. Explain that prokaryotes usually have one cell, although a few have multicellular life stages. Eukaryotes have one or more cells. **Ask:** Which organism is usually larger, a prokaryote or a eukaryote? Why? A eukaryote is usually larger because it can have many more cells. Last, put the label *Living* above the entire chart. Next to the chart, write *Nonliving*. Under *Nonliving*, write *Viruses*. Refer back to the chart as needed as you work through the lesson.

Interpreting Visuals

Analyzing Invite students to examine the illustration of a prokaryotic cell and a eukaryotic cell. **Ask:** What differences do you see between these two cells? The prokaryotic cell does not have a nucleus or membrane-bound organelles. **Ask:** Are both of these cells living? How do you know? Yes, all cells are living. Both prokaryotic cells and eukaryotic cells are able to move, get energy, and reproduce.

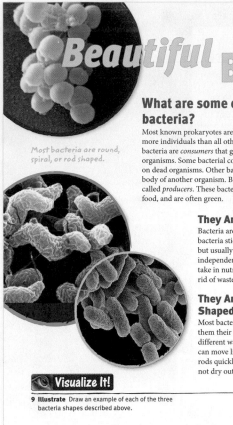

Beautiful Bacteria

Most bacteria are round, spiral, or rod shaped.

What are some characteristics of bacteria?

Most known prokaryotes are bacteria. The domain Bacteria has more individuals than all other domains combined do. Many bacteria are *consumers* that get their nutrients by feeding on other organisms. Some bacterial consumers are *decomposers*, which feed on dead organisms. Other bacterial consumers live in or on the body of another organism. Bacteria that make their own food are called *producers*. These bacteria use energy from sunlight to make food, and are often green.

They Are Single-Celled

Bacteria are small, single-celled organisms. Some bacteria stick together to form strands or films, but usually each bacterium still functions as an independent organism. Each bacterium must take in nutrients, release energy from food, get rid of wastes, and grow on its own.

They Are Round, Spiral, or Rod Shaped

Most bacteria have a rigid cell wall that gives them their shape. Each shape helps bacteria in a different way. Bacteria that are shaped like spirals can move like corkscrews. Bacteria shaped like rods quickly absorb nutrients. Round bacteria do not dry out quickly.

Visualize It!

9 Illustrate Draw an example of each of the three bacteria shapes described above.

82 Unit 2 Earth's Organisms

They Live Everywhere

Bacteria can be found almost everywhere on Earth. They can be found breaking down dead material in soil, making nitrogen available inside plant roots, and breaking down nutrients in animal intestines. They can be found at the tops of mountains and even in Antarctic ice. Some bacteria can survive during periods when environmental conditions become harsh by forming *endospores*. An endospore is made up of a thick, protective coating, the bacteria's genetic material, and cytoplasm. Many endospores can survive in hot, cold, and very dry places. When conditions improve, the endospores break open, and the bacteria become active again.

Active Reading

10 Relate What is the advantage for bacteria that form endospores?

A close-up look at leaves from this pond reveals that bacteria live here.

Visualize It!

11 Predict This pond is full of decaying leaves and wood as well as living aquatic plants and animals. In what parts of the pond do you think bacteria might live?

83

Answers

9. Student drawings should include round, rod, and spiral shaped bacteria.

10. Sample answer: Bacteria that form endospores can survive through harsh environmental conditions.

11. Sample answer: Bacteria probably live in the soil, the decaying leaves and wood, and the living plants and animals.

Probing Questions

Analyzing Information **Ask:** Spherical bacteria do not dry out quickly. Where do you think such bacteria might be found? They might be in places that are sometimes wet and sometimes dry. If they don't dry out quickly, they can survive until the area becomes wet again. **Ask:** Rod-shaped bacteria quickly absorb nutrients. Why might this be? Because they have more surface area than spherical bacteria, they can absorb more nutrients from outside the cell. This might give them an advantage over other bacteria in nutrient-poor places.

Learning Alert

Helping or Harming? Students may think that all bacteria are harmful, or pathogenic. Explain that it is true that bacteria can cause many illnesses, but many species help other living things or cause no harm. For example, human beings have bacteria living inside their digestive tracts that aid in digestion. Students may be interested to know that so far, researchers have discovered no pathogenic archaea.

SPLIT Personality

How do bacteria reproduce?

Bacteria grow if they have the space and food they need. When a bacterial cell has reached its full size, it will generally begin to reproduce. Bacteria reproduce by dividing in two. Some bacteria can divide every 20 minutes!

By Binary Fission

 Active Reading **12 Identify** As you read, underline the steps that occur when a bacterium reproduces using binary fission.

Both archaea and bacteria reproduce by binary fission. **Binary fission** is reproduction in which one single-celled organism splits into two single-celled organisms. The first step in bacterial reproduction is copying the cell's genetic information. Bacteria have their genetic information in the form of a long, circular strand of DNA. This loop, called a *chromosome*, is copied. Then the two chromosomes separate, with one on each side of the cell. Next, the cell's membrane starts to grow inward, separating the two halves of the cell. Finally, a new cell wall forms and separates the two new cells. At the end of binary fission, there are two identical bacterial cells, each with identical DNA. This type of reproduction, in which one parent produces offspring that are genetically identical to the parent, is called *asexual reproduction*. The cells will grow until they reach full size, and the process will begin again.

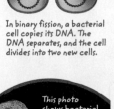

In binary fission, a bacterial cell copies its DNA. The DNA separates, and the cell divides into two new cells.

This photo shows bacterial binary fission.

 **Do the Math** **You Try It**

13 A bacterium undergoes binary fission. After thirty minutes, both new cells are ready to divide again. If this generation divides, and so does the following generation, how many total bacteria will there be? You may want to draw a diagram to check your answer.

84

How do bacteria exchange DNA?

How do bacteria get new genes? There are three ways that bacteria can acquire new genetic information. One way, called *transformation*, occurs when bacteria take up DNA from the environment. Another way, *transduction*, happens when a virus injects DNA into a bacterium. Sometimes the DNA is incorporated into the cell and may be useful. The third way is called *conjugation*. Some bacteria have a second loop of DNA, smaller than the main chromosome, called a plasmid. During conjugation, a plasmid is transferred from one bacterium to another when the two bacteria temporarily join together. The bacterium that gets the plasmid now has new genes that it can use. An example of a trait found on plasmid DNA is antibiotic resistance.

This photo shows bacterial conjugation.

 Visualize It!

14 Diagram Fill in the missing labels in this flow chart to complete the description of conjugation.

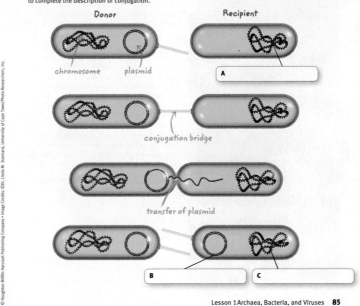

Donor   Recipient

chromosome   plasmid

A

conjugation bridge

transfer of plasmid

B   C

Lesson 1 Archaea, Bacteria, and Viruses **85**

Answers

12. *See students' pages for annotations.*

13. 8 cells; student diagrams should show one cell dividing into 2 cells, the 2 cells both dividing, to produce 4 cells, and the 4 cells all dividing, to produce 8 cells.

14. A: chromosome; B: plasmid; C: chromosome

Interpreting Visuals

Synthesizing **Ask:** Describe in your own words what happens during binary fission. Sample answer: The DNA is copied to make two loops. Then the cell divides so that one loop of DNA is in each cell. **Ask:** Describe in your own words what happens during conjugation. Sample answer: Two cells join together. A plasmid is copied and then transferred from one cell to the other. The genes in the plasmid may be useful to a new cell.

Do the Math

Ask: How did you figure out the answer to this question? Sample answer: I drew a diagram. **Ask:** What if the question asked how many cells there were after 10 divisions? Instead of drawing, I could just write the number of cells for each generation. The cells double with each generation.

Formative Assessment

Ask: What are characteristics of bacteria? They are almost all single-celled; lack a nucleus or organelles; are spherical, rod-shaped, or spiral-shaped; and live everywhere.

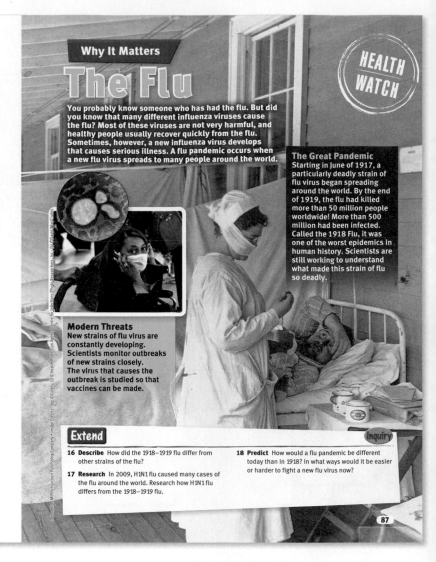

Alive *or* NOT Alive?

Virus Shapes
These microscopic images show some viruses with different shapes.

Crystals

Cylinders

Spheres

Phages

What are some characteristics of viruses?

A **virus** is a microscopic particle that cannot replicate on its own. It either gets inside a cell or injects a cell with its DNA, often destroying the cell. Many viruses cause diseases, such as the common cold, flu, and acquired immune deficiency syndrome (AIDS). People, plants, animals, and prokaryotes can all be infected by viruses. Viruses are made of a protein coat and genetic material. The genetic material can be either DNA or RNA. The protein coat gives the virus its shape. Most viruses are smaller than the smallest bacteria. About 5 billion virus particles could fit in a single drop of blood.

Are viruses living?

All living things are made of cells that contain genetic material, protein, and other chemicals. Like living things, viruses contain genetic material and protein. But, unlike living things, viruses do not perform any life functions. Viruses do not use energy from nutrients. Viruses do not maintain homeostasis. A virus can't grow. Viruses do not respond to stimuli such as light, sound, or touch. In fact, a virus cannot function on its own. A virus can replicate only inside a cell it infects. As a result, viruses are not considered living.

Active Reading 15 **Identify** List three reasons viruses are not living things.

_____
_____
_____
_____
_____

86   Unit 2 Earth's Organisms

Why It Matters

The Flu

You probably know someone who has had the flu. But did you know that many different influenza viruses cause the flu? Most of these viruses are not very harmful, and healthy people usually recover quickly from the flu. Sometimes, however, a new influenza virus develops that causes serious illness. A flu pandemic occurs when a new flu virus spreads to many people around the world.

HEALTH WATCH

The Great Pandemic
Starting in June of 1917, a particularly deadly strain of flu virus began spreading around the world. By the end of 1919, the flu had killed more than 50 million people worldwide! More than 500 million had been infected. Called the 1918 Flu, it was one of the worst epidemics in human history. Scientists are still working to understand what made this strain of flu so deadly.

Modern Threats
New strains of flu virus are constantly developing. Scientists monitor outbreaks of new strains closely. The virus that causes the outbreak is studied so that vaccines can be made.

Extend   Inquiry

16 **Describe** How did the 1918–1919 flu differ from other strains of the flu?

17 **Research** In 2009, H1N1 flu caused many cases of the flu around the world. Research how H1N1 flu differs from the 1918–1919 flu.

18 **Predict** How would a flu pandemic be different today than in 1918? In what ways would it be easier or harder to fight a new flu virus now?

87

Answers

15. Sample answer: Viruses do not get energy from nutrients, maintain homeostasis, or grow.

16. Sample answer: The 1918–1919 flu was more deadly than other strains of the flu. It killed more than 50 million people worldwide.

17. Students' answers should demonstrate an understanding that both pandemics were variants of Influenza A (subtype H1N1), but the 2009 outbreak was less severe.

18. Sample answer: A new flu virus would spread more easily today because people travel more extensively. It would also be easier to fight with modern vaccines and disease prevention methods.

Interpreting Visuals

Classifying Direct students to look at the images of viruses. **Ask:** Why might viruses have so many different shapes? Their shapes might help them latch on to the different kinds of cells that they use to replicate themselves, or perhaps they are like bacteria in that their shapes help them survive in different conditions.

Why It Matters

Ask: The flu is transmitted easily from person to person. How do you think a flu pandemic today would be similar to or different from the 1918 flu pandemic? Because people travel more today, the flu would spread more quickly than it did in 1918. Today a vaccine could be developed more quickly after a new strain of the flu emerged. There are anti-viral medicines available today that might lessen the severity of the flu. **Ask:** If most people recover quickly from the flu, why do we worry about flu pandemics? The flu can be dangerous to some people, such as pregnant women, the young and the old, or people who have other medical problems. Not all strains of the flu are the same; some strains can be deadly.

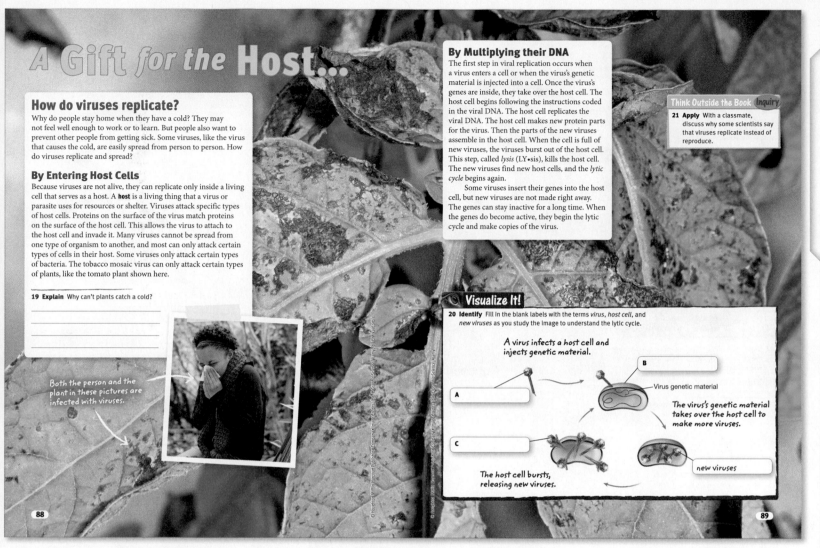

A Gift for the Host...

How do viruses replicate?

Why do people stay home when they have a cold? They may not feel well enough to work or to learn. But people also want to prevent other people from getting sick. Some viruses, like the virus that causes the cold, are easily spread from person to person. How do viruses replicate and spread?

By Entering Host Cells

Because viruses are not alive, they can replicate only inside a living cell that serves as a host. A **host** is a living thing that a virus or parasite uses for resources or shelter. Viruses attack specific types of host cells. Proteins on the surface of the virus match proteins on the surface of the host cell. This allows the virus to attach to the host cell and invade it. Many viruses cannot be spread from one type of organism to another, and most can only attack certain types of cells in their host. Some viruses only attack certain types of bacteria. The tobacco mosaic virus can only attack certain types of plants, like the tomato plant shown here.

19 Explain Why can't plants catch a cold?

Both the person and the plant in these pictures are infected with viruses.

By Multiplying their DNA

The first step in viral replication occurs when a virus enters a cell or when the virus's genetic material is injected into a cell. Once the virus's genes are inside, they take over the host cell. The host cell begins following the instructions coded in the viral DNA. The host cell replicates the viral DNA. The host cell makes new protein parts for the virus. Then the parts of the new viruses assemble in the host cell. When the cell is full of new viruses, the viruses burst out of the host cell. This step, called *lysis* (LY•sis), kills the host cell. The new viruses find new host cells, and the *lytic cycle* begins again.

Some viruses insert their genes into the host cell, but new viruses are not made right away. The genes can stay inactive for a long time. When the genes do become active, they begin the lytic cycle and make copies of the virus.

Think Outside the Book (Inquiry)

21 Apply With a classmate, discuss why some scientists say that viruses replicate instead of reproduce.

Visualize It!

20 Identify Fill in the blank labels with the terms *virus*, *host cell*, and *new viruses* as you study the image to understand the lytic cycle.

A virus infects a host cell and injects genetic material.

A

B — Virus genetic material

The virus's genetic material takes over the host cell to make more viruses.

C

The host cell bursts, releasing new viruses.

new viruses

88 · 89

Answers

19. Sample answer: Many viruses cannot be spread from one type of organism to another, so the cold virus probably can't spread to plants.

20. A: virus; B: host cell; C: new viruses

21. Student output should demonstrate an understanding that reproduction only applies to living things that can produce new individuals on their own, so when viruses make copies of themselves by depending on a host cell, it is not reproduction.

Interpreting Visuals

Classifying **Ask:** What happens during the lytic cycle? The virus attaches to a host. It enters the host or injects its genetic material into the host. The host's cells replicate the virus's genes. The new viruses burst out of the host cell, usually killing it, and the cycle begins again.

Formative Assessment

Ask: What are characteristics of viruses? They are microscopic; they are made of DNA or RNA and a protein coat; they are not living; they have different shapes, such as geometric forms, cylinders, and spheres. **Ask:** How do viruses replicate? One method is a process called the lytic cycle, in which a virus attaches to a host cell. The virus then either enters the cell or injects its genetic material into the host cell. The host cell replicates the DNA and viral proteins. Viruses are assembled inside the host cell. The new viruses burst out of the host cell, generally killing it when they do.

Visual Summary

To complete this summary, circle the correct word or words. Then use the key below to check your answers. You can use this page to review the main concepts of the lesson.

Archaea are prokaryotes with variable cell walls made up of unique molecules.

22 Archaea are more/less similar to eukaryotes than bacteria are.

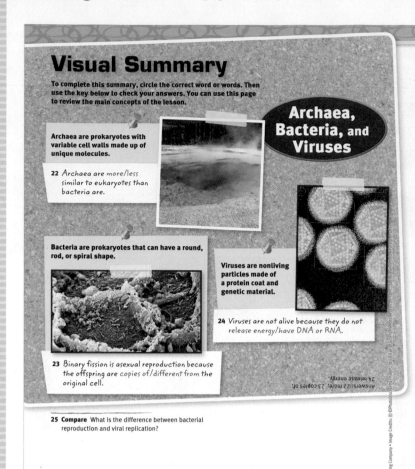

Archaea, Bacteria, and Viruses

Bacteria are prokaryotes that can have a round, rod, or spiral shape.

Viruses are nonliving particles made of a protein coat and genetic material.

24 Viruses are not alive because they do not release energy/have DNA or RNA.

23 Binary fission is asexual reproduction because the offspring are copies of/different from the original cell.

Answers: 22 more; 23 copies of; 24 release energy.

25 Compare What is the difference between bacterial reproduction and viral replication?

Lesson Review

Lesson ①

Vocabulary

Fill in the blanks with the terms that best complete the following sentences.

1 A(n) _____ is made of genetic material and a protein coat.

2 _____ is when one cell reproduces by dividing in half to become two cells.

3 A virus needs a(n) _____ to reproduce.

Key Concepts

4 Compare How do prokaryotes and eukaryotes differ?

5 Describe What are the characteristics of archaea?

6 Identify In the lytic cycle, the host cell

  A destroys the virus

  B becomes a virus

  C is destroyed

  D undergoes cell division

7 Explain How do the cell walls of archaea and bacteria differ?

Critical Thinking

Use the image below to answer the question that follows.

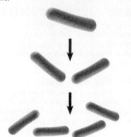

8 Explain Describe the process illustrated in the diagram above. How many individuals would exist if the process continued for one more generation?

9 Apply Unlike some archaea, most bacteria die when their environment reaches extremely high temperature. How can people kill harmful bacteria that might live in some human foods?

Visual Summary Answers

22. more

23. copies of

24. release energy

25. Sample answer: Bacteria copy their genetic material and then split in two through binary fission, a type of asexual reproduction. Viruses infect a cell and cause the cell to make new viruses in the lytic cycle, a type of replication.

Lesson Review Answers

1. virus

2. binary fission

3. host

4. Prokaryotes do not have a nucleus or membrane-bound organelles, and most of them are single-celled organisms. Eukaryotes have a nucleus and membrane-bound organelles and can be either single-celled or multicellular.

5. Archaea are prokaryotic organisms that can live in extreme environments. They are chemically different from bacteria.

6. C

7. The cell walls of archaea are chemically different from those of bacteria.

8. In binary fission, a bacterial cell copies its DNA. The cell splits so that each new cell gets one copy of the DNA. If this process continued for one more generation beyond what is shown in the image, 8 individuals would exist.

9. Sample answer: People can heat the food to very high temperatures to kill any bacteria that might live in the food.

Protists and Fungi

Essential Question What are protists and fungi?

 Professional Development

For more detailed information about the topics in this lesson, refer to the Content Refresher in the Unit Opener pages.

Opening Your Lesson

Begin the lesson by assessing students' prerequisite and prior knowledge.

Prerequisite Knowledge

- Basic knowledge of cell structures and cell processes, including mitosis and meiosis
- Definitions of *haploid, diploid,* and *zygote*
- Methods by which autotrophs and heterotrophs obtain food

Accessing Prior Knowledge

KWL Invite students to complete a KWL chart to access prior knowledge about protists and fungi. Have students put what they **K**now in the first column and what they **W**ant to know in the second column. After they have finished the lesson, they can complete the third column with what they **L**earned.

⊘ *Optional Online resource: KWL*

Customize Your Opening

☐ **Accessing Prior Knowledge,** above
☐ **Print Path** Engage Your Brain, SE p. 93
☐ **Print Path** Active Reading, SE p. 93
☐ **Digital Path** Lesson Opener

Key Topics/Learning Goals	Supporting Concepts
Characteristics of Protists 1 Describe the characteristics of kingdom Protista.	• Protista is a kingdom of eukaryotic organisms that cannot be classified as fungi, plants, or animals. • Protists have membrane-bound organelles and may also have complex cilia and flagella for movement and haploid gametes for reproduction.
Reproduction and Diversity in Protists 1 Describe how protists reproduce. 2 Describe the different types of protists.	• Protists can reproduce sexually (by fusion of gametes) or asexually (by budding, binary fission, and fragmentation). • Plant-like protists make nutrients through photosynthesis. Animal-like protists obtain nutrients by ingesting other organisms. Fungus-like protists absorb nutrients from their environment.
Characteristics of Fungi 1 Describe the characteristics of the kingdom Fungi. 2 Explain how hyphae make up the bodies of many fungi.	• Fungi are spore-producing organisms that absorb nutrients from their environment. They often have threadlike bodies, and many have cell walls that contain the protein chitin. • Many fungi are made of threadlike strands called hyphae. Hyphae form a tangled mass called a mycelium that makes up the body.
Reproduction and Diversity in Fungi 1 Describe how fungi reproduce. 2 Describe the different types of fungi.	• In fungi sexual reproduction, a hypha from one fungus joins with a hypha from another. They produce a structure in which genetic material is fused, meiosis occurs, and spores are released. In fungi asexual reproduction, hyphae produce a long stalk. Spores are produced by mitosis and released. • The three main types of fungi are zygote fungi, sac fungi, and club fungi.

Options for Instruction

Two parallel paths provide coverage of the Essential Questions, with a strong **Inquiry** strand woven into each.
Follow the **Print Path,** the **Digital Path,** or your customized combination of print, digital, and inquiry.

 **Print Path**
Teaching support for the Print Path appears with the Student Pages.

 Inquiry Labs and Activities

 **Digital Path**
Digital Path shortcut: TS673068

On the Move!, SE pp. 94–95 **What are some characteristics of protists?** • They Have One or More Cells • They Have Membrane-bound... • They Have Complex Structures for...	**Activity** The Truth About Protists and Fungi **Activity** Fungi or Protist?	**Characteristics of Protists** Interactive Graphics
Protist Production, SE pp. 96–97 **How can protists reproduce?** **A Diverse Group,** SE pp. 98–99 **What are different kinds of protists?**	**Quick Lab** What Do Protists Look Like? **Daily Demo** Culture of Diversity	**Reproduction in Protists** Graphic Sequence
Lots of Fun(gi)!, SE p. 100 **What are some characteristics of fungi?**	**Quick Lab** Observing a Mushroom's Spores and Hyphae	**Parts of a Fungus** Interactive Graphics
Lots of Fun(gi)!, SE pp. 101–103 **How can fungi reproduce?** **What are some kinds of fungi?** • Zygote Fungi • Sac Fungi • Club Fungi **How do fungi form partnerships?**	**Exploration Lab** Survey of Reproduction in Protists and Fungi	**Asexual and Sexual Reproduction** Interactive Graphics **Types of Fungi** Slideshow

Options for Assessment

See the Evaluate page for options, including Formative Assessment, Summative Assessment, and Unit Review.

Engage and Explore

Activities and Discussion

Probing Questions *Plant-like or Animal-like?*

Reproduction and Diversity in Protists

whole class
10 min
DIRECTED inquiry

Evaluating Tell students that euglenoids are single-celled protists. Many euglenoids are producers. When there is not enough sunlight to make food however, these euglenoids can get food as heterotrophs. Show students an illustration of a euglena, a common euglenoid. Point out the flagellum (used for movement) and the chloroplasts (used for photosynthesis). **Ask:** Do you think euglenoids like this one should be grouped with animal-like protists or plant-like protists? Why? Sample answer: Euglenoids should be grouped with plant-like protists because they have chloroplasts. **Ask:** Do you think grouping protists by how they obtain nutrients is a good system? Can you think of a better way? Have students share their viewpoints and suggestions. Discuss the limitations of any alternative systems suggested by students.

Variation For more individual accountability, these questions can be answered by students at the beginning of class in their notebooks or journals or on slips of paper to be handed in at the end of class.

Take It Home *Hungry for Algae*

Characteristics of Protists

adult-student pairs
20 min
GUIDED inquiry

Students work with an adult to research the ingredients found in foods in their home to determine if the foods contain algae derivatives such as alginate, carrageenan, or agar. Explain that these substances are common ingredients in many foods. Alginate, which comes from brown algae, and carrageenan and agar, which come from red algae, are used as thickeners, stabilizers, and emulsifiers. They are found in products such as ice cream, pie fillings, pudding, brownie mix, chocolate milk, sauces, sour cream, and yogurt.

🌐 *Optional Online resource: student worksheet*

Activity *The Truth About Protists and Fungi*

Characteristics of Protists and Fungi, Reproduction and Diversity in Protists and Fungi

whole class
ongoing
GUIDED inquiry

Card Responses Have students make "true" and "false" answer cards. Prepare a series of true/false statements about protists and fungi. Read a statement aloud. At a signal from you, students should hold up a card indicating  whether the statement is true or false. As you move through the lesson, occasionally ask questions about the lesson content. If the class's accuracy is less than 90 percent, it might be helpful to reemphasize the material or to reteach the material using a different approach. This technique also helps you identify those students who need individual help.

Discussion *Allergies and Molds*

Reproduction and Diversity in Fungi

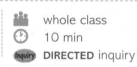
whole class
10 min
DIRECTED inquiry

Ask students if they or people they know are allergic to molds. **Ask:** Why do you think mold allergies are so common? Sample answer: because molds are very common **Ask:** What types of environments or substances do you think mold-sensitive people should avoid? Why? Sample answer: damp basements, damp soil, leaf litter, and other decaying organic matter because molds flourish in such places and materials

Customize Your Labs

📄 *See the Lab Manual for lab datasheets.*

💿 *Go Online for editable lab datasheets.*

Levels of **Inquiry**

DIRECTED inquiry
introduces inquiry skills within a structured framework.

GUIDED inquiry
develops inquiry skills within a supportive environment.

INDEPENDENT inquiry
deepens inquiry skills with student-driven questions or procedures.

Labs and Demos

Daily Demo *Culture of Diversity*

Engage

Introducing Key Topics

 small groups, whole class
 20 min
 GUIDED inquiry

Use this short demo before students begin the lesson.

PURPOSE **To demonstrate protist and fungi diversity**

MATERIALS

- 1 live algae culture
- 1 live ciliate culture
- 1 live fungal culture, such as bread mold
- 3 microscopes (projection microscope if available)
- 3 microscope slides with coverslips
- 3 plastic droppers

1 Set up the microscopes at different locations around the classroom. Label the stations 1 through 3.

2 Prepare slides of each culture to view under the microscopes.

3 **Observing** Direct students to circulate from station to station. Encourage students to record their observations using notes or drawings.

4 **Communicating** Ask students to describe characteristics of the organisms, including any similarities and differences.

5 **Predicting** Tell students that the organisms they observed come from two kingdoms: kingdom Protista and kingdom Fungi. **Ask:** Of the organisms, which two do you think come from the same kingdom? Because ciliates move, some students may assume that they belong to their own group, and that the algae and mold should be grouped together.

6 **Assessing** Explain that the ciliates and algae are protists, and that the mold is a fungus. **Ask:** What does this tell you about the organisms in kingdom Protista? Sample answer: It tells me that the organisms may be very different from one another.

Exploration Lab *Survey of Reproduction in Protists and Fungi*

Reproduction and Diversity in Protists and Fungi

 pairs
45 min
GUIDED/INDEPENDENT inquiry

Students will examine prepared slides that show the different methods of protist reproduction and the types of spores produced by fungi, as well as observe yeast budding.

PURPOSE **To demonstrate how some protists and fungi reproduce**

MATERIALS

- eyedropper
- microscope, compound
- microscope slide
- microscope slides, prepared, *Paramecium* binary fission and conjugation
- microscope slide, prepared, *Rhisopus* sexual reproduction
- yeast, active dry

Quick Lab *Observing a Mushroom's Spores and Hyphae*

PURPOSE **To examine and describe the parts of a mushroom**

See the Lab Manual or go Online for planning information.

Quick Lab *What Do Protists Look Like?*

PURPOSE **To examine and describe various protists**

See the Lab Manual or go Online for planning information.

Activities and Discussion

- ☐ **Probing Questions** Plant-like or Animal-like?
- ☐ **Take It Home** Hungry for Algae
- ☐ **Activity** The Truth About...
- ☐ **Discussion** Allergies and Molds

Labs and Demos

- ☐ **Daily Demo** Culture of Diversity
- ☐ **Exploration Lab** Survey of Reproduction in Protists and Fungi
- ☐ **Quick Lab** Observing a Mushroom...
- ☐ **Quick Lab** What Do Protists...?

Your Resources

Explain Science Concepts

Key Topics	📖 Print Path	💻 Digital Path
Characteristics of Protists	☐ **On the Move!,** SE pp. 94–95 • Compare, #5 • Visualize It!, #6 • Identify, #7	☐ **Characteristics of Protists** Describe the characterisics of the kingdom Protista, and describe characteristics of three main types of protists.
Reproduction and Diversity in Protists	☐ **Protist Production,** SE pp. 96–97 • Active Reading (Annotation strategy), #8 • Think Outside the Book, #9 • Visualize It!, #10 ☐ **A Diverse Group,** SE pp. 98–99 • Active Reading (Annotation strategy), #11 • Infer, #12 • Summarize, #13	☐ **Reproduction in Protists** Contrast asexual and sexual reproduction in protists.
Characteristics of Fungi	☐ **Lots of Fun(gi)!,** SE p. 100 • Visualize It!, #14	☐ **Parts of a Fungus** Describe characteristics of the kingdom Fungi, and identify the structure that makes up the body of these organisms.
Reproduction and Diversity in Fungi	☐ **Lots of Fun(gi)!,** SE pp. 101–103 • Active Reading, #15 • Inquiry, #16 • Active Reading (Annotation strategy), #17 • Infer, #18	☐ **Asexual and Sexual Reproduction** Describe sexual and asexual reproduction a fungus. ☐ **Types of Fungi** Describe different kinds of fungi and explain their importance in the environment.

Differentiated Instruction

Basic *Comparing Characteristics*

Synthesizing Key Topic

 individuals or pairs
⏱ 15–20 min

Two-Panel Flip Chart Invite students to create a Two-Panel Flip Chart FoldNote to compare the characteristics of protists and fungi. Students can write each kingdom and its major characteristics on the outside of each panel. Then, students can write descriptions of how the organisms in each kingdom reproduce on the top inside of each panel and include examples from the kingdom on the bottom inside of each panel. Encourage students to include illustrations in their charts. Have students use their completed flip charts as study aids.

 Online resource: Two-Panel Flip Chart support

Advanced *Ciliated Presentations*

Reproduction and Diversity in Protists

 individuals or pairs
⏱ varied

Presentations Ciliates are described as the most animal-like members of the kingdom Protista. Have students research a ciliate of their choice and then prepare a presentation for delivery to the class. Presentations should include information about where the ciliate lives, what it eats, how it moves, and how it reproduces, along with other interesting information about its biology. Encourage students to include drawings and photographs.

 Optional Online rubric: Oral Presentations

ELL *Protist Posters*

Reproduction and Diversity in Protists

 pairs
⏱ varied

Posters Have students work in pairs to create posters that describe the major groupings of protists based on how they obtain nutrients: animal-like protists, fungus-like protists, or plant-like protists. Posters should show examples of each protist type and describe how they obtain nutrients. Students should write labels and simple captions for images.

⊙ *Optional Online resources: Writing for Displays: Labels, Captions, Summaries, Posters and Displays rubric*

Lesson Vocabulary

| Protista | gamete | spore | algae |
| Fungi | hyphae | mycorrhiza | lichen |

Previewing Vocabulary

 whole class
⏱ 10 min

Word Origins Share the following to help students remember terms:
- **Hyphae** comes from a Greek term that means "web." Have students look at the fungus illustration in the lesson that shows the branching, weblike structure of the hyphae.
- **Mycorrhiza** is made up of two word parts: *myco-*, meaning "fungus," and *rhiza,* the Greek word for "root." Tell students that a mycorrhiza is a relationship between a fungus and a plant's roots.

Reinforcing Vocabulary

 individuals
⏱ 30 min

Word Triangle To help students remember vocabulary terms in the lesson, provide them with the Word Triangle graphic organizer. Students write the term and its definition in the bottom section. In the middle, they write a sentence in which the term is used correctly. At the top, they draw a small picture to illustrate the term.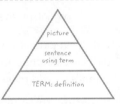

⊙ *Optional Online resource: Word Triangle support*

Customize Your Core Lesson

Core Instruction
☐ **Print Path** choices
☐ **Digital Path** choices

Vocabulary
☐ **Previewing Vocabulary** Word Origins
☐ **Reinforcing Vocabulary** Word Triangle

Your Resources

Differentiated Instruction
☐ **Basic** Comparing Characteristics
☐ **Advanced** Ciliated Presentations
☐ **ELL** Protist Posters

Extend Science Concepts

Reinforce and Review

Activity *Fungi or Protist?*

Synthesizing Key Topics whole class
10 min

Tell students that a scientist has discovered a fungus-like organism on the forest floor. It could be an actual fungus, or it could be a fungus-like protist. The scientist makes a series of observations to try to classify the organism. Write the following observations on the board, reading them aloud as you go. Instruct students to raise their hands when they have enough information to make a classification.

1 The organism lives in a moist environment.

2 The organism is yellow-brown in color.

3 The organism absorbs nutrients from its environment.

4 The organism produces spores.

5 The organism can move during one stage of its life.

6 The organism does not have hyphae.

Call on volunteers to explain why they raised their hands when they did. Discuss their rationales. Guide the class to conclude that the scientist could make a definitive classification after observation #5.

Variation This activity can also be used before students read the lesson in order to assess what they already know.

Graphic Organizer

**Reproduction and
Diversity in Protists** individuals
15 min

Cycle Diagram After students have finished the lesson, have them create a Cycle Diagram graphic organizer that shows how some protists reproduce through the process of alternation of generations.

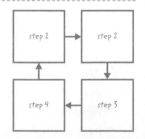

🌐 *Optional Online resource: Cycle Diagram support*

Going Further

Health Connection

Characteristics of Protists individuals or pairs
varied

Research Project Native Hawaiians have historically used a species of brown algae from the genus *Sargassum* to heal cuts caused by corals. Other seaweeds contain compounds that may have medicinal values as well. About 20 different seaweeds are used in preparations for treating diseases, including intestinal parasite infections and cancer. Allow interested students to research specific examples of medicinal uses for seaweed and create a brief multimedia presentation on their example. Then combine all presentations into one presentation for the class.

🌐 *Optional Online rubric: Multimedia Presentation*

Math Connection

Characteristics of Fungi whole class
10 min

Calculation Truffles are a kind of sac fungi that are prized as an ingredient in French cooking. Tell students that in western France an unusually dry summer produced a smaller-than-usual harvest. Prices of top-quality truffles rose from $535 per kilogram to $625 per kilogram. **Ask:** What percentage increase does this price difference represent? $625 − $535 = $90; ($90 ÷ $535) × 100 = 16.8 percent increase Tell students to imagine that they are chefs and need to make a new dish with a recipe that calls for 1 lb of truffles. **Ask:** How many kilograms of truffles will you need to buy, and what will it cost at the new price? 1 kg = 2.2 lb. Students will need 0.45 kg for the recipe. The cost would be $625 × 0.45 = $281.25.

Customize Your Closing

 See the Assessment Guide for quizzes and tests.

🌐 *Go Online to edit and create quizzes and tests.*

Reinforce and Review

☐ **Activity** Fungi or Protist?

☐ **Graphic Organizer** Cycle Diagram

☐ **Print Path** Visual Summary, SE p. 104

☐ **Digital Path** Lesson Closer

Evaluate Student Mastery

Formative Assessment

See the teacher support below the Student Pages for additional Formative Assessment questions.

Ask the following questions to assess student mastery of the material. **Ask:** How are algae similar to plants? **Sample answer:** They both make food through photosynthesis. **Ask:** A single-celled protist reproduces by copying its DNA and then dividing into two cells. **Ask:** What is the name for this type of reproduction? **binary fission** **Ask:** What are two characteristics that fungi share? They absorb nutrients from the environment and produce spores.

Reteach

Formative assessment may show that students need reinforcement for certain topics. The resources below are recommended for reteaching. If students were introduced to a topic through the Print Path, you can also use the Digital Path to reteach, and vice versa.

🎧 *Can be assigned to individual students*

Characteristics of Protists
Basic Comparing Characteristics 🎧

Reproduction and Diversity in Protists
ELL Protist Posters 🎧

Graphic Organizer Cycle Diagram 🎧

Characteristics of Fungi
Quick Lab Observing a Mushroom's Spores and Hyphae

Reproduction and Diversity in Fungi
Daily Demo Culture of Diversity

Exploration Lab Survey of Reproduction in Protists and Fungi

Summative Assessment

Alternative Assessment
Show What You Know About Protists and Fungi

🌐 *Online resources: student worksheet, optional rubrics*

Protists and Fungi

Climb the Pyramid: *Show What You Know about Protists and Fungi*

1. Work on your own, with a partner, or with a small group.

2. Choose one item from each layer of the pyramid. Check your choices.

3. Have your teacher approve your plan.

4. Submit or present your results.

___ **Make a Pop-up Book**

Make a pop-up book about protists. Create a separate chapter for each of the three protist groups (animal-like protists, fungus-like protists, and plant-like protists). Be creative and write text for your book.

___ **Walk in the Woods**

Write a short story about finding several fungi during a walk through a forest. In your story, describe each of the fungi, tell about the environment where they live, and explain their role in the forest ecosystem. Make sure you identify the group that each fungus belongs to.

___ **Fungi Models**

Research a species of sac or club fungus on the Internet, in an encyclopedia, or in a book about fungi. Create a colorful, lifelike model of the fungus you investigated.

___ **Pretty Protists**

Protists are found in countless shapes, sizes, and colors. Find pictures of magnified protists on the Internet or at a library. Choose five organisms that are pretty or interesting and recreate the pictures of those protists on a poster using your imagination. Then include information that describes each protist.

___ **Doing Away with Mildew**

Mildew is a type of fungus that can cause problems for homeowners. It can grow on walls, rugs, and other surfaces in the interior of houses. Research mildew and then create a pamphlet for homeowners that describes what mildew is, the conditions it needs to grow, and how it reproduces and spreads. The pamphlet should also provide tips on preventing mildew.

___ **Amoeboid Movement**

Amoebas are soft, jellylike protists that have the ability to move using pseudopodia, or "false feet." Research the manner in which amoebas move, and then create a flipbook, or a sequence of drawings, that shows the steps in amoeboid movement. Use labels and captions to explain what is happening in each drawing.

Going Further
- [ ] **Health Connection**
- [ ] **Math Connection**

Formative Assessment
- [ ] **Strategies** Throughout TE
- [ ] **Lesson Review** SE

Summative Assessment
- [ ] **Alternative Assessment** Show What You Know About Protists and Fungi
- [ ] **Lesson Quiz**
- [ ] **Unit Tests A and B**
- [ ] **Unit Review** SE End-of-Unit

Your Resources

_____

_____

Answers

Answers for 1–3 should represent students' current thoughts, even if incorrect.

1. False; True; False; True

2. Sample answer: Seaweed is a multicellular protist that can grow to be quite large.

3. Sample answers: A spore is a reproductive cell. Hyphae are threadlike fibers that make up fungi.

4. Students' annotations will vary.

Opening Your Lesson

Discuss student responses to item 1 to assess students' prerequisite knowledge and to estimate what they already know about protists and fungi.

Prerequisites Students should already have some knowledge of cell structure and cell processes, such as mitosis, meiosis, and photosynthesis. In this lesson, students will apply this knowledge as they learn how protists and fungi grow and reproduce.

Learning Alert

Diversity of Protists As students learn the material in this lesson, they may be confused about what characteristics unite the organisms in the kingdom Protista. You may want to stress that this group is unique in that the organisms in the kingdom Protista are united more by their differences from other groups than by their similarities with each other. Many of the organisms in kingdom Protista are only distantly related to each other, and scientists do not agree on how to classify the members of this kingdom.

On the Move!

What are some characteristics of protists?

The kingdom **Protista** is a group of eukaryotic organisms that cannot be classified as fungi, plants, or animals. Members of the kingdom Protista are called protists. Protists are a very diverse group of organisms. Many members of this kingdom are not closely related to each other and some are more closely related to members of other kingdoms. As a result, classification of protists is likely to change. So are there traits that are shared by all protists? As eukaryotes, they all have a nucleus and membrane-bound organelles.

5 Compare The two organisms shown below look very different. Why do scientists classify both as protists?

_____

_____

_____

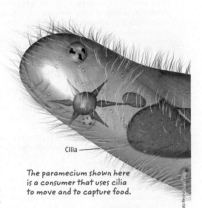

Cilia

The paramecium shown here is a consumer that uses cilia to move and to capture food.

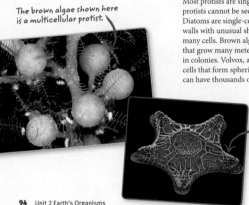

The brown algae shown here is a multicellular protist.

They Have One or Many Cells

Most protists are single-celled organisms. These protists cannot be seen without a microscope. Diatoms are single-celled protists that have cell walls with unusual shapes. Some protists have many cells. Brown algae are multicellular protists that grow many meters long. Other protists live in colonies. Volvox, a kind of green algae, has cells that form spherical colonies. These colonies can have thousands of cells that all work together.

The diatom shown here is a microscopic single-celled protist.

They Have Membrane-Bound Organelles

Like all eukaryotes, protists have membrane-bound organelles. Organelles are structures that carry out jobs inside a cell. For example, some protists have chloroplasts that make food from the sun's energy. Many protists have contractile vacuoles that remove excess water from the cell. Some protists have organelles that sense light.

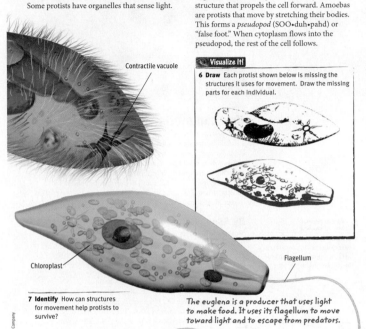

Contractile vacuole

Chloroplast

7 Identify How can structures for movement help protists to survive?

_____

_____

_____

_____

They Have Complex Structures for Movement

Some protists have structures for movement. Most protists that move do so in order to find food. Some protists use cilia to move. Cilia are hairlike structures that beat rapidly back and forth. Other protists use a flagellum or many flagella to move. A flagellum is a whiplike structure that propels the cell forward. Amoebas are protists that move by stretching their bodies. This forms a *pseudopod* (SOO•duh•pahd) or "false foot." When cytoplasm flows into the pseudopod, the rest of the cell follows.

Visualize It!

6 Draw Each protist shown below is missing the structures it uses for movement. Draw the missing parts for each individual.

Flagellum

The euglena is a producer that uses light to make food. It uses its flagellum to move toward light and to escape from predators.

94   Unit 2 Earth's Organisms

Lesson 2 Protists and Fungi   95

Answers

5. Sample answer: Both organisms are protists because they don't fit in any other eukaryotic groups.

6. Students should draw cilia on the top protist and a flagellum on the bottom protist.

7. Sample answer: Structures for movement allow protists to move towards food or light.

Interpreting Visuals

To help students better understand the images of flagella and cilia movement, make two simple line drawings on the board. The first drawing should show the outline of a boat as seen from overhead, with numerous oars sticking out from the sides. The second drawing should show a boat outline with a single engine and propeller at the back. Encourage students to compare the drawings with the images on the page. **Ask:** Which drawing is a model for the way cilia move a protist? the boat with oars **Ask:** Which drawing is a model for the way a flagellum moves a protist? the boat with a propeller

Formative Assessment

Ask: What characteristics do all protists share? Sample answer: All protists have a nucleus and membrane-bound organelles. **Ask:** What are three ways in which protists can differ from one another? Sample answer: Some are single-celled, others are multicellular; some make their own food, others can't; some can direct their own movement, others can't.

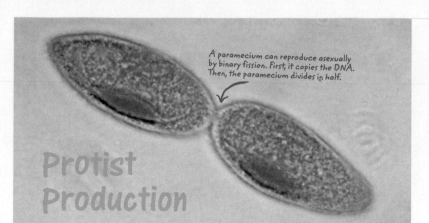

A paramecium can reproduce asexually by binary fission. First, it copies the DNA. Then, the paramecium divides in half.

Protist Production

How can protists reproduce?

Some protists reproduce only asexually. Others reproduce asexually at one stage in their life cycle and sexually at another stage. For some protists, the type of reproduction alternates by generation. For example, a parent reproduces asexually, and its offspring reproduce sexually. Then the cycle starts again. Other protists reproduce asexually until environmental conditions become stressful. A lack of food or water can trigger these protists to reproduce sexually until conditions improve.

Active Reading

8 Identify On this page and the next, underline the benefits of asexual reproduction and the benefits of sexual reproduction.

By Asexual Reproduction

Most protists can reproduce asexually. In asexual reproduction, the offspring come from just one parent. So every organism can produce offspring on its own. These offspring are genetically identical to the parent. When environmental conditions are favorable and there is plenty of food and water, asexual reproduction produces many offspring very quickly.

Protists can reproduce asexually in different ways. These include binary fission and fragmentation. During binary fission, a single-celled protist copies its DNA. The protist then divides into two cells. Each new cell has a copy of the DNA. The paramecium shown above is splitting through binary fission. Fragmentation is a process in which a piece breaks off of an organism and develops into a new individual. Many multicellular protists can reproduce by fragmentation.

Think Outside the Book

9 Compare Both protists and bacteria can reproduce asexually using binary fission. Research to find out how protist fission differs from bacterial fission.

96 Unit 2 Earth's Organisms

By Sexual Reproduction

Some protists reproduce sexually. In sexual reproduction, two cells, called **gametes** , join together. Each gamete contains a single copy of the genes for the organism. A cell with only one copy of genetic material is described as being *haploid*. A cell with two copies is *diploid*. Each gamete comes from a different parent. When the haploid gametes join, the diploid offspring have a unique combination of genetic material. Genetic diversity increases a species' chance of survival when the environment changes.

In some protists, generations alternate between using sexual or asexual reproduction. The haploid generation adults are called *gametophytes* (guh•MEET•uh•fyts). The diploid generation adults are called *sporophytes* (SPOHR•uh•fyts). Diploid adults undergo meiosis to make haploid spores. **Spores** are reproductive cells that are resistant to stressful environmental conditions. These spores develop into haploid adults. The haploid adults undergo mitosis to form haploid gametes. Two gametes join to form a diploid zygote. The zygote then grows into a diploid adult. This continuing cycle is called *alternation of generations*.

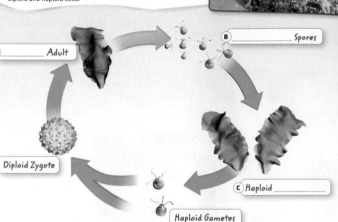

Ulva, or sea lettuce, is an algae that reproduces by alternation of generations.

Visualize It!

10 Draw Use the terms *diploid*, *haploid*, and *adult* to fill in the blanks describing how *Ulva* reproduces with alternating generations of diploid and haploid cells.

A _____ Adult

B _____ Spores

C Haploid _____

Haploid Gametes

Diploid Zygote

Lesson 2 Protists and Fungi **97**

Answers

8. *See students' pages for annotations.*

9. Sample answer: Protists are eukaryotes, whereas bacteria are prokaryotes. Protists must undergo division of the nucleus. In contrast, bacterial DNA adheres to the cell membrane after it is replicated, and the DNA is divided by the bacterial cell growing longer and dividing into two parts.

10. A: Diploid; B: Haploid; C: Adult

Building Math Skills

Explain to students that *Plasmodium vivax*, the protist that causes the disease malaria, reproduces asexually using multiple fission. A single spore of a *P. vivax* organism can produce 40,000 offspring. Researchers have determined that when a mosquito that is infected with *P. vivax* inserts its proboscis into a human blood vessel, the mosquito injects about a thousand spores. **Ask:** How many *P. vivax* spores could be present in a person's body after just one division by multiple fission? 1,000 spores × 40,000 offspring = 40,000,000 spores

Interpreting Visuals

To help students interpret the chart showing alternation of generations, **Ask:** What process happens between step A and step B to produce haploid spores? meiosis **Ask:** What process happens after step C to produce haploid gametes? mitosis **Ask:** Why are there two arrows pointing to "Diploid Zygote"? The arrows indicate that two gametes join together to form a diploid zygote. **Ask:** What do you call the process in which two haploid gametes join to form a diploid zygote? sexual reproduction (or fertilization)

A Diverse Group

What are different kinds of protists?

Because protists are so diverse, grouping them can be difficult. One useful way to group protists is by how they get food. Some capture food, like animals do. Some absorb nutrients, like fungi do. Some make food, like plants do.

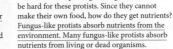 **11 Identify** On this page and the next, underline how each kind of protist gets its food.

Animal-like Protists

Animal-like protists cannot make their own food. Instead, they get nutrients by ingesting other organisms. Many animal-like protists eat small organisms such as bacteria, yeast, or other protists.

Most animal-like protists can move around their environment. This allows them to search for food in the environment. Sometimes, the same structures that aid movement can also help protists get food. For example, cilia sweep food toward a paramecium's food passageway. Amoebas use their pseudopodia to engulf their food.

Fungus-like Protists

Usually, fungus-like protists cannot move on their own. So capturing live organisms would be hard for these protists. Since they cannot make their own food, how do they get nutrients? Fungus-like protists absorb nutrients from the environment. Many fungus-like protists absorb nutrients from living or dead organisms.

Fungus-like protists produce spores that are used in reproduction. The protists release the spores into the environment, and the spores can survive through periods of harsh conditions. When the spores land on a good source of nutrients, they develop into an adult.

Amoebas capture their food by surrounding it with a pseudopod.

This water mold absorbs nutrients from the body of a fish.

98 Unit 2 Earth's Organisms

Plant-like Protists

Plant-like protists are producers. This means they use the sun's energy to make food through photosynthesis. Single-celled, free-floating, plant-like protists are a main part of the ocean's phytoplankton. Phytoplankton are tiny, floating organisms that provide food for many larger organisms. They also produce much of the world's oxygen.

Multicellular plant-like protists are called **algae** . All algae have the green pigment chlorophyll in their cells. Many also have other pigments. Algae are grouped by color. The three main groups of algae are brown algae, red algae, and green algae. The pigment color determines what wavelengths of light the algae can absorb.

12 Infer Because plant-like protists make their own food from sunlight, in what kind of environment would they not be able to survive? Why?

Red algae live in tropical water.

Some brown algae can grow to be many meters long.

This green algae lives in shallow tide pools.

13 Summarize For each kind of protist on the chart below, list three characteristics.

Animal-like Protists	Fungus-like Protists	Plant-like Protists

99

Answers

11. *See students' pages for annotations.*

12. Plant-like protists could not survive in dark environments without enough sunlight for photosynthesis.

13. Sample answer: Animal-like protists cannot make their own food; can move; some are parasites; some eat other organisms. Fungus-like protists cannot move; absorb nutrients; complex life cycle; many are parasites; produce spores. Plant-like protists make their own food; cannot move; grouped by color; most are multicellular.

Using Annotations

Text Structure: Comparison/Contrast The annotation asks students to underline text describing how each type of protist gets its food. After students complete the annotation, have them rewrite the information into a Concept Map graphic organizer. They can use "Protists can be grouped by how they get food" as the key topic and use descriptions of each of three ways as details. Remind students to include linking words on the arrows. Encourage them to use the map as a study aid to compare and contrast the three protist groups.

🌐 *Optional Online resources: Text Structure: Compare/Contrast, Concept Map support*

Formative Assessment

Ask: How are phytoplankton similar to plants? Sample answer: Both make food through photosynthesis. **Ask:** How are phytoplankton different from plants? Sample answer: Phytoplankton are single-celled, while plants are multicellular.

Probing Question DIRECTED Inquiry

Evaluating Why is algae important to the survival of other organisms? Sample answer: Algae provides food and oxygen for other organisms.

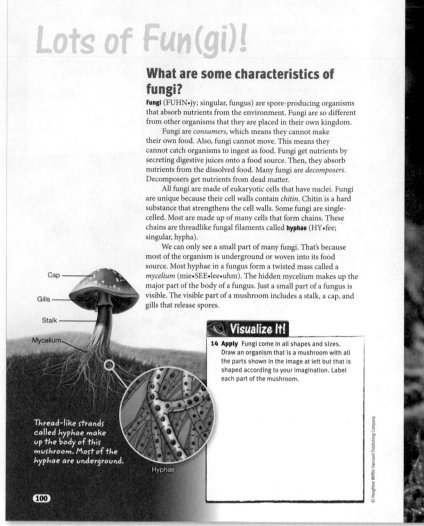

Lots of Fun(gi)!

What are some characteristics of fungi?

Fungi (FUHN•jy; singular, fungus) are spore-producing organisms that absorb nutrients from the environment. Fungi are so different from other organisms that they are placed in their own kingdom.

Fungi are *consumers*, which means they cannot make their own food. Also, fungi cannot move. This means they cannot catch organisms to ingest as food. Fungi get nutrients by secreting digestive juices onto a food source. Then, they absorb nutrients from the dissolved food. Many fungi are *decomposers*. Decomposers get nutrients from dead matter.

All fungi are made of eukaryotic cells that have nuclei. Fungi are unique because their cell walls contain *chitin*. Chitin is a hard substance that strengthens the cell walls. Some fungi are single-celled. Most are made up of many cells that form chains. These chains are threadlike fungal filaments called **hyphae** (HY•fee; singular, hypha).

We can only see a small part of many fungi. That's because most of the organism is underground or woven into its food source. Most hyphae in a fungus form a twisted mass called a *mycelium* (mie•SEE•lee•uhm). The hidden mycelium makes up the major part of the body of a fungus. Just a small part of a fungus is visible. The visible part of a mushroom includes a stalk, a cap, and gills that release spores.

Cap

Gills

Stalk

Mycelium

Thread-like strands called hyphae make up the body of this mushroom. Most of the hyphae are underground.

Hyphae

Visualize It!

14 Apply Fungi come in all shapes and sizes. Draw an organism that is a mushroom with all the parts shown in the image at left but that is shaped according to your imagination. Label each part of the mushroom.

100

© Houghton Mifflin Harcourt Publishing Company

How can fungi reproduce?

Fungi reproduce both asexually and sexually. In asexual reproduction, offspring are genetically identical to the parent. In sexual reproduction, offspring are genetically unique.

By Asexual Reproduction

Asexual reproduction in fungi occurs in three ways. In fragmentation, hyphae break apart, and each piece becomes a new fungus. In budding, a small portion of a parent cell pinches off to become a new individual. In asexual reproduction by spores, hyphae produce a long stalk called a *sporangium* (spuh•RAN•jee•uhm). Here, spores develop through mitosis. Spores are light and easily spread by wind. So spores can travel long distances even though fungi cannot move on their own. When conditions are favorable, a spore develops into a new fungus.

By Sexual Reproduction

In most fungi, sexual reproduction occurs when hyphae from two individuals join together. The fused hyphae produce a special reproductive structure, such as a mushroom. Genetic material from both individuals fuse to form diploid cells. Then the cells undergo meiosis to become haploid again. The spores are then released. These spores are much like asexual spores. Both can spread easily through the environment and survive until favorable conditions arise.

Active Reading 15 Identify Describe the role of spores in both asexual and sexual fungus reproduction.

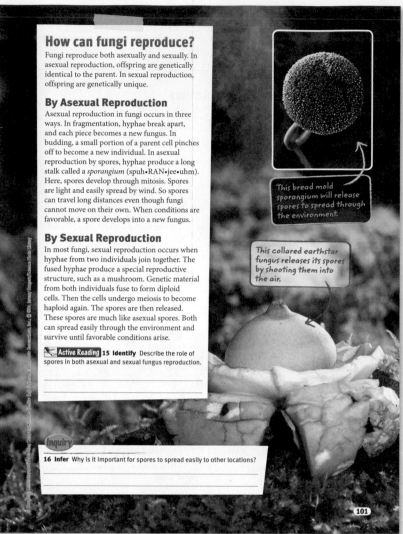

This bread mold sporangium will release spores to spread through the environment.

This collared earthstar fungus releases its spores by shooting them into the air.

Inquiry

16 Infer Why is it important for spores to spread easily to other locations?

101

Answers

14. Student labels should include the cap, gills, stalk, and mycelium.

15. Sample answer: In both asexual and sexual reproduction, spores can spread to new environments and wait for favorable conditions to grow.

16. Sample answer: Sreading to new locations allows fungi to grow in a variety of environments. This gives the fungi more opportunities to grow and reproduce successfully.

Interpreting Visuals

Direct students to locate the mycelium in the illustration showing the parts of a fungus.

Ask: Based on the illustration, what is the function of the mycelium? Sample answer: The mycelium absorbs nutrients from organic matter in the soil.

Probing Question   DIRECTED *Inquiry*

Predicting A homeowner discovers a poisonous type of mushroom growing in many places in her yard. She gets rid of all the caps and stems she can see by pulling them up like weeds. Will this permanently rid her yard of the mushrooms? Why or why not? No. Mushrooms are fungi, and the largest part of a fungus is underground.

Formative Assessment

Ask: What are two ways that fungi can reproduce asexually? 1. Hyphae can break apart; each piece then becomes a new fungus. 2. A fungus can produce spores; the spores spread and then develop into new fungi. Note that yeast can reproduce by budding.

What are some kinds of fungi?

Fungi are classified based on their shape and the way they reproduce. Many species of fungi fit into three main groups. These groups are zygote fungi, sac fungi, and club fungi.

Active Reading **17 Identify** On this page and the next, underline the characteristics that define each kind of fungus.

These mushrooms are club fungi.

Zygote Fungi

Zygote fungi are named for sexual reproductive structures that produce zygotes inside a tough capsule. Most of the fungi in this group live in the soil and are decomposers. Some zygote fungi are used to process foods like soybeans. Other types of zygote fungi are used to fight bacterial infections. However, some zygote fungi can cause problems for people. Have you ever seen moldy bread? A mold is a fast-growing, fuzzy fungus that reproduces asexually. Bread mold and molds that rot fruits and vegetables are examples of this asexual stage of a zygote fungus life cycle. Some molds also have a stage during which they reproduce sexually.

This bread mold is a fuzzy example of a zygote fungus.

Sac Fungi

Sac fungi are the largest group of fungi. Sac fungi include yeasts, powdery mildews, morels, and bird's-nest fungi. Sac fungi reproduce asexually and sexually. Sexually produced spores develop within a microscopic sac that then opens to release the spores. This structure gives sac fungi their name. Most sac fungi are multicellular. Yeasts are typically single-celled sac fungi that usually reproduce asexually by budding. Budding occurs when a new cell pinches off from an existing cell. Under certain conditions a yeast will reproduce sexually and form spores in sacs. Yeasts are used to make bread and alcohol. Other sac fungi make antibiotics and vitamins.

Morels are an edible type of sac fungus that grow at the base of trees.

Club Fungi

Mushrooms, bracket fungi, puffballs, smuts, and rusts are club fungi. Club fungi are named for the microscopic structures in which the spores develop. Only the spore-producing part of a club fungus is visible. These structures usually grow at the edges of the mycelium. A fungal mycelium can be incredibly large. One of the world's largest living organisms is a honey mushroom in Oregon whose mycelium spans almost 9 km².

Club fungi are very important decomposers of wood. Without fungi, the nutrients in wood could not be recycled. Smuts and rusts are plant parasites. They often attack crops such as corn and wheat.

These red **Amanita** are highly toxic, yet beautiful, club fungi.

How do fungi form partnerships?

Fungi form two very important partnerships. Some fungi grow on or in the roots of plants. These plants provide nutrients to the fungus. In return, the fungus usually helps the roots absorb minerals. This partnership is called a **mycorrhiza** (my•kuh•RY•zuh).

A **lichen** is a partnership between a fungus and a green alga or cyanobacterium. They are so inseparable that scientists give lichens their own scientific names. The alga or cyanobacterium uses photosynthesis to make food. The fungus gives protection, water, and minerals. Lichens provide food for animals in polar climates. Also, because lichens are very sensitive to pollution, the presence of lichens indicates that an environment has clean air.

18 Infer Suppose that the number of kinds of lichens at a city park is decreasing each year. What might explain this disappearance?

_____

_____

Lichens can grow on rocks. They release acids that break down rock over time to make soil.

102 Unit 2 Earth's Organisms

Lesson 2 Protists and Fungi 103

Answers

17. *See students' pages for annotations.*

18. Sample answer: Air pollution in the city might be increasing, since air pollution kills lichens.

Building Reading Skills

Pyramid Guide students as they make a Pyramid FoldNote graphic organizer. Then have them use the Pyramid for taking notes as they read the section on types of fungi. Each side of the Pyramid should summarize information on one type of fungi (zygote fungi, sac fungi, or club fungi). Encourage students to include illustrations.

🌐 *Online resource: Pyramid support*

Learning Alert

Diversity of Fungi Because there are so many different types of fungi, their common characteristics will need to be emphasized so that students remember that they are all in one kingdom. Have students look at the images of fungi on these and other pages. Ask students to name characteristics that all of the fungi have in common, and list them on the board. Review the list to make sure that each characteristic applies to all fungi.

Probing Question GUIDED Inquiry

Predicting Describe how the world would be different without fungi. Sample answer: Without fungi, we wouldn't have certain types of food or medicine. Dead organic matter might build up and many plants would grow poorly without mycorrhizae.

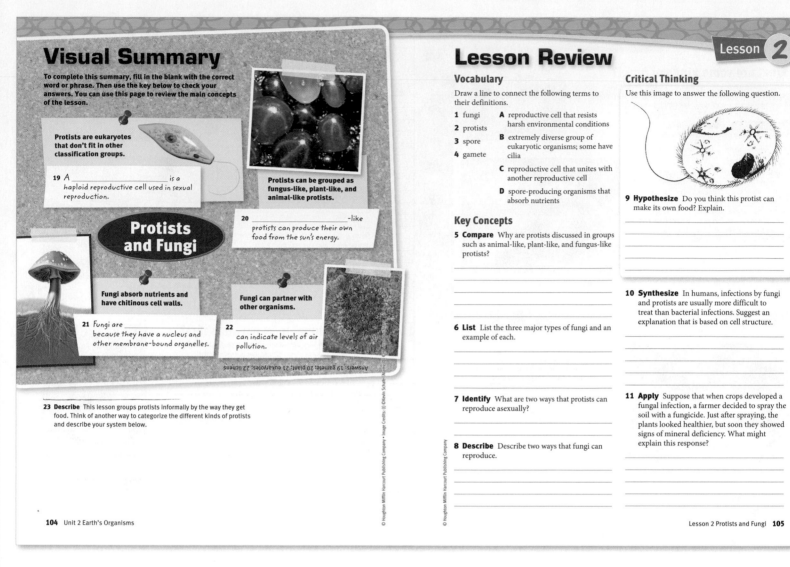

Visual Summary Answers

19. gamete

20. plant

21. eukaryotes

22. lichens

23. Student answers should describe a way to categorize protists. They could use the ways that protists move, the ways they reproduce, or their DNA as characteristics that can organize this diverse group into categories.

Lesson Review Answers

1. D

2. B

3. A

4. C

5. A helpful way to distinguish between diverse protists is the way they get nutrients. Some protists ingest food, like animals do, some make food, like plants do, and some absorb nutrients, like fungi do.

6. zygote fungi (bread mold); sac fungi (morels); club fungi (mushrooms)

7. fragmentation; binary fission

8. Sample answer: To reproduce sexually, fungi can fuse hyphae from different individuals and release sexual spores. To reproduce asexually, fungi can use fragmentation or budding or produce asexual spores.

9. Sample answer: No. This protist has cilia and a flagellum. These structures help the organism move, so the organism probably has to get food from its environment.

10. Sample answer: Humans and fungi are both eukaryotes, whereas bacteria are prokaryotes. Therefore, humans and fungi have more similar cell structures, so it is more difficult to develop a treatment that destroys fungus cells without also destroying human cells.

11. Sample answer: The fungicide might have killed not only the fungal infection but also helpful fungi that formed mycorrhizae with the plant roots.

Teacher Notes

Introduction to Plants

Essential Question What are plants?

 Professional Development

For more detailed information about the topics in this lesson, refer to the Content Refresher in the Unit Opener pages.

Opening Your Lesson

Begin the lesson by assessing students' prerequisite and prior knowledge.

Prerequisite Knowledge

- A general understanding of living things and the theory of evolution
- An understanding of the classification of living things

Accessing Prior Knowledge

To gauge what students know about plants, have them make a Description Wheel. In the center, have them write *PLANTS*. On the wheel's spokes, have them write what they know about the characteristics of plants.

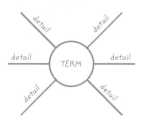

Customize Your Opening

- ☐ **Accessing Prior Knowledge,** above
- ☐ **Print Path** Engage Your Brain, SE p. 107
- ☐ **Print Path** Active Reading, SE p. 107
- ☐ **Digital Path** Lesson Opener

Key Topics/Learning Goals

Characteristics of Plants

1. Describe the common characteristics of all plants.
2. Describe the process of photosynthesis.
3. Describe the significance of chlorophyll in plants.

Structure and Function in Plants

1. List characteristics of non-vascular and vascular plants.
2. Identify three organs found in vascular plants and describe their functions.

Classification of Plants

1. Explain reproduction in seedless plants.
2. Describe reproduction in seed plants.
3. List the major groups of plants.

Supporting Concepts

- Plants are multicellular eukaryotes. Most plants are producers. Plant cells have cell walls. Plant life cycles include two stages.
- During photosynthesis, plants use energy from sunlight to produce glucose from carbon dioxide and water.
- Chlorophyll is a green pigment that plants use to capture energy from sunlight.

- Nonvascular plants lack a vascular system and rely on diffusion to transport water and nutrients. Vascular plants have a vascular system to transport water and nutrients.
- Most vascular plants have roots, stems, and leaves. Roots supply plants with water and minerals from soil. Stems support the plant. Leaves make food for the plant, prevent water loss, and allow for gas exchange.

- In plants, fertilization results in a zygote, which develops into an embryo.
- All nonvascular plants and some vascular plants are seedless. They depend on water to allow their sperm to swim and fertilize eggs.
- Most vascular plants produce seeds, which consist of the embryo and a protective coating. Seed plants also produce pollen.
- The major groups of plants are seedless nonvascular plants, seedless vascular plants, gymnosperms, and angiosperms.

Options for Instruction

Two parallel paths provide coverage of the Essential Questions, with a strong **Inquiry** strand woven into each. Follow the **Print Path,** the **Digital Path,** or your customized combination of print, digital, and inquiry.

 Print Path
Teaching support for the Print Path appears with the Student Pages.

 Inquiry Labs and Activities

Digital Path
Digital Path shortcut: TS663354

Plants Alive, SE pp. 108–109
What are the characteristics of plants?

Activity
What Makes a Plant a Plant?

Activity
Card Responses

What Is a Plant?
Interactive Graphics

Photosynthesis
Video

A Wide World of Plants,
SE pp. 110–111
What are the two main groups of plants?

Quick Lab
Observing Transport

Nonvascular Plants
Video

Vascular Plants
Interactive Graphics

Spore Power to Ya!,
SE pp. 112–113
How are seedless nonvascular plants classified?
How are seedless vascular plants classified?

Seeds of Success,
SE pp. 114–116
How are seed plants classified?

Daily Demo
How Are Flowers Pollinated?

Activity
Diagramming a Seed or a Cone

Activity
Is It Really a Fruit?

Quick Lab
Investigating Flower Parts

Seed and Seedless Plants
Interactive Images

Angiosperms and Gymnosperms
Slideshow

Options for Assessment

See the Evaluate page for options, including Formative Assessment, Summative Assessment, and Unit Review.

Engage and Explore

Activities and Discussion

Activity *What Makes a Plant a Plant?*

 Engage

Characteristics of Plants

 whole class
 10 min
 GUIDED inquiry

Think Fast Pose the following question to get students thinking about characteristics of plants. Encourage students to quickly raise their hands to respond to each question. **Ask:** What do you know about plants? Sample answers: Plants have roots and leaves. Plants do not move. Plants are made of cells. Plants make sugars through photosynthesis. Many plants are green. **Ask:** How are plants different from animals? Sample answers: Plants are rooted in one spot. Plants do not make noise. Plants do not have a nervous system. Animals eat and move, plants make their own food.

Activity *Diagramming a Seed or a Cone*

Classification of Plants

 pairs or small groups
 15 min
 GUIDED inquiry

Give students a seed or pine cone. Invite them to examine it closely and diagram it. Have students identify and label the embryo and protective coating of the seed or cone. Have groups share their results and identify the type of seed they have.

Activity *Is It Really a Fruit?*

Classification of Plants

 individuals, then pairs
 10 min
 GUIDED inquiry

Think, Pair, Share Tell students that a fruit surrounds and protects seeds. Have  individuals list fruits and vegetables they like to eat. Then, have them decide whether each food is a fruit. Next, pairs can share their ideas. Finally, invite pairs to share their lists with the class.

Take It Home *Plants at Home*

 Engage

Classification of Plants

 adult-student pairs
 ongoing
 INDEPENDENT inquiry

Students and adults can work together to identify and classify plants according to their characteristics. Classifications do not need to be scientific categories. For example, pairs might classify them by indoor and outdoor plants, leafy plants, grassy plants, mossy plants, green plants, brown plants, and so on.

Probing Questions *Roots, Stems, and Leaves*

 Engage

Structure and Function in Plants

whole class
10 min
GUIDED inquiry

Invite a volunteer to draw a picture of a plant, showing roots, stem(s), and leaves. Invite another volunteer to label the roots, stem, and leaves. **Ask:** What do roots do? Sample answers: Most roots are underground. They take up water, and carry it to the rest of the plant. **Ask:** What is a leaf like? Sample answers: Leaves are often green. They can dry up and turn brown. In autumn, some change color and drop off a tree or bush. **Ask:** How would you describe a stem? Sample answers: Stems are long and round. They hold up a flower or leaves. Add to these ideas as students progress through the lesson.

Customize Your Labs

See the Lab Manual for lab datasheets.

Go Online for editable lab datasheets.

©Comstock/Getty Images

Levels of **Inquiry**

DIRECTED inquiry
introduces inquiry skills within a structured framework.

GUIDED inquiry
develops inquiry skills within a supportive environment.

INDEPENDENT inquiry
deepens inquiry skills with student-driven questions or procedures.

Labs and Demos

Daily Demo *How Are Flowers Pollinated?*

Engage

Classification of Plants

👥 whole class
🕐 10 min
 DIRECTED inquiry

PURPOSE **To show how flowers reproduce**

MATERIALS

• flowers

• hand lenses

1 Pass out some flowers to groups of students.

2 Explain that flowers are the reproductive structures of vascular plants called angiosperms.

3 Ask students to describe what they see. Point out the stamen, pistil, and ovary. Explain what each part does.

4 **Applying** Explain that pollen produces sperm. Encourage students to suggest ways that the pollen can be carried from plant to plant. Sample answers: Wind, water, or animals can carry pollen.

5 **Comparing** How are the reproductive systems of angiosperms different than most animals? Sample answers: Angiosperms have both male and female reproductive organs. Most animals have either male or female reproductive organs only.

©Corbis

Quick Lab *Investigating Flower Parts*

Classification of Plants

👥 individuals
🕐 30 min
 GUIDED inquiry

Students will observe flowers with a hand lens and draw and label what they see. They will then take apart the flower and make observations of each of its parts and draw and label what they see.

PURPOSE **To observe and identify the different parts of a flower**

MATERIALS

• flowers

• hand lens

• scalpel

Quick Lab *Observing Transport*

Structure and Function in Plants

👥 individuals
🕐 35 min
 GUIDED inquiry

Students will observe vascular transport in a celery stalk placed in a glass of colored water. They will make a connection between the function of the plant's stem and what they observed.

PURPOSE **To identify the function of the stem of a plant**

MATERIALS

• beaker

• blue food coloring

• celery stalk with leaves

• colored pencils

• water

• knife (for teacher)

Activities and Discussion

☐ **Activity** What Makes a Plant a Plant?
☐ **Activity** Diagramming a Seed or Cone
☐ **Activity** Is It Really a Fruit?
☐ **Take It Home** Plants at Home
☐ **Probing Questions** Roots, Stems, and Leaves

Labs and Demos

☐ **Daily Demo** How Are Flowers Pollinated?
☐ **Quick Lab** Investigating Flower Parts
☐ **Quick Lab** Observing Transport

Your Resources

Explain Science Concepts

Key Topics	📖 Print Path	💻 Digital Path
Characteristics of Plants	☐ **Plants Alive,** SE pp. 108–109 • Think Outside the Book, #5 • Active Reading, #6 • Visualize It!, #7 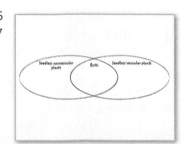	☐ **What Is a Plant?** • Explore the basic characteristics of plants. ☐ **Photosynthesis** • Learn about the process of photosynthesis.
Structure and Function in Plants	☐ **A Wide World of Plants,** SE pp. 110–111 • Explain, #8 • Active Reading (Annotation strategy), #9 • Compare, #10	☐ **Nonvascular Plants** • Explore the structures of nonvascular plants. ☐ **Vascular Plants** • Learn about the structures of vascular plants.
Classification of Plants	☐ **Spore Power to Ya!,** SE pp. 112–113 • Active Reading (Annotation strategy), #11 • Visualize It!, #12 • Venn Diagram, #13 ☐ **Seeds of Success,** SE pp. 114–116 • Active Reading (Annotation strategy), #14 • Identify, #15 • Visualize It!, #16 • Visualize It!, #17	☐ **Seed and Seedless Plants** • Compare and contrast reproduction in seed and seedless plants. ☐ **Angiosperms and Gymnosperms** • Learn about the different varieties of plants. 

Basic *Comparing Leaves*

Structure and Function in Plants

 individuals or pairs

 10 min

Venn Diagram Provide leaves from different environments, such as a desert plant and a deciduous tree, to students. Have students use a hand lens to compare the two leaves. Encourage students to notice the cuticles, stomata, and other similarities and differences between the two leaves. Have students use a Venn diagram to compare the two leaves.

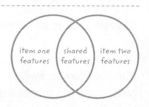

item one features | shared features | item two features

Advanced *Designing an Experiment*

Characteristics of Plants

 individuals

 20 min

Invite students to design an experiment that provides evidence about what happens during photosynthesis. For example, can they show that plants give off oxygen when exposed to carbon dioxide, water, and light? Can they test to see if carbon dioxide is needed for photosynthesis? (Hint: Boiling water removes carbon dioxide.) How does the amount of light, the size of plant, the number of leaves, disease, or the age of plant affect photosynthesis? Have students select one question to answer and then design an experiment to answer the question. Review the experiments to be sure they are safe and feasible. Then, encourage students to perform their experiments.

ELL *Roots, Stems, or Leaves*

Structure and Function in Plants

 pairs

 10 min

Provide students with examples of roots, stems, and leaves. Have students classify each item as a root, stem, or leaf. Provide some items that students may use to discuss, such as broccoli, potatoes, onions, carrots, cauliflower, cabbage, lettuce, parsley, and so on. **Sample answers: broccoli/cauliflower—stem and flower; potato—stem tuber; carrots—roots; lettuce/cabbage—leaves; onions—underground stems**

producers **photosynthesis** **chlorophyll**
vascular system **seed** **pollen**
gymnosperm **angiosperm**

Previewing Vocabulary

 whole class

 10 min

Word Origins and Word Parts
- **chlorophyll** *Chloro-* comes from the Greek word *khloros*, which means "green." *Phyll-* comes from the Greek word *phullon*, which means "leaf." Chlorophyll makes leaves green.
- **gymnosperm** *Gymno-* means "naked" and *-sperm* means "seed." The seeds of a gymnosperm are not enclosed in fruit.
- **angiosperm** Tell students that *angio-* means "a vessel" or "a case." The seeds of an angiosperm are encased in fruit.

Reinforcing Vocabulary

 individuals

 ongoing

Word Squares Have students use Word Squares for some of the terms in the lesson. Students will write each term in one square; a diagram or sketch in another square; a definition in a third square; and a sentence using the term in the last square.

TERM translation	symbol or picture
my meaning dictionary definition	sentence

Customize Your Core Lesson

Core Instruction
☐ **Print Path** choices
☐ **Digital Path** choices

Vocabulary
☐ **Previewing Vocabulary** Word Origins and Word Parts
☐ **Reinforcing Vocabulary** Word Squares

Differentiated Instruction
☐ **Basic** Comparing Leaves
☐ **Advanced** Designing an Experiment
☐ **ELL** Roots, Stems, or Leaves

Your Resources

Extend Science Concepts

Reinforce and Review

Activity *Card Responses*

Synthesizing Key Topics | 👥 individuals
🕐 ongoing

1 Have students make answer cards for questions you will ask about the lesson. Cards can be true/false, yes/no/maybe, A/B/C/D, or whatever fits your questions.

2 Ask a question. At your signal, students hold up their cards. To help students answer individually, be very clear about the signal and have everyone raise their cards at the same time—for example, "Ready, one, two, three, cards up!"

3 Every ten minutes or so during the class, ask a few recall questions about the lesson. Have students answer by holding up a card. If the class's accuracy rate is less than 90 percent, it might be time to reteach another way. This technique also helps you pinpoint those who need individual help.

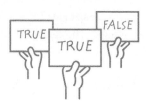

Graphic Organizer

Synthesizing Key Topics | 👥 individuals
🕐 10 min

Cluster Diagram Have students make a cluster diagram that shows how plants are classified. For example, in the top circle, have students write *Plants*. Below this, they can draw two circles to show that plants are classified as *Vascular* or *Nonvascular*. Additional circles can show how each is further categorized into *Seed Plants* and *Seedless Plants*.

🎧 *Optional Online resource: Cluster Diagram support*

Going Further

Fine Arts Connection

Classification of Plants | 👥 individuals
🕐 20 min

Make a Flower Invite interested students to use paper and other materials to make a flower model. Encourage students to include the sepals, petals, stamen, pistil, seed, ovary, or fruit. Have students include labels or a key to identify the flower's parts.

Real World Connection

Structure and Function in Plants | 👥 individuals
🕐 ongoing

Growing Plants Encourage interested students to plant seeds in soil from the school yard and organic soil from a store. In which soil do the seeds grow better? Ask students to think about what other variables could be influencing the seed growth? Encourage students to find out how these two types of soil are different. Based on the differences, why do they think the seeds grew differently?

Customize Your Closing

📖 *See the Assessment Guide for quizzes and tests.*

🎧 *Go Online to edit and create quizzes and tests.*

Reinforce and Review

☐ **Activity** Card Responses

☐ **Graphic Organizer** Cluster Diagram

☐ **Print Path** Visual Summary, SE p. 118

☐ **Print Path** Lesson Review, SE p. 119

☐ **Digital Path** Lesson Closer

Evaluate Student Mastery

See the teacher support below the Student Pages for additional Formative Assessment questions.

Ask the following questions to assess student mastery of the material. **Ask:** What are some common characteristics of all plants? Sample answer: They are multicellular producers, their life cycles have two stages, they use photosynthesis to make glucose, and they have chlorophyll. **Ask:** What are the three main plant organs? roots, stems, leaves **Ask:** What is a nonvascular plant? a plant that depends on diffusion to move water and nutrients through the plant **Ask:** How are seed plants classified? by whether or not their seeds are enclosed by fruit **Ask:** What are some major plant groups? mosses, liverworts and hornworts, ferns, club mosses, seed plants, flowering plants

Reteach

Formative assessment may show that students need reinforcement for certain topics. The resources below are recommended for reteaching. If students were introduced to a topic through the Print Path, you can also use the Digital Path to reteach, and vice versa.
🎧 *Can be assigned to individual students*

Characteristics of Plants

Activity What Makes a Plant a Plant?

Structure and Function in Plants

Basic Comparing Leaves 🎧

ELL Roots, Stems, or Leaves

Classifications of Plants

Graphic Organizer Cluster Diagram 🎧

Daily Demo How Are Flowers Pollinated?

Summative Assessment

Alternative Assessment
Plants, Plants, and More Plants!

🎮 *Online resources: student worksheet; optional rubrics*

Introduction to Plants

Climb the Ladder: *Plants, Plants, and More Plants!*
Complete the following to show what you have learned about plants.

1. Work on your own, with a partner, or with a small group.
2. Choose one item from each rung of the ladder. Check your choices.
3. Have your teacher approve your plan.
4. Submit or present your results.

__ **Make a Field Guide**	__ **Plant Reproduction**
Make a field guide that identifies the major groups of plants. Draw a picture of each type of plant, and explain how you would identify this type of plant in the field.	Write and put on a play or skit that explains how seed plants and seedless plants reproduce. Assign roles, such as seedless plant, gymnosperm, and angiosperm. Perform your skit for the class.
__ **Singing About Plants**	__ **Making Models**
Write a song or poem that compares the features of vascular and nonvascular plants.	Make models of a vascular and a nonvascular plant. Label the features that make the plants vascular or nonvascular.
__ **Characteristics of Plants**	__ **Plants Made Simple**
Make a poster or multimedia display that describes the characteristics of plants.	Write a science chapter for a third grader about the characteristics of plants. Make the chapter fun to read!

Going Further

- ☐ **Fine Arts Connection**
- ☐ **Real World Connection**
- ☐ **Print Path** Why It Matters, SE p. 117

Formative Assessment

- ☐ **Strategies** Throughout TE
- ☐ **Lesson Review** SE

Summative Assessment

- ☐ **Alternative Assessment** Plants, Plants, and More Plants!
- ☐ **Lesson Quiz**
- ☐ **Unit Tests A and B**
- ☐ **Unit Review** SE End-of-Unit

Your Resources

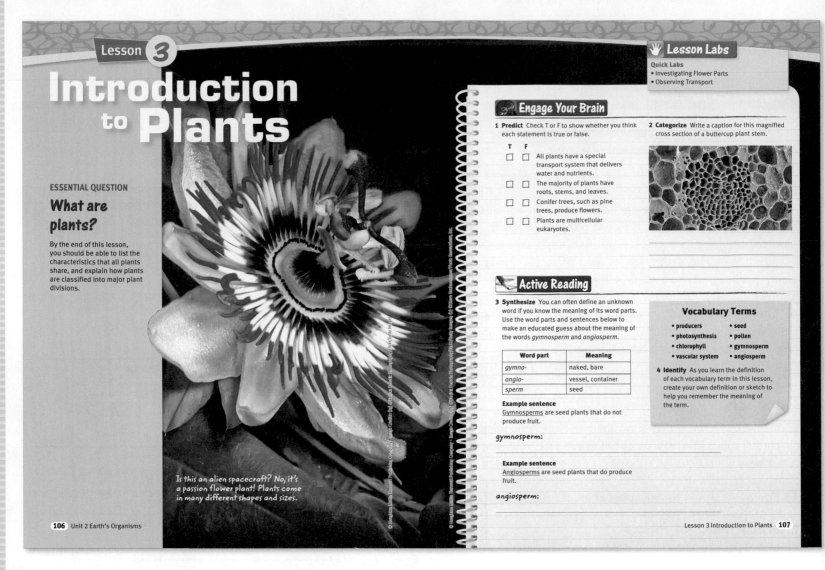

Answers

Answers for 1–3 should represent students' current thoughts, even if incorrect.

1. F; T; F; T

2. Sample answer: Water flows through the open spaces in this plant stem.

3. gymnosperm: naked seed

   angiosperm: seed in a vessel or container

Opening Your Lesson

Discuss student answers to the true-or-false questions to assess their prior knowledge about the key topics.

Accessing Prior Knowledge Read aloud the title of the lesson. Invite students to discuss what they know about plants in general, and how the plant in the image is unusual. Invite them to explain how the plant shows characteristics that all plants share.

Prerequisites Students should already have some understanding of what living things are, how living things are classified, and the history of life on Earth.

Learning Alert

Difficult Concepts Students may think that plants take in through their roots all the substances they need to grow. To help them understand that plants need more than this, ask students what plant roots do. Answer: Plant roots take in water and minerals. **Ask:** Are water and minerals all that plants need to survive? Invite volunteers to explain that during photosynthesis, plants make their own food by capturing energy from the sun and using it to produce sugar (glucose) from carbon dioxide and water.

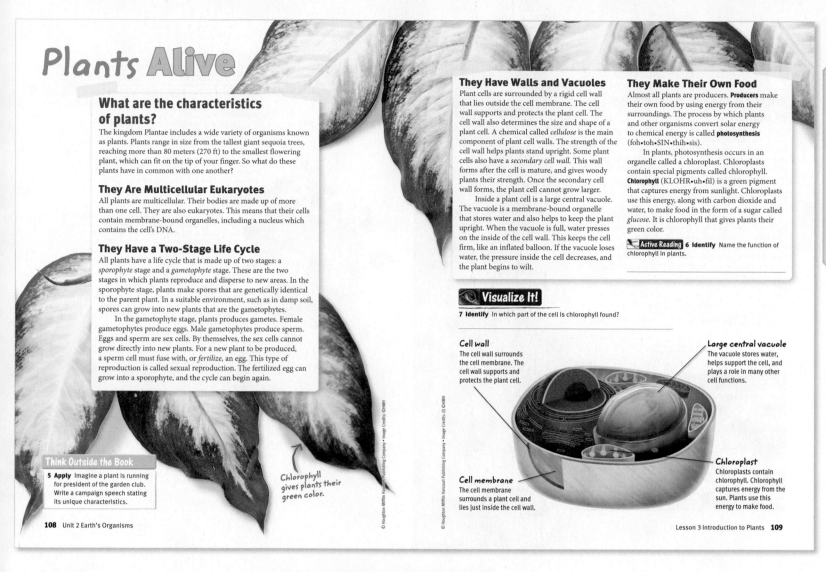

Plants Alive

What are the characteristics of plants?

The kingdom Plantae includes a wide variety of organisms known as plants. Plants range in size from the tallest giant sequoia trees, reaching more than 80 meters (270 ft) to the smallest flowering plant, which can fit on the tip of your finger. So what do these plants have in common with one another?

They Are Multicellular Eukaryotes

All plants are multicellular. Their bodies are made up of more than one cell. They are also eukaryotes. This means that their cells contain membrane-bound organelles, including a nucleus which contains the cell's DNA.

They Have a Two-Stage Life Cycle

All plants have a life cycle that is made up of two stages: a *sporophyte* stage and a *gametophyte* stage. These are the two stages in which plants reproduce and disperse to new areas. In the sporophyte stage, plants make spores that are genetically identical to the parent plant. In a suitable environment, such as in damp soil, spores can grow into new plants that are the gametophytes.

In the gametophyte stage, plants produces gametes. Female gametophytes produce eggs. Male gametophytes produce sperm. Eggs and sperm are sex cells. By themselves, the sex cells cannot grow directly into new plants. For a new plant to be produced, a sperm cell must fuse with, or *fertilize*, an egg. This type of reproduction is called sexual reproduction. The fertilized egg can grow into a sporophyte, and the cycle can begin again.

Think Outside the Book

5 Apply Imagine a plant is running for president of the garden club. Write a campaign speech stating its unique characteristics.

Chlorophyll gives plants their green color.

108 Unit 2 Earth's Organisms

They Have Walls and Vacuoles

Plant cells are surrounded by a rigid cell wall that lies outside the cell membrane. The cell wall supports and protects the plant cell. The cell wall also determines the size and shape of a plant cell. A chemical called *cellulose* is the main component of plant cell walls. The strength of the cell wall helps plants stand upright. Some plant cells also have a *secondary cell wall*. This wall forms after the cell is mature, and gives woody plants their strength. Once the secondary cell wall forms, the plant cell cannot grow larger.

Inside a plant cell is a large central vacuole. The vacuole is a membrane-bound organelle that stores water and also helps to keep the plant upright. When the vacuole is full, water presses on the inside of the cell wall. This keeps the cell firm, like an inflated balloon. If the vacuole loses water, the pressure inside the cell decreases, and the plant begins to wilt.

They Make Their Own Food

Almost all plants are producers. **Producers** make their own food by using energy from their surroundings. The process by which plants and other organisms convert solar energy to chemical energy is called **photosynthesis** (foh•toh•SIN•thih•sis).

In plants, photosynthesis occurs in an organelle called a chloroplast. Chloroplasts contain special pigments called chlorophyll. **Chlorophyll** (KLOHR•uh•fil) is a green pigment that captures energy from sunlight. Chloroplasts use this energy, along with carbon dioxide and water, to make food in the form of a sugar called *glucose*. It is chlorophyll that gives plants their green color.

Active Reading 6 Identify Name the function of chlorophyll in plants.

Visualize It!

7 Identify In which part of the cell is chlorophyll found?

Cell wall
The cell wall surrounds the cell membrane. The cell wall supports and protects the plant cell.

Large central vacuole
The vacuole stores water, helps support the cell, and plays a role in many other cell functions.

Cell membrane
The cell membrane surrounds a plant cell and lies just inside the cell wall.

Chloroplast
Chloroplasts contain chlorophyll. Chlorophyll captures energy from the sun. Plants use this energy to make food.

Lesson 3 Introduction to Plants 109

Answers

5. Students' speeches will vary, but should include the key characteristics of plants.

6. Chlorophyll captures energy from sunlight.

7. chloroplasts

Interpreting Visuals

Invite students to examine the image of the cell. **Ask:** Why is chlorophyll so important to plants? Sample answer: Chlorophyll captures energy from the sun. Plants use this energy to make their food. Without chlorophyll, plants could not survive. **Ask:** How are a cell wall and a cell membrane different? Sample answer: The cell wall is rigid and is outside the cell membrane. The cell wall supports and protects the cell, including the membrane.

Building Reading Skills

Process Notes Help students use a Process Notes chart to describe the life cycle of a plant. **Ask:** What happens first in the life cycle of a plant? Sample answer: First, plants have a sporophyte stage in which they make spores. **Ask:** What happens next? Sample answer: The spores grow to become gametophytes, which produce eggs or sperm. **Ask:** What happens next? Sample answer: If a sperm fertilizes an egg, and the fertilized egg grows into a sporophyte, then the cycle begins again.

🌐 *Optional Online resource: Process Notes support*

A Wide World of Plants

What are the two main groups of plants?

Plants can be grouped into two broad categories: nonvascular plants and vascular plants. A plant that has a vascular system is called a vascular plant. A **vascular system** is a system of tube-like tissues that transports water, nutrients, and other materials from one part of an organism to another part. Nonvascular plants do not have a vascular system.

Nonvascular Plants

Have you ever walked through a cool forest with a moist green carpet on the ground? Chances are, the green "carpet" was made up of tiny plants called moss. Mosses, and their relatives such as liverworts and hornworts, are nonvascular plants. Nonvascular plants do not have vascular systems to transport water and nutrients throughout their bodies. Instead, water must move from the environment and throughout the plant by a process called *diffusion*. If nonvascular plants were large, the cells of the plants that are far from the ground would not get enough water. Likewise, cells that are far from the leaves would not get enough nutrients. For this reason, nonvascular plants are all fairly small.

Active Reading **8 Explain** Why are nonvascular plants so small?

This liverwort is a type of nonvascular plant. The liverwort stalks are about 1 cm tall.

110 Unit 2 Earth's Organisms

This giant sequoia transports water and nutrients through a vascular system. The materials move between the roots and the leaves, nearly 72 m (200 ft) above ground.

Active Reading

9 List As you read, underline the importance of a plant's vascular system.

Vascular Plants

Vascular plants have a vascular system that transports water and nutrients throughout the plant's body. The vascular system allows these plants to grow large and still move water and materials effectively. As a result, many vascular plants are very tall. Some, such as the giant redwoods of California, reach heights of over 91 meters (300 ft)!

The body of a vascular plant is divided into two systems: the root system and the shoot system. The root system is made up of roots and other underground structures. The above ground structures, such as stems, leaves and flowers, make up the shoot system. Roots, stems, and leaves are the three major kinds of organs in vascular plants. Water and materials are transported between the roots and the shoots through vascular tissue.

Leaves
Most leaves grow above ground. They make food for the plant by photosynthesis. The outer surfaces of a leaf are covered by a waxy cuticle that prevents water loss. Tiny openings in leaves, called *stomata*, allow for gas exchange.

Stem
Stems are usually above ground. They provide support, and they transport water and minerals from the roots up to the leaves. Stems also transport the glucose that is made in the leaves to other parts of the plant. Some stems store materials, such as water.

Roots
Most roots are underground. They supply plants with water and minerals from the soil. Roots also anchor plants in the soil and can store extra food made through photosynthesis.

10 Compare In the table below, compare the functions of the three parts of the plant.

Roots	Stems	Leaves

Lesson 3 Introduction to Plants 111

Answers

8. Nonvascular plants do not have specialized tissue to move materials; diffusion allows the plants to absorb water from the ground.

9. *See students' pages for annotations.*

10. Roots: supply plant with water and minerals; anchor plant in ground

   Stems: provide support; transport water; minerals; and sugars

   Leaves: where food is made; help prevent water loss

Probing Questions GUIDED Inquiry

To help students understand the characteristics of nonvascular plants, ask the following questions. **Ask:** Why can't nonvascular plants be large? Sample answer: They would not be able to transport enough water or nutrients to the parts of the plant that are far away from the source, since these plants depend on diffusion to move materials throughout the plant. **Ask:** Why do mosses need to live in wet places? Sample answer: They depend on water for reproduction.

Using Annotations

As students complete the annotation activity, encourage them to find and underline two statements telling the importance of a plant's vascular system. Extend the activity by having students write a two- or three-sentence comparison of the function of a vascular system in plants and the function of one of the systems, such as the circulatory or digestive sytem, in their own bodies.

Formative Assessment

Ask: Why can vascular plants grow tall? Sample answer: They have a vascular system to transport water and nutrients throughout the plant. **Ask:** What are the three groups of vascular plants? Sample answer: seedless vascular plants, gymnosperms, angiosperms

Spore Power to Ya!

How are seedless nonvascular plants classified?

When you think of growing a plant, you probably imagine planting a seed. But not all plants make seeds. In fact, all nonvascular plants and some vascular plants are seedless. These plants, like all plants, spread by producing spores.

Mosses

Active Reading

11 Identify As you read, underline the structure in nonvascular plants that is like a root.

Mosses grow on moist soil or on rocks, forming a fuzzy mat of tiny green plants. Mosses have leafy stalks and rhizoids (RY•zoydz). A *rhizoid* is a nonvascular rootlike structure that helps mosses attach to surfaces such as rocks and trees. Rhizoids help the plants get water and nutrients. Mosses can grow even in harsh environments. They have been found above the tree line on mountains and can survive even the freezing temperatures of Antarctica!

Liverworts and Hornworts

Mosses and other nonvascular seedless plants dominated the land for many millions of years.

Like mosses, liverworts and hornworts are small nonvascular plants that usually live in damp environments. Liverworts can be leafy and mosslike or broad and flattened. Hornworts also have broad, flattened leaflike structures. Both liverworts and hornworts have rhizoids to hold them in place.

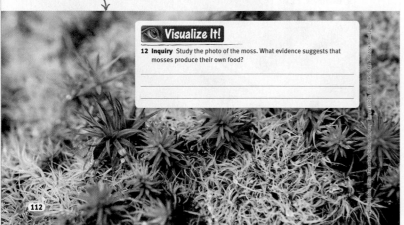

Visualize It!

12 Inquiry Study the photo of the moss. What evidence suggests that mosses produce their own food?

112

How are seedless vascular plants classified?

Seedless vascular plants include ferns, horsetails, and club mosses. These plants all have vascular tissue, and generally have roots, stems, and leaves. Like seedless nonvascular plants, seedless vascular plants reproduce using spores.

Ferns and Whisk Ferns

Ferns are seedless vascular plants often grown as house plants. Ferns have roots, and most ferns also have rhizomes that help them spread. A *rhizome* (RY•zohm) is an underground stem from which new leaves and roots grow. Ferns have leaves, called *fronds*, that uncurl as they grow. Whisk ferns are related to ferns, but look very different. They have rhizoids instead of roots, and small growths that look like buttons instead of leaves.

Horsetails

Horsetails have cane-like stems with leaves that grow in a unique whorl pattern around the stems. Horsetails can be up to eight meters tall, but many are smaller. They usually grow in wet, marshy places. Their stems are hollow and contain silica. The silica gives horsetails a gritty, rough texture. In fact, early American pioneers used horsetails to scrub pots and pans.

Club Mosses

Club mosses look similar to true mosses. But unlike true mosses, club mosses have vascular tissue, roots, stems, and tiny leaves. Prehistoric club mosses were tall trees. Some even grew up to 40 m tall! Today's club mosses are small. An example of a modern club moss is the ground pine. Like the name suggests, the ground pine looks like a miniature pine tree. Club mosses grow in woodlands and near streams and marshes.

Ferns are easily recognized by their leaves, or fronds.

On the underside of a fern frond are clusters of spore-producing containers called sori.

13 Compare In the graphic organizer below, compare seedless nonvascular plants to seedless vascular plants. How are they similar and different?

Seedless nonvascular plants — Both — Seedless vascular plants

Lesson 3 Introduction to Plants 113

Answers

11. *See students' pages for annotations.*

12. Sample answer: Their green color shows that they contain chlorophyll.

13. Seedless nonvascular plants: do not have vascular tissues, tend to be small, transport water and materials by diffusion; Both: multicellular eukaryotes, two-stage life cycle, cell walls, photosynthesis, reproduce with spores to make new plants; Seedless vascular plants: have vascular tissue, bodies made up of root and shoot system, have roots, stems, and leaves, grow tall

Building Reading Skills

Outline Have students make an Outline to organize the information on these pages. Tell students to organize the outline using the headings on the page as headings in their outlines. Then, have students add details under each of the headings.

⊙ *Optional Online resource: Outline support*

Probing Questions **GUIDED Inquiry**

Synthesizing Have students look at the Venn diagram. **Ask:** How are seedless vascular plants and seedless nonvascular plants alike? Sample answer: They require water to allow sperm to swim to an egg, and they use spores to spread. **Ask:** How are mosses similar to liverworts and hornworts? Sample answers: They are nonvascular and they have rhizoids to hold them in place. **Ask:** How are ferns, horsetails, and club mosses alike? Sample answers: They are seedless vascular plants. They all have roots and shoots. **Ask:** Are club mosses really mosses? Explain. Sample answers: No, because mosses are nonvascular, and club mosses are vascular plants.

Seeds of Success

How are seed plants classified?

Seed plants are vascular plants that reproduce by making seeds. A **seed** is a plant embryo enclosed in a protective coating. Seed plants also produce **pollen**, a tiny structure in which sperm forms. A sperm cell from pollen fertilizes an egg cell, which develops into an embryo inside a seed. Seed plants are classified based on whether or not their seeds are enclosed in a fruit.

Active Reading

14 Identify As you read, underline the characteristics of gymnosperms.

Gymnosperms

Gymnosperms (JIM•nuh•spermz) are plants that produce seeds that are not enclosed in a fruit. This group includes cycads (SY•kadz), ginkgoes (GING•kohz), and conifers. Cycads produce seeds in large, woody structures called *cones* that grow at the center of a thick trunk. Ginkgoes produce round, grape-like seeds that are not covered by a cone. Ginkgo seeds smell like rotting butter. The word *conifer* comes from two words that mean "cone-bearing." Conifers, such as pine trees, also produce cones. The wood of conifer trees is used for building and for paper products. Pine trees also produce a sticky fluid called resin used to make soap, paint, and ink.

Cycads are gymnosperms found in the tropics that have short stems and palm-like leaves. Cycads produce seeds on large, protective cones. Only about 140 species of cycads still exist.

Ginkgoes are gymnosperms that are pollution tolerant and are used in traditional medicine. Only the *Ginkgo biloba* is still alive today. Its leaves are fan-shaped, and its seeds are round and not covered by a cone.

Conifers are the most common type of gymnosperm. This group includes pine trees, cedars, redwoods, and junipers. They produce seeds in cones and have needle-like leaves. Many are green all year.

15 Identify Which type of gymnosperm does not reproduce with cones?

114 Unit 2 Earth's Organisms

Angiosperms

Angiosperms (AN•jee•uh•spermz) are vascular plants that produce flowers, and fruits which surround and protect seeds. Angiosperms are the most abundant type of plant alive today. At least 260,000 living species of angiosperms are known, and new species are still being discovered. They can be found in almost every ecosystem.

Flowers are the reproductive structures of angiosperms. Flowers are typically made up of sepals, petals, stamens, and a pistil. Sepals are modified leaves that cover and protect the flower while it is budding. Flower petals are often colorful and fragrant. A stamen is the male reproductive structure in a flower. It is made up of an anther, which is attached to a filament. Pollen is made in the anther. A pistil is the female reproductive structure in a flower. The seed develops within the ovary at the base of the pistil. As the seed develops, the ovary matures into a fruit which covers the seed.

Visualize It!

16 Label Fill in the structure of each of the flower parts described below.

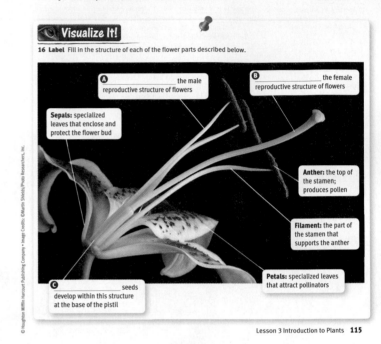

A _____ the male reproductive structure of flowers

B _____ the female reproductive structure of flowers

Sepals: specialized leaves that enclose and protect the flower bud

Anther: the top of the stamen; produces pollen

Filament: the part of the stamen that supports the anther

Petals: specialized leaves that attract pollinators

C _____ seeds develop within this structure at the base of the pistil

Lesson 3 Introduction to Plants 115

Answers

14. *See students' pages for annotations.*

15. ginkgoes

16. A: stamen; B: pistil; C: ovary

Formative Assessment

Ask: Do flowering plants have fruit? Sample answer: Yes. **Ask:** What is another name for a flowering plant? Sample answer: an angiosperm **Ask:** Do nonflowering plants have fruit? Sample answer: No, nonflowering plants have no fruit. **Ask:** What is another name for a nonflowering plant? Sample answer: a gymnosperm

Interpreting Visuals

Invite students to look at the image that shows a close-up look at a flower. **Ask:** What is the purpose of the stamen and pistil? Sample answer: Reproduction; these are the male and female reproductive structures of a flower. **Ask:** What does the anther do? Sample answer: It produces pollen. **Ask:** Why is pollen important? Sample answers: It contains the sperm. **Ask:** How does pollen travel from one flower to another? Sample answer: It is carried by wind, animals, or water.

Visualize It!

17 Compare Compare vascular and nonvascular plants, seedless and seed vascular plants, and nonflowering and flowering plants.

Nonvascular plants — Moss

Vascular plants — Potato plant

A Summarize the similarities and differences.

_____

_____

Seedless vascular plants — Horsetail

Seed vascular plants — Pea plant

B Summarize the similarities and differences.

_____

_____

Gymnosperms (nonflowering plants) — Conifer

Angiosperms (flowering plants) — Hibiscus

C Summarize the similarities and differences.

_____

_____

116 Unit 2 Earth's Organisms

Why It Matters

Pharmaceuticals and Plants

Throughout history, plants have played an important role in medicine. Many modern medicines are derived from chemicals found in plants. Tropical rain forests are a source of many potential medicinal plants. For example, the cat's claw shown here is a woody vine found in the Amazon rain forest. It is used by local tribes to treat arthritis and some viral infections. Research is under way to find out if cat's claw might be useful for treating a variety of diseases. Scientists have discovered many useful compounds in rain-forest plants, and are likely to discover many more.

Cat's claw

White Willow Tree
The white willow tree is native to Europe and Asia. The medicinal value of white willow bark goes back to ancient Egyptians, who used white willow to treat inflammation. A compound in white willow, salicin, led to the development of aspirin.

Foxglove
Foxglove is a flowering plant commonly grown in gardens. This plant produces uncommon compounds that are used to make medicine for the heart.

Extend   **Inquiry**

18 Summarize How are the compounds derived from the foxglove plant and the white willow tree used in medicine?

19 Research Find out how another plant is used in modern medicine.

20 Propose How can we protect medicinal plants in rain forests?

117

Answers

17. **A:** Nonvascular plants are smaller and don't have true roots, stems, or leaves. Both are multicellular eukaryotes and have cell walls and chloroplasts. **B:** Seedless plants need water so sperm can swim and fertilize eggs. Seed plants produce pollen. Both have two-stage life cycles. **C:** Gymnosperms don't have flowers or fruits. Both are vascular plants and reproduce by making seeds.

18. Foxglove is used in heart medicine; the white willow tree is used in aspirin.

19. Research should show an understanding of plants used for medicinal purposes.

20. Sample answer: Protect indigenous people with knowledge of plants; create incentives for protecting these plants.

Formative Assessment

Ask: What are three possible classification groups for a plant that does not have flowers? nonvascular, seedless vascular, gymnosperm (nonflowering vascular seed plant) **Ask:** How are vascular seedless plants different from vascular seed plants? Sample answer: Seedless plants depend on water to allow their sperm to fertilize eggs. Seed plants produce pollen. Seedless plants spread by spores. Seed plants spread by seeds. **Ask:** How many possible categories could a plant that produces naked seeds inside cones belong to? one (gymnosperm)

Why It Matters

Invite students to look at the photos and read the descriptions on this page. **Ask:** Why are the plants on this page important? Sample answer: They have medicinal uses. **Ask:** Why are white willows important? Sample answer: The bark contains salicin, which treats inflammation and is found in aspirin. **Ask:** Why are foxglove plants important? Sample answer: They can be used to make heart medicines. **Ask:** Why are cat's claw vines important? Sample answer: They may be useful for treating a variety of diseases.

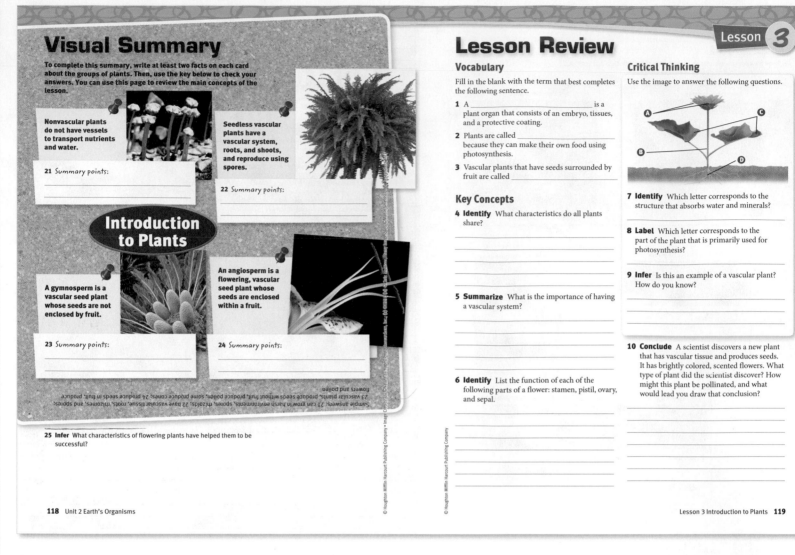

Visual Summary Answers

Sample answers:

21. can grow in harsh environments; spores; rhizoids

22. have vascular tissue; roots; rhizomes; spores

23. vascular plants; produce seeds without fruit; produce pollen; some produce cones

24. produce seeds in fruit; produce flowers and pollen

25. They have their own vascular system for transporting water and nutrients, they do not need water to reproduce, and they have protected seeds.

Lesson Review Answers

1. seed

2. producers

3. angiosperms

4. multicellular eukaryotes; two-stage life cycle; cell wall; large vacuoles; make their own food

5. A vascular system allows materials to be transported efficiently through the plant so it can grow tall and reach sunlight for photosynthesis.

6. stamen: the male reproductive structure of flowers; pistil: the female reproductive structure of flowers; ovary: structure at the base of the pistil in which seeds develop; sepal: specialized leaves that enclose and protect the flower bud

7. D

8. C

9. Possible answers: Yes, it is a flowering plant, or angiosperm; all angiosperms contain vascular tissues; roots, stems, and leaves are vascular tissues in plants.

10. Sample answer: The plant is an angiosperm because it has flowers. It is most likely pollinated by animals, because the flowers would attract birds and insects.

Plant Processes

Essential Question How do plants stay alive?

 Professional Development

For more detailed information about the topics in this lesson, refer to the Content Refresher in the Unit Opener pages.

Opening Your Lesson

Begin the lesson by assessing students' prerequisite and prior knowledge.

Prerequisite Knowledge

- An understanding of plant structures
- Some knowledge about photosynthesis, chlorophyll, seeds, and pollen

Accessing Prior Knowledge

Ask: How does a house plant change if it doesn't get the water it needs? Sample answer: It wilts.

Ask: What happens to a houseplant that faces a sunny window? Sample answer: It grows toward the window.

Explain to students that these are just some of the ways that plants respond to their environment. Tell students that they will learn more about plant responses and other plant processes in this lesson.

Customize Your Opening

- ☐ **Accessing Prior Knowledge,** above
- ☐ **Print Path** Engage Your Brain, SE p. 121
- ☐ **Print Path** Active Reading, SE p. 121
- ☐ **Digital Path** Lesson Opener

Key Topics/Learning Goals

Plants and Energy

1. Describe photosynthesis.
2. Describe the role of chloroplasts and chlorophyll.
3. Explain how plants get chemical energy from glucose through cellular respiration.

Plant Reproduction

1. Describe the phases of plant life cycles.
2. Compare sexual reproduction in seedless and seed plants.
3. Identify the roles of the parts of a flower in reproduction.

Plant Responses

1. Identify the types of stimuli that plants respond to.
2. Relate transpiration to a plant's ability to maintain an internal balance of water.
3. Describe two types of plant tropisms.
4. Describe the triggers and the benefits of winter dormancy for some plants.

Supporting Concepts

- During photosynthesis, plants use the energy in sunlight to make glucose, which stores energy in its chemical bonds.
- Photosynthesis takes place in chloroplasts, which contain chlorophyll, a green pigment.
- Plants release the energy in the bonds of glucose through cellular respiration. Cellular respiration also produces carbon dioxide and water.

- Plant life cycles include two phases: the sporophyte and the gametophyte.
- Seedless plants require standing water for sperm to swim to eggs during reproduction.
- Seed plants produce pollen, which is passed from male to female reproductive structures.
- In flowering plants, reproduction involves the stamen, pistil, and seeds.

- Plants respond to internal and external stimuli.
- During transpiration, water vapor is released into the air through stomata. Stomata can be opened or closed to conserve water.
- A tropism is a change in the direction of plant growth in response to a stimulus. Hormones control tropisms.
- Phototropism is a change in plant growth in response to light. Gravitropism is growth in response to gravity.
- Dormancy is a slowing of plant growth triggered by shorter days and longer nights. This helps plants survive winter.

Options for Instruction

Two parallel paths provide coverage of the Essential Questions, with a strong **Inquiry** strand woven into each. Follow the **Print Path,** the **Digital Path,** or your customized combination of print, digital, and inquiry.

 Print Path
Teaching support for the Print Path appears with the Student Pages.

 Inquiry Labs and Activities

 **Digital Path**
Digital Path Shortcut: TS663364

Fueled By the Sun,
SE pp. 122–123
How do plants obtain and use energy?

Virtual Lab
What Affects Photosynthesis Rate?
Quick Lab
Investigating Plant Pigments
Activity
Photosynthesis and Cellular Respiration

Photosynthesis
Video

Cellular Respiration
Interactive Graphics

A Plant's Life, SE pp. 124–127
What are the phases of a plant's life cycle?
How do seedless plants reproduce?
How do seed plants reproduce?
How do flowering plants reproduce?
How do plants reproduce asexually?

Exploration Lab
Fertilization in Angiosperms

Life Cycle
Interactive Graphics

Plant Reproduction
Interactive Images

Asexual Reproduction
Slideshow

Action, Reaction,
SE pp. 128–130
What are some ways plants respond to their environment?

Quick Lab
Observing Stomata

Activity
Fast Reaction!

Activity
Plant Processes

Daily Demo
Where Does the Water Come From?

Plant Responses
Interactive Graphics

Options for Assessment

See the Evaluate page for options, including Formative Assessment, Summative Assessment, and Unit Review.

Engage and Explore

Activities and Discussion

Activity *Photosynthesis and Cellular Respiration*

Engage

Plants and Energy

 whole class
 10 min
 GUIDED inquiry

Prepare index cards with questions about photosynthesis and cellular respiration. (Sample questions are listed below.) Prepare a unique card for each student. Distribute the cards, and have students write an answer to their question on the back of the card. As students progress through the lesson, have them add additional insights to the card. You may want to have students use the card for review after they complete the lesson.

Sample questions:

- What are the products of cellular respiration?
- What are the products of photosynthesis?
- What are the starting materials of cellular respiration?
- What are the starting materials of photosynthesis?
- What form of energy is an input during photosynthesis?
- What form of energy is light energy converted to during photosynthesis?
- What plant process gives off oxygen?
- In what organelle does photosynthesis occur?
- In what organelle does cellular respiration occur?
- What green pigment in plants absorbs light energy?

Activity *Fast Reaction!*

Plant Responses

 whole class
 10 min
 GUIDED inquiry

Think Fast Pose the following questions to help students explore the concept of plant reactions to their environments. After posing each question, call on a variety of students to share their responses. **Ask:** What happens if a plant loses too much water? Sample answer: The plant droops, and the stomata close to prevent more water from being lost. **Ask:** What happens if a plants doesn't get enough light? Sample answer: The plant goes dormant or dies.

Labs and Demos

Daily Demo *Where Does the Water Come From?*

Engage

Plant Responses

 whole class
 10 min
 Directed inquiry

PURPOSE **To introduce the process of transpiration**

MATERIALS

- recently watered plant
- sunny windowsill or bright desk lamp
- plastic sandwich bag with zipper closure

1 Set the plant on the windowsill or under the bright light.

2 Seal the sandwich bag very tightly around the base of one leaf so that an entire leaf is enclosed in the bag.

3 Allow the plant to sit for about five minutes, or until water droplets appear in the bag.

4 **Observing** What do you observe? Sample answer: Water in the bag.

5 **Analyzing** Why does this happen? Sample answer: The plant is giving off water; water is evaporating.

6 **Predicting** If this plant had not been watered recently, how do you think our results would be different? Sample answer: There might be little or no water in the bag.

Explain that students will learn about why this happens in greater detail in the lesson. Use their responses to reinforce the idea that plants respond to stimuli.

⊘ ▣ Quick Lab *Observing Stomata*

PURPOSE **To observe stomata and guard cells in a leaf**

See the Lab Manual or go Online for planning information.

Levels of **Inquiry**

DIRECTED inquiry
introduces inquiry skills within a structured framework.

GUIDED inquiry
develops inquiry skills within a supportive environment.

INDEPENDENT inquiry
deepens inquiry skills with student-driven questions or procedures.

Quick Lab *Investigating Plant Pigments*

Plants and Energy

👥 pairs
🕐 45 min
Inquiry **DIRECTED** inquiry

Students will analyze the colors found in plant leaves.

PURPOSE To observe how pigments separate based on molecular size and to demonstrate that plants contain several pigments

MATERIALS

- 2 beakers, 250 mL
- filter paper strip, 12 cm x 3 cm
- gloves
- hair dryer, optional
- isopropyl alcohol
- mortar and pestle
- Pasteur pipette
- 5 spinach leaves
- metric ruler
- transparent tape
- stirring rod

Exploration Lab *Fertilization in Angiosperms*

Plant Reproduction

👥 pairs
🕐 45 min
Inquiry **DIRECTED/GUIDED** inquiry

Students will obtain pollen from a flower's anthers and observe the pollen under a microscope.

PURPOSE To germinate pollen grains and draw conclusions about how pollen grains fertilize an egg

MATERIALS

- colored pencils
- cover slips
- cup
- eyedropper
- microscope
- microscope slides
- paper
- petri dish with cover
- pollen from a flowering plant
- stirring rod
- sugar, 3.5 g
- water

Virtual Lab *What Affects Photosynthesis Rate?*

Plants and Energy

👥 flexible
🕐 45 min
Inquiry **GUIDED** inquiry

Students will use a model to explore how carbon dioxide levels, light, and temperature affect the photosynthesis rate.

PURPOSE To analyze factors that affect photosynthesis

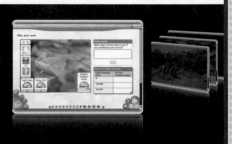

Customize Your Labs

📖 *See the Lab Manual for lab datasheets.*

🌐 *Go Online for editable lab datasheets.*

Activities and Discussion

☐ **Activity** Photosynthesis and Cellular Respiration

☐ **Activity** Fast Reaction!

Labs and Demos

☐ **Daily Demo** Where Does the Water Come From?

☐ **Quick Lab** Investigating Plant Pigments

☐ **Quick Lab** Observing Stomata

☐ **Exploration Lab** Fertilization in Angiosperms

☐ **Virtual Lab** What Affects Photosynthesis Rate?

Your Resources

Explain Science Concepts

Key Topics	📖 Print Path	🖥 Digital Path
Plants and Energy	☐ **Fueled By the Sun,** SE pp. 122–123 • Visualize It!, #5 • Relate, #6 	☐ **Photosynthesis** Learn about the process of photosynthesis. ☐ **Cellular Respiration** Explore the process of cellular respiration. 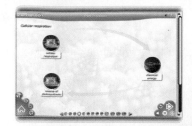
Plant Reproduction	☐ **A Plant's Life,** SE pp. 124–127 • Visualize It!, #7 • Venn Diagram, #8 • Visualize It!, #9 • Visualize It!, #10 • Think Outside the Book, #11 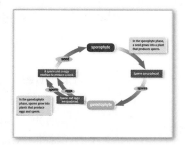	☐ **Life Cycle** Study the two-part life cycle of plants. ☐ **Plant Reproduction** Explore how seed, seedless, and flowering plants reproduce. ☐ **Asexual Reproduction** Learn how most plants also reproduce asexually.
Plant Responses	☐ **Action, Reaction,** SE pp. 128–130 • Infer, #12 • Active Reading (Annotation strategy), #13 • Visualize It!, #14 • Inquiry, #15 • Summarize, #16 • Think Outside the Book, #17 <table><tr><td>Stimulus</td><td>Response</td></tr><tr><td></td><td>closing stomata to preserve water</td></tr><tr><td></td><td>growth of roots downward</td></tr><tr><td>direction of light</td><td></td></tr></table>	☐ **Plant Responses** Identify ways that plants respond to their environment. 

Basic *Modeling Photosynthesis and Cellular Respiration*

Plants and Energy   small groups   10 min

Prepare index cards for each member of the group. Each member should have a set of cards with the following terms and symbols listed one per card:
- carbon dioxide
- water
- glucose
- oxygen
- energy
- → [make 1 card or note with this symbol]
- + [make 3 cards or notes with this symbol]

Have students arrange the cards to show the process of photosynthesis. Then have students rearrange the cards to show cellular respiration. Point out that the starting materials for one process are the ending materials of the other process.

Advanced *A Plant's Point of View*

Plant Responses   individuals   30 min

Short Story Have each student write a short story from the point of view of a plant. In the story, the plant must describe an internal or external stimulus and the plant's response to that stimulus. Encourage students to think creatively about writing from a plant's point of view, but to include factual information from the lesson. Encourage motivated students to perform additional research about plant responses to add information to their stories.

ELL *Plant Process Pictures*

Synthesizing Key Topics   individuals, then pairs   10 min

Write the following terms on the board: *photosynthesis, cellular respiration, pollination, transpiration, tropism, dormant.* Have each student select two of these terms. For the terms they select, have students make a drawing, diagram, or other illustration that helps them remember information associated with these terms. Then, have students form pairs and discuss one of their drawings with their partner.

| cellular respiration | pollination | stamen | pistil |
| stimulus | transpiration | tropism | dormant |

Previewing Vocabulary

 whole class   15 min

Relating Vocabulary to Lesson Topics Write the following three questions on the board:
How do plants obtain and use energy?
How do plants reproduce?
What are some ways plants respond to their environment?
Have students look through the lesson to find terms related to each question. Record their ideas under each question. Call on volunteers to anticipate the terms' meanings based on how they are categorized.

Reinforcing Vocabulary

individuals, then groups of four   15 min

Word Triangle Distribute to each student a blank Word Triangle. Have students complete Word Triangles for the lesson vocabulary. For each term, they will write a definition, write a sentence using the term, and draw an illustration that represents the term.

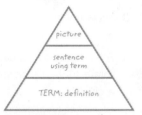

Customize Your Core Lesson

Core Instruction
- [ ] **Print Path** choices
- [ ] **Digital Path** choices

Vocabulary
- [ ] **Previewing Vocabulary** Relating Vocabulary to Lesson Topics
- [ ] **Reinforcing Vocabulary** Word Triangle

Your Resources

Differentiated Instruction
- [ ] **Basic** Modeling Photosynthesis and Cellular Respiration
- [ ] **Advanced** A Plant's Point of View
- [ ] **ELL** Plant Process Pictures

Extend Science Concepts

Reinforce and Review

Activity *Plant Processes*

Synthesizing Key Topics   small groups

🕐 20 min

Carousel Review Help students review the material by following these steps:

1 After students have read the lesson, prepare four pieces of chart paper with the following questions:

- How are the processes of photosynthesis and cellular respiration related?

- How are reproduction in a seedless plant and reproduction in a seed plant different? How are they similar?

- What are the stages in a plant's two-part life cycle?

- How do plants respond to light, changing day length, and gravity?

2 Divide students into small groups and assign each group a chart. Give each group a different colored marker.

3 Have the groups review their question, discuss their answer, and write a response.

4 After five minutes, each group should rotate to the next chart. Groups should put a check by each answer they agree with, comment on answers they don't agree with, and add their own answers. Continue until all groups have reviewed all charts.

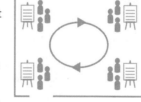

5 Invite each group to share information with the class.

Graphic Organizer

Synthesizing Key Topics   individuals

🕐 10 min

Idea Wheel Have students draw a small circle and insert the following label "Plant Processes." Then have students draw a much larger circle around the smaller circle. Have students divide the larger circle into three sections. Encourage students to label the sections as follows: *Energy, Reproduction, Reaction.* Model this on the board if needed. Then ask students to add details, examples, diagrams, and other notes to each section of the circle.

Going Further

Earth Science Connection

Plants and Energy   small groups

🕐 20 min

Posters Point out that plant processes play critical roles in the carbon cycle and the water cycle. Have students perform quick research to learn more about these cycles and the part that plants play in them. Then have each group choose one cycle to illustrate on a poster, highlighting how plants are related to the cycle. Invite each group to share its completed poster with the class.

Real World Connection

Plant Reproduction   small groups

🕐 20 min

Quick Research Point out to students that some fruits at the store, such as some grapes and oranges, are seedless. Have students think back to the information in the lesson about plant reproduction, and the role of seeds in this process. Then have each group research to learn how seedless fruits are produced. Encourage each group to prepare a short presentation to share what they learn with the class.

Customize Your Closing

📖 *See the Assessment Guide for quizzes and tests.*

⊘ *Go Online to edit and create quizzes and tests.*

Reinforce and Review

☐ **Activity** Plant Processes

☐ **Graphic Organizer** Idea Wheel

☐ **Print Path** Visual Summary, SE p. 132

☐ **Print Path** Lesson Review, SE p. 133

☐ **Digital Path** Lesson Closer

Evaluate Student Mastery

Formative Assessment

See the teacher support below the Student Pages for additional Formative Assessment questions.

Ask the following questions to assess student mastery of the material. **Ask:** What process allows plants to store energy from sunlight? photosynthesis **Ask:** Why must plants also carry out cellular respiration? to release the energy stored during photosynthesis **Ask:** What are two types of reproduction plants can undergo? sexual and asexual **Ask:** What are some ways that plants respond to their environment? Sample answer: phototropism, gravitropism, and going dormant

Reteach

Formative assessment may show that students need reinforcement for certain topics. The resources below are recommended for reteaching. If students were introduced to a topic through the Print Path, you can also use the Digital Path to reteach, or vice versa.
 Can be assigned to individual students

Plants and Energy
Virtual Lab What Affects Photosynthesis Rates?

Plant Reproduction
Exploration Lab Fertilization in Angiosperms

Plant Responses
Daily Demo Where Does the Water Come From?

Summative Assessment

Alternative Assessment
Design a Website

⊘ *Online resources: student worksheet; optional rubrics*

Plant Processes

Tic-Tac-Toe: *Design a Website*
You are developing a website to help students learn about plant processes.

1. Work on your own, with a partner, or with a small group.

2. The boxes below describe tasks associated with developing the website. Check the boxes you plan to complete. They must form a line in any direction.

3. Have your teacher approve your plan.

4. Do each activity, and turn in your results. All activities should be completed on paper; you are not being asked to create an actual website.

__ Home Page Writer	__ Game Designer	__ Illustrator
You are a writer asked to help develop the home page for the website. Develop short written summaries of five different plant processes to include on the home page of the website.	You are developing a game in which students match plant structures and processes. List at least five plant processes. Identify at least one structure involved in each process. Provide an answer key for the game.	You are an artist asked to make illustrations representing photosynthesis, phototropism, gravitropism, reproduction, and cellular respiration to include on the website. Include labels and short descriptions of each diagram.
__ Illustrator	__ Teacher	__ Game Designer
Make two cycle diagrams to include on the website. Indicate the plant processes the cycle diagrams will relate to. Show labels, illustrations, and other information that should be included with each cycle diagram.	You are a teacher asked to write a memo to the website designers identifying what you feel are the five most important facts about plant processes that students should learn. Briefly explain why each fact is important.	You are a game designer asked to make a crossword puzzle to include on the website that includes terms related to plant reproduction. On paper, show the crossword puzzle, the clues, and the solutions.
__ Game Designer	__ Game Designer	__ Quiz Writer
Design a drag-and-drop activity to help students learn about the equations for photosynthesis and cellular respiration. List the words or formulas that students will drag to make the equations. Provide an answer key for the activity.	Design an interactive game that students can use to simulate phototropism. Write a detailed description of your game, including how students will be able to adjust the stimuli (light), and how the activity will simulate the plant's response to the stimuli.	Create an interactive quiz that students can take after completing the activities on the website. Include ten questions and answers that span all the topics on the website. For each question, write a clue for students who give an incorrect response.

Going Further
- [ ] **Earth Science Connection**
- [ ] **Real World Connection**
- [ ] **Print Path** Why It Matters, SE p. 131

Formative Assessment
- [ ] **Strategies** Throughout TE
- [ ] **Lesson Review** SE

Summative Assessment
- [ ] **Alternative Assessment** Design a Website
- [ ] **Lesson Quiz**
- [ ] **Unit Tests A and B**
- [ ] **Unit Review** SE End-of-Unit

Your Resources

Lesson ④

Plant Processes

ESSENTIAL QUESTION

How do plants stay alive?

By the end of this lesson, you should be able to describe the processes through which plants obtain energy, reproduce, and respond to their environments.

The Venus flytrap responds to touch. When the leaf is triggered by an insect, the trap snaps shut in 0.1 second!

120 Unit 2 Earth's Organisms

Lesson Labs

Quick Labs
• Investigating Plant Pigments
• Observing Stomata

Exploration Lab
• Fertilization in Angiosperms

Engage Your Brain

1 Identify Read over the following vocabulary terms. In the spaces provided, place a + if you know the term well, a – if you have heard the term but are not sure what it means, and a ? if you are unfamiliar with the term. Then write a sentence that includes one of the words you are most familiar with.

_____ cellular respiration

_____ transpiration

_____ tropism

_____ pollination

Sentence using known word:

2 Describe Finish the caption for this photo.

The vine responds to the wire by

_____

Active Reading

3 Synthesize You can often define an unknown word if you know the meaning of its word parts. Use the word parts and sentence below to make an educated guess about the meaning of the word *photosynthesis*.

Word part	Meaning
photo-	light
synthesis	putting together

Example sentence:
Plants die without sunlight because they are unable to carry out photosynthesis.

photosynthesis:

Vocabulary Terms

• cellular respiration   • stimulus
• pollination   • transpiration
• stamen   • tropism
• pistil   • dormant

4 Apply As you learn the definition of each vocabulary term in this lesson, create your own definition or sketch to help you remember the meaning of the term.

Lesson 4 Plant Processes 121

Answers

Answers for 1–3 should represent students' current thoughts, even if incorrect.

1. Students' answers should reflect their current understanding of the terms.

2. Sample answer: wrapping around it as it grows.

3. Sample answer: Photosynthesis is a process that uses light energy to make sugars.

4. Students should define or sketch each vocabulary term in the lesson.

Opening Your Lesson

Accessing Prior Knowledge Use a DRTA activity to help students access prior knowledge related to plant processes. Distribute to each student a blank DRTA worksheet. Have students preview the Essential question, the Engage Your Brain questions, and the Active Reading activities for this lesson. After students have previewed these components, ask them to complete the first three boxes of the DRTA worksheet. Call on several volunteers to share what they have written, and use students' response to assess their prior knowledge of plant processes. Remind students to complete the fourth box of the DRTA activity after they have read the lesson. At the conclusion of the lesson, ask volunteers to share what they have learned about plant processes and to state whether their responses to either of the Engage Your Brain questions or the Active Reading activities has changed as a result of reading the lesson.

🌐 *Online resource: Textbook DRTA*

Prerequisites Students should already know the terms *photosynthesis*, *chlorophyll*, *seed*, and *pollen* and should have an understanding of the structure of plants.

Fueled By the Sun

How do plants obtain and use energy?

Plants, like all living things, need energy to survive. But plants don't exactly "eat" to get energy. Plants get energy from sunlight during the process of photosynthesis.

Plants Capture Light Energy in Chloroplasts

Plants use photosynthesis to change light energy to chemical energy in the form of sugar. Unlike animal cells, plant cells have organelles called *chloroplasts* [KLOHR•uh•plasts], where photosynthesis takes place. Chloroplasts are made up of two membranes that surround stacks of smaller, circular membranes. These smaller membranes contain chlorophyll, which is a green pigment. Chlorophyll absorbs light energy from the sun.

Sunlight is made up of various wavelengths of light. Different wavelengths of visible light are seen as different colors. Chlorophyll absorbs many wavelengths, but it reflects more green light than other colors of light. As a result, most plants look green.

Visualize It!

5 Describe Fill in the captions to describe how plants obtain energy from sunlight.

Light energy

Carbon dioxide

Oxygen

Water

A For photosynthesis to occur, plants must take in light energy, carbon dioxide, and water. In addition to sugar, plants produce _____

Chloroplasts Use Light Energy to Make Sugar

The light energy captured in chloroplasts is changed and stored in the bonds of a sugar called glucose. In the same process, oxygen gas is released. Many chemical reactions occur during photosynthesis. The process can be summarized by the following equation:

Photosynthesis
$$6CO_2 + 6H_2O \xrightarrow{\text{light energy}} C_6H_{12}O_6 + 6O_2$$

This equation shows that light energy is used to change six molecules of carbon dioxide and six molecules of water into one molecule of glucose and six molecules of oxygen gas.

Chloroplast

B Plant cells have organelles called chloroplasts, where photosynthesis takes place. These organelles contain a pigment called _____ that absorbs light.

Plant cell

Mitochondria Release Energy from Sugar

In plants, extra glucose is stored as starch or changed to other types of sugar such as fructose or sucrose. **Cellular respiration** [SEL•yuh•luhr res•puh•RAY•shun] is the process by which cells use oxygen to release the stored energy from the bonds of sugar molecules. This process occurs in mitochondria. Cellular respiration also produces carbon dioxide and water.

Cellular respiration
$$C_6H_{12}O_6 + 6O_2 \longrightarrow 6CO_2 + 6H_2O + \text{energy}$$

In cellular respiration, one molecule of glucose and six molecules of oxygen are changed into six molecules of carbon dioxide and six molecules of water. The reaction changes the energy in sugar into energy that can be used to power cell processes.

6 Relate How is cellular respiration the reverse of photosynthesis?

_____
_____
_____

Mitochondrion

C Cellular respiration occurs in organelles called mitochondria. Cellular respiration uses oxygen to release energy from glucose. It also releases _____ and _____

122 Unit 2 Earth's Organisms

Lesson 4 Plant Processes 123

Answers

5. A: oxygen.; B: chlorophyll.; C: carbon dioxide and water

6. Sample answer: Photosynthesis uses energy from the sun, carbon dioxide, and water, and produces glucose and oxygen. Cellular respiration uses glucose and oxygen to release energy and produce carbon dioxide and water.

Interpreting Visuals

Have students examine the illustration. **Ask:** What are the cellular structures involved in photosynthesis and cellular respiration? Sample answer: Chloroplasts are involved in photosynthesis; mitochondria are involved in cellular respiration.

Learning Alert

Respiration and Breathing The term *respiration* is sometimes used to refer to breathing. Remind students that cellular respiration is a chemical reaction that occurs in cells and releases stored energy. The fact that plants carry out cellular respiration does not mean that plants breathe, which is a physical action, in the way that many animals do.

Formative Assessment

Ask: By what process do plants obtain and store energy? Answer: photosynthesis **Ask:** By what process do plants release stored energy? Answer: cellular respiration **Ask:** In the bonds of what molecule is chemical energy stored at the end of photosynthesis? Answer: glucose **Ask:** Animal cells contain mitochondria but not chloroplasts. Using this information, what can you infer about processes carried out in animal cells? Answer: Animals carry out cellular respiration but not photosynthesis.

A Plant's Life

What are the phases of a plant's life cycle?

All plants complete their life cycles by alternating between two phases, the sporophyte phase and the gametophyte phase. These two phases look different from each other.

In one phase, plants called sporophytes [SPOHR•uh•fyts] produce spores by meiosis. Meiosis is a process of cell division in which each daughter cell receives half the chromosomes of the parent cell. The products of meiosis in plant sporophytes are spores. The spores are then released.

Under the right conditions, spores grow into plants called gametophytes [guh•MEET•uh•fyts]. Female gametophytes make eggs. Male gametophytes make sperm. When a sperm fertilizes an egg, they combine to form an embryo. The embryo develops into a seed, which is released and can grow into a new sporophyte.

Visualize It!

7 Contrast Use the diagram to explain how spores differ from seeds.

_____

_____

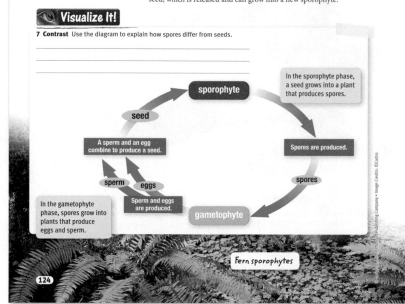

In the sporophyte phase, a seed grows into a plant that produces spores.

Spores are produced.

spores

In the gametophyte phase, spores grow into plants that produce eggs and sperm.

Sperm and eggs are produced.

A sperm and an egg combine to produce a seed.

sporophyte · seed · sperm · eggs · gametophyte

Fern sporophytes

124

How do seedless plants reproduce?

The gametophyte generation in plants makes eggs and sperm. In seedless plants, sperm are released in the presence of water. Sperm have whip-like tails. The sperm swim to the eggs and fertilize them. The fertilized eggs then grow into sporophytes.

Some seedless plants, such as mosses, have a visible gametophyte phase. The short, dense plant you think of as moss is the gametophyte. Sometimes you can also see the sporophytes of moss if you look closely. They are thin, brown stems topped by a small, brown capsule.

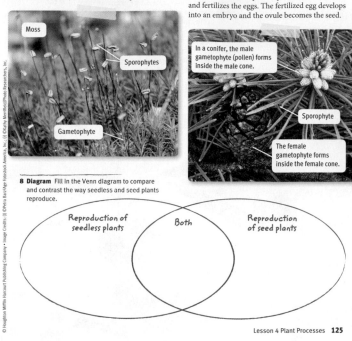

Moss

Sporophytes

Gametophyte

In a conifer, the male gametophyte (pollen) forms inside the male cone.

Sporophyte

The female gametophyte forms inside the female cone.

How do seed plants reproduce?

The sporophyte is what you see in seed plants. In most seed plants, the sporophyte makes two types of spores, male and female, that grow into microscopic male and female gametophytes. The male gametophyte is pollen, a tiny structure in which sperm form. Pollen may be carried by wind, water, or animals to the female plant reproductive structure. The female gametophyte develops inside an ovule, which is part of the sporophyte. Within the ovule the gametophyte produces eggs. **Pollination** happens when pollen lands on the female plant reproductive structure and fertilizes the eggs. The fertilized egg develops into an embryo and the ovule becomes the seed.

8 Diagram Fill in the Venn diagram to compare and contrast the way seedless and seed plants reproduce.

Reproduction of seedless plants | Both | Reproduction of seed plants

Lesson 4 Plant Processes **125**

Answers

7. Sample answer: Spores grow into a gametophyte, which makes eggs or sperm. Seeds grow into sporophytes, which produce spores.

8. Sample answer: Reproduction of seedless plants: no pollen, need water to reproduce; Both: reproduce sexually, involve egg and sperm, have two-part life cycle; Reproduction of seed plants: use pollen, don't need water to reproduce

Building Reading Skills

Two-panel Flip Chart After students have read the information about the two-part life cycle of plants, direct them to make a Two-panel Flip Chart comparing the sporophyte phase and the gametophyte phase. Encourage students to add words, phrases, or illustrations under each panel of the flip chart. Students can use this flip chart to review key information about plant reproduction after they have completed the lesson.

⊙ *Optional Online resource: Two-panel Flip Chart support*

Probing Question GUIDED Inquiry

Relating Some plants rely on animals such as birds and bees for pollination; others rely on water or wind. **Ask:** How do you think the method of pollination relates to the structure of pollen? Sample answer: Pollen spread by animals might be on a flower that produces nectar or some other substance that draws pollinators. Pollen spread by wind might have a shape that makes it float better in the air. Pollen spread by water would need to be waterproof and would probably float.

How do flowering plants reproduce?

In flowering plants, sexual reproduction takes place inside the flowers. Flowers are reproductive structures that have specialized leaves called sepals and petals, which often attract animal pollinators such as insects.

A **stamen** is the male reproductive structure of flowers. At the tip of each stamen is an *anther,* where pollen is produced. A **pistil** is the female reproductive structure of flowers. When a pollen grain reaches the tip of the pistil, called the *stigma,* pollination occurs. A pollen tube grows down through the pistil into the ovary. Within the ovary are one or more ovules containing eggs. Sperm travel down the tube, into the ovary, and fertilize the eggs.

A fertilized egg develops into an embryo, a tiny, undeveloped plant. The ovule develops into a seed that surrounds and protects the embryo. The ovary becomes a fruit, which protects the seeds and helps seeds to spread. When conditions are right, seeds will sprout and grow into new plants.

Visualize It!

9 Identify Circle the two labels of gametophyte structures in the illustration.

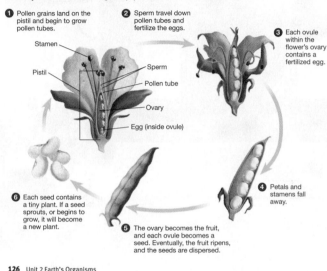

① Pollen grains land on the pistil and begin to grow pollen tubes.

② Sperm travel down pollen tubes and fertilize the eggs.

③ Each ovule within the flower's ovary contains a fertilized egg.

④ Petals and stamens fall away.

⑤ The ovary becomes the fruit, and each ovule becomes a seed. Eventually, the fruit ripens, and the seeds are dispersed.

⑥ Each seed contains a tiny plant. If a seed sprouts, or begins to grow, it will become a new plant.

Stamen
Pistil
Sperm
Pollen tube
Ovary
Egg (inside ovule)

© Houghton Mifflin Harcourt Publishing Company

How do plants reproduce asexually?

Most plants can also reproduce asexually. Asexual reproduction allows a plant to reproduce without seeds or spores. During asexual reproduction, part of a parent plant, such as a stem or root, produces a new plant. Some examples of structures that plants use to reproduce asexually include plantlets, tubers, and runners.

- Plantlets are tiny plants that grow along the edges of a plant's leaves. These plantlets fall off and grow on their own.
- Tubers are underground stems that store nutrients and can grow into new plants. A potato is a tuber. Each "eye" can grow into a new plant.
- Runners are above-ground stems that can grow into new plants. Strawberries send out lots of runners.

11 Apply Write a play that compares and contrasts the results of sexual and asexual reproduction in plants.

Visualize It!

10 Label Under each example of asexual reproduction, write the type of structure used for this purpose.

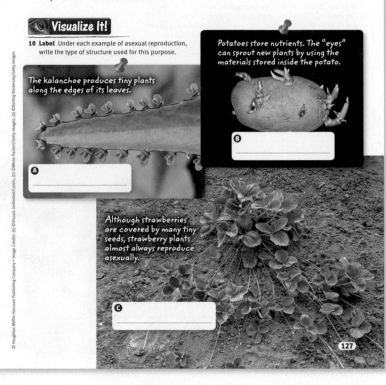

The kalanchoe produces tiny plants along the edges of its leaves.

A

Potatoes store nutrients. The "eyes" can sprout new plants by using the materials stored inside the potato.

B

Although strawberries are covered by many tiny seeds, strawberry plants almost always reproduce asexually.

C

Image Credits: (tl) ©Visuals Unlimited/Corbis; (tr) ©White Packert/Corbis; (b) ©Dorling Kindersley/Getty Images

© Houghton Mifflin Harcourt Publishing Company • Image Credits

127

Answers

9. Sperm, Egg (also accept *pollen* in captions)

10. A: plantlet; B: tuber;

   C: runner

11. Answers will vary.

Interpreting Visuals

Point out the cycle diagram that illustrates the life cycle of a flowering plant. Remind students that cycle diagrams show repeating events that happen one after another, and that there is no designated beginning or ending in a cycle diagram.

Learning Alert

Distinguishing Pollen and Seeds Students may confuse pollen and seeds. There are some similarities: both pollen and seeds are moved by wind, water, and animals. Point out that pollen is the male gametophyte, while a seed develops from a fertilized ovule (the result of sperm from the male gametophyte fertilizing the egg from the female gametophyte). Pollen germinates to produce a tiny male gametophyte and sperm. A seed germinates to produce a new plant.

Formative Assessment

Ask: What are three structures that plants use to reproduce asexually? Answer: plantlets, tubers, runners **Ask:** What is one advantage to a plant reproducing asexually? Sample answer: The plant can produce many copies of itself.

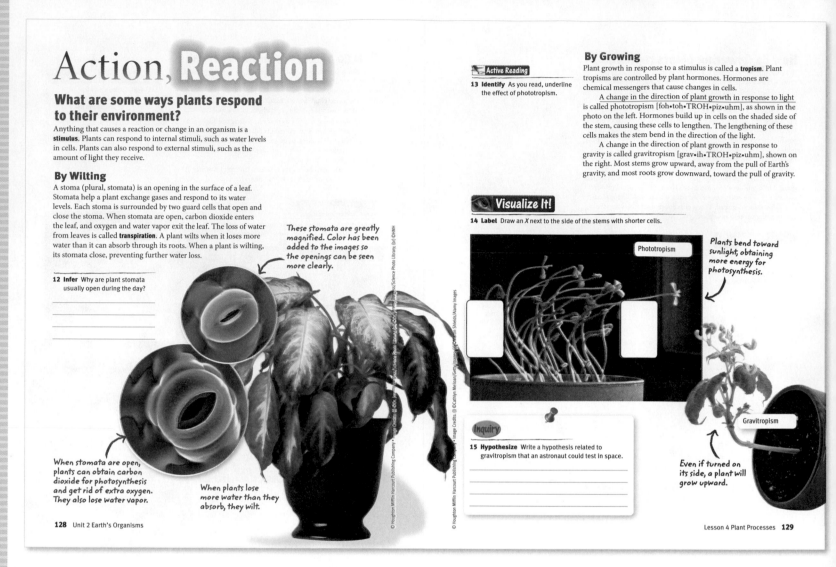

Action, Reaction

What are some ways plants respond to their environment?

Anything that causes a reaction or change in an organism is a **stimulus**. Plants can respond to internal stimuli, such as water levels in cells. Plants can also respond to external stimuli, such as the amount of light they receive.

By Wilting

A stoma (plural, stomata) is an opening in the surface of a leaf. Stomata help a plant exchange gases and respond to its water levels. Each stoma is surrounded by two guard cells that open and close the stoma. When stomata are open, carbon dioxide enters the leaf, and oxygen and water vapor exit the leaf. The loss of water from leaves is called **transpiration**. A plant wilts when it loses more water than it can absorb through its roots. When a plant is wilting, its stomata close, preventing further water loss.

12 Infer Why are plant stomata usually open during the day?

These stomata are greatly magnified. Color has been added to the images so the openings can be seen more clearly.

When stomata are open, plants can obtain carbon dioxide for photosynthesis and get rid of extra oxygen. They also lose water vapor.

When plants lose more water than they absorb, they wilt.

📖 **Active Reading**

13 Identify As you read, underline the effect of phototropism.

By Growing

Plant growth in response to a stimulus is called a **tropism**. Plant tropisms are controlled by plant hormones. Hormones are chemical messengers that cause changes in cells.

A change in the direction of plant growth in response to light is called phototropism [foh•toh•TROH•piz•uhm], as shown in the photo on the left. Hormones build up in cells on the shaded side of the stem, causing these cells to lengthen. The lengthening of these cells makes the stem bend in the direction of the light.

A change in the direction of plant growth in response to gravity is called gravitropism [grav•ih•TROH•piz•uhm], shown on the right. Most stems grow upward, away from the pull of Earth's gravity, and most roots grow downward, toward the pull of gravity.

👁 **Visualize It!**

14 Label Draw an *X* next to the side of the stems with shorter cells.

Phototropism

Plants bend toward sunlight, obtaining more energy for photosynthesis.

Gravitropism

Even if turned on its side, a plant will grow upward.

Inquiry

15 Hypothesize Write a hypothesis related to gravitropism that an astronaut could test in space.

128 Unit 2 Earth's Organisms

Lesson 4 Plant Processes 129

Answers

12. Sample answer: Stomata are opened during the day so that photosynthesis can occur while there is sunshine available.

13. *See students' pages for annotations.*

14. Students should draw an *X* on the right side of the plant.

15. Sample answer: My hypothesis is that in space, where the gravitational pull is zero, the roots of plants would grow randomly in different directions.

Learning Alert

Homeostasis Homeostasis, the maintenance of a stable internal environment, requires responses to changing external and internal conditions. Students will probably be familiar with some animal responses to changing conditions; for example, shivering is a response to cold temperatures, and thirst is a response to decreased water levels in the body. Plants also respond to the environment and maintain homeostasis. Although plants do not have nervous systems to sense changes, or muscular systems to move and respond, they are able to sense and respond to changes in their internal and external environments.

Probing Questions   INDEPENDENT (Inquiry)

Investigating What is a specific question you have about phototropism in plants? How could you design an experiment to find the answer to this question? Sample answer: The question I have about phototropism is, *Is root growth also affected by phototropism?* I would grow two plants, one with a light overhead and one with a light to the side. After the stems show the effects of phototropism, I would carefully remove the soil around the roots to see if their growth was also affected.

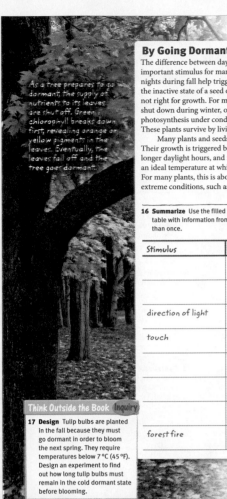

As a tree prepares to go dormant, the supply of nutrients to its leaves are shut off. Green chlorophyll breaks down first, revealing orange or yellow pigments in the leaves. Eventually, the leaves fall off and the tree goes dormant.

By Going Dormant

The difference between day length and night length is an important stimulus for many plants. Shorter days and longer nights during fall help trigger winter dormancy. **Dormant** describes the inactive state of a seed or other plant part when conditions are not right for growth. For many plants, it is more energy-efficient to shut down during winter, or during a dry season, than to continue photosynthesis under conditions of reduced sunlight and rain. These plants survive by living off of stored sugars.

Many plants and seeds come out of dormancy in the spring. Their growth is triggered by the return of more direct sunlight, longer daylight hours, and increased rain. Each plant species has an ideal temperature at which most of its seeds begin to grow. For many plants, this is about 27 °C (80 °F). But some seeds need extreme conditions, such as forest fires, to break their dormancy.

16 Summarize Use the filled in boxes as clues to help you complete the table with information from the lesson. Some terms will appear more than once.

Stimulus	Response
	closing stomata to preserve water
	growth of roots downward
direction of light	
touch	growth of stem around a wire
	growth of stems upward
	seed growth
	changing leaf color, losing leaves
forest fire	

Think Outside the Book (Inquiry)

17 Design Tulip bulbs are planted in the fall because they must go dormant in order to bloom the next spring. They require temperatures below 7 °C (45 °F). Design an experiment to find out how long tulip bulbs must remain in the cold dormant state before blooming.

130

Why It Matters

In Season

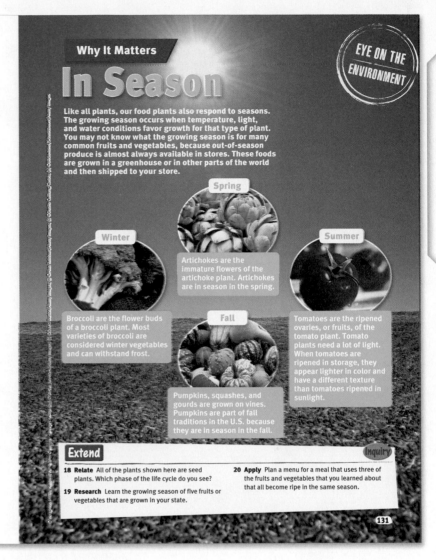

Like all plants, our food plants also respond to seasons. The growing season occurs when temperature, light, and water conditions favor growth for that type of plant. You may not know what the growing season is for many common fruits and vegetables, because out-of-season produce is almost always available in stores. These foods are grown in a greenhouse or in other parts of the world and then shipped to your store.

Spring

Artichokes are the immature flowers of the artichoke plant. Artichokes are in season in the spring.

Winter

Broccoli are the flower buds of a broccoli plant. Most varieties of broccoli are considered winter vegetables and can withstand frost.

Fall

Pumpkins, squashes, and gourds are grown on vines. Pumpkins are part of fall traditions in the U.S. because they are in season in the fall.

Summer

Tomatoes are the ripened ovaries, or fruits, of the tomato plant. Tomato plants need a lot of light. When tomatoes are ripened in storage, they appear lighter in color and have a different texture than tomatoes ripened in sunlight.

Extend (Inquiry)

18 Relate All of the plants shown here are seed plants. Which phase of the life cycle do you see?

19 Research Learn the growing season of five fruits or vegetables that are grown in your state.

20 Apply Plan a menu for a meal that uses three of the fruits and vegetables that you learned about that all become ripe in the same season.

131

Answers

16. too little water; gravity; bending toward light; gravity; warm weather, more light, rain; cold weather, less light; seeds grow

17. Sample answer: Split the bulbs into four groups. Plant them in shallow soil. Place group 1 in a warm greenhouse. Place the other groups in a refrigerator. Leave group 2 in the fridge for 1 month and group 3 in the fridge for 2 months. After the allotted time, move the pots to the greenhouse. Leave group 4 in the fridge until the end of the experiment. Times for groups 2 and 3 may have to be modified.

18. sporophyte

19. Answers will vary.

20. Students should plan a meal that uses locally grown produce that is in season.

Building Reading Skills

Supporting Main Ideas Distribute to each student a blank Supporting Main Ideas Diagram. Have each student complete his or her diagram with information about ways that plants respond to their environment. Then have students work in groups of three or four to compare and discuss their completed diagrams. Finally, call on each group of students to share a detail from one of their completed diagrams.

Online resource: Supporting Main Ideas

Why It Matters

Students might not have an understanding of the seasonal nature of fruit production because of the year-round availability of many fruits in the supermarket. Point out that fruits available year-round are shipped from many different locations, or are grown in artificial conditions such as greenhouses. Use the information in the Why It Matters feature to emphasize seasonal changes in plants. Then ask students to identify any additional examples of seasonal fruits with which they are familiar.

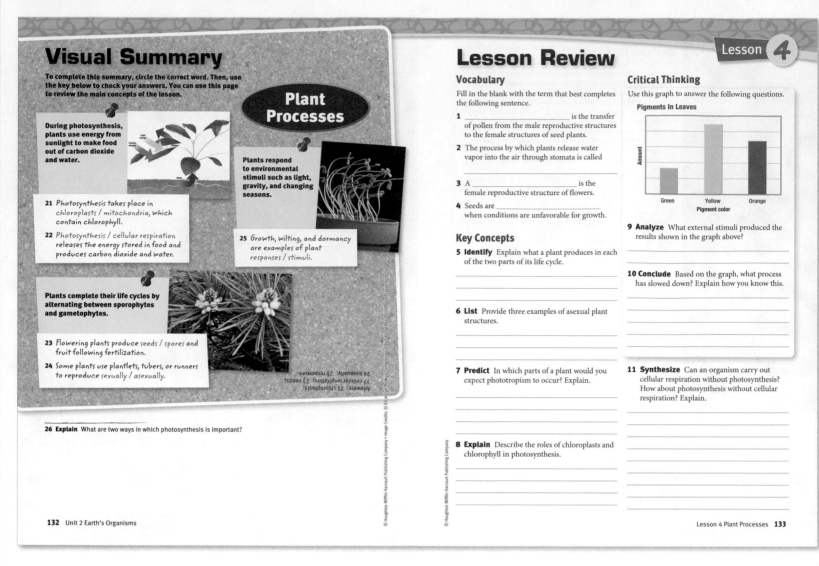

Visual Summary Answers

21. chloroplasts
22. cellular respiration
23. seeds
24. asexually
25. responses
26. Sample answer: Photosynthesis produces sugars using light energy. This food is the source of energy that every other organism uses for their life processes. Photosynthesis also produces oxygen, which animals breathe. Oxygen is used during cellular respiration to make use of the energy stored in chemical bonds.

Lesson Review Answers

1. Pollination
2. transpiration
3. pistil
4. dormant
5. In the sporophyte phase: spores; In the gametophyte phase: eggs and sperm
6. plantlets, tubers, and runners
7. in the green parts of the plant that carry out photosynthesis, such as leaves
8. Photosynthesis takes place in chloroplasts. Chlorophyll is the pigment that absorbs the sunlight needed for photosynthesis.
9. Sample answer: cold weather and reduced length of daylight
10. Sample answer: Photosynthesis; The amount of chlorophyll is less than of the yellow and orange pigments, so less photosynthesis is going on.
11. Sample answer: Organisms can carry out cellular respiration without photosynthesis because they get food from eating plants or animals. No organism can carry out photosynthesis without cellular respiration because cellular respiration is required to release the energy stored in food.

S.T.E.M. Engineering & Technology

Analyzing a Greenhouse

Purpose To identify inputs and to differentiate between convective and radiative energy transfer in a greenhouse

Learning Goals

- Construct a mini-greenhouse.
- Plot temperature versus time on a graph.
- Identify inputs, outputs, and system processes in a greenhouse.

Informal Vocabulary

convection, radiation, agriculture, horticulture

Prerequisite Knowledge

- Basic understanding of plants and plant processes

Materials

small box, approximately 8 in. (length) × 5 in. (width) ×
    3 in. (height)

thermometer

brown or black markers

clear plastic wrap

tape or rubber bands

aluminum foil

lamp

Caution! Lamps can get hot and could burn the plastic wrap if placed too close or left unattended.

Content Refresher

Transfer of Energy as Heat There are three methods of transferring energy as heat: convection, radiation, and conduction.

Convection achieves energy transfer by the movement of a fluid, such as a liquid or a gas. Air currents and water currents are examples of energy transfer through convection. In a greenhouse, convection occurs when warm air rises while cooler air sinks. This movement creates air currents.

Radiation is the transfer of energy by electromagnetic waves. At the temperatures common in a greenhouse, these waves are in the infrared portion of the electromagnetic spectrum. Therefore, the radiation is not visible to the human eye. If an object gets hot enough (such as a red-hot electric element on the top of a stove), the electromagnetic radiation emitted can be visible to the human eye.

Conduction is the transfer of energy as heat due to a temperature difference between two touching surfaces. Energy flows from the warmer object to the cooler object. Conduction can occur in solids, liquids, and gases. In solids, molecules vibrate faster to transfer energy from a warm section to a cooler section. In gases and liquids, energy transfer occurs when molecules collide during their random motion. In a greenhouse, the warm inner air transfers energy as heat to the cooler glass. Then the glass, now warm, transfers energy to the cooler outside air.

21st Century SKILLS   Theme: Environmental Literacy

Activities focusing on 21st Century Skills are included for this feature and can be found on the following pages.

These activities focus on the following skills:

- **Critical Thinking and Problem Solving**
- **ICT (Information, Communications, and Technology) Literacy**
- **Productivity and Accountability**

You can learn more about the 21st Century Skills in the front matter of this Teacher's Edition.

S.T.E.M. Engineering & Technology

Evaluating Technological Systems

Skills
✔ Identify inputs
✔ Identify outputs
✔ Identify system processes
✔ Identify system feedback
Examine system interactions
Apply system controls
✔ Communicate results

Objectives
• Identify inputs and outputs of a physical system.
• Differentiate between convective and radiative heat transfer.
• Graph temperature data versus time.
• Analyze and communicate results of an experiment.

Analyzing a Greenhouse

A greenhouse is an enclosed space that maintains a consistent environment and temperature to let people grow plants where the natural climate is not ideal. A greenhouse system needs to heat up and cool off in order to effectively grow plants. How the sun warms a greenhouse involves both radiation and convection. Objects on the ground absorb sunlight and become warm. At the same time, objects cool off primarily in two ways: (1) they get rid of heat by transferring energy as visible light or infrared (in•fruh•RED) light (radiation), or (2) they transfer energy in the form of heat to the air, which then carries it away (convection). A greenhouse retains energy in the form of heat primarily because its roof and walls prevent its warmed air from moving out into the atmosphere.

1 Infer Identify the processes shown at labels A and B as either convection or radiation.

A _____

B _____

Infer Why is convection the main process regulating the temperature in a greenhouse?

_____
_____
_____

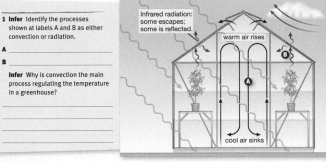

Infrared radiation: some escapes; some is reflected.

warm air rises

cool air sinks

134 Unit 2 Earth's Organisms

Greenhouse Systems

Greenhouses are systems that have inputs and outputs. The inputs are air, water, sunlight, young plants or seeds, and plant nutrients. The outputs are energy in the form of heat and mature plants, fruits, or vegetables. The main uses of greenhouses are agriculture (farming) and horticulture (HOHR•tih•kuhl•cher) (gardening). Typical outputs of agricultural greenhouses are fruits and vegetables. Typical outputs of horticultural greenhouses are ornamental plants and flowers. Greenhouses can vary in size from very large to the size of a shoebox. Gardeners call small greenhouses *cold frames*.

2 Infer Three different types of greenhouses are shown here. Label each type of greenhouse agriculture, horticulture, or cold frame, and list the likely outputs of each.

A _____

B _____

C _____

✋ You Try It!
Now it's your turn to make a greenhouse and analyze how it works.

135

Answers

1. A: convection; B: radiation

   Sample answer: The air in a greenhouse is unevenly warmed by the energy it receives from the sun. The walls and the roof of the greenhouse prevent most of this warmed air from escaping. This allows convection to occur as warmer air rises and cooler air sinks, and is therefore the main process that regulates the temperature in a greenhouse.

2. A: agriculture: the one with vegetables growing; its likely output is crops that many people eat, such as peppers, lettuce, and tomatoes

   B: horticulture: the one with people that looks like a place to visit; its likely output is flowers or special plants

   C: cold frame: the one for the home garden; its likely output is vegetables that people like to grow at home, such as tomatoes, lettuce, or green beans

Evaluating Technological Systems

✋ You Try It!

Now it's your turn to construct a mini-greenhouse and analyze its inputs, how it heats up, and how its temperature is regulated.

1 Identify Inputs

What are the inputs of your greenhouse?

2 Identify Outputs

What are the outputs of your greenhouse?

3 Identify System Processes

A First, record the room-temperature reading of your thermometer.

B Then, begin to construct your greenhouse using the materials listed. With a marking pen, color the inside of your box to simulate the color of dirt.

C Place your thermometer in the box so that it does not touch any part of the box but so that you can still read it. Why should the thermometer not touch the box?

D Using the foil, make a tent-style barrier in the box to shade the thermometer so the lamp does not directly shine on it. Why is it important to shade the thermometer?

E Cover the box with clear plastic wrap, and seal it as best you can with tape or a rubber band to minimize air leaks. Place the lamp above the box to act as the sun.

You Will Need

✓ small box, 8 in. (length) x 5 in. (width) x 3 in. (height)
✓ thermometer, digital if possible (1)
✓ marking pens, brown or black
✓ clear plastic wrap
✓ tape or rubber bands
✓ aluminum foil
✓ lamp

S.T.E.M. Engineering & Technology

F What physical processes are involved in your greenhouse system as it accumulates heat energy?

4 Identify System Feedbacks

Record the temperature of the air in the greenhouse every 5 minutes for at least 30 minutes. Add scale values on tick marks to both axes. Then, graph the temperature versus time in the space provided.

5 Communicate Results

Describe what you learned from your greenhouse experiment.

Answers

1. visible and invisible radiation (i.e., energy), air

2. Sample answer: My greenhouse doesn't seem to output much of anything, unless you count my learning from it. Maybe some of its heat escapes to heat up the room.

3. D: Sample answer: I want to measure the temperature of the air, not the temperature of the side of the box.

   E: Sample answer: To protect the thermometer from direct radiation from the lamp, otherwise the thermometer would be directly heated by the lamp rather than by the air in the box.

F: Sample answer: Light enters the box, and some of it is absorbed by the walls or floor of the box. This makes the molecules in the box vibrate more, which means they are hotter. Some of the heat of the box is transferred to the air in the box when air molecules touch the box molecules. The box can also radiate heat, but some of the heat that is radiated inside the box may be absorbed or reflected by the plastic film so that not all of it gets out.

4. Students should have a graph that shows the temperature increasing with observation time.

21st Century SKILLS

Learning and Innovation Skills

 individuals   🕐 15 min

Critical Thinking and Problem Solving Based on the results of the greenhouse experiment, have students design a terrarium in which they could grow plants indoors year round. Encourage students to think about the inputs and physical processes in the terrarium. What effect does the addition of soil have on the terrarium? How is this different from the mini-greenhouse in the experiment?

Information, Media, and Technology Skills

 pairs or small groups   🕐 20 min

ICT (Information, Communications, and Technology) Literacy Invite small groups of students to talk about and compare greenhouse technology. In the real world, how would a greenhouse be different from their mini-greenhouses? What technological challenges might you encounter when building a real greenhouse? How might you design a greenhouse if you wanted to grow plants that required two different temperatures to thrive? How might you design an automatic watering system? How could you ensure proper drainage? Encourage students to share their ideas with the class.

Life and Career Skills

 pairs or small groups   🕐 ongoing

Productivity and Accountability Invite students to plan and manage additional mini-greenhouse experiments. Encourage all students to participate actively and to collaborate and cooperate effectively within their group. Tell students that they should solicit and implement ideas from all group members, and all members will be accountable for their end result. If something doesn't work as planned, group members should set and meet new goals based on what they learned. Invite group members to share their results with the class in a professional manner.

Differentiated Instruction

Basic *A Hotter Greenhouse*

 individuals or pairs   🕐 45 min

Challenge students to make a mini-greenhouse in which the air temperature is warmer than the highest temperatures recorded during the greenhouse experiment. Encourage students to think about how they could make the air temperature warmer. Have students share their ideas and then conduct the new experiment.

Advanced *Visit a Greenhouse*

 individuals or pairs   🕐 varied

Invite interested students to visit a working greenhouse. During the visit, have students list the inputs and system processes they notice. Based on what they see and what they learned from the mini-greenhouse experiment, encourage students to draw a plan for a greenhouse that could grow vegetables or flowers that do not normally thrive in the region.

ELL *Showing Energy Transfer in a Greenhouse*

 pairs or small groups   🕐 20 min

Have students draw a sketch of their mini-greenhouses, using arrows to show how energy is transferred through convection. Then have students draw another sketch that shows how energy would be transferred through both convection and radiation in a real greenhouse.

Customize Your Feature

- [ ] **21st Century Skills** Learning and Innovation Skills
- [ ] **21st Century Skills** Information, Media, and Technology Skills
- [ ] **21st Century Skills** Life and Career Skills
- [ ] **Basic** A Hotter Greenhouse
- [ ] **Advanced** Visit a Greenhouse
- [ ] **ELL** Showing Energy Transfer in a Greenhouse

Introduction to Animals

Essential Question What are animals?

 Professional Development

For more detailed information about the topics in this lesson, refer to the Content Refresher in the Unit Opener pages.

Opening Your Lesson

Begin the lesson by assessing students' prerequisite and prior knowledge.

Prerequisite Knowledge

- Multicellular organisms are made up of more than one cell.
- Scientists classify organisms according to shared characteristics.

Accessing Prior Knowledge

Invite students to make a Tri-fold KWL chart to access prior knowledge about animals. Have students put what they know in the first column and what they want to know in the second column. After they have finished the lesson, they can complete the third column with what they learned.

🌐 *Online resource: Tri-fold FoldNote support*

Customize Your Opening

☐ **Accessing Prior Knowledge,** above

☐ Print Path Engage Your Brain, SE p. 139

☐ Print Path Active Reading, SE p. 139

☐ **Digital Path** Lesson Opener

Key Topics/Learning Goals	Supporting Concepts
Animal Characteristics 1 List six characteristics that most animals share.	• All animals are multicellular, consume other organisms to get energy, have specialized parts, have the ability to move, and need to maintain their own body temperature. • Most animals reproduce sexually, though some use asexual reproduction.
Animal Diversity 1 Describe the diversity of the animal kingdom. 2 Explain the difference between an invertebrate and a vertebrate.	• Animals are the most physically diverse kingdom of organisms. They vary in size, shape, body covering, and body plan. • An invertebrate is an animal that does not have a backbone. A vertebrate is an animal that does have an internal segmented backbone.
Invertebrates 1 Describe the main characteristics of each invertebrate animal phylum.	• Invertebrates are included in the following phyla based on their characteristics: Porifera, Cnidaria, Ctenophora, Platyhelminthes, Mollusca, Annelida, Nematoda, Arthropoda, and Echinodermata. • Some invertebrates have a hard, external supporting structure called an exoskeleton.
Vertebrates 1 Describe the main characteristics of the vertebrate animal phylum, Chordata. 2 Describe the most familiar vertebrates—fish, amphibians, reptiles, birds, and mammals.	• All vertebrates are chordates, which have a notochord, a hollow nerve tube, pharyngeal slits, and a tail at some point in development. Tunicates and lancelets are invertebrates that are also chordates. • Vertebrates have an endoskeleton, a braincase, vertebrae, and bones. • Vertebrates include fish, amphibians, reptiles, birds, and mammals.

Options for Instruction

Two parallel paths provide coverage of the Essential Questions, with a strong **Inquiry** strand woven into each. Follow the **Print Path,** the **Digital Path,** or your customized combination of print, digital, and inquiry.

 Print Path
Teaching support for the Print Path appears with the Student Pages.

 Inquiry Labs and Activities

Digital Path
Digital Path shortcut: TS663424

You Are an Animal!
SE pp. 140–141
What characteristics do animals share?

Quick Lab
Characteristics of Animals

Activity
Human Body Organization

Which Are Animals?
Interactive Images

Characteristics of Animals
Video

Such Diversity! SE pp. 142–143
What groups make up the diversity of animals?

Quick Lab
Form and Motion

Activity
That's Diversity!

Animal Diversity
Slideshow

Vertebrates and Invertebrates
Interactive Images

Soft and Squishy?
SE pp. 144–145
What are some different kinds of invertebrates?

Daily Demo
Sponge Expansion

Invertebrate Phyla
Interactive Graphics

Some Familiar Faces...
SE pp. 146–147
What are some different kinds of vertebrates?

Activity
Finding Personal Vertebrae

Chordata
Slideshow

Vertebrate Groups
Interactive Images

Options for Assessment

See the Evaluate page for options, including Formative Assessment, Summative Assessment, and Unit Review.

Engage and Explore

Activities and Discussion

Discussion *Animals*

Introducing Key Topics

 whole class
 10 min
 GUIDED inquiry

Ask students to name as many animals as they can. Encourage them to think of unusual animals. List their responses on the board. Ask students how they know if something is an animal. Guide students to understand that all animals have the ability to move and consume food to get energy. Lead a discussion about some of the other shared characteristics of animals, such as being multicellular, having specialized parts, reproduction, and maintaining body temperature.

Activity *Human Body Organization*

Animal Characteristics

 individuals or pairs
 30 min
 DIRECTED inquiry

The human body has trillions of cells, thousands of different tissues, numerous organs, and many major organ systems. Help students understand the levels of organization in the human body by having them list specific cells, tissues, and organs in a particular organ system. Allow students to use reference materials or the Internet to complete this activity.

Activity *That's Diversity!*

Engage

Animal Diversity

 small groups
 15 min
 DIRECTED inquiry

Ask students to write down two examples of each of the following: *animals that crawl, animals that fly, animals that do not have bones, animals that live in the soil,* and *animals that live in the ocean.* Tell students that answers should be specific. For example, an answer should be *a praying mantis* rather than *an insect.* As each group shares its answers with the class, others should cross out matches on their own lists. Explain to students that the number of different animals students can think of illustrates animal diversity.

Probing Question *Making Inferences*

Invertebrates

 whole class
 10 min
 DIRECTED inquiry

Inferring Jellyfish, sponges, and octopuses are among the many invertebrates that live in the ocean. How do you think living in a water environment might affect their body shapes? Samples answers: Some of these animals have a streamlined body shape to move quickly in the water. Some are porous so they can filter water to get food.

Activity *Finding Personal Vertebrae*

Engage

Vertebrates

 whole class
 5 min
 DIRECTED inquiry

Make sure students realize that they have vertebrae and know how to find them. Ask students to stand up. Have them put one hand at the center base of their skulls and feel the bumpy bones. Then, have them place the other hand at their center backs below their waists and feel their bumpy bones. Then, have them move their two hands towards each other along their spines, feeling the bumpy bones as they go. Explain that these bones are our vertebrae and that similar structures can be found in all other vertebrates.

©Melba Photo Agency/Alamy Images

Customize Your Labs

 See the Lab Manual for lab datasheets.

 Go Online for editable lab datasheets.

Labs and Demos

Daily Demo *Sponge Expansion*

Engage

Invertebrates

👥 whole class
🕐 10 min
🔵 **GUIDED** inquiry

PURPOSE **To show how a sponge absorbs water**

MATERIALS

- natural sponge
- microscope

1 Place a thin, dry slice of a natural sponge under a microscope. Allow students to examine the spongin fiber network. Explain to students that sponges do not have true circulatory or digestive systems. Instead, sponges need to have a constant flow of water through their bodies. This flow of water brings them food and carries away wastes.

2 Add a few drops of water to the sponge, and have students re-examine the slice. Students should see how the fibers take up the water (the fibers will swell slightly) and how the water moves into the spaces between the fibers.

3 **Applying** Based on what you have observed, explain how you think sponges take in nutrients. Water that contains nutrients flows into the sponge. When water flows out, the nutrients are filtered out and absorbed by the sponge.

4 **Synthesizing** In what way do you think sponges are less complex than most other animals? They move very little and their bodies are not very specialized.

Quick Lab *Form and Motion*

Animal Diversity

👥 small groups
🕐 15 min
🔵 **DIRECTED** inquiry

Students will investigate the relationships between animals' body forms and the ways in which they move.

PURPOSE **To observe how animal form relates to motion**

MATERIALS

- animal photograph
- animal video footage

Quick Lab *Characteristics of Animals*

Animal Characteristics

👥 individuals
🕐 25 min
🔵 **INDEPENDENT** inquiry

Students will create a sketch of a fictional animal with the characteristics that most animals share, and then they will identify and label the specific and unique characteristics of their animal.

PURPOSE **To brainstorm, create, and label a sketch of an animal that does not actually exist, but which has the six characteristics that most animals share**

MATERIALS

- paper
- colored pencils

Activities and Discussion

☐ **Discussion** Animals

☐ **Activity** Human Body Organization

☐ **Activity** That's Diversity!

☐ **Probing Question** Making Inferences

☐ **Activity** Finding Personal Vertebrae

Labs and Demos

☐ **Daily Demo** Sponge Expansion

☐ **Quick Lab** Form and Motion

☐ **Quick Lab** Characteristics of Animals

Your Resources

_____

_____

_____

Explain Science Concepts

Key Topics	📖 **Print Path**	🖥 **Digital Path**
Animal Characteristics	☐ **You Are an Animal!,** SE pp. 140–141 • Visualize It!, #5 • Active Reading (Annotation strategy), #6 • Infer, #7	☐ **Which Are Animals?** Discover which living things are animals. ☐ **Character-istics of Animals** Learn what all animals have in common.
Animal Diversity	☐ **Such Diversity!,** SE pp. 142–143 • Visualize It!, #8 • Active Reading (Annotation strategy), #9 • Visualize It!, #10 	☐ **Animal Diversity** Explore the diversity of the animal kingdom. ☐ **Vertebrates and Invertebrates** Learn about the two major groups of animals.
Invertebrates	☐ **Soft and Squishy?,** SE pp. 144–144 • Active Reading (Annotation strategy), #11 • Inquiry, #12 • Think Outside the Book, #13	☐ **Invertebrate Phyla** Learn about invertebrates.
Vertebrates	☐ **Some Familiar Faces...,** SE pp. 146–147 • Active Reading (Annotation strategy), #14 • Relate, #15 • Visualize It!, #16 	☐ **Chordata** Explore the characteristics all vertebrates share. ☐ **Vertebrate Groups** Learn about invertebrate chordates and vertebrates.

Differentiated Instruction

Basic *Animal Study*

Animal Characteristics

 individuals or pairs
 varies

After students have learned about animal characteristics, ask them to research the physical structure of one particular animal. Studying one animal can help students recognize the common characteristics that all animals share. Then, direct students to design a poster that diagrams the anatomy of their chosen animal. Tell students to include in their poster the characteristics that classify their particular animal.

Advanced *Observing Hydras*

Invertebrates

 pairs
 varies

Obtain live hydras and water fleas *(Daphnia)* from a biological supply house. Distribute the hydras in water-filled specimen dishes. Have pairs of students study the hydras under a dissecting microscope. Add a few water fleas to each dish, and have students observe how hydras use their tentacles to capture and subdue prey. Encourage students to draw the hydras and to record their observations of how hydras move and manipulate captured prey into their mouths.

ELL *Vertebrate Body Coverings*

Vertebrates

 individuals or pairs
 15 min

Make a Table Ask students to draw a table with two columns. They should title the left column "Type of Vertebrate" and the right column "Body Covering." In the left column, have students list the following types of vertebrates: *fish, reptiles, amphibians, birds,* and *mammals*. Then have students use animal picture books to find out about different types of body coverings that vertebrates have and use this information to fill in the chart. fish: mucous-covered scales; reptiles: dry scales; amphibians: mucous-covered skin; birds: feathers; mammals: hair

Lesson Vocabulary

consumer	**invertebrate**	**exoskeleton**
vertebrate	**endoskeleton**	

Previewing Vocabulary

 whole class
 10 min

Word Origins Share the following to help students remember terms:

- **Consumer** is from the Latin word *consumere,* which means "to use up, eat, waste."
- **Invertebrate** is derived from the Latin prefix *in-,* which means "not," and the Latin word *vertebra,* which means "joint."
- **Exoskeleton** contains the prefix *exo-,* which means "outside" or "external."
- **Endoskeleton** contains the prefix *endo-,* which means "within" or "internal."

Reinforcing Vocabulary

individuals ongoing

Four Square To help students remember the vocabulary terms in the lesson, have them use a four square. After they draw the four square, guide students to write the term in the center. They should then fill in the surrounding cells with the types of information shown.

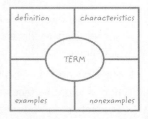

Customize Your Core Lesson

Core Instruction

- ☐ **Print Path** choices
- ☐ **Digital Path** choices

Vocabulary

- ☐ **Previewing Vocabulary** Word Origins
- ☐ **Reinforcing Vocabulary** Four Square

Your Resources

Differentiated Instruction

- ☐ **Basic** Animal Study
- ☐ **Advanced** Observing Hydras
- ☐ **ELL** Vertebrate Body Coverings

Extend Science Concepts

Reinforce and Review

Activity *Animals*

Synthesizing Key Topics
 small groups
🕐 15 min

Inside/Outside Circles Help students review the material by following these steps:

1   After students have read the lesson, give each an index card with a question from the text or one that you have written. Have students write the answer on the back of their index cards. Check the answers or provide a key to make sure they are correct. Have students adjust incorrect answers.

2   Students pair up and form two circles one inside the other. One partner is in an inside circle; the other is in an outside circle. The students in the inside circle face out, and the students in the outside circle face in.

3   Each student in the inside circle asks his or her partner the question on the index card. The partner answers. If the answer is incorrect, the student in the inside circle teaches the other student the correct answer. Repeat this step with the outside-circle students asking the questions.

4   Have each student on the outside circle rotate one person to the right. He or she faces a new partner and gets a new question. Students rotate after each pair of questions. (You can vary the rotation by moving more than one person, moving to the left, and so on, but make sure that partners are always new.)

FoldNote

Synthesizing Key Topics
 individuals
🕐 10 min

Layered Book FoldNote Have students create a Layered Book FoldNote that includes a page for each of the following: *animal characteristics, animal diversity, invertebrates,* and *vertebrates.* Students should include a diagram or illustration on each page and a description for each topic.

🌐 *Optional Online resource: Layered Book FoldNote support*

Going Further

Health Connection

Invertebrates
 whole class
🕐 varies

Research Project Sponges have few predators. The sharp spicules and tough fibers in the bodies of sponges discourage aquatic organisms from eating sponges. Many sponges also produce toxic chemicals that deter predators and keep other sponges from growing too close. A chemical produced by a Caribbean sponge, *Cryptothethya crypta,* was one of the first marine chemicals to be used in chemotherapy. Currently, many other chemicals produced by sponges are being tested as anticancer and antiviral drugs. Have students use the Internet to research other modern uses for chemicals produced by sponges.

Math Connection

Vertebrates
 individuals or pairs
🕐 15 min

Shark Teeth *Carcharodon megalodon* is an extinct shark that existed in the Miocene era. Its teeth could be as long as 16.8 centimeters. Based on the shark's tooth length, scientists estimate that this shark was probably 16 meters long, which is about twice as long as today's great white shark. Ask students to imagine that they have discovered some shark teeth with the following lengths: 33.6 cm, 67.2 cm, and 8.4 cm. Have students use the ratio that the megalodon scientists would have used to estimate the sizes of the sharks that these teeth came from. 32 m, 64 m, and 8 m Students can then measure these lengths on the floor to get a feel for how long these animals were.

Customize Your Closing

🗨 *See the Assessment Guide for quizzes and tests.*

🌐 *Go Online to edit and create quizzes and tests.*

Reinforce and Review

☐ **Activity** Animals

☐ **FoldNote** Layered Book FoldNote

☐ **Print Path** Visual Summary, SE p. 148

☐ **Print Path** Lesson Review, SE p. 149

☐ **Digital Path** Lesson Closer

Evaluate Student Mastery

Formative Assessment

See the teacher support below the Student Pages for additional Formative Assessment questions.

Ask students the following questions to assess their mastery of key topics. **Ask:** What characteristics do animals share? All animals are multicellular, reproduce, have specialized parts, have the ability to move, maintain body temperature, and consume other organisms to get energy. **Ask:** What makes animals diverse? Animals have a variety of body coverings, sizes, plans, and shapes. **Ask:** What are some different kinds of invertebrates? Sample answer: sea stars, comb jellies, butterflies, and tapeworms **Ask:** What are some different kinds of vertebrates? Sample answer: fish, reptiles, birds, and mammals

Reteach

Formative assessment may show that students need reinforcement for certain topics. The resources below are recommended for reteaching. If students were introduced to a topic through the Print Path, you can also use the Digital Path to reteach, or vice versa.
🎧 *Can be assigned to individual students*

Animal Characteristics
Activity Human Body Organization 🎧

Animal Diversity
Activity That's Diversity!

Invertebrates
Daily Demo Sponge Expansion

Vertebrates
Activity Finding Personal Vertebrae 🎧

Summative Assessment

Alternative Assessment
Amazing Animals!

🌐 *Online resources: student worksheet, optional rubrics*

Introduction to Animals

Take Your Pick: *Amazing Animals!*

1. Work on your own or with a partner.
2. Choose items from below for a total of 10 points. Check your choices.
3. Have your teacher approve your plan.
4. Submit or present your results.

2 Points

_____ **Exploring Your Home** List all of the animals that you find around your home. Do you have pets? Are there any spiders in spider webs outside? Can you see any animals from your window? When you have finished writing your list, make a poster about the animals you found. Classify each animal as a vertebrate or invertebrate and identify another group it belongs to.

_____ **Mollusk Menus** Research how people use mollusks for food. Look for recipes for snails, clams, squids, and other mollusks. Create a menu that features an appetizer and a main dish made from mollusks.

5 Points

_____ **Skin vs. Exoskeleton** Compare the functions of an exoskeleton to the functions of skin, the body covering of vertebrates. Write a paragraph describing the differences, or create a chart showing the functions shared and not shared by exoskeletons and skin.

_____ **Underwater Breathing** Learn more about the way that fish breathe underwater. Research how fish use their gills to breathe, or remove oxygen from the water. Create a presentation describing this process.

8 Points

_____ **Invertebrate Report** Choose a type of invertebrate to research and write a short report about. In the report, describe the animal's habitat and food sources. Also tell how the animal obtains food and avoids predators. Include one unusual fact about your chosen invertebrate.

_____ **Observing Animals** Go outside and find two different animals to observe. Watch them quietly for ten minutes each. Record your observations. Compare the two animals. How are their body parts alike? How do the animals move? Can you tell what each animal eats and how it finds food? Design a slideshow using presentation software that shares this information.

Going Further
☐ Health Connection
☐ Math Connection

Formative Assessment
☐ **Strategies** Throughout TE
☐ **Lesson Review** SE

Summative Assessment
☐ **Alternative Assessment** Amazing Animals!
☐ **Lesson Quiz**
☐ **Unit Tests A and B**
☐ **Unit Review** SE End-of-Unit

Your Resources

_____   _____

_____   _____

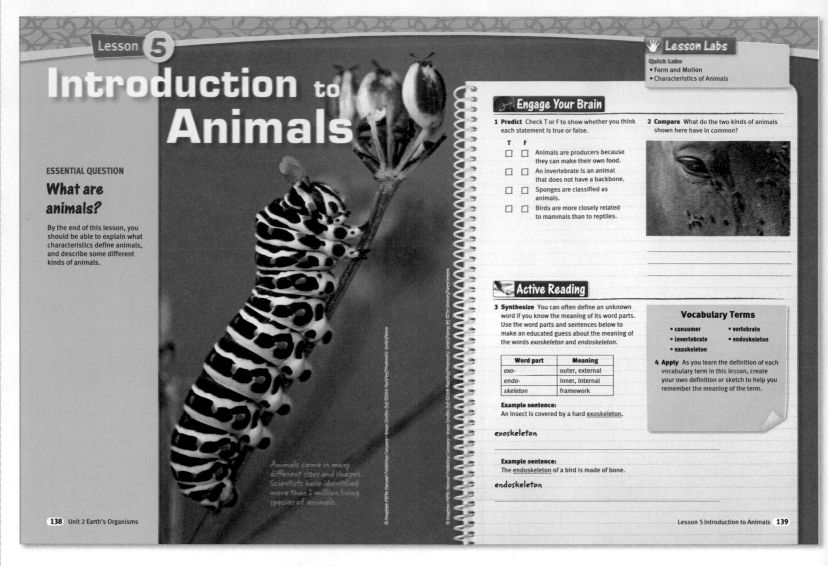

Lesson **5**

Introduction to Animals

ESSENTIAL QUESTION

What are animals?

By the end of this lesson, you should be able to explain what characteristics define animals, and describe some different kinds of animals.

Animals come in many different sizes and shapes. Scientists have identified more than 1 million living species of animals.

138 Unit 2 Earth's Organisms

✋ Lesson Labs

Quick Labs
• Form and Motion
• Characteristics of Animals

🐛 Engage Your Brain

1 Predict Check T or F to show whether you think each statement is true or false.

T F

☐ ☐ Animals are producers because they can make their own food.

☐ ☐ An invertebrate is an animal that does not have a backbone.

☐ ☐ Sponges are classified as animals.

☐ ☐ Birds are more closely related to mammals than to reptiles.

2 Compare What do the two kinds of animals shown here have in common?

_____

_____

_____

📖 Active Reading

3 Synthesize You can often define an unknown word if you know the meaning of its word parts. Use the word parts and sentences below to make an educated guess about the meaning of the words *exoskeleton* and *endoskeleton*.

Word part	Meaning
exo-	outer, external
endo-	inner, internal
skeleton	framework

Example sentence:
An insect is covered by a hard <u>exoskeleton</u>.

exoskeleton

_____

Example sentence:
The <u>endoskeleton</u> of a bird is made of bone.

endoskeleton

_____

Vocabulary Terms

• consumer   • vertebrate
• invertebrate   • endoskeleton
• exoskeleton

4 Apply As you learn the definition of each vocabulary term in this lesson, create your own definition or sketch to help you remember the meaning of the term.

Lesson 5 Introduction to Animals 139

Answers

Answers for 1–3 should represent students' current thoughts, even if incorrect.

1. F; T; T; F

2. Sample answer: Both flies and horses are multicellular organisms, have specialized parts, reproduce through sexual reproduction, can move around, respond to stimuli, and eat food.

3. Sample answer: An exoskeleton is a hard external covering. An endoskeleton is an internal skeleton.

4. Students should define or sketch each vocabulary term in the lesson.

Opening Your Lesson

Discuss students' responses to items 1 and 2 to assess their prerequisite knowledge and to estimate what they already know about animals.

Prerequisites Students should already know that multicellular organisms are organisms that are made up of more than one cell. Students should also know that scientists classify organisms according to shared characteristics.

Learning Alert

Some students may think that all animals have two eyes, a nose, and a mouth. Prompt students to challenge this misconception by asking questions such as: "Is a worm an animal?" "Is a bacterium an animal?" "Is a coral an animal?" "Is a jellyfish an animal?" "Is a fungus an animal?" Discuss with students some characteristics that distinguish animals from other organisms. Make a list of the six characteristics of animals. Explain to students that animals share these characteristics, but they are further classified into groups based on other characteristics they share as a group. For example, bees and ants are both insects, and sharks and goldfish are both fish.

You Are an Animal!

What characteristics do animals share?

Animals come in many shapes and sizes. Pets, such as dogs and cats, are animals. Some sponges used in the shower are the remains of an animal. Some animals are too small to be seen without a microscope. Yet all animals share six characteristics.

Many Cells

Like other organisms, animals are made up of cells. All animals are *multicellular* organisms, which means that they are made up of many cells. Similar cells work together to perform the animal's life functions. Animal cells are eukaryotic, so they have a nucleus. In animals, all of the cells work together to perform the life functions of the animal.

Specialized Parts

The cells in a multicellular organism develop into different kinds of cells. This process is called differentiation. Some cells may become skin cells, and others may become gut cells. Each type of cell has a special function to play in an organism. For example, retinal cells of the eye function in vision.

© Visualize It!

5 Infer These photos show different kinds of animal cells. Write down three other specialized cells that you think would be found in animal bodies.

_____

_____

_____

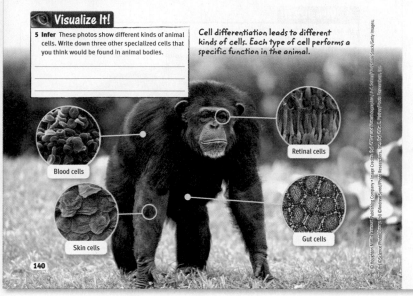

Cell differentiation leads to different kinds of cells. Each type of cell performs a specific function in the animal.

Blood cells

Retinal cells

Skin cells

Gut cells

Movement

Animals move in various ways such as running, flying, and swimming. Some animals move to find food, shelter, and mates. Some animals move during only part of their life cycle. For example, the immature stage of a barnacle, the larva, swims around to find food. But adult barnacles are permanently attached to a hard surface, such as a rock, and catch food that passes by.

Reproduction

Most animals use sexual reproduction. In sexual reproduction, a male sex cell, the sperm, fertilizes a female sex cell, the egg. Then the fertilized egg, or zygote, divides many times to form an embryo. Sexual reproduction leads to genetically diverse offspring. Some animals, such as hydras and sponges, can also reproduce asexually. Offspring of asexual reproduction are genetically identical to their parent.

Consume Food

Active Reading **6 Identify** As you read, underline the different kinds of food animals eat.

All organisms need energy to survive. Animals cannot produce their own food, so they are consumers. A **consumer** is an animal that eats other organisms, or parts of organisms, to get the energy it needs for life processes. Animals eat many kinds of food. Some animals eat plants, some eat animals or animal products, and some eat both plants and animals.

Maintain Body Temperature

To function well, all animals need to maintain their bodies within a specific range of temperatures. Birds and mammals maintain their own body temperatures by using some of the energy released by chemical reactions. Other animals rely on their environment to maintain their body temperature.

Some animals, like barnacles, can move from place to place only during the early larval stage of their life cycle.

Adult barnacles

Barnacle larva

Some animals have specialized diets. South American vampire bats feed only on blood.

7 Infer How might an organism that relies on the environment to maintain body temperature do so?

_____

_____

_____

Lesson 5 Introduction to Animals **141**

Answers

5. Sample answer: kidney, hair, and bone cells

6. *See students' pages for annotations.*

7. Sample answer: Some lizards sit in the sun to warm themselves. When the weather gets too hot, the lizard may burrow underground to stay cool.

Interpreting Visuals

Have students look at the visual showing the different types of cells found in a single animal. **Ask:** How are these cells similar? Because these cells are eukaryotic cells, they all have a nucleus and organelles. **Ask:** How are they different? The shapes and functions of the cells are different. **Ask:** If these cells are all animal cells, why are they so different? Cell differentiation leads to different types of cells that are specialized to perform different functions.

Formative Assessment

Ask: What are the six characteristics of animals? Animals are multicellular, reproduce, have specialized parts, move, consume food, and maintain body temperature. Do all animals reproduce in the same way? No, some animals reproduce sexually, while other reproduce asexually. Some use both methods of reproduction.

Probing Questions GUIDED Inquiry

Inferring Looking at a slide of cells from an organism under a microscope, how could you begin to classify the organism? Sample answer: If the cells have a nucleus and no cell walls, then the organism is probably an animal and not a plant.

Such Diversity!

What groups make up the diversity of animals?

Animals live in nearly every ecosystem on Earth. They are the most physically diverse kingdom of organisms. Some animals have four legs and some have none. Others, like rotifers, are smaller than the period ending this sentence. Blue whales are as big as two school buses! Besides shape and size, animals have body coverings that vary from feathers to hard shells to soft tissues.

One way to categorize animals is by symmetry or body plan. Some animals, such as sponges, are asymmetrical. You cannot draw a straight line to divide its body into equal parts. Animals like the sea anemone have a radial body plan, organized like the spokes of a wheel. Animals such as tortoises have bilateral symmetry with two mirror-image sides. Animals can also be categorized by internal traits, such as whether or not they have a backbone.

Outer Coverings

A _____

B _____

C _____

👁 **Visualize It!**

8 Identify Name the outer covering of each animal on the lines provided.

D _____

Body Plans

Asymmetry In asymmetry, the animal is irregular in shape and, therefore, lacks symmetry.

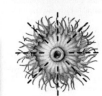

Radial symmetry The bodies of animals with radial symmetry are organized like spokes on a wheel.

Bilateral symmetry Animals with bilateral symmetry have two sides that mirror each other along one plane through the central axis.

142 Unit 2 Earth's Organisms

Active Reading **9 Compare** As you read, underline the characteristics of invertebrates and vertebrates.

Invertebrates

An **invertebrate** is an animal without a backbone. In fact, invertebrates do not have any bones. Instead, many invertebrates have a hard, external covering, which supports the body, called an **exoskeleton**. Most animals on Earth—over 95% of all animal species—are invertebrates.

Asexual reproduction is more common in invertebrates than in other animals. For example, the phyla that include animals such as sponges, jellyfish, flatworms, and segmented worms use both sexual and asexual reproduction.

Two special kinds of invertebrates are tunicates and lancelets. Tunicates, such as sea squirts, are small, sac-shaped animals. Lancelets are small, fish-shaped animals as shown below. These invertebrate animals are unique because they share some characteristics with vertebrates.

Vertebrates

Tunicates and lancelets, along with vertebrates, are part of a group of animals called *chordates* (KOHR•dayts). Chordates have four traits at some point in their life: a notochord, a hollow nerve cord, pharyngeal (fuh•RIN•jee•uhl) slits, and a tail.

Animals that have a backbone are called **vertebrates**. The backbone is a part of an endoskeleton. An **endoskeleton** is an internal skeleton that supports an animal's body. The backbone is made up of bones called *vertebrae* (VER•tuh•bray) that protect part of the nervous system. Vertebrates also have a braincase, or skull, that protects their large brains. Almost all vertebrates reproduce sexually. In a few species, a female's egg can develop into an individual without being fertilized.

👁 **Visualize It!**

10 Apply You may be unfamiliar with the lancelet shown here, but since lancelets are animals, what six things do you know must be true about them?

_____

_____

_____

_____

_____

_____

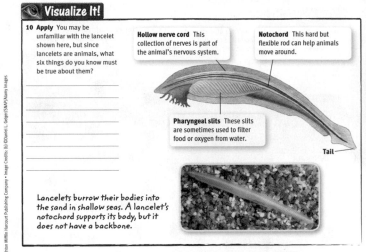

Hollow nerve cord This collection of nerves is part of the animal's nervous system.

Notochord This hard but flexible rod can help animals move around.

Pharyngeal slits These slits are sometimes used to filter food or oxygen from water.

Tail

Lancelets burrow their bodies into the sand in shallow seas. A lancelet's notochord supports its body, but it does not have a backbone.

Lesson 5 Introduction to Animals 143

Answers

8. Sample answers: A: hard exoskeleton; B: feathers; C: soft flesh; D: tough skin

9. *See students' pages for annotations.*

10. Students should note that the lancelets must have many cells, specialized parts, movement, sexually reproduce, consume food, and maintain a body temperature.

Interpreting Visuals

Have students look at the images showing different body plans. **Ask:** Why did the illustrator use dotted lines on the images that show radial symmetry and bilateral symmetry? The dotted lines show you that if you could fold the animal in half along the dotted lines like a piece of paper, then the two sides would match up exactly.

Have students study the images of the animals with different body coverings. **Ask:** Besides differences in body coverings, how else are these animals different? They are different in size and shape. They probably also have very different internal structures and move in different ways.

Building Reading Skills

Three-panel Flip Chart After students have read the section on animal diversity, direct them to make a Three-panel Flip Chart comparing vertebrates, invertebrates, and invertebrate chordates. Have students record details from the text on their charts, and include illustrations of animals from each group.

🌐 *Optional Online resource: Three-panel Flip Chart support*

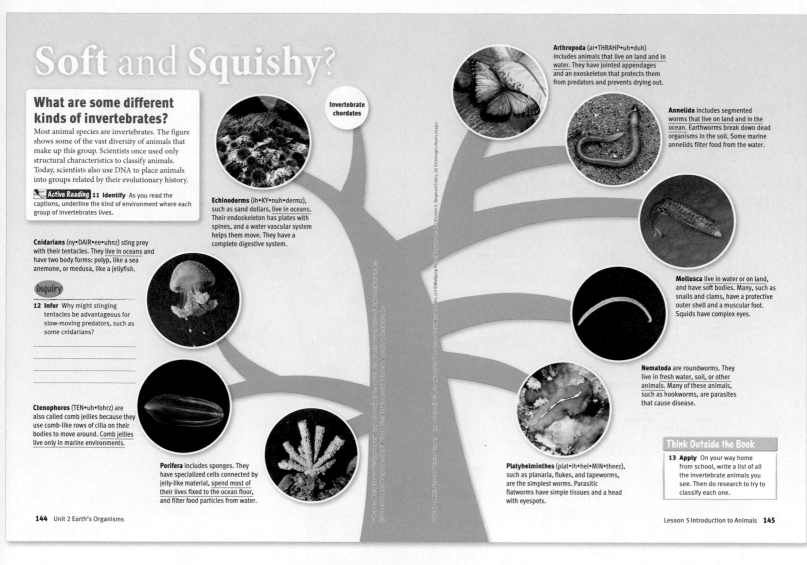

Answers

11. *See students' pages for annotations.*

12. Sample answer: Slow-moving predators can't capture prey by chasing them or capturing them in fast-snapping jaws. Having stinging cells to discharge when prey are close by allows slow-moving predators to immobilize their prey.

13. Student answers should identify common local invertebrates.

Interpreting Visuals

Talk with students about how a branching diagram helps organize different types of information. **Ask:** What do the different branches on this diagram represent? Each branch of the diagram represents a different kind of invertebrate. Animals grouped together before a branch in the diagram share similar characteristics and DNA.

Learning Alert

Classification Students may not realize that the characteristics used for the classification of animals have changed as advancements in technology and new scientific discoveries have been made. Today, DNA and the principles of genetics are also used to classify organisms. As advancements are made in these areas, the classification of some organisms may change. Have interested students research the history of biological classification and present their findings to the class.

Mnemonics To help students remember the two different body plans of cnidarians, provide them with the following mnemonics. Write the words *medusa* and *polyp* on the board. Point out that *medusa* contains the letter **d** and that this form of a cnidarian has tentacles that hang **d**own from the animal's body. Then, point out that the word *polyp* contains the letter **p**, and that this form of a cnidarian has tentacles that project u**p**.

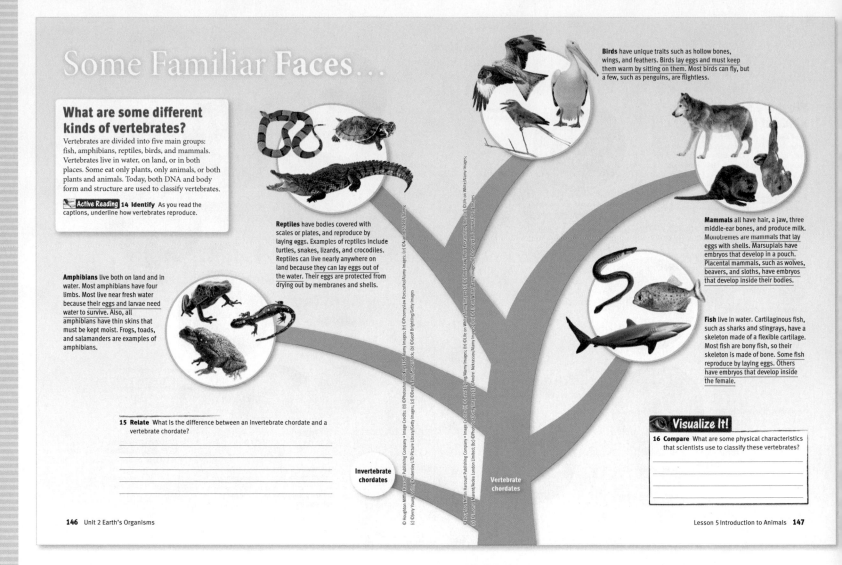

Some Familiar Faces...

What are some different kinds of vertebrates?

Vertebrates are divided into five main groups: fish, amphibians, reptiles, birds, and mammals. Vertebrates live in water, on land, or in both places. Some eat only plants, only animals, or both plants and animals. Today, both DNA and body form and structure are used to classify vertebrates.

Active Reading **14 Identify** As you read the captions, underline how vertebrates reproduce.

Amphibians live both on land and in water. Most amphibians have four limbs. Most live near fresh water because their eggs and larvae need water to survive. Also, all amphibians have thin skins that must be kept moist. Frogs, toads, and salamanders are examples of amphibians.

Reptiles have bodies covered with scales or plates, and reproduce by laying eggs. Examples of reptiles include turtles, snakes, lizards, and crocodiles. Reptiles can live nearly anywhere on land because they can lay eggs out of the water. Their eggs are protected from drying out by membranes and shells.

Birds have unique traits such as hollow bones, wings, and feathers. Birds lay eggs and must keep them warm by sitting on them. Most birds can fly, but a few, such as penguins, are flightless.

Mammals all have hair, a jaw, three middle-ear bones, and produce milk. Monotremes are mammals that lay eggs with shells. Marsupials have embryos that develop in a pouch. Placental mammals, such as wolves, beavers, and sloths, have embryos that develop inside their bodies.

Fish live in water. Cartilaginous fish, such as sharks and stingrays, have a skeleton made of a flexible cartilage. Most fish are bony fish, so their skeleton is made of bone. Some fish reproduce by laying eggs. Others have embryos that develop inside the female.

15 Relate What is the difference between an invertebrate chordate and a vertebrate chordate?

Invertebrate chordates

Vertebrate chordates

Visualize It!

16 Compare What are some physical characteristics that scientists use to classify these vertebrates?

146 Unit 2 Earth's Organisms

Lesson 5 Introduction to Animals **147**

Answers

14. *See students' pages for annotations.*

15. Sample answer: Invertebrate chordates have a hollow nerve cord, notochord, pharyngeal slits, and tail at some point in their life, as all chordates do. However, they don't have a backbone as vertebrate chordates do.

16. Sample answer: habitat; type of skeleton; outer body covering; type of reproduction

Interpreting Visuals

Talk with students about how this branching diagram is similar to the diagram on the previous pages. **Ask:** What do the different branches on this diagram represent? Each branch of the diagram represents a different kind of vertebrate. **Ask:** What structure of body support do vertebrates have in common? Vertebrates have an endoskeleton that gives their body support and provides a place for muscles to attach.

Using Annotations

Cluster Diagrams The annotation asks students to underline the characteristics that define each group of vertebrates. After students complete the annotation, have them work in small groups to create a cluster diagram for each vertebrate group. In the center circle of each diagram, students should write the name of the vertebrate group. In the surrounding circles, they should list the characteristics that they underlined in the text.

Formative Assessment

Ask: What characteristic separates vertebrates from invertebrates? Vertebrates have a backbone, and they are all chordates. **Ask:** What characteristics do chordates have? At some point in their life, they have a notochord, a hollow nerve cord, pharyngeal slits, and a tail. **Ask:** Are invertebrates also chordates? only lancelets and tunicates are

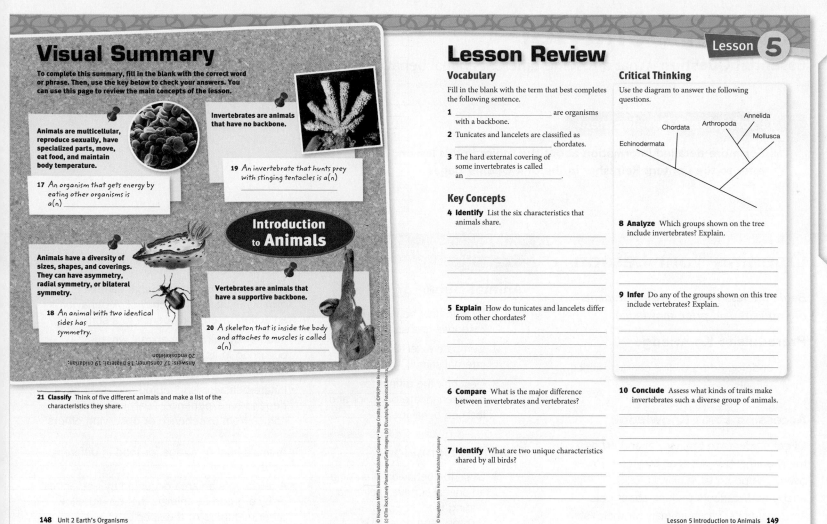

Visual Summary

To complete this summary, fill in the blank with the correct word or phrase. Then, use the key below to check your answers. You can use this page to review the main concepts of the lesson.

Animals are multicellular, reproduce sexually, have specialized parts, move, eat food, and maintain body temperature.

Invertebrates are animals that have no backbone.

17 An organism that gets energy by eating other organisms is a(n) _____

19 An invertebrate that hunts prey with stinging tentacles is a(n) _____

Introduction to Animals

Animals have a diversity of sizes, shapes, and coverings. They can have asymmetry, radial symmetry, or bilateral symmetry.

18 An animal with two identical sides has _____ symmetry.

Vertebrates are animals that have a supportive backbone.

20 A skeleton that is inside the body and attaches to muscles is called a(n) _____

Answers: 17 consumer; 18 bilateral; 19 cnidarian; 20 endoskeleton

21 Classify Think of five different animals and make a list of the characteristics they share.

Lesson Review

Vocabulary

Fill in the blank with the term that best completes the following sentence.

1 _____ are organisms with a backbone.

2 Tunicates and lancelets are classified as _____ chordates.

3 The hard external covering of some invertebrates is called an _____.

Key Concepts

4 Identify List the six characteristics that animals share.

_____

_____

_____

_____

_____

5 Explain How do tunicates and lancelets differ from other chordates?

_____

_____

_____

_____

_____

6 Compare What is the major difference between invertebrates and vertebrates?

_____

_____

_____

7 Identify What are two unique characteristics shared by all birds?

_____

_____

_____

Critical Thinking

Use the diagram to answer the following questions.

Echinodermata · Chordata · Arthropoda · Annelida · Mollusca

8 Analyze Which groups shown on the tree include invertebrates? Explain.

_____

_____

_____

9 Infer Do any of the groups shown on this tree include vertebrates? Explain.

_____

_____

_____

10 Conclude Assess what kinds of traits make invertebrates such a diverse group of animals.

_____

_____

_____

_____

_____

Visual Summary Answers

17. consumer

18. bilateral

19. cnidarian

20. endoskeleton

21. Answers will vary but all animals are multicellular organisms, have specialized parts, can move, reproduce through sexual reproduction, eat food, and maintain their body temperature.

Lesson Review Answers

1. Vertebrates

2. invertebrate

3. exoskeleton

4. Animals are multicellular, reproduce sexually, have specialized parts, have the ability to move, and are consumers.

5. Tunicates and lancelets do not have a backbone, so they are not vertebrates.

6. Vertebrates have a backbone, while invertebrates do not.

7. Birds have hollow bones and feathers.

8. All of the groups shown are or include invertebrates, but chordata also includes vertebrates.

9. Yes. Chordata includes vertebrates, but also invertebrate chordates.

10. Sample answer: Invertebrates include many phyla with different sizes, shapes, body coverings, and body plans.

Animal Behavior

Essential Question What are some different animal behaviors?

 Professional Development

For more detailed information about the topics in this lesson, refer to the Content Refresher in the Unit Opener pages.

Opening Your Lesson

Begin the lesson by assessing students' prerequisite and prior knowledge.

Prerequisite Knowledge

- An understanding of the characteristics of animals

Accessing Prior Knowledge

Direct students to brainstorm and list as many animal behaviors as they can. To overcome potential thinking blocks, encourage students to think about pets and/or domesticated animals for their lists.

Customize Your Opening

☐ **Accessing Prior Knowledge,** above

☐ **Print Path** Engage Your Brain, SE p. 151

☐ **Print Path** Active Reading, SE p. 151

☐ **Digital Path** Lesson Opener

Key Topics/Learning Goals	Supporting Concepts
Animal Behavior 1 Explain how behavior is the response to a stimulus. 2 Compare external and internal stimuli. 3 Describe the difference between innate behavior and learned behavior.	• A stimulus is information that can make an organism change its behavior. A behavior is an action taken in response to a stimulus. • Internal stimuli tell an animal what is occurring in its body. External stimuli give an animal information about its surroundings. • Innate behavior is inherited and does not depend on experience. Learned behavior comes from experience or observing others.
Survival Behaviors 1 Describe behaviors that help an animal survive, including finding food, keeping a territory, and defensive behaviors.	• Animals hunt or forage for food in different ways. • A territory is an area occupied by one animal or by a group of animals that do not allow other members of the species to enter. Animals mark territories in different ways. • Defensive behaviors can be used to protect resources such as food, mates, and territory, or to protect themselves against predators.
Reproductive and Seasonal Behaviors 1 Explain the functions of courtship and parenting. 2 Describe migration, hibernation, and estivation.	• Courtship behaviors help animals find mates. Parenting refers to behaviors animals use to raise their young. Not all animals parent. • Migration is the movement from one place to another during certain times. Hibernation is a period of inactivity experienced in winter. Estivation is a period of inactivity experienced during hot and dry conditions.
Social Behaviors 1 Describe social behaviors including communication, living in groups, and social hierarchy.	• Animals may communicate by sound, touch, and chemicals. There are benefits and drawbacks for animals living in groups. Social hierarchies are found among species that have dominant-subordinate behaviors.

Options for Instruction

Two parallel paths provide coverage of the Essential Questions, with a strong **Inquiry** strand woven into each. Follow the **Print Path,** the **Digital Path,** or your customized combination of print, digital, and inquiry.

 Print Path
Teaching support for the Print Path appears with the Student Pages.

 Inquiry Labs and **Activities**

 Digital Path
Digital Path shortcut: TS663436

How Stimulating! SE pp. 152–153 What is behavior? How does behavior develop?	**Activity** Linking Stimuli and Behaviors **Activity** Learned or Innate? **Quick Lab** At a Snail's Pace	**Types of Stimulus and Behavior** Interactive Graphics
Survival Skills, SE pp. 154–155 What behaviors help animals survive?	**Daily Demo** Observing Group Behaviors **Activity** Identifying Survival Skills **Quick Lab** Modeling Predator-Prey Scenarios	**Finding Food** Interactive Images **Protecting and Defense Behaviors** Slideshow
A Success Story, SE pp. 156–157 What behaviors help animals reproduce successfully? What behaviors help animals survive seasonal change?	**Virtual Lab** Animal Migration	**Courtship and Parenting** Graphic Sequence **Seasonal Behaviors** Interactive Images
Social Structure, SE pp. 158–159 What are some social animal behaviors?	**Daily Demo** Observing Group Behaviors	**Social Behaviors** Interactive Images

Options for Assessment

See the Evaluate page for options, including Formative Assessment, Summative Assessment, and Unit Review.

Engage and Explore

Activities and Discussion

Activity *Linking Stimuli and Behaviors*

> Engage

Animal Behavior

 individuals, then whole class
 15 min
 GUIDED inquiry

Direct students to make a list of stimuli they have experienced so far today. Then have students write how each stimulus changed (or perhaps did not change) their behavior. Finally, review student lists as a class and work together to classify the different types of stimuli as internal or external. **Ask:** Overall, do you think people experience more internal or external stimuli on an average day? Student answers will vary.

Activity *Identifying Survival Skills*

Survival Behaviors

 pairs
 15 min
 GUIDED inquiry

Think, Pair, Share Ask students to think of examples of animal survival skills. Tell them that these should be specific behaviors that help specific types of animals survive. Then, have students work in pairs to list as many animal survival skills as possible. Allow students to use their texts for ideas and inspiration if necessary. Write the following four categories on the board: *Finding Food, Marking Territories, Defending Resources,* and *Avoiding Danger*. As students describe their examples, work as a class to place each example into one of the categories.

Take It Home *Observing Animal Behavior*

Introducing Key Topics

 student-adult pairs
 30 min
 GUIDED inquiry

Have students work with an adult to locate and observe animals near their homes. Animals can be wild or domesticated. Student-adult pairs should choose one animal and complete the worksheet together.

 Optional Online resource: student worksheet

Discussion *Fight or Flight Response*

Animal Behavior

 whole class
 10 min
 GUIDED inquiry

Explain that the "fight or flight" response is a response to an external stimulus that may be triggered by the sound of a predator. Use the example of the European hare from the text. Tell students that humans experience this response as well. Have students describe a situation in which they experienced the "fight or flight" response and have them describe physical responses they felt. Answers will vary but might include descriptions of increased heart rate, sweating, or a shaky feeling.

Probing Question *Animal Communication*

Social Behaviors

 whole class
 15 min
 GUIDED inquiry

Play a tape of various bird songs and calls. (Recordings of birds can be found in libraries or on the Internet.) **Ask:** What types of information do you think birds communicate through their songs and calls? Guide students to understand that birds communicate for many reasons, including to attract a mate, mark territory, alert others to the presence of a predator, and convey information about food. Then ask students to compare bird communication and human communication. **Ask:** How are they similar? How are they different? Sample answer: Both birds and humans communicate to share information and to get what they need to survive. Human communication may be more complex and is not always related to survival.

Customize Your Labs

 See the Lab Manual for lab datasheets.

 Go Online for editable lab datasheets.

Levels of  | DIRECTED inquiry | GUIDED inquiry | INDEPENDENT inquiry

introduces inquiry skills within a structured framework. | develops inquiry skills within a supportive environment. | deepens inquiry skills with student-driven questions or procedures.

Labs and Demos

Daily Demo *Observing Group Behaviors*

Engage

Survival Behaviors/ Social Behaviors

 whole class
 20 min
 DIRECTED inquiry

Use this demo after introducing social and survival behaviors.

PURPOSE **To demonstrate the survival skills and social behaviors of certain groups of animals**

MATERIALS

- a nature video showing lionesses' social and hunting behaviors and herd animals' social and survival behaviors

1 Show a 2- to 3-minute video segment to demonstrate social and survival behaviors in predators and prey.

2 Have students work with a partner to list the various social and survival behaviors they witnessed while watching the video.

3 Discuss with the class the behaviors seen by students. Help students identify the purposes behind each behavior. Ask students to identify the benefits and drawbacks of living in a group. Identify and explain which animal group in the video has a social hierarchy. Correct any misconceptions that students may have.

Quick Lab *At a Snail's Pace*

Animal Behavior

 small groups
 30 min
 GUIDED inquiry

Students develop an experiment to test how snails respond to light.

PURPOSE **To observe how snails respond to light and identify a relationship between light stimulus and animal behavior**

MATERIALS

- books
- flashlight
- marker, permanent
- picture frame, 20 cm x 20 cm
- ruler
- snail
- tape, masking

Virtual Lab *Animal Migration*

Reproductive and Seasonal Behaviors

 flexible
45 min
GUIDED inquiry

Students investigate bird migration through geographical flyways.

PURPOSE To learn about different types of animal migrations

©Getty Images

Quick Lab *Modeling Predator-Prey Scenarios*

PURPOSE **To model predator-prey relationships and recognize a relationship between group size and survival rate**

See the lab manual or go Online for planning information.

Activities and Discussion

☐ **Activity** Linking Stimuli and Behaviors
☐ **Activity** Identifying Survival Skills
☐ **Take It Home** Observing Behaviors
☐ **Discussion** Fight or Flight Response
☐ **Probing Question** Communication

Labs and Demos

☐ **Daily Demo** Observing Group Behaviors
☐ **Quick Lab** At a Snail's Pace
☐ **Quick Lab** Predator-Prey Scenarios
☐ **Virtual Lab** Animal Migration

Your Resources

_____

_____

_____

Explain Science Concepts

Key Topics	📖 Print Path	💻 Digital Path
Animal Behavior	☐ **How Stimulating!,** SE pp. 152–153 • Active Reading, #5 • Visualize It!, #6 • Think Outside the Book, #7 • Identify, #8 **8 Identify** Which human behaviors are innate, and which are learned? List some examples below. Innate / Learned laughing / playing the piano	☐ **Types of Stimulus and Behaviors** Learn about stimuli and innate and learned behaviors.
Survival Behaviors	☐ **Survival Skills,** SE pp. 154–155 • Identify, #9 • Active Reading, #10 • Inquiry, #11	☐ **Finding Food** Explore behaviors that help animals survive, such as behaviors for finding food. ☐ **Protecting and Defense Behaviors** Learn about how animals defend themselves and their territories.
Reproductive and Seasonal Behaviors	☐ **A Success Story,** SE pp. 156–157 • Visualize It!, #12 • Active Reading (Annotation strategy), #13 • Infer, #14	☐ **Courtship and Parenting** Explore how courtship and parenting are important for a species' survival. ☐ **Seasonal Behaviors** Learn how an animal's biological clock can affect survival behaviors, such as migration, hibernation, and estivation.
Social Behaviors	☐ **Social Structure,** SE pp. 158–159 • Active Reading, #15 • Infer, #16 • Compare, #17	☐ **Social Behaviors** Explore the social behaviors of animals.

Differentiated Instruction

Basic *Survival and Reproductive Behaviors*

Synthesizing Key Topics

 small groups

🕐 15 min

Have student groups find three photographs of animals exhibiting various survival behaviors and/or reproductive behaviors. Examples include a predator hunting prey, an animal making use of camouflage, and a primate carrying her baby. Each group should identify the behavior and write a short summary describing the purpose of the behavior. Support students as needed.

Advanced *Seasonal Behavior Patterns*

Reproductive and Seasonal Behaviors

 small groups

🕐 varies

Quick Research The migratory and hibernating/estivating patterns of animals are governed by various environmental stimuli. Invite small groups to research an animal that exhibits one of these types of seasonal behavior. Groups should investigate and report on the environmental triggers that cause the animal to prepare for migration, hibernation, or estivation. Groups should prepare a multimedia presentation to present to the class.

ELL *Body Language*

Social Behaviors

 small groups

🕐 20 min

Students may struggle with the concept that some animals use visual communication (such as the "waggle dance" of bees) to communicate. Explain to students that this kind of visual communication is similar to the body language that most humans use every day. To demonstrate body language, put a finger over your lips. **Ask:** What did I just communicate to you? Sample answer: that you want us to be quiet Have students work in small groups to come up with additional examples of body language used by humans. Have the groups act out their examples, and have the rest of the class guess what messages the group is sending. Some messages that students could use include "look at that" (point), "I'm angry" (fist), "come here" (wiggle finger), and "stop!" (raised hand, palm out).

Lesson Vocabulary

stimulus	innate behavior	learned behavior
territory	migration	hibernation
estivation	social behavior	

Previewing Vocabulary

 whole class   🕐 10 min

Predicting Meaning After an initial review of the lesson vocabulary, discuss the following with students. **Ask:** How are the words *migration, hibernation,* and *estivation* related? Students should be able to identify that each word describes a way in which animals survive seasonal changes. **Ask:** How are these words different? Students should be able to identify that each word describes a different way of coping with seasonal change.

Reinforcing Vocabulary

 individuals   🕐 15 min

Four Square To help students remember the vocabulary terms in the lesson, have them use a four square. After they draw the four square, guide students to write the term in the center. They should then fill in the surrounding cells with the types of information shown. Students may add illustrations in any of the four squares.

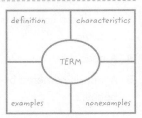

Customize Your Core Lesson

Core Instruction

☐ **Print Path** choices

☐ **Digital Path** choices

Vocabulary

☐ **Previewing Vocabulary** Predicting Meaning

☐ **Reinforcing Vocabulary** Four Square

Your Resources

Differentiated Instruction

☐ **Basic** Survival and Reproductive Behaviors

☐ **Advanced** Seasonal Behavior Patterns

☐ **ELL** Body Language

Extend Science Concepts

Reinforce and Review

Activity *Learned or Innate?*

Animal Behavior

 whole class

🕐 15 min

Two Sides Have students stand in the center of the classroom. Explain that the front of the room is the "learned behavior side," while the back of the room is the "innate behavior side." Then explain that you will read a series of statements describing animal behavior. Students will listen to each statement and decide if the behavior is learned or innate. After they decide, students will walk to the side of the room that reflects their choice. Once all students have made their decisions, discuss student choices in relation to the correct answer.

Statements

1. Your neighbor's dog responds to the commands to "sit" and "shake" by sitting and lifting its paw. **Answer: learned behavior**

2. A baby gorilla clings to its mother's belly. **Answer: innate behavior**

3. A newborn calf stands within minutes of its birth. **Answer: innate behavior**

4. A bear cub traps salmon in its paws. **Answer: learned behavior**

5. A wolf is cornered by a bear. It growls and attacks. **Answer: innate behavior**

FoldNote

Summarizing Key Concepts

 individuals

🕐 ongoing

Layered Book FoldNote Have students develop a Layered Book FoldNote to summarize information about the four main categories of behaviors covered in the lesson: survival behaviors, reproductive behaviors, seasonal behaviors, and social behaviors. When students have completed their layered books, have them compare their summaries with a partner to correct any errors and add any missing information. Support students throughout the writing process.

Going Further

Human Biology Connection

Animal Behavior

 individuals or small groups

🕐 varies

Quick Research Have students research human reflexes, such as the suckling reflex, the rooting reflex, or the Moro reflex. Have students choose one human reflex to research. Then have students create a poster, diagram, or multimedia presentation to present their findings to the class. Students should address how their chosen reflexes improve the odds for human survival.

Social Studies Connection

Social Behaviors

👥 whole class

🕐 varies

Discussion Explain that humans have the most complex social structure of all animals. Guide a discussion of human social structure. **Ask:** What is the basic unit of human social structure? the family **Ask:** What factors make human social structure more complex than other animal social structures? Answers will vary but should include a discussion of human intelligence levels as compared to other animals. **Ask:** How would you describe the social structure of school? Family? Athletic teams or extracurricular clubs? Answers will vary based on students' experiences.

To extend the activity have interested students choose to investigate human social structures by comparing them across cultural lines or investigating the development of human social structure over time.

Customize Your Closing

🗨 *See the Assessment Guide for quizzes and tests.*

⟳ *Go Online to edit and create quizzes and tests.*

Reinforce and Review

☐ **Activity** Learned or Innate?

☐ **FoldNote** Layered Book FoldNote

☐ **Print Path** Visual Summary, SE p. 160

☐ **Print Path** Lesson Review, SE p. 161

☐ **Digital Path** Lesson Closer

Evaluate Student Mastery

Formative Assessment

See the teacher support below the Student Pages for additional Formative Assessment questions.

Ask the following questions to assess student mastery of the material. **Ask:** Define the term *innate behavior* in your own words. Sample answer: An innate behavior is a behavior that an animal knows from the moment it is born. **Ask:** What are two behaviors that help animals reproduce successfully? courtship and parenting **Ask:** What behaviors indicate a response to seasonal changes? migration, estivation, and hibernation **Ask:** What are some social behaviors? living in groups, communicating, forming a pecking order, and living with set structure

Reteach

Formative assessment may show that students need reinforcement for certain topics. The resources below are recommended for reteaching. If students were introduced to a topic through the Print Path, you can also use the Digital Path to reteach, or vice versa.
🎧 *Can be assigned to individual students*

Animal Behavior
Activity Linking Stimuli and Behaviors 🎧

Survival Behaviors
Activity Identifying Survival Skills

Reproductive and Seasonal Behaviors
Virtual Lab Animal Migration

Social Behaviors
FoldNote Layered Book FoldNote 🎧

Summative Assessment

Alternative Assessment
How Animals Behave

⊙ *Online resources: student worksheet, optional rubrics*

Animal Behavior

Mix and Match: *How Animals Behave*
Mix and match ideas to show what you've learned about animal behavior.

1. Work on your own, with a partner, or with a small group.
2. Choose one information source from Column A, two topics from Column B, and one option from Column C. Check your choices.
3. Have your teacher approve your plan.
4. Submit or present your results.

A. Choose One Information Source	B. Choose Two Things to Analyze	C. Choose One Way to Communicate Analysis
___ observations of an aquarium	___ behavioral interactions between animals of the same species	___ series of illustrations with captions
___ observations of a pet	___ behavioral interactions between animals of different species	___ model, such as drawings or descriptions connected by strings
___ observations of a zoo exhibit	___ survival behaviors exhibited by a species	___ booklet, such as a field guide
___ observations of an aquarium exhibit	___ seasonal behaviors exhibited by a species	___ journal or essay
___ observations of wild animals in a local park	___ parenting behaviors exhibited by a species	___ game
___ observations of wild animals during a neighborhood walk	___ social behaviors exhibited by a species	___ story, song, or poem with supporting details
___ observations of a nature video showing behaviors of specific animals	_____	___ skit, chant, or dance with supporting details
_____		___ puppet show
		___ multimedia presentation
		___ video
		_____

Going Further
- ☐ **Human Biology Connection**
- ☐ **Social Studies Connection**

Formative Assessment
- ☐ **Strategies** Throughout TE
- ☐ **Lesson Review** SE

Summative Assessment
- ☐ **Alternative Assessment** How Animals Behave
- ☐ **Lesson Quiz**
- ☐ **Unit Tests A and B**
- ☐ **Unit Review** SE End-of-Unit

Your Resources

_____   _____

_____   _____

Lesson ⑥

Animal Behavior

ESSENTIAL QUESTION

What are some different animal behaviors?

By the end of this lesson, you should be able to describe some behaviors that help animals to survive and reproduce.

Male bower birds build stunning nests with colorful objects, such as berries and flowers, to attract females. This male also collected a brightly colored pen!

150 Unit 2 Earth's Organisms

Lesson Labs

Quick Labs
• At a Snail's Pace
• Modeling Predator-Prey Scenarios

Engage Your Brain

1 Identify Unscramble the letters below to find four behaviors that help animals survive and reproduce. Write your words on the blank lines.

TANIGE _____

LGIENRNA _____

TNARPEIGN _____

TIMNAG _____

2 Describe Write your own caption to this photo.

Active Reading

3 Synthesize Many English words have their roots in other languages. Use the Latin words below to make an educated guess about the meaning of the words *hibernation* and *estivation*.

Root word	Meaning
hibernus	of winter
aestas	of summer

Example sentence:
The snakes were hibernating to avoid the cold.

hibernation _____

Example sentence:
The frogs were estivating to avoid the heat.

estivation _____

Vocabulary Terms

• stimulus   • migration
• innate behavior   • hibernation
• learned behavior • estivation
• territory   • social behavior

4 Apply As you learn the definition of each vocabulary term in this lesson, create your own definition or sketch to help you remember the meaning of the term.

Lesson 6 Animal Behavior 151

Answers

Answers for 1–3 should represent students' current thoughts, even if incorrect.

1. eating, learning, parenting, mating

2. Sample answer: Sea turtles lay their eggs in holes they dig in the sand.

3. Sample answer: a period of inactivity during the winter; a period of inactivity during the summer

4. Students should define or sketch each vocabulary term in the lesson.

Opening Your Lesson

Discuss students' responses to the Engage Your Brain activity. Have them read aloud their captions describing the turtles' nesting behaviors. Then ask students to think about how the turtles know where to travel when nesting time comes. Ask volunteers to share their ideas.

Prerequisites Students should understand that animals exhibit different behaviors based on the adaptations they have developed. For example, most female birds sit on their eggs during the gestational period to protect them and keep them warm until they hatch.

Probing Questions GUIDED (Inquiry)

Analyzing What have you noticed about the behaviors of some of the animals that you see in the area where you live? Students should identify a common animal and a behavior. For example, squirrels gather and store food in various locations during the cooler autumn months and dig it up to eat when food is scarce. Spiders build webs in certain places to catch prey. If students have difficulty answering the question, provide them with a short list of animals that are common to their area and guide them to correct answers by asking appropriate questions.

How Stimulating!

What is behavior?

If your stomach grumbles when you wake up in the morning, you might go eat breakfast. Hunger is a **stimulus**, which is a type of information that causes a reaction or change in an organism. In this case, the response is a behavioral change. You go from lying in bed to looking for food. Behavior is the set of actions taken by an organism in response to stimuli.

Stimuli can be internal or external. An internal stimulus, such as feeling sick or feverish, comes from within an animal's body. When you get sick, your behavior can change. For example, you may choose to rest or no longer eat whatever caused your sickness.

An external stimulus comes from outside the body. These stimuli give animals information about their surroundings. If a rabbit hears a fox hunting nearby, the rabbit might run away. The sound of a fox is an external stimulus.

Active Reading

5 Identify What are the two categories of stimuli that can cause a change in behavior?

Visualize It!

6 Infer Consider the colorful individual below. How might color vision help mantis shrimp survive?

Animal sensory systems detect external stimuli. Mantis shrimp eyes distinguish more colors than human eyes can detect.

Think Outside the Book

7 Compare Do some research on an animal that can sense external stimuli that people cannot sense, such as electric pulses (electric fish), magnetic fields (homing pigeons), infrared radiation (snakes), or UV light (bees). Write a report describing how these animals respond to these external stimuli with behavior.

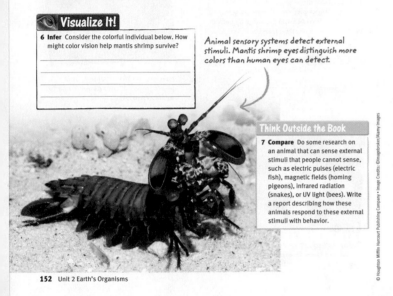

152 Unit 2 Earth's Organisms

How does behavior develop?

Animals are born knowing how to perform certain behaviors. A calf knows how to nurse as soon as it is born. All calves perform this behavior when they are born. However, some behaviors occur only if they are learned during an animal's life. A pet dog can learn to sit in response to its owner's command. But dogs will sit on command only if they are trained.

Some Behaviors Are Innate

Behavior that develops without depending on learning or experience is **innate behavior**. Animals perform an innate behavior completely the first time they try it. For example, a person's first yawn is just like every other time he or she yawns. A mother goose retrieves any eggs that roll from her nest by rolling them back to the nest with her bill. She does not need another goose to show her how to act this way. This behavior is known by the goose without any learning or previous experience.

Newborn whales have the innate ability to swim. They know how to swim without learning!

Some Behaviors Are Learned

A behavior that develops through experience or from observing the actions of other animals is a **learned behavior**. Many animals learn through experience which places are most likely to have food available. Some birds learn their songs by listening to other individuals. Young dolphins can learn how to hunt by watching adults. Some dolphins learn to push sponges along the ocean floor to stir up food, but not all dolphins behave this way.

Lyrebirds learn their songs by imitating sounds in the environment. They even imitate sounds such as cameras and chainsaws!

8 Identify Which human behaviors are innate, and which are learned? List some examples below.

Innate	Learned
laughing	playing the piano

Lesson 6 Animal Behavior 153

Answers

5. internal; external

6. Sample answer: Seeing a wide range of colors might help mantis shrimp recognize and communicate with other mantis shrimp.

7. Student answers should clearly indicate an external stimulus and a behavioral response.

8. Sample answers: Innate: eating, sleeping, yawning; Learned: speaking a certain language, playing a sport, reading

Building Reading Skills

Text Structure: Main Idea and Details Have students read the section "What is behavior?" Then have them analyze the text to identify and circle the main idea. Tell students to review the section again and identify the supporting details. Have students underline or highlight the supporting details. **Ask:** What clues in the text helped you identify the main idea? Sample answer: The section heading helped me identify the main idea. The heading asks what behavior is, so I knew that the sentence that defines behavior was the main idea. Ask volunteers to name important details that support the main idea.

Formative Assessment

Ask: What is the difference between an innate behavior and a learned behavior? Sample answer: An innate behavior is one that an animal knows from birth, such as a dolphin's ability to swim. A learned behavior is one that an animal is not born with but learns either from experience or from observation. An example is a bear cub learning to fish by watching its mother. **Ask:** What is an innate behavior that you have? Sample answers: yawning, sleeping, eating **Ask:** What is a learned behavior that you have? Sample answer: learning how to eat using utensils

Survival Skills

What behaviors help animals survive?

In order to survive, animals need to be able to avoid danger. They must also be able to find food and water. Animals have a variety of behaviors to stay safe and to find and defend food, water, shelter, and mates. Behaviors used to find food are called *foraging* behaviors.

Finding Food

All animals need food to survive. Animals that eat plants must find and identify the right plants. Getting enough food can take a lot of time. Giant pandas need to spend up to 14 hours a day eating bamboo. Squirrels bury food to store it for eating at a later time when food is hard to find.

Predators are animals that eat other individuals, called prey. Predators have different strategies to capture their prey. Some use speed and strength to catch prey. But others use lures, tools, or traps. The alligator snapping turtle has a pink, worm-like lure in its mouth. It waits with its mouth open to lure fish to the "worm." When a fish comes close, the turtle snaps it up.

Spiders build webs to trap their prey. When an insect hits the web, the spider moves quickly to find its meal.

9 Identify What are two strategies that predators use to capture prey?

_____

Marking Territories

Many animals must protect mates, offspring, or resources such as food. To do this, some animals mark a **territory**, an area occupied by a group or an individual. Marking a territory signals others of the same species not to enter the area. Birds mark territories by singing. Mammals rub the bark from trees or release chemical signals.

Cheetahs have a territorial imperative, which means they need to mark a territory. They do so by leaving a scent on trees.

Defending Resources

Many animals must defend their food, mates, and offspring from competition. Sometimes animals will fight to defend their resources. But usually they have behaviors that help them avoid fighting. Fighting is dangerous for both the winners and the losers. A common strategy to avoid fighting is trying to look bigger. Looking bigger can convince the competition to give up.

Avoiding Danger

Avoiding danger is an important part of survival. Some animals are fast and can run away to escape predators. The European hare can run as fast as 72 kilometers per hour! A few animals can change color to blend in to the environment and avoid predators. Octopi and cuttlefish can change their color to quickly match a background. Some animals avoid predators by releasing toxic chemicals. Skunks and stinkbugs release a chemical that drives predators away. Some animals can trick predators by appearing too big to eat. Pufferfish can avoid predation by puffing up their bodies when threatened.

Many male **Anolis** lizards puff out colorful throat flaps, called dewlaps, to threaten other males.

Active Reading 10 Identify What are three behaviors that animals use to avoid danger?

_____

_____

Can you see the octopus in this photograph? It uses camouflage to avoid predators.

Octopi can squirt ink to confuse predators. This allows them to escape unharmed.

Inquiry

11 Infer Not many animals can change color to camouflage themselves against a background. What is another behavior that animals could use to be camouflaged against a background?

_____

_____

Answers

9. Sample answer: chase prey with speed and strength; trap prey in a web

10. run away; change color; release toxic chemicals

11. Sample answer: Animals can move to environments that match their color. For example, a butterfly can land on a plant that is the same color as its wings.

Building Reading Skills

Idea Wheel Direct students to create an Idea Wheel to organize the information on animal survival skills. First, ask students to draw a large circle with a smaller circle inside. Students should label the smaller circle "Survival Skills." Then, have them divide the outer ring into four sections and label the sections "Finding Food," "Marking Territories," "Defending Resources," and "Avoiding Danger." Students should write short descriptions for each survival skill under the corresponding topic head within the wheel. Students can share their wheels with a partner to check for errors or missing information.

Optional Online resource: Idea Wheel support

Probing Questions GUIDED Inquiry

Hypothesizing How do you think animal species develop their specific survival skills? What do these skills depend on? Sample answer: Each animal species develops its survival skills over a long period of time. Animals inherit both physical characteristics and behavioral characteristics. If an animal attempts a survival technique that fails, the animal may die or fail to reproduce. Such a behavior pattern would not be passed on to future generations. Survival techniques that are consistently successful will be passed on to future generation of animals within the species.

A Success Story

What behaviors help animals reproduce successfully?

Animals have behaviors that help them reproduce successfully. Courtship behaviors help individuals find a mate. Parenting behaviors help animals raise healthy young. Many strange and beautiful animal behaviors relate to courtship and parenting.

Courtship

Many of the bright colors and complex calls of animals are used to help find a mate. Males use a variety of behaviors to try attracting females. Some birds and fish build eye-catching nests. Some insects bring gifts of food to convince females to mate. Many males have displays that stand out and get a female's attention. Adelie penguins call loudly, lift their head, and flap their flippers. Male jumping spiders perform fast dances that attract nearby females. Some females participate in courtship behaviors, too. Male and female sandhill cranes dance together by running, jumping, and flapping their wings.

Male and female fireflies "flash" each other to signal that they are ready to mate.

Parenting

Parents can help their young survive in many ways. Young killer whales learn to hunt by watching the adults. Many kinds of bird parents bring food to babies that are too weak to leave the nest. Mother killdeer birds behave as though their wing is broken to lure predators away from the nest.

Parents may help their young for just a short time or for quite a while. Some animals parent only long enough to lay eggs in a protected place. Mother chimpanzees parent their daughters for many years. Not all animals exhibit parenting behaviors.

Many birds hatch as helpless young that depend upon their parents to feed them.

Visualize It!

12 Apply How do you think the young in the photo let the parents know that they need food?

_____

_____

_____

156 Unit 2 Earth's Organisms

Active Reading

13 Identify As you read, underline the key terms that describe important seasonal animal behaviors.

Humpback whales move between cold, northern waters where they feed and warm, southern waters where they give birth.

What behaviors help animals survive seasonal change?

Seasonal changes can make survival difficult. A change in temperature can make it hard to find food or raise young. Animals have a few strategies to survive seasonal changes. Both daily cycles, or *circadian rhythms* (ser•KAY•dee•uhn RITH•uhmz), and seasonal cycles of behavior are controlled by biological clocks. A *biological clock* is an internal control of an animal's natural cycles.

Moving to Good Conditions

When seasonal weather changes make it hard to survive, some animals migrate. **Migration** is a seasonal movement from one place to another. Monarch butterflies cannot survive cold, northern winters. So they fly south when the weather cools. In the spring, they mate and fly north again. Many kinds of invertebrates, fish, amphibians, reptiles, birds, and mammals migrate. Animals that migrate depend on a biological clock to signal when to move.

Waiting for Good Conditions

Animals that don't migrate can become inactive until seasonal conditions improve. **Hibernation** is a period of inactivity and decreased body temperature that some animals experience in winter. **Estivation** is a period of inactivity experienced during hot and dry summers. A biological clock signals when to begin and end these seasonal behaviors.

A hibernating dormouse's temperature can drop to just above the environmental temperature.

14 Infer What do people do to make it through seasonal conditions such as cold winters or hot summers?

_____

_____

_____

Lesson 6 Animal Behavior 157

Answers

12. Sample answer: The open mouths signal hunger to the parents.

13. *See students' pages for annotations.*

14. Sample answer: People control the environment they live in by heating or cooling their houses.

Building Reading Skills

Everyday Definitions Students may be unfamiliar with the everyday definition of the word *courtship*. If this is the case, explain that *courtship* is an old-fashioned form of dating. Men used to court women they were interested in marrying, attempting to attract women with gifts and special, affectionate treatment. Ask students to apply this concept to animal behavior and discuss their interpretations of the term.

Interpreting Visuals

Direct students to examine the map showing the migratory paths of humpback whales. **Ask:** As the weather warms, the whales travel to different places. Is there a pattern to their movements? Yes. The whales generally travel north.

Learning Alert ⚠ MISCONCEPTION ⚠

Hibernation Students may think that hibernation is the same as sleeping. Hibernation is not sleeping; it is a period of inactivity and lowered body temperature that helps animals conserve energy during winter. Animals do not hibernate continuously through winter. Periods in which the animals' temperature rises to normal may last for days. Remind students that some animals in warm climates use estivation to conserve energy. Estivation is characterized by inactivity and lowered body temperature during hot, dry weather.

Social Structure

What are some social animal behaviors?

Animals have many social behaviors, such as those to communicate, hunt, and reproduce. **Social behavior** is the set of interactions that occur among animals of the same species.

Living in Groups

Many animals live in groups. A group of lions is called a *pride*. A group of geese is called a *gaggle*. Living in a group has some advantages. A group can spot a predator more quickly than an individual can. Groups can coordinate hunting and foraging, so everyone has a better chance of getting food.

Living in a group also has disadvantages. Individuals in groups compete for mates and food. And close contact with so many other animals can spread disease.

Active Reading 15 Compare List one advantage and one disadvantage of living in a group.

Communicating

Animals communicate to influence the behavior of others. Many signals relate to danger, food, and mating. Many male birds perform colorful dance displays to catch a female's eye. Bees signal where to find food with both sound and scent in a "waggle dance."

Some animals communicate by sound, sight, or touch. Elephants make sounds that are too low for humans to hear. Some animals communicate with chemicals. *Pheromones* (FEHR•uh•mohnz) are chemicals released by one animal that affect the behavior of others. Moths release pheromones to attract a mate. Ants leave pheromone paths to help others find food.

Meerkats make many kinds of calls to communicate with other meerkats in their large social groups.

16 Infer Meerkats make different alarm calls for different types of predators. How do you think this could help meerkats survive?

Forming a "Pecking Order"

People who own chickens can easily recognize a pecking order. One bird is the most dominant and has first access to food. Another is the bottom bird who lets all of the other birds get food before it has a turn. Groups that have clearly dominant individuals have a *social hierarchy* (SOH•shuhl HY•uh•rar•kee). Wolves also have a social hierarchy. The dominant male and female pair is called the alpha pair. All of the other wolves in the pack will follow the alpha pair's lead. The alpha pair decides when to hunt and when to rest. In a social hierarchy, individuals can sometimes fight to change their status.

Living Within a Set Structure

Some animals have a social structure that is determined from birth. In a honeybee colony, one individual is the queen. She is the only bee that lays eggs, and her position lasts her entire life. All bees in the colony come from her eggs, so all the bees are closely related. The queen's offspring include workers that clean, feed larvae, build, and find food. The workers do each job at a different stage of life. Young workers clean the hive. Older workers forage for food that they share. A bee colony is an example of a set social structure. Several insects that are very closely related have this type of social organization.

When dominant baboons approach, less dominant animals move away.

17 Compare How are social hierarchies different from set social structures?

These weaver ants are workers that are building a safe nest for the colony.

159

Answers

15. Sample answer: greater chance of spotting a predator (advantage); greater chance of disease (disadvantage)

16. Sample answer: If meerkats know which kind of predator is coming, they can respond correctly. So, if a hawk comes, they can hide under a bush. If a snake comes, they can move to high ground.

17. Sample answer: Animals with a social hierarchy can fight to change their dominance position. Animals with a set social structure have roles that are set from birth.

Formative Assessment

Ask: What is an example of an animal that lives in a group? Sample answers: bees, elephants, antelope, zebra, many types of fish **Ask:** Name two reasons why living in a group can be a disadvantage for animals. Sample answer: Individuals living in a group compete for mates and food. **Ask:** What is one advantage to living in groups? Sample answer: Adult animals can share parenting duties. **Ask:** How is a queen bee different from every other bee in a colony? The queen bee can lay eggs.

Interpreting Visuals

Have students examine the photo of the group of baboons. **Ask:** How do animals' physical characteristics contribute to a group's social hierarchy? Sample answer: Physical characteristics such as size or various physical markings could influence an animal's place in the social hierarchy.

Visual Summary

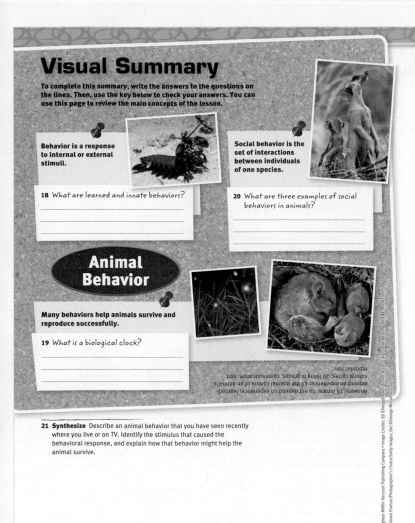

To complete this summary, write the answers to the questions on the lines. Then, use the key below to check your answers. You can use this page to review the main concepts of the lesson.

Behavior is a response to internal or external stimuli.

18 What are learned and innate behaviors?

Social behavior is the set of interactions between individuals of one species.

20 What are three examples of social behaviors in animals?

Animal Behavior

Many behaviors help animals survive and reproduce successfully.

19 What is a biological clock?

Answers: 18 innate: do not depend on experience; learned: depend on experience; 19 the internal control of an animal's natural cycles; 20 living in groups, communication, and reproduction

21 Synthesize Describe an animal behavior that you have seen recently where you live or on TV. Identify the stimulus that caused the behavioral response, and explain how that behavior might help the animal survive.

Lesson Review

Lesson **6**

Vocabulary

Draw a line to connect the following terms to their definitions.

1 territory   **A** a behavior that does not depend on experience

2 innate

3 estivation   **B** a period of inactivity that occurs during hot and dry conditions

    C an area occupied by one or more animals that do not allow other members of the species to enter

Key Concepts

4 Identify What is the difference between internal stimuli and external stimuli?

5 Describe Choose one animal and describe how it marks its territory.

6 Explain How do animals use pheromones?

7 Compare What are the advantages and disadvantages of living in a group?

Critical Thinking

Use this map to answer the following questions.

8 Analyze Which of the following behaviors could be represented by the arrows: migration, hibernation, or estivation?

9 Infer How would the birds traveling along this path know when to move from place to place?

10 Relate What behaviors do humans use to find food, parent their offspring, and court each other?

11 Apply Explain how looking bigger by spreading its wings might help a bird avoid predation.

Visual Summary Answers

18. innate: do not depend on experience; learned: depend on experience

19. the internal control of an animal's natural cycles

20. living in groups; communication; reproduction

21. Sample answer: A squirrel ran up a tree when a dog approached. Stimulus: dog approaching. This behavior might help the squirrel survive because it is avoiding danger by escaping the dog.

Lesson Review Answers

1. C

2. A

3. B

4. Sample answer: internal stimuli come from within the body; external stimuli come from outside the body

5. Sample answer: A songbird marks its territory by singing.

6. Sample answer: Animals release pheromones to signal that they are ready to mate, to mark their territory, or to leave a path to food.

7. Living in a group helps animals detect predators and find food. But it also means competition for food and mates, and it helps disease spread.

8. migration

9. a biological clock

10. Sample answer: Humans garden, hunt, and visit grocery stores for food; feed and shelter their offspring; sometimes give gifts when courting.

11. Sample answer: Spreading its wings may trick a predator into thinking the bird is too big to eat.

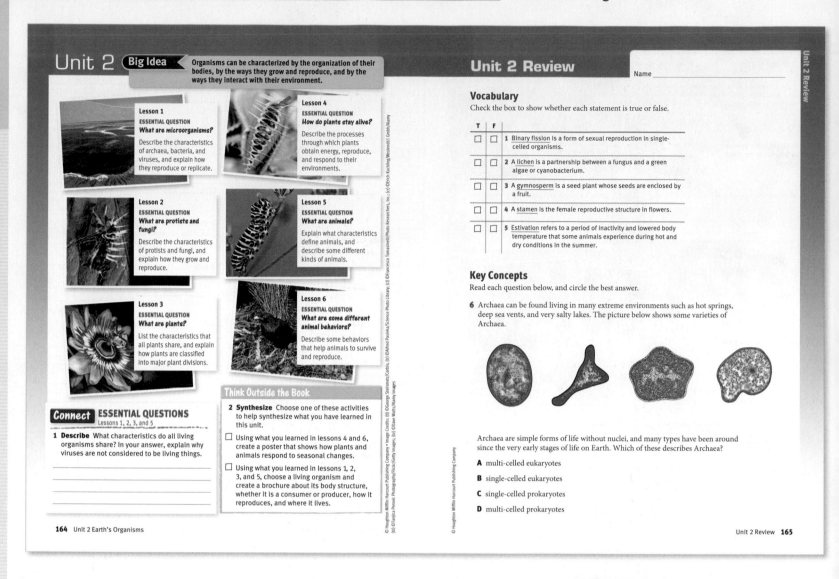

Unit Summary Answers

1. Sample answer: All organisms are made of cells, respond to stimuli, reproduce, grow, and use energy obtained from their environment. Viruses are not considered living because they do not perform any life functions and cannot function on their own.

2. Option 1: Students' posters should include such things as changes in foliage/leaf loss or flowering and seed production in plants. Animal seasonal responses include hibernation, estivation, breeding, migration, and coat changes. Students should identify how or why such behaviors are advantageous to the organisms.

   Option 2: Students' brochures should include accurate depictions of the plant or animal they have chosen to study. The brochures should highlight how the body of their chosen organism is adapted to the role it has in the environment (such as a consumer or producer).

Unit Review Response to Intervention

A Quick Grading Chart follows the Answers. See the Assessment Guide for more detail about correct and incorrect answer choices. Refer back to the Lesson Planning pages for activities and assignments that can be used as remediation for students who answer questions incorrectly.

Answers

1. False This statement is false because binary fission is a form of asexual reproduction in single-celled organisms by which one cell divides into two cells of the same size. (Lesson 1)

2. True This statement is true because a lichen is the combination of a fungus with a green algae or cyanobacterium. (Lesson 2)

3. False This statement is false because gymnosperms do not have fruit, angiosperms do. (Lesson 4)

4. False This statement is false because a stamen is the male reproductive structure in flowers; the pistil is the female reproductive structure. (Lesson 4)

Unit 2 Review continued

7 The picture below shows a virus.

Virus

Which of the following is a task the host cell has during the replication of viruses?

A The host cell destroys the virus.

B The host cell replicates the virus's genetic material.

C The host cell is destroyed and viral replication stops.

D The host cell's proteins block the replication of the viral proteins.

8 Which of the following is true of protists?

A Protists reproduce only by asexual reproduction.

B Some protists can photosynthesize.

C Protists cannot move on their own.

D Protists are prokaryotic.

9 Fungi that exist mostly in a unicellular state and reproduce by budding are called what?

A molds **C** spores

B hyphae **D** yeasts

10 Where would you expect to see a plant that does not have a vascular system?

A in a botanical museum, because they are all extinct

B deeply rooted in a forest with a trunk that reaches 20 meters or more

C low and close to the ground

D climbing high while circling the branches of another plant

11 Which of the following is a plant structure that is involved in asexual reproduction?

A stigma **C** pistil

B stamen **D** tuber

12 The diagram below shows a cycle of energy flowing between living organisms.

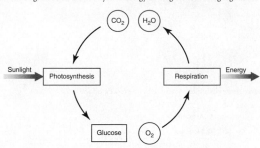

Which of the following could the two sides of the diagram represent?

A The left side represents a producer, and the right side represents a consumer.

B The left side represents a consumer, and the right side represents a producer.

C The left side represents an animal that eats plants, and the right side represents a plant.

D The left side represents energy created, and the right side represents energy destroyed.

13 Which of the following is true of all animals?

A They are producers.

B They are multicellular.

C They reproduce asexually.

D They are unicellular.

Answers *(continued)*

5. **True** This statement is true because estivation is like hibernation, but, unlike hibernation, occurs only in the summertime. (Lesson 6)

6. **Answer C is correct** because Archaea are single-celled and prokaryotic since they have no nuclei or other membrane-bound organelles. (Lesson 1)

7. **Answer B is correct** because this is part of the replication process. (Lesson 1)

8. **Answer B is correct** because there are plant-like protists (algae) that photosynthesize. (Lesson 2)

9. **Answer D is correct** because yeasts are mostly unicellular and reproduce by budding. (Lesson 2)

10. **Answer C is correct** because nonvascular plants depend on diffusion to move water and nutrients. (Lesson 3)

11. **Answer D is correct** because a tuber is a structure that allows a plant to reproduce asexually. (Lesson 4)

12. **Answer A is correct** because plants are photosynthetic, and the other side could represent a respiring consumer. (Lesson 4)

13. **Answer B is correct** because a key characteristic of animals is that they are multicellular. (Lesson 5)

14. **Answer C is correct** because insects, such as the preserved ant within the amber, are arthropods, as are crabs and lobsters. (Lesson 5)

15. **Answer D is correct** because the circadian rhythm is the daily cycle of an animal's activity. (Lesson 6)

16. **Answer B is correct** because the butterflies inherently know to migrate without being taught. (Lesson 6)

17. **Answer A is correct** because Chordata is made up of vertebrates and some invertebrates, which all have a notochord at some point in their development. (Lesson 5)

18. **Key Elements:**

   • The male reproductive structure, the stamen, produces pollen. Pollinators, such as insects, or the wind carry the pollen to the female reproductive structure, the pistil.

Unit 2 Review continued

Name _____

14 The fossil below shows a well-preserved invertebrate with an exoskeleton and jointed appendages.

Which of these invertebrate phyla is characterized by an exoskeleton and jointed legs?

A Cnidara **C** Arthropoda

B Ctenophora **D** Mollusca

15 Which of the following phrases describes the cycle of activity that an animal has during any 24-hour period?

A the animal's hibernation period

B the animal's estivation period

C the animal's biological clock

D the animal's circadian rhythm

16 Which of the following describes an innate animal behavior?

A a pet dog shaking hands on its owner's command

B Monarch butterflies migrating southward

C squirrels in a park approaching people for food

D a horse being ridden through an obstacle course

17 The diagram below shows the relationships among some members of the phylum Chordata.

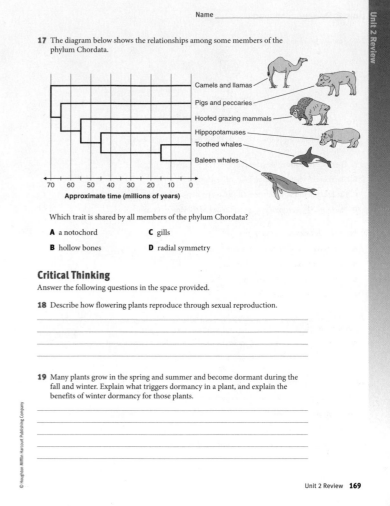

Camels and llamas
Pigs and peccaries
Hoofed grazing mammals
Hippopotamuses
Toothed whales
Baleen whales

70 60 50 40 30 20 10 0
Approximate time (millions of years)

Which trait is shared by all members of the phylum Chordata?

A a notochord **C** gills

B hollow bones **D** radial symmetry

Critical Thinking
Answer the following questions in the space provided.

18 Describe how flowering plants reproduce through sexual reproduction.

_____

_____

_____

19 Many plants grow in the spring and summer and become dormant during the fall and winter. Explain what triggers dormancy in a plant, and explain the benefits of winter dormancy for those plants.

_____

_____

_____

_____

_____

_____

Answers *(continued)*

- After fertilization of the ova by the sperm nuclei, seeds develop in the ovaries. The ovaries become fruit that protects the seeds. The seeds are genetically different from each other and both parents. (Lesson 4)

19. Key Elements:

- Shorter days and longer nights during the fall help trigger the release of hormones that cause winter dormancy in the plants. In the spring when there are more hours of sunlight, the plants come out of dormancy.

- With fewer hours of sunlight during the winter, it is more energy efficient for these plants to shut down and use up stored sugars than it is for them to photosynthesize. (Lesson 4)

20. Key Elements:

- photosynthesis

- chloroplasts

- The energy is stored in the chemical bonds of glucose molecules, which the plant can either use for its own cellular functions or store in its roots.

- producer (Lesson 4)

21. Key Elements:

Student answers may vary. Answers should contain the following points:

- The vascular system of plants is the means by which plants move water and minerals up from the roots to the branches.

- Vascular systems allow trees to grow very tall relative to nonvascular plants.

Unit 2 Review continued

20 The diagram below shows the process in which plants use energy from the sun.

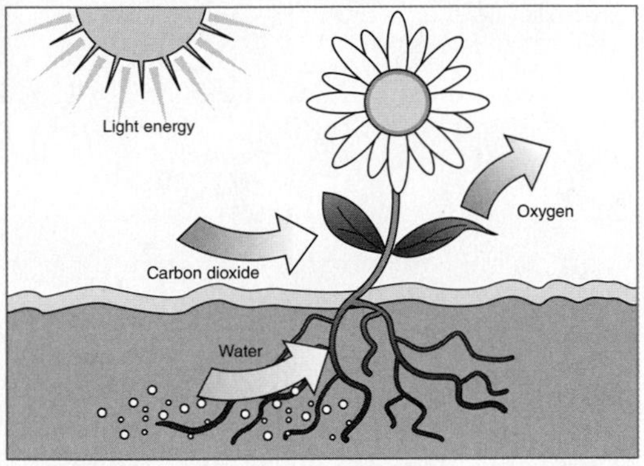

Light energy

Oxygen

Carbon dioxide

Water

What is this process called? _____

In which plant organelle does this process occur? _____

How does the plant store the energy it gets from the sun?

_____

_____

Is a plant a producer, consumer, or decomposer? _____

Connect **ESSENTIAL QUESTIONS**
Lessons 3, 5, and 6

Answer the following question in the space provided.

21 Explain how the vascular systems of plants in the rainforests might have affected animal behavior and the diversity of life in the rainforests.

_____

_____

_____

_____

_____

170 Unit 2 Earth's Organisms

© Houghton Mifflin Harcourt Publishing Company

Quick Grading Chart

Use the chart below for quick test grading. The lesson correlations can help you target reteaching for missed items.

Item	Answer	Cognitive Complexity	Lesson
1.	—	Low	1
2.	—	Low	2
3.	—	Low	4
4.	—	Low	4
5.	—	Low	6
6.	C	Moderate	1
7.	B	Moderate	1
8.	B	Moderate	2
9.	D	Low	2
10.	C	Moderate	3
11.	D	Moderate	4
12.	A	Moderate	4
13.	B	Moderate	5
14.	C	Moderate	5
15.	D	Moderate	6
16.	B	Moderate	6
17.	A	Moderate	5
18.	—	Moderate	4
19.	—	Moderate	4
20.	—	Moderate	4
21.	—	High	3

Cognitive Complexity refers to the demand on thinking associated with an item, and may vary with the answer choices, the number of steps required to arrive at an answer, and other factors, but not the ability level of the student.

Answers *(continued)*

- Tall trees provide new habitats, challenges, and modes of transportation for many animals.
- Tall trees in the rain forest create layers of ecosystems that allow for more diversity and interactions to develop.
  (Lesson 3)

Teacher Notes

Resources

Handbook

References

Mineral Properties

Here are five steps to take in mineral identification:

1 Determine the color of the mineral. Is it light-colored, dark-colored, or a specific color?

2 Determine the luster of the mineral. Is it metallic or non-metallic?

3 Determine the color of any powder left by its streak?

4 Determine the hardness of your mineral. Is it soft, hard, or very hard? Using a glass plate, see if the mineral scratches it.

5 Determine whether your sample has cleavage or any special properties.

TERMS TO KNOW	DEFINITION
adamantine	a non-metallic luster like that of a diamond
cleavage	how a mineral breaks when subject to stress on a particular plane
luster	the state or quality of shining by reflecting light
streak	the color of a mineral when it is powdered
submetallic	between metallic and nonmetallic in luster
vitreous	glass-like type of luster

Silicate Minerals					
Mineral	Color	Luster	Streak	Hardness	Cleavage and Special Properties
Beryl	deep green, pink, white, bluish green, or yellow	vitreous	white	7.5–8	1 cleavage direction; some varieties fluoresce in ultraviolet light
Chlorite	green	vitreous to pearly	pale green	2–2.5	1 cleavage direction
Garnet	green, red, brown, black	vitreous	white	6.5–7.5	no cleavage
Hornblende	dark green, brown, or black	vitreous	none	5–6	2 cleavage directions
Muscovite	colorless, silvery white, or brown	vitreous or pearly	white	2–2.5	1 cleavage direction
Olivine	olive green, yellow	vitreous	white or none	6.5–7	no cleavage
Orthoclase	colorless, white, pink, or other colors	vitreous	white or none	6	2 cleavage directions
Plagioclase	colorless, white, yellow, pink, green	vitreous	white	6	2 cleavage directions
Quartz	colorless or white; any color when not pure	vitreous or waxy	white or none	7	no cleavage

Nonsilicate Minerals					
Mineral	Color	Luster	Streak	Hardness	Cleavage and Special Properties
Native Elements					
Copper	copper-red	metallic	copper-red	2.5–3	no cleavage
Diamond	pale yellow or colorless	adamantine	none	10	4 cleavage directions
Graphite	black to gray	submetallic	black	1–2	1 cleavage direction
Carbonates					
Aragonite	colorless, white, or pale yellow	vitreous	white	3.5–4	2 cleavage directions; reacts with hydrochloric acid
Calcite	colorless or white to tan	vitreous	white	3	3 cleavage directions; reacts with weak acid; double refraction
Halides					
Fluorite	light green, yellow, purple, bluish green, or other colors	vitreous	none	4	4 cleavage directions; some varieties fluoresce
Halite	white	vitreous	white	2.0–2.5	3 cleavage directions
Oxides					
Hematite	reddish brown to black	metallic to earthy	dark red to red-brown	5.6–6.5	no cleavage; magnetic when heated
Magnetite	iron-black	metallic	black	5.5–6.5	no cleavage; magnetic
Sulfates					
Anhydrite	colorless, bluish, or violet	vitreous to pearly	white	3–3.5	3 cleavage directions
Gypsum	white, pink, gray, or colorless	vitreous, pearly, or silky	white	2.0	3 cleavage directions
Sulfides					
Galena	lead-gray	metallic	lead-gray to black	2.5–2.8	3 cleavage directions
Pyrite	brassy yellow	metallic	greenish, brownish, or black	6–6.5	no cleavage

References

Geologic Time Scale

Geologists developed the geologic time scale to represent the 4.6 billion years of Earth's history that have passed since Earth formed. This scale divides Earth's history into blocks of time. The boundaries between these time intervals (shown in millions of years ago or mya in the table below), represent major changes in Earth's history. Some boundaries are defined by mass extinctions, major changes in Earth's surface, and/or major changes in Earth's climate.

The four major divisions that encompass the history of life on Earth are Precambrian time, the Paleozoic era, the Mesozoic era, and the Cenozoic era. The largest divisions are eons. **Precambrian time** is made up of the first three eons, over 4 billion years of Earth's history.

The **Paleozoic era** lasted from 542 mya to 251 mya. All major plant groups, except flowering plants, appeared during this era. By the end of the era, reptiles, winged insects, and fishes had also appeared. The largest known mass extinction occurred at the end of this era.

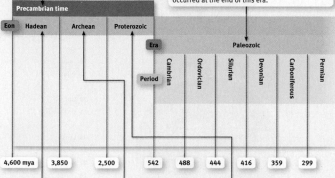

The **Hadean eon** lasted from about 4.6 billion years ago (bya) to 3.85 bya. It is described based on evidence from meterorites and rocks from the moon.

The **Archean eon** lasted from 3.85 bya to 2.5 bya. The earliest rocks from Earth that have been found and dated formed at the start of this eon.

The **Proterozoic eon** lasted from 2.5 bya to 542 mya. The first organisms, which were single-celled organisms, appeared during this eon. These organisms produced so much oxygen that they changed Earth's oceans and Earth's atmosphere.

© Houghton Mifflin Harcourt Publishing Company

Divisions of Time

The divisions of time shown here represent major changes in Earth's surface and when life developed and changed significantly on Earth. As new evidence is found, the boundaries of these divisions may shift. The Phanerozoic eon is divided into three eras. The beginning of each of these eras represents a change in the types of organisms that dominated Earth. And, each era is commonly characterized by the types of organisms that dominated the era. These eras are divided into periods, and periods are divided into epochs.

The **Mesozoic era** lasted from 251 mya to 65.5 mya. During this era, many kinds of dinosaurs dominated land, and giant lizards swam in the ocean. The first birds, mammals, and flowering plants also appeared during this time. About two-thirds of all land species went extinct at the end of this era.

The **Phanerozoic eon** began 542 mya. We live in this eon.

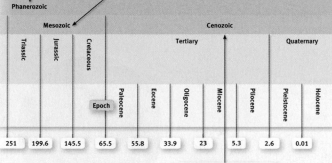

The **Cenozoic era** began 65.5 mya and continues today. Mammals dominate this era. During the Mesozoic era, mammals were small in size but grew much larger during the Cenozoic era. Primates, including humans, appeared during this era.

© Houghton Mifflin Harcourt Publishing Company

Star Charts for the Northern Hemisphere

A star chart is a map of the stars in the night sky. It shows the names and positions of constellations and major stars. Star charts can be used to identify constellations and even to orient yourself using Polaris, the North Star.

Because Earth moves through space, different constellations are visible at different times of the year. The star charts on these pages show the constellations visible during each season in the Northern Hemisphere.

Spring

Autumn

Summer

Winter

Constellations

1 Ursa Minor
2 Draco
3 Cepheus
4 Cassiopeia
5 Auriga
6 Ursa Major
7 Boötes
8 Hercules
9 Cygnus
10 Perseus
11 Gemini
12 Cancer
13 Leo
14 Serpens
15 Sagitta
16 Pegasus
17 Pisces

Constellations

18 Aries
19 Taurus
20 Orion
21 Virgo
22 Libra
23 Ophiuchus
24 Aquila
25 Lepus
26 Canis Major
27 Hydra
28 Corvus
29 Scorpius
30 Sagittarius
31 Capricornus
32 Aquarius
33 Cetus
34 Columba

References

World Map

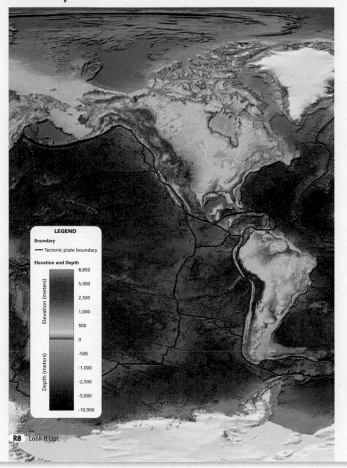

LEGEND

Boundary
— Tectonic plate boundary

Elevation and Depth

Elevation (meters)
8,850
5,000
2,500
1,000
500
0

Depth (meters)
-500
-1,000
-2,500
-5,000
-10,900

© Houghton Mifflin Harcourt Publishing Company

© Houghton Mifflin Harcourt Publishing Company

R8   Look It Up!

Look It Up!   R9

References

Classification of Living Things

Domains and Kingdoms

All organisms belong to one of three domains: Domain Archaea, Domain Bacteria, or Domain Eukarya. Some of the groups within these domains are shown below. (Remember that genus names are italicized.)

Domain Archaea

The organisms in this domain are single-celled prokaryotes, many of which live in extreme environments.

Archaea		
Group	**Example**	**Characteristics**
Methanogens	*Methanococcus*	produce methane gas; can't live in oxygen
Thermophiles	*Sulpholobus*	require sulphur; can't live in oxygen
Halophiles	*Halococcus*	live in very salty environments; most can live in oxygen

Domain Bacteria

Organisms in this domain are single-celled prokaryotes and are found in almost every environment on Earth.

Bacteria		
Group	**Example**	**Characteristics**
Bacilli	*Escherichia*	rod shaped; some bacilli fix nitrogen; some cause disease
Cocci	*Streptococcus*	spherical shaped; some cause disease; can form spores
Spirilla	*Treponema*	spiral shaped; cause diseases such as syphilis and Lyme disease

Domain Eukarya

Organisms in this domain are single-celled or multicellular eukaryotes.

Kingdom Protista Many protists resemble fungi, plants, or animals, but are smaller and simpler in structure. Most are single celled.

Protists		
Group	**Example**	**Characteristics**
Sarcodines	*Amoeba*	radiolarians; single-celled consumers
Ciliates	*Paramecium*	single-celled consumers
Flagellates	*Trypanosoma*	single-celled parasites
Sporozoans	*Plasmodium*	single-celled parasites
Euglenas	*Euglena*	single celled; photosynthesize
Diatoms	*Pinnularia*	most are single celled; photosynthesize
Dinoflagellates	*Gymnodinium*	single celled; some photosynthesize
Algae	*Volvox*	single celled or multicellular; photosynthesize
Slime molds	*Physarum*	single celled or multicellular; consumers or decomposers
Water molds	powdery mildew	single celled or multicellular; parasites or decomposers

Kingdom Fungi Most fungi are multicellular. Their cells have thick cell walls. Fungi absorb food from their environment.

Fungi		
Group	**Examples**	**Characteristics**
Threadlike fungi	bread mold	spherical; decomposers
Sac fungi	yeast; morels	saclike; parasites and decomposers
Club fungi	mushrooms; rusts; smuts	club shaped; parasites and decomposers
Lichens	British soldier	a partnership between a fungus and an alga

Kingdom Plantae Plants are multicellular and have cell walls made of cellulose. Plants make their own food through photosynthesis. Plants are classified into divisions instead of phyla.

Plants		
Group	**Examples**	**Characteristics**
Bryophytes	mosses; liverworts	no vascular tissue; reproduce by spores
Club mosses	*Lycopodium;* ground pine	grow in wooded areas; reproduce by spores
Horsetails	rushes	grow in wetland areas; reproduce by spores
Ferns	spleenworts; sensitive fern	large leaves called fronds; reproduce by spores
Conifers	pines; spruces; firs	needlelike leaves; reproduce by seeds made in cones
Cycads	*Zamia*	slow growing; reproduce by seeds made in large cones
Gnetophytes	*Welwitschia*	only three living families; reproduce by seeds
Ginkgoes	*Ginkgo*	only one living species; reproduce by seeds
Angiosperms	all flowering plants	reproduce by seeds made in flowers; fruit

Kingdom Animalia Animals are multicellular. Their cells do not have cell walls. Most animals have specialized tissues and complex organ systems. Animals get food by eating other organisms.

Animals		
Group	**Examples**	**Characteristics**
Sponges	glass sponges	no symmetry or specialized tissues; aquatic
Cnidarians	jellyfish; coral	radial symmetry; aquatic
Flatworms	planaria; tapeworms; flukes	bilateral symmetry; organ systems
Roundworms	*Trichina;* hookworms	bilateral symmetry; organ systems
Annelids	earthworms; leeches	bilateral symmetry; organ systems
Mollusks	snails; octopuses	bilateral symmetry; organ systems
Echinoderms	sea stars; sand dollars	radial symmetry; organ systems
Arthropods	insects; spiders; lobsters	bilateral symmetry; organ systems
Chordates	fish; amphibians; reptiles; birds; mammals	bilateral symmetry; complex organ systems

References

Periodic Table of the Elements

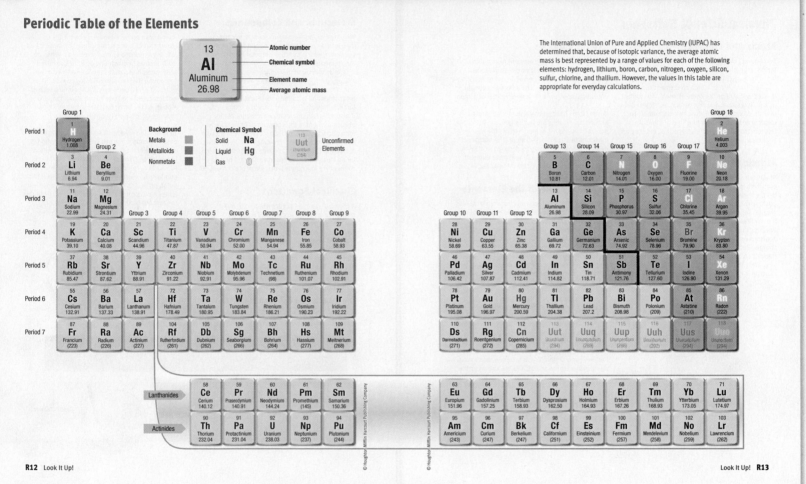

The International Union of Pure and Applied Chemistry (IUPAC) has determined that, because of isotopic variance, the average atomic mass is best represented by a range of values for each of the following elements: hydrogen, lithium, boron, carbon, nitrogen, oxygen, silicon, sulfur, chlorine, and thallium. However, the values in this table are appropriate for everyday calculations.

© Houghton Mifflin Harcourt Publishing Company

References

Physical Science Refresher

Atoms and Elements

Every object in the universe is made of matter. **Matter** is anything that takes up space and has mass. All matter is made of atoms. An **atom** is the smallest particle into which an element can be divided and still be the same element. An **element**, in turn, is a substance that cannot be broken down into simpler substances by chemical means. Each element consists of only one kind of atom. An element may be made of many atoms, but they are all the same kind of atom.

Atomic Structure

Atoms are made of smaller particles called **electrons**, **protons**, and **neutrons**. Electrons have a negative electric charge, protons have a positive charge, and neutrons have no electric charge. Together, protons and neutrons form the **nucleus**, or small dense center, of an atom. Because protons are positively charged and neutrons are neutral, the nucleus has a positive charge. Electrons move within an area around the nucleus called the **electron cloud**. Electrons move so quickly that scientists cannot determine their exact speeds and positions at the same time.

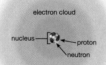

electron cloud

nucleus → proton

neutron

Atomic Number

To help distinguish one element from another, scientists use the atomic numbers of atoms. The **atomic number** is the number of protons in the nucleus of an atom. The atoms of a certain element always have the same number of protons.

When atoms have an equal number of protons and electrons, they are uncharged, or electrically neutral. The atomic number equals the number of electrons in an uncharged atom. The number of neutrons, however, can vary for a given element. Atoms of the same element that have different numbers of neutrons are called **isotopes**.

Periodic Table of the Elements

In the periodic table, each element in the table is in a separate box. And the elements are arranged from left to right in order of increasing atomic number. That is, an uncharged atom of each element has one more electron and one more proton than an uncharged atom of the element to its left. Each horizontal row of the table is called a **period**. Changes in chemical properties of elements across a period correspond to changes in the electron arrangements of their atoms.

Each vertical column of the table is known as a **group**. A group lists elements with similar physical and chemical properties. For this reason, a group is also sometimes called a family. The elements in a group have similar properties because their atoms have the same number of electrons in their outer energy level. For example, the elements helium, neon, argon, krypton, xenon, and radon all have similar properties and are known as the noble gases.

Molecules and Compounds

When two or more elements join chemically, they form a **compound**. A compound is a new substance with properties different from those of the elements that compose it. For example, water, H_2O, is a compound formed when hydrogen (H) and oxygen (O) combine. The smallest complete unit of a compound that has the properties of that compound is called a **molecule**. A chemical formula indicates the elements in a compound. It also indicates the relative number of atoms of each element in the compound. The chemical formula for water is H_2O. So, each water molecule consists of two atoms of hydrogen and one atom of oxygen. The subscript number after the symbol for an element shows how many atoms of that element are in a single molecule of the compound.

Chemical Equations

A chemical reaction occurs when a chemical change takes place. A chemical equation describes a chemical reaction using chemical formulas. The equation indicates the substances that react and the substances that are produced. For example, when carbon and oxygen combine, they can form carbon dioxide, shown in the equation below: $C + O_2 \longrightarrow CO_2$

Acids, Bases, and pH

An **ion** is an atom or group of chemically bonded atoms that has an electric charge because it has lost or gained one or more electrons. When an acid, such as hydrochloric acid, HCl, is mixed with water, it separates into ions. An **acid** is a compound that produces hydrogen ions, H^+, in water. The hydrogen ions then combine with a water molecule to form a hydronium ion, H_3O^+. A **base**, on the other hand, is a substance that produces hydroxide ions, OH^-, in water.

To determine whether a solution is acidic or basic, scientists use pH. The **pH** of a solution is a measure of the hydronium ion concentration in a solution. The pH scale ranges from 0 to 14. Acids have a pH that is less than 7. The lower the number, the more acidic the solution. The middle point, pH = 7, is neutral, neither acidic nor basic. Bases have a pH that is greater than 7. The higher the number is, the more basic the solution.

The pH of Some Common Materials

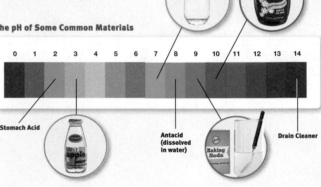

0 1 2 3 4 5 6 7 8 9 10 11 12 13 14

Stomach Acid

Antacid (dissolved in water)

Drain Cleaner

References

Physical Laws and Useful Equations

Law of Conservation of Mass

Mass cannot be created or destroyed during ordinary chemical or physical changes.

The total mass in a closed system is always the same no matter how many physical changes or chemical reactions occur.

Law of Conservation of Energy

Energy can be neither created nor destroyed.

The total amount of energy in a closed system is always the same. Energy can be changed from one form to another, but all of the different forms of energy in a system always add up to the same total amount of energy, no matter how many energy conversions occur.

Law of Universal Gravitation

All objects in the universe attract each other by a force called gravity. The size of the force depends on the masses of the objects and the distance between the objects.

The first part of the law explains why lifting a bowling ball is much harder than lifting a marble. Because the bowling ball has a much larger mass than the marble does, the amount of gravity between Earth and the bowling ball is greater than the amount of gravity between Earth and the marble.

The second part of the law explains why a satellite can remain in orbit around Earth. The satellite is placed at a carefully calculated distance from Earth. This distance is great enough to keep Earth's gravity from pulling the satellite down, yet small enough to keep the satellite from escaping Earth's gravity and wandering off into space.

Newton's Laws of Motion

Newton's first law of motion states that an object at rest remains at rest, and an object in motion remains in motion at constant speed and in a straight line unless acted on by an unbalanced force.

The first part of the law explains why a football will remain on a tee until it is kicked off or until a gust of wind blows it off. The second part of the law explains why a bike rider will continue moving forward after the bike comes to an abrupt stop. Gravity and the friction of the sidewalk will eventually stop the rider.

Newton's second law of motion states that the acceleration of an object depends on the mass of the object and the amount of force applied.

The first part of the law explains why the acceleration of a 4 kg bowling ball will be greater than the acceleration of a 6 kg bowling ball if the same force is applied to both balls. The second part of the law explains why the acceleration of a bowling ball will be greater if a larger force is applied to the bowling ball. The relationship of acceleration (a) to mass (m) and force (F) can be expressed mathematically by the following equation:

$$acceleration = \frac{force}{mass}, \text{ or } a = \frac{F}{m}$$

This equation is often rearranged to read $force = mass \times acceleration$, or $F = m \times a$

Newton's third law of motion states that whenever one object exerts a force on a second object, the second object exerts an equal and opposite force on the first.

This law explains that a runner is able to move forward because the ground exerts an equal and opposite force on the runner's foot after each step.

Average speed

$$average\ speed = \frac{total\ distance}{total\ time}$$

Example:
A bicycle messenger traveled a distance of 136 km in 8 h. What was the messenger's average speed?

$$\frac{136\ km}{8\ h} = 17\ km/h$$

The messenger's average speed was **17 km/h.**

Average acceleration

$$average\ acceleration = \frac{final\ velocity - starting\ velocity}{time\ it\ takes\ to\ change\ velocity}$$

Example:
Calculate the average acceleration of an Olympic 100 m dash sprinter who reached a velocity of 20 m/s south at the finish line. The race was in a straight line and lasted 10 s.

$$\frac{20\ m/s - 0\ m/s}{10\ s} = 2\ m/s/s$$

The sprinter's average acceleration was **2 m/s/s south.**

Pressure

Pressure is the force exerted over a given area. The SI unit for pressure is the pascal. Its symbol is Pa.

$$pressure = \frac{force}{area}$$

Net force

Forces in the Same Direction

When forces are in the same direction, add the forces together to determine the net force.

Example:
Calculate the net force on a stalled car that is being pushed by two people. One person is pushing with a force of 13 N northwest, and the other person is pushing with a force of 8 N in the same direction.

$$13\ N + 8\ N = 21\ N$$

The net force is **21 N northwest.**

Forces in Opposite Directions

When forces are in opposite directions, subtract the smaller force from the larger force to determine the net force. The net force will be in the direction of the larger force.

Example:
Calculate the net force on a rope that is being pulled on each end. One person is pulling on one end of the rope with a force of 12 N south. Another person is pulling on the opposite end of the rope with a force of 7 N north.

$$12\ N - 7\ N = 5\ N$$

The net force is **5 N south.**

Example:
Calculate the pressure of the air in a soccer ball if the air exerts a force of 10 N over an area of 0.5 m².

$$pressure = \frac{10N}{0.5\ m^2} = \frac{20N}{m^2} = 20\ Pa$$

The pressure of the air inside the soccer ball is **20 Pa.**

A How-To Manual for Active Reading

This book belongs to you, and you are invited to write in it. In fact, the book won't be complete until you do. Sometimes you'll answer a question or follow directions to mark up the text. Other times you'll write down your own thoughts. And when you're done reading and writing in the book, the book will be ready to help you review what you learned and prepare for tests.

Active Reading Annotations

Before you read, you'll often come upon an Active Reading prompt that asks you to underline certain words or number the steps in a process. Here's an example.

Active Reading

12 Identify In this paragraph, number the sequence of sentences that describe replication.

Marking the text this way is called **annotating,** and your marks are called **annotations.** Annotating the text can help you identify important concepts while you read.

There are other ways that you can annotate the text. You can draw an asterisk (*) by vocabulary terms, mark unfamiliar or confusing terms and information with a question mark (?), and mark main ideas with a <u>double underline</u>. And you can even invent your own marks to annotate the text!

Other Annotating Opportunities

Keep your pencil, pen, or highlighter nearby as you read, so you can make a note or highlight an important point at any time. Here are a few ideas to get you started.

- Notice the headings in red and blue. The blue headings are questions that point to the main idea of what you're reading. The red headings are answers to the questions in the blue ones. Together these headings outline the content of the lesson. After reading a lesson, you could write your own answers to the questions.

- Notice the bold-faced words that are highlighted in yellow. They are highlighted so that you can easily find them again on the page where they are defined. As you read or as you review, challenge yourself to write your own sentence using the bold-faced term.

- Make a note in the margin at any time. You might
  - Ask a "What if" question
  - Comment on what you read
  - Make a connection to something you read elsewhere
  - Make a logical conclusion from the text

Use your own language and abbreviations. Invent a code, such as using circles and boxes around words to remind you of their importance or relation to each other. Your annotations will help you remember your questions for class discussions, and when you go back to the lesson later, you may be able to fill in what you didn't understand the first time you read it. Like a scientist in the field or in a lab, you will be recording your questions and observations for analysis later.

Active Reading Questions

After you read, you'll often come upon Active Reading questions that ask you to think about what you've just read. You'll write your answer underneath the question. Here's an example.

Active Reading

8 Describe Where are phosphate groups found in a DNA molecule?

_____

_____

This type of question helps you sum up what you've just read and pull out the most important ideas from the passage. In this case the question asks you to **describe** the structure of a DNA molecule that you have just read about. Other times you may be asked to do such things as **apply** a concept, **compare** two concepts, **summarize** a process, or **identify a cause-and-effect** relationship. You'll be strengthening those critical thinking skills that you'll use often in learning about science.

Reading and Study Skills

Using Graphic Organizers to Take Notes

Graphic organizers help you remember information as you read it for the first time and as you study it later. There are dozens of graphic organizers to choose from, so the first trick is to choose the one that's best suited to your purpose. Following are some graphic organizers to use for different purposes.

To remember lots of information	To relate a central idea to subordinate details	To describe a process	To make a comparison
• Arrange data in a Content Frame • Use Combination Notes to describe a concept in words and pictures	• Show relationships with a Mind Map or a Main Idea Web • Sum up relationships among many things with a Concept Map	• Use a Process Diagram to explain a procedure • Show a chain of events and results in a Cause-and-Effect Chart	• Compare two or more closely related things in a Venn Diagram

Content Frame

1 Make a four-column chart.

2 Fill the first column with categories (e.g., snail, ant, earthworm) and the first row with descriptive information (e.g., group, characteristic, appearance).

3 Fill the chart with details that belong in each row and column.

4 When you finish, you'll have a study aid that helps you compare one category to another.

Invertebrates

NAME	GROUP	CHARACTERISTICS	DRAWING
snail	mollusks	mangle	
ant	arthropods	six legs, exoskeleton	
earthworm	segmented worms	segmented body, circulatory and digestive systems	
heartworm	roundworms	digestive system	
sea star	echinoderms	spiny skin, tube feet	
jellyfish	cnidarians	stinging cells	

Combination Notes

1 Make a two-column chart.

2 Write descriptive words and definitions in the first column.

3 Draw a simple sketch that helps you remember the meaning of the term in the second column.

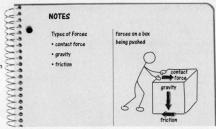

Mind Map

1 Draw an oval, and inside it write a topic to analyze.

2 Draw two or more arms extending from the oval. Each arm represents a main idea about the topic.

3 Draw lines from the arms on which to write details about each of the main ideas.

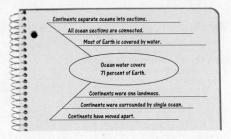

Main Idea Web

1 Make a box and write a concept you want to remember inside it.

2 Draw boxes around the central box, and label each one with a category of information about the concept (e.g., definition, formula, descriptive details).

3 Fill in the boxes with relevant details as you read.

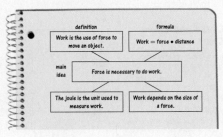

Reading and Study Skills

Concept Map

1 Draw a large oval, and inside it write a major concept.

2 Draw an arrow from the concept to a smaller oval, in which you write a related concept.

3 On the arrow, write a verb that connects the two concepts.

4 Continue in this way, adding ovals and arrows in a branching structure, until you have explained as much as you can about the main concept.

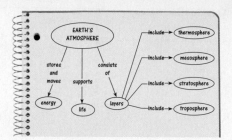

Venn Diagram

1 Draw two overlapping circles or ovals—one for each topic you are comparing—and label each one.

2 In the part of each circle that does not overlap with the other, list the characteristics that are unique to each topic.

3 In the space where the two circles overlap, list the characteristics that the two topics have in common.

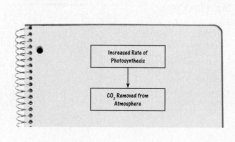

Cause-and-Effect Chart

1 Draw two boxes and connect them with an arrow.

2 In the first box, write the first event in a series (a cause).

3 In the second box, write a result of the cause (the effect).

4 Add more boxes when one event has many effects, or vice versa.

Process Diagram

A process can be a never-ending cycle. As you can see in this technology design process, engineers may backtrack and repeat steps, they may skip steps entirely, or they may repeat the entire process before a useable design is achieved.

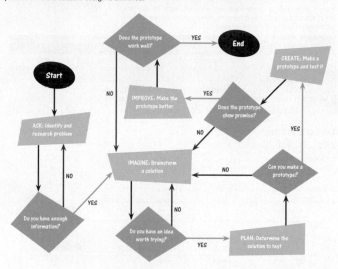

Reading and Study Skills

Using Vocabulary Strategies

Important science terms are highlighted where they are first defined in this book. One way to remember these terms is to take notes and make sketches when you come to them. Use the strategies on this page and the next for this purpose. You will also find a formal definition of each science term in the Glossary at the end of the book.

Description Wheel

1 Draw a small circle.

2 Write a vocabulary term inside the circle.

3 Draw several arms extending from the circle.

4 On the arms, write words and phrases that describe the term.

5 If you choose, add sketches that help you visualize the descriptive details or the concept as a whole.

Four Square

1 Draw a small oval and write a vocabulary term inside it.

2 Draw a large rectangle around the oval, and divide the rectangle into four smaller squares.

3 Label the smaller squares with categories of information about the term, such as: definition, characteristics, examples, non-examples, appearance, and root words.

4 Fill the squares with descriptive words and drawings that will help you remember the overall meaning of the term and its essential details.

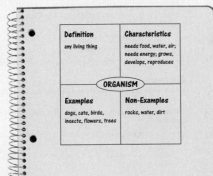

Frame Game

1 Draw a small rectangle, and write a vocabulary term inside it.

2 Draw a larger rectangle around the smaller one. Connect the corners of the larger rectangle to the corners of the smaller one, creating four spaces that frame the word.

3 In each of the four parts of the frame, draw or write details that help define the term. Consider including a definition, essential characteristics, an equation, examples, and a sentence using the term.

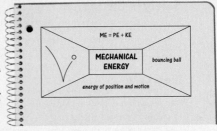

Magnet Word

1 Draw horseshoe magnet, and write a vocabulary term inside it.

2 Add lines that extend from the sides of the magnet.

3 Brainstorm words and phrases that come to mind when you think about the term.

4 On the lines, write the words and phrases that describe something essential about the term.

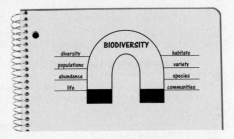

Word Triangle

1 Draw a triangle, and add lines to divide it into three parts.

2 Write a term and its definition in the bottom section of the triangle.

3 In the middle section, write a sentence in which the term is used correctly.

4 In the top section, draw a small picture to illustrate the term.

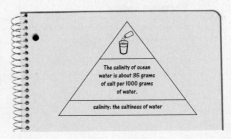

Science Skills

Safety in the Lab

Before you begin work in the laboratory, read these safety rules twice. Before starting a lab activity, read all directions and make sure that you understand them. Do not begin until your teacher has told you to start. If you or another student are injured in any way, tell your teacher immediately.

Dress Code

Eye Protection

Hand Protection

Clothing Protection

- Wear safety goggles at all times in the lab as directed.
- If chemicals get into your eyes, flush your eyes immediately.
- Do not wear contact lenses in the lab.
- Do not look directly at the sun or any intense light source or laser.
- Do not cut an object while holding the object in your hand.
- Wear appropriate protective gloves as directed.
- Wear an apron or lab coat at all times in the lab as directed.
- Tie back long hair, secure loose clothing, and remove loose jewelry.
- Do not wear open-toed shoes, sandals, or canvas shoes in the lab.

Glassware and Sharp Object Safety

Glassware Safety

Sharp Objects Safety

- Do not use chipped or cracked glassware.
- Use heat-resistant glassware for heating or storing hot materials.
- Notify your teacher immediately if a piece of glass breaks.
- Use extreme care when handling all sharp and pointed instruments.
- Cut objects on a suitable surface, always in a direction away from your body.

Chemical Safety

Chemical Safety

- If a chemical gets on your skin, on your clothing, or in your eyes, rinse it immediately (shower, faucet or eyewash fountain) and alert your teacher.
- Do not clean up spilled chemicals unless your teacher directs you to do so.
- Do not inhale any gas or vapor unless directed to do so by your teacher.
- Handle materials that emit vapors or gases in a well-ventilated area.

Electrical Safety

Electrical Safety

- Do not use equipment with frayed electrical cords or loose plugs.
- Do not use electrical equipment near water or when clothing or hands are wet.
- Hold the plug housing when you plug in or unplug equipment.

Heating and Fire Safety

Heating Safety

- Be aware of any source of flames, sparks, or heat (such as flames, heating coils, or hot plates) before working with any flammable substances.
- Know the location of lab fire extinguishers and fire-safety blankets.
- Know your school's fire-evacuation routes.
- If your clothing catches on fire, walk to the lab shower to put out the fire.
- Never leave a hot plate unattended while it is turned on or while it is cooling.
- Use tongs or appropriate insulated holders when handling heated objects.
- Allow all equipment to cool before storing it.

Plant and Animal Safety

Plant Safety

Animal Safety

- Do not eat any part of a plant.
- Do not pick any wild plants unless your teacher instructs you to do so.
- Handle animals only as your teacher directs.
- Treat animals carefully and respectfully.
- Wash your hands thoroughly after handling any plant or animal.

Wafting

Cleanup

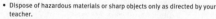
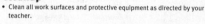
Proper Waste Disposal

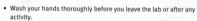

Hygienic Care

- Clean all work surfaces and protective equipment as directed by your teacher.
- Dispose of hazardous materials or sharp objects only as directed by your teacher.
- Keep your hands away from your face while you are working on any activity.
- Wash your hands thoroughly before you leave the lab or after any activity.

Science Skills

Designing, Conducting, and Reporting an Experiment

An experiment is an organized procedure to study something under specific conditions. Use the following steps of the scientific method when designing or conducting a controlled experiment.

1 Identify a Research Problem

Every day, you make observations by using your senses to gather information. Careful observations lead to good questions, and good questions can lead you to an experiment. Imagine, for example, that you pass a pond every day on your way to school, and you notice green scum beginning to form on top of it. You wonder what it is and why it seems to be growing. You list your questions, and then you do a little research to find out what is already known. A good place to start a research project is at the library. A library catalog lists all of the resources available to you at that library and often those found elsewhere. Begin your search by using:

- keywords or main topics.
- similar words, or synonyms, of your keyword.

The types of resources that will be helpful to you will depend on the kind of information you are interested in. And, some resources are more reliable for a given topic than others. Some different kinds of useful resources are:

- magazines and journals (or periodicals)—articles on a topic.
- encyclopedias—a good overview of a topic.
- books on specific subjects—details about a topic.
- newspapers—useful for current events.

The Internet can also be a great place to find information. Some of your library's reference materials may even be online. When using the Internet, however, it is especially important to make sure you are using appropriate and reliable sources. Websites of universities and government agencies are usually more accurate and reliable than websites created by individuals or businesses. Decide which sources are relevant and reliable for your topic. If in doubt, check with your teacher.

Take notes as you read through the information in these resources. You will probably come up with many questions and ideas for which you can do more research as needed. Once you feel you have enough information, think about the questions you have on the topic. Then, write down the problem that you want to investigate. Your notes might look like these.

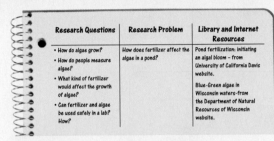

Research Questions	Research Problem	Library and Internet Resources
• How do algae grow? • How do people measure algae? • What kind of fertilizer would affect the growth of algae? • Can fertilizer and algae be used safely in a lab? How?	How does fertilizer affect the algae in a pond?	Pond fertilization: initiating an algal bloom – from University of California Davis website. Blue-Green algae in Wisconsin waters–from the Department of Natural Resources of Wisconsin website.

As you gather information from reliable sources, record details about each source, including author name(s), title, date of publication, and/or web address. Make sure to also note the specific information that you use from each source. Staying organized in this way will be important when you write your report and create a bibliography or works cited list. Recording this information and staying organized will help you credit the appropriate author(s) for the information that you have gathered.

Representing someone else's ideas or work as your own, (without giving the original author credit), is known as plagiarism. Plagiarism can be intentional or unintentional. The best way to make sure that you do not commit plagiarism is to always do your own work and to always give credit to others when you use their words or ideas.

Current scientific research is built on scientific research and discoveries that have happened in the past. This means that scientists are constantly learning from each other and combining ideas to learn more about the natural world through investigation. But, a good scientist always credits the ideas and research that they have gathered from other people to those people. There are more details about crediting sources and creating a bibliography under step 9.

2 Make a Prediction

A prediction is a statement of what you expect will happen in your experiment. Before making a prediction, you need to decide in a general way what you will do in your procedure. You may state your prediction in an if-then format.

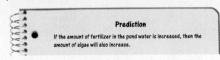

Prediction

If the amount of fertilizer in the pond water is increased, then the amount of algae will also increase.

Science Skills

3 Form a Hypothesis

Many experiments are designed to test a hypothesis. A hypothesis is a tentative explanation for an expected result. You have predicted that additional fertilizer will cause additional algae growth in pond water; your hypothesis should state the connection between fertilizer and algal growth.

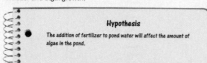

Hypothesis

The addition of fertilizer to pond water will affect the amount of algae in the pond.

4 Identify Variables to Test the Hypothesis

The next step is to design an experiment to test the hypothesis. The experimental results may or may not support the hypothesis. Either way, the information that results from the experiment may be useful for future investigations.

Experimental Group and Control Group

An experiment to determine how two factors are related has a control group and an experimental group. The two groups are the same, except that the investigator changes a single factor in the experimental group and does not change it in the control group.

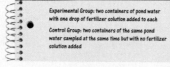

Experimental Group: two containers of pond water with one drop of fertilizer solution added to each

Control Group: two containers of the same pond water sampled at the same time but with no fertilizer solution added

Variables and Constants

In a controlled experiment, a variable is any factor that can change. Constants are all of the variables that are kept the same in both the experimental group and the control group.

The independent variable is the factor that is manipulated or changed in order to test the effect of the change on another variable. The dependent variable is the factor the investigator measures to gather data about the effect.

Independent Variable	Dependent Variable	Constants
Amount of fertilizer in pond water	Growth of algae in the pond water	• Where and when the pond water is obtained • The type of container used • Light and temperature conditions where the water is stored

© Houghton Mifflin Harcourt Publishing Company

5 Write a Procedure

Write each step of your procedure. Start each step with a verb, or action word, and keep the steps short. Your procedure should be clear enough for someone else to use as instructions for repeating your experiment.

Procedure

1. Use the masking tape and the marker to label the containers with your initials, the date, and the identifiers "Jar 1 with Fertilizer," "Jar 2 with Fertilizer," "Jar 1 without Fertilizer," and "Jar 2 without Fertilizer."

2. Put on your gloves. Use the large container to obtain a sample of pond water.

3. Divide the water sample equally among the four smaller containers.

4. Use the eyedropper to add one drop of fertilizer solution to the two containers labeled, "Jar 1 with Fertilizer," and "Jar 2 with Fertilizer".

5. Cover the containers with clear plastic wrap. Use the scissors to punch ten holes in each of the covers.

6. Place all four containers on a window ledge. Make sure that they all receive the same amount of light.

7. Observe the containers every day for one week.

8. Use the ruler to measure the diameter of the largest clump of algae in each container, and record your measurements daily.

© Houghton Mifflin Harcourt Publishing Company

Science Skills

6 Experiment and Collect Data

Once you have all of your materials and your procedure has been approved, you can begin to experiment and collect data. Record both quantitative data (measurements) and qualitative data (observations), as shown below.

Algal Growth and Fertilizer

Date and Time	Experimental Group		Control Group		Observations
	Jar 1 with Fertilizer (diameter of algal clump in mm)	Jar 2 with Fertilizer (diameter of algal clump in mm)	Jar 1 without Fertilizer (diameter of algal clump in mm)	Jar 2 without Fertilizer (diameter of algal clump in mm)	
5/3 4:00 p.m.	0	0	0	0	condensation in all containers
5/4 4:00 p.m.	0	3	0	0	tiny green blobs in Jar 2 with fertilizer
5/5 4:15 p.m.	4	5	0	3	green blobs in Jars 1 and 2 with fertilizer and Jar 2 without fertilizer
5/6 4:00 p.m.	5	6	0	4	water light green in Jar 2 with fertilizer
5/7 4:00 p.m.	8	10	0	6	water light green in Jars 1 and 2 with fertilizer and Jar 2 without fertilizer
5/8 3:30 p.m.	10	18	0	6	cover off of Jar 2 with fertilizer
5/9 3:30 p.m.	14	23	0	8	drew sketches of each container

Drawings of Samples Viewed Under Microscope on 5/9 at 100x

Jar 1 with fertilizer Jar 2 with fertilizer Jar 1 without fertilizer Jar 2 without fertilizer

7 Analyze Data

After you complete your experiment, you must analyze all of the data you have gathered. Tables, statistics, and graphs are often used in this step to organize and analyze both the qualitative and quantitative data. Sometimes, your qualitative data are best used to help explain the relationships you see in your quantitative data.

Computer graphing software is useful for creating a graph from data that you have collected. Most graphing software can make line graphs, pie charts, or bar graphs from data that has been organized in a spreadsheet. Graphs are useful for understanding relationships in the data and for communicating the results of your experiment.

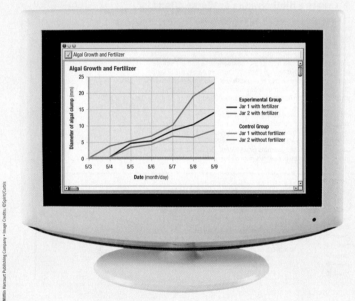

Science Skills

8 Make Conclusions

To draw conclusions from your experiment, first, write your results. Then, compare your results with your hypothesis. Do your results support your hypothesis? What have you learned?

Conclusion

More algae grew in the pond water to which fertilizer had been added than in the pond water to which fertilizer had not been added. My hypothesis was supported. I conclude that it is possible that the growth of algae in ponds can be influenced by the input of fertilizer.

9 Create a Bibliography or Works Cited List

To complete your report, you must also show all of the newspapers, magazines, journals, books, and online sources that you used at every stage of your investigation. Whenever you find useful information about your topic, you should write down the source of that information. Writing down as much information as you can about the subject can help you or someone else find the source again. You should at least record the author's name, the title, the date and where the source was published, and the pages in which the information was found. Then, organize your sources into a list, which you can title Bibliography or Works Cited.

Usually, at least three sources are included in these lists. Sources are listed alphabetically, by the authors' last names. The exact format of a bibliography can vary, depending on the style preferences of your teacher, school, or publisher. Also, books are cited differently than journals or websites. Below is an example of how different kinds of sources may be formatted in a bibliography.

BOOK: Hauschultz, Sara. *Freshwater Algae.* Brainard, Minnesota: Northwoods Publishing, 2011.

ENCYCLOPEDIA: Lasure, Sedona. "Algae is not all just pond scum." *Encyclopedia of Algae.* 2009.

JOURNAL: Johnson, Keagan. "Algae as we know it." *Sci Journal,* vol 64. (September 2010): 201-211.

WEBSITE: Dout, Bill. "Keeping algae scum out of birdbaths." *Help Keep Earth Clean. News.* January 26, 2011. <www.SaveEarth.org>.

Using a Microscope

Scientists use microscopes to see very small objects that cannot easily be seen with the eye alone. A microscope magnifies the image of an object so that small details may be observed. A microscope that you may use can magnify an object 400 times—the object will appear 400 times larger than its actual size.

Body The body separates the lens in the eyepiece from the objective lenses below.

Nosepiece The nosepiece holds the objective lenses above the stage and rotates so that all lenses may be used.

High-Power Objective Lens This is the largest lens on the nosepiece. It magnifies an image approximately 40 times.

Stage The stage supports the object being viewed.

Diaphragm The diaphragm is used to adjust the amount of light passing through the slide and into an objective lens.

Mirror or Light Source Some microscopes use light that is reflected through the stage by a mirror. Other microscopes have their own light sources.

Eyepiece Objects are viewed through the eyepiece. The eyepiece contains a lens that commonly magnifies an image ten times.

Coarse Adjustment This knob is used to focus the image of an object when it is viewed through the low-power lens.

Fine Adjustment This knob is used to focus the image of an object when it is viewed through the high-power lens.

Low-Power Objective Lens This is the smallest lens on the nosepiece. It magnifies images about 10 times.

Arm The arm supports the body above the stage. Always carry a microscope by the arm and base.

Stage Clip The stage clip holds a slide in place on the stage.

Base The base supports the microscope.

Science Skills

Measuring Accurately

Precision and Accuracy

When you do a scientific investigation, it is important that your methods, observations, and data be both precise and accurate.

Low precision: The darts did not land in a consistent place on the dartboard.

Precision, but not accuracy: The darts landed in a consistent place, but did not hit the bull's eye.

Precision and accuracy: The darts landed consistently on the bull's eye.

Precision

In science, *precision* is the exactness and consistency of measurements. For example, measurements made with a ruler that has both centimeter and millimeter markings would be more precise than measurements made with a ruler that has only centimeter markings. Another indicator of precision is the care taken to make sure that methods and observations are as exact and consistent as possible. Every time a particular experiment is done, the same procedure should be used. Precision is necessary because experiments are repeated several times and if the procedure changes, the results might change.

Example

Suppose you are measuring temperatures over a two-week period. Your precision will be greater if you measure each temperature at the same place, at the same time of day, and with the same thermometer than if you change any of these factors from one day to the next.

Accuracy

In science, it is possible to be precise but not accurate. *Accuracy* depends on the difference between a measurement and an actual value. The smaller the difference, the more accurate the measurement.

Example

Suppose you look at a stream and estimate that it is about 1 meter wide at a particular place. You decide to check your estimate by measuring the stream with a meter stick, and you determine that the stream is 1.32 meters wide. However, because it is difficult to measure the width of a stream with a meter stick, it turns out that your measurement was not very accurate. The stream is actually 1.14 meters wide. Therefore, even though your estimate of about 1 meter was less precise than your measurement, your estimate was actually more accurate.

Graduated Cylinders

How to Measure the Volume of a Liquid with a Graduated Cylinder

- Be sure that the graduated cylinder is on a flat surface so that your measurement will be accurate.

- When reading the scale on a graduated cylinder, be sure to have your eyes at the level of the surface of the liquid.

- The surface of the liquid will be curved in the graduated cylinder. Read the volume of the liquid at the bottom of the curve, or meniscus (muh-NIHS-kuhs).

- You can use a graduated cylinder to find the volume of a solid object by measuring the increase in a liquid's level after you add the object to the cylinder.

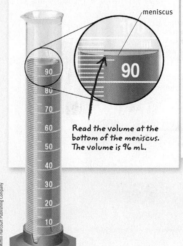

meniscus

Read the volume at the bottom of the meniscus. The volume is 96 mL.

Metric Rulers

How to Measure the Length of a Leaf with a Metric Ruler

1 Lay a ruler flat on top of the leaf so that the 1-centimeter mark lines up with one end. Make sure the ruler and the leaf do not move between the time you line them up and the time you take the measurement.

2 Look straight down on the ruler so that you can see exactly how the marks line up with the other end of the leaf.

3 Estimate the length by which the leaf extends beyond a marking. For example, the leaf below extends about halfway between the 4.2-centimeter and 4.3-centimeter marks, so the apparent measurement is about 4.25 centimeters.

4 Remember to subtract 1 centimeter from your apparent measurement, since you started at the 1-centimeter mark on the ruler and not at the end. The leaf is about 3.25 centimeters long (4.25 cm − 1 cm = 3.25 cm).

Triple Beam Balance

This balance has a pan and three beams with sliding masses, called riders. At one end of the beams is a pointer that indicates whether the mass on the pan is equal to the masses shown on the beams.

How to Measure the Mass of an Object

1 Make sure the balance is zeroed before measuring the mass of an object. The balance is zeroed if the pointer is at zero when nothing is on the pan and the riders are at their zero points. Use the adjustment knob at the base of the balance to zero it.

2 Place the object to be measured on the pan.

3 Move the riders one notch at a time away from the pan. Begin with the largest rider. If moving the largest rider one notch brings the pointer below zero, begin measuring the mass of the object with the next smaller rider.

4 Change the positions of the riders until they balance the mass on the pan and the pointer is at zero. Then add the readings from the three beams to determine the mass of the object.

300 g	position of largest rider
90 g	position of middle rider
+ 3 g	position of smallest rider
393 g	mass of beaker and water

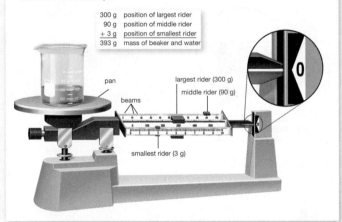

pan

beams

largest rider (300 g)

middle rider (90 g)

smallest rider (3 g)

Using the Metric System and SI Units

Scientists use International System (SI) units for measurements of distance, volume, mass, and temperature. The International System is based on powers of ten and the metric system of measurement.

Basic SI Units		
Quantity	Name	Symbol
length	meter	m
volume	liter	L
mass	gram	g
temperature	kelvin	K

SI Prefixes		
Prefix	Symbol	Power of 10
kilo-	k	1000
hecto-	h	100
deca-	da	10
deci-	d	0.1 or $\frac{1}{10}$
centi-	c	0.01 or $\frac{1}{100}$
milli-	m	0.001 or $\frac{1}{1000}$

Changing Metric Units

You can change from one unit to another in the metric system by multiplying or dividing by a power of 10.

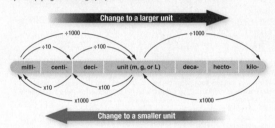

Change to a larger unit

milli- centi- deci- unit (m, g, or L) deca- hecto- kilo-

Change to a smaller unit

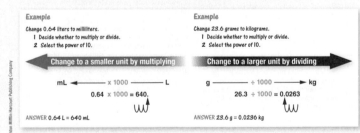

Example

Change 0.64 liters to milliliters.
1 Decide whether to multiply or divide.
2 Select the power of 10.

Change to a smaller unit by multiplying

mL ◄──── x 1000 ──── L

0.64 x 1000 = 640.

ANSWER 0.64 L = 640 mL

Example

Change 23.6 grams to kilograms.
1 Decide whether to multiply or divide.
2 Select the power of 10.

Change to a larger unit by dividing

g ──── ÷ 1000 ──► kg

26.3 ÷ 1000 = 0.0263

ANSWER 23.6 g = 0.0236 kg

Science Skills

Converting Between SI and U.S. Customary Units

Use the chart below when you need to convert between SI units and U.S. customary units.

SI Unit	From SI to U.S. Customary			From U.S. Customary to SI		
Length	When you know	multiply by	to find	When you know	multiply by	to find
kilometer (km) = 1000 m	kilometers	0.62	miles	miles	1.61	kilometers
meter (m) = 100 cm	meters	3.28	feet	feet	0.3048	meters
centimeter (cm) = 10 mm	centimeters	0.39	inches	inches	2.54	centimeters
millimeter (mm) = 0.1 cm	millimeters	0.04	inches	inches	25.4	millimeters
Area	When you know	multiply by	to find	When you know	multiply by	to find
square kilometer (km^2)	square kilometers	0.39	square miles	square miles	2.59	square kilometers
square meter (m^2)	square meters	1.2	square yards	square yards	0.84	square meters
square centimeter (cm^2)	square centimeters	0.155	square inches	square inches	6.45	square centimeters
Volume	When you know	multiply by	to find	When you know	multiply by	to find
liter (L) = 1000 mL	liters	1.06	quarts	quarts	0.95	liters
	liters	0.26	gallons	gallons	3.79	liters
	liters	4.23	cups	cups	0.24	liters
	liters	2.12	pints	pints	0.47	liters
milliliter (mL) = 0.001 L	milliliters	0.20	teaspoons	teaspoons	4.93	milliliters
	milliliters	0.07	tablespoons	tablespoons	14.79	milliliters
	milliliters	0.03	fluid ounces	fluid ounces	29.57	milliliters
Mass	When you know	multiply by	to find	When you know	multiply by	to find
kilogram (kg) = 1000 g	kilograms	2.2	pounds	pounds	0.45	kilograms
gram (g) = 1000 mg	grams	0.035	ounces	ounces	28.35	grams

Temperature Conversions

Even though the kelvin is the SI base unit of temperature, the degree Celsius will be the unit you use most often in your science studies. The formulas below show the relationships between temperatures in degrees Fahrenheit (°F), degrees Celsius (°C), and kelvins (K).

$$°C = \frac{5}{9} \ (°F - 32) \qquad °F = \frac{9}{5} \ °C + 32 \qquad K = °C + 273$$

Examples of Temperature Conversions		
Condition	Degrees Celsius	Degrees Fahrenheit
Freezing point of water	0	32
Cool day	10	50
Mild day	20	68
Warm day	30	86
Normal body temperature	37	98.6
Very hot day	40	104
Boiling point of water	100	212

Math Refresher

Performing Calculations

Science requires an understanding of many math concepts. The following pages will help you review some important math skills.

Mean

The mean is the sum of all values in a data set divided by the total number of values in the data set. The mean is also called the *average*.

Example

Find the mean of the following set of numbers: 5, 4, 7, and 8.

Step 1   Find the sum.

5 + 4 + 7 + 8 = 24

Step 2   Divide the sum by the number of numbers in your set. Because there are four numbers in this example, divide the sum by 4.

24 ÷ 4 = 6

Answer The average, or mean, is 6.

Median

The median of a data set is the middle value when the values are written in numerical order. If a data set has an even number of values, the median is the mean of the two middle values.

Example

To find the median of a set of measurements, arrange the values in order from least to greatest. The median is the middle value.

13 mm   14 mm   16 mm   21 mm   23 mm

Answer The median is 16 mm.

Mode

The mode of a data set is the value that occurs most often.

Example

To find the mode of a set of measurements, arrange the values in order from least to greatest and determine the value that occurs most often.

13 mm, 14 mm, 14 mm, 16 mm, 21 mm, 23 mm, 25 mm

Answer The mode is 14 mm.

A data set can have more than one mode or no mode. For example, the following data set has modes of 2 mm and 4 mm:

2 mm   2 mm   3 mm   4 mm   4 mm

The data set below has no mode, because no value occurs more often than any other.

2 mm   3 mm   4 mm   5 mm

Math Refresher

Ratios

A **ratio** is a comparison between numbers, and it is usually written as a fraction.

Example
Find the ratio of thermometers to students if you have 36 thermometers and 48 students in your class.

Step 1   Write the ratio.

$$\frac{36 \text{ thermometers}}{48 \text{ students}}$$

Step 2   Simplify the fraction to its simplest form.

$$\frac{36}{48} = \frac{36 \div 12}{48 \div 12} = \frac{3}{4}$$

The ratio of thermometers to students is 3 to 4 or 3:4.

Proportions

A **proportion** is an equation that states that two ratios are equal.

$$\frac{3}{1} = \frac{12}{4}$$

To solve a proportion, you can use cross-multiplication. If you know three of the quantities in a proportion, you can use cross-multiplication to find the fourth.

Example
Imagine that you are making a scale model of the solar system for your science project. The diameter of Jupiter is 11.2 times the diameter of the Earth. If you are using a plastic-foam ball that has a diameter of 2 cm to represent the Earth, what must the diameter of the ball representing Jupiter be?

$$\frac{11.2}{1} = \frac{x}{2 \text{ cm}}$$

Step 1   Cross-multiply.

$$\frac{11.2}{1} = \frac{x}{2}$$

$$11.2 \times 2 = x \times 1$$

Step 2   Multiply.

$$22.4 = x \times 1$$

$$x = 22.4 \text{ cm}$$

You will need to use a ball that has a diameter of 22.4 cm to represent Jupiter.

Rates

A **rate** is a ratio of two values expressed in different units. A unit rate is a rate with a denominator of 1 unit.

Example
A plant grew 6 centimeters in 2 days. The plant's rate of growth was $\frac{6 \text{ cm}}{2 \text{ days}}$.

To describe the plant's growth in centimeters per day, write a unit rate.

Divide numerator and denominator by 2:

$$\frac{6 \text{ cm}}{2 \text{ days}} = \frac{6 \text{ cm} \div 2}{2 \text{ days} \div 2}$$

Simplify: $= \frac{3 \text{ cm}}{1 \text{ day}}$

Answer   The plant's rate of growth is 3 centimeters per day.

Percent

A **percent** is a ratio of a given number to 100. For example, 85% = 85/100. You can use percent to find part of a whole.

Example
What is 85% of 40?

Step 1   Rewrite the percent as a decimal by moving the decimal point two places to the left.

0.85

Step 2   Multiply the decimal by the number that you are calculating the percentage of.

$$0.85 \times 40 = 34$$

85% of 40 is 34.

Decimals

To **add** or **subtract decimals**, line up the digits vertically so that the decimal points line up. Then, add or subtract the columns from right to left. Carry or borrow numbers as necessary.

Example
Add the following numbers: 3.1415 and 2.96.

Step 1   Line up the digits vertically so that the decimal points line up.

```
  3.1415
+ 2.96
```

Step 2   Add the columns from right to left, and carry when necessary.

```
  3.1415
+ 2.96
  6.1015
```

The sum is 6.1015.

Fractions

A **fraction** is a ratio of two nonzero whole numbers.

Example
Your class has 24 plants. Your teacher instructs you to put 5 plants in a shady spot. What fraction of the plants in your class will you put in a shady spot?

Step 1   In the denominator, write the total number of parts in the whole.

$$\frac{?}{24}$$

Step 2   In the numerator, write the number of parts of the whole that are being considered.

$$\frac{5}{24}$$

So, $\frac{5}{24}$ of the plants will be in the shade.

Math Refresher

Simplifying Fractions

It is usually best to express a fraction in its simplest form. Expressing a fraction in its simplest form is called **simplifying a fraction**.

Example

Simplify the fraction $\frac{30}{45}$ to its simplest form.

Step 1 Find the largest whole number that will divide evenly into both the numerator and denominator. This number is called the greatest common factor (GCF).

Factors of the numerator 30:
1, 2, 3, 5, 6, 10, 15, 30

Factors of the denominator 45:
1, 3, 5, 9, 15, 45

Step 2 Divide both the numerator and the denominator by the GCF, which in this case is 15.

$$\frac{30}{45} = \frac{30 \div 15}{45 \div 15} = \frac{2}{3}$$

Thus, $\frac{30}{45}$ written in its simplest form is $\frac{2}{3}$.

Adding and Subtracting Fractions

To **add** or **subtract** fractions that have the same denominator, simply add or subtract the numerators.

Examples

$\frac{3}{5} + \frac{1}{5} = ?$ and $\frac{3}{4} - \frac{1}{4} = ?$

Step 1 Add or subtract the numerators.

$\frac{3}{5} + \frac{1}{5} = \frac{4}{5}$ and $\frac{3}{4} - \frac{1}{4} = \frac{2}{4}$

Step 2 Write in the common denominator, which remains the same.

$\frac{3}{5} + \frac{1}{5} = \frac{4}{5}$ and $\frac{3}{4} - \frac{1}{4} = \frac{2}{4}$

Step 3 If necessary, write the fraction in its simplest form.

$\frac{4}{5}$ cannot be simplified, and $\frac{2}{4} = \frac{1}{2}$.

To **add** or **subtract** fractions that have **different denominators**, first find the least common denominator (LCD).

Examples

$\frac{1}{2} + \frac{1}{6} = ?$ and $\frac{3}{4} - \frac{2}{3} = ?$

Step 1 Write the equivalent fractions that have a common denominator.

$\frac{3}{6} + \frac{1}{6} = ?$ and $\frac{9}{12} - \frac{8}{12} = ?$

Step 2 Add or subtract the fractions.

$\frac{3}{6} + \frac{1}{6} = \frac{4}{6}$ and $\frac{9}{12} - \frac{8}{12} = \frac{1}{12}$

Step 3 If necessary, write the fraction in its simplest form.

$\frac{4}{6} = \frac{2}{3}$, and $\frac{1}{12}$ cannot be simplified.

Multiplying Fractions

To **multiply fractions**, multiply the numerators and the denominators together, and then simplify the fraction to its simplest form.

Example

$\frac{5}{9} \times \frac{7}{10} = ?$

Step 1 Multiply the numerators and denominators.

$$\frac{5}{9} \times \frac{7}{10} = \frac{5 \times 7}{9 \times 10} = \frac{35}{90}$$

Step 2 Simplify the fraction.

$$\frac{35}{90} = \frac{35 \div 5}{90 \div 5} = \frac{7}{18}$$

© Houghton Mifflin Harcourt Publishing Company

Dividing Fractions

To **divide fractions**, first rewrite the divisor (the number you divide by) upside down. This number is called the reciprocal of the divisor. Then multiply and simplify if necessary.

Example

$\frac{5}{8} \div \frac{3}{2} = ?$

Step 1 Rewrite the divisor as its reciprocal.

$$\frac{3}{2} \rightarrow \frac{2}{3}$$

Step 2 Multiply the fractions.

$$\frac{5}{8} \times \frac{2}{3} = \frac{5 \times 2}{8 \times 3} = \frac{10}{24}$$

Step 3 Simplify the fraction.

$$\frac{10}{24} = \frac{10 \div 2}{24 \div 2} = \frac{5}{12}$$

Using Significant Figures

The **significant figures** in a decimal are the digits that are warranted by the accuracy of a measuring device.

When you perform a calculation with measurements, the number of significant figures to include in the result depends in part on the number of significant figures in the measurements. When you multiply or divide measurements, your answer should have only as many significant figures as the measurement with the fewest significant figures.

Examples

Using a balance and a graduated cylinder filled with water, you determined that a marble has a mass of 8.0 grams and a volume of 3.5 cubic centimeters. To calculate the density of the marble, divide the mass by the volume.

Write the formula for density: $\text{Density} = \frac{\text{mass}}{\text{volume}}$

Substitute measurements: $= \frac{8.0\,g}{3.5\,cm^3}$

Use a calculator to divide: $\approx 2.285714286\ g/cm^3$

Answer Because the mass and the volume have two significant figures each, give the density to two significant figures. The marble has a density of 2.3 grams per cubic centimeter.

Using Scientific Notation

Scientific notation is a shorthand way to write very large or very small numbers. For example, 73,500,000,000,000,000,000,000 kg is the mass of the moon. In scientific notation, it is 7.35×10^{22} kg. A value written as a number between 1 and 10, times a power of 10, is in scientific notation.

Examples

You can convert from standard form to scientific notation.

Standard Form	Scientific Notation
720,000	7.2×10^5
5 decimal places left	Exponent is 5.
0.000291	2.91×10^{-4}
4 decimal places right	Exponent is -4.

You can convert from scientific notation to standard form.

Scientific Notation	Standard Form
4.63×10^7	46,300,000
Exponent is 7.	7 decimal places right
1.08×10^{-6}	0.00000108
Exponent is -6.	6 decimal places left

© Houghton Mifflin Harcourt Publishing Company

Math Refresher

Making and Interpreting Graphs

Circle Graph

A circle graph, or pie chart, shows how each group of data relates to all of the data. Each part of the circle represents a category of the data. The entire circle represents all of the data. For example, a biologist studying a hardwood forest in Wisconsin found that there were five different types of trees. The data table at right summarizes the biologist's findings.

Wisconsin Hardwood Trees	
Type of tree	Number found
Oak	600
Maple	750
Beech	300
Birch	1,200
Hickory	150
Total	3,000

How to Make a Circle Graph

1 To make a circle graph of these data, first find the percentage of each type of tree. Divide the number of trees of each type by the total number of trees, and multiply by 100%.

$$\frac{600 \text{ oak}}{3,000 \text{ trees}} \times 100\% = 20\%$$

$$\frac{750 \text{ maple}}{3,000 \text{ trees}} \times 100\% = 25\%$$

$$\frac{300 \text{ beech}}{3,000 \text{ trees}} \times 100\% = 10\%$$

$$\frac{1,200 \text{ birch}}{3,000 \text{ trees}} \times 100\% = 40\%$$

$$\frac{150 \text{ hickory}}{3,000 \text{ trees}} \times 100\% = 5\%$$

2 Now, determine the size of the wedges that make up the graph. Multiply each percentage by 360°. Remember that a circle contains 360°.

$20\% \times 360° = 72°$ $25\% \times 360° = 90°$

$10\% \times 360° = 36°$ $40\% \times 360° = 144°$

$5\% \times 360° = 18°$

3 Check that the sum of the percentages is 100 and the sum of the degrees is 360.

$20\% + 25\% + 10\% + 40\% + 5\% = 100\%$

$72° + 90° + 36° + 144° + 18° = 360°$

4 Use a compass to draw a circle and mark the center of the circle.

5 Then, use a protractor to draw angles of 72°, 90°, 36°, 144°, and 18° in the circle.

6 Finally, label each part of the graph, and choose an appropriate title.

A Community of Wisconsin Hardwood Trees

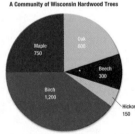

Line Graphs

Line graphs are most often used to demonstrate continuous change. For example, Mr. Smith's students analyzed the population records for their hometown, Appleton, between 1910 and 2010. Examine the data at right.

Because the year and the population change, they are the variables. The population is determined by, or dependent on, the year. Therefore, the population is called the **dependent variable,** and the year is called the **independent variable.** Each year and its population make a **data pair.** To prepare a line graph, you must first organize data pairs into a table like the one at right.

Population of Appleton, 1910–2010	
Year	Population
1910	1,800
1930	2,500
1950	3,200
1970	3,900
1990	4,600
2010	5,300

How to Make a Line Graph

1 Place the independent variable along the horizontal (x) axis. Place the dependent variable along the vertical (y) axis.

2 Label the x-axis "Year" and the y-axis "Population." Look at your greatest and least values for the population. For the y-axis, determine a scale that will provide enough space to show these values. You must use the same scale for the entire length of the axis. Next, find an appropriate scale for the x-axis.

3 Choose reasonable starting points for each axis.

4 Plot the data pairs as accurately as possible.

5 Choose a title that accurately represents the data.

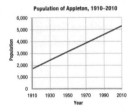

How to Determine Slope

Slope is the ratio of the change in the y-value to the change in the x-value, or "rise over run."

1 Choose two points on the line graph. For example, the population of Appleton in 2010 was 5,300 people. Therefore, you can define point A as (2010, 5,300). In 1910, the population was 1,800 people. You can define point B as (1910, 1,800).

2 Find the change in the y-value.
(y at point A) − (y at point B) = 5,300 people − 1,800 people = 3,500 people

3 Find the change in the x-value.
(x at point A) − (x at point B) = 2010 − 1910 = 100 years

4 Calculate the slope of the graph by dividing the change in y by the change in x.

$$slope = \frac{change\ in\ y}{change\ in\ x}$$

$$slope = \frac{3,500 \text{ people}}{100 \text{ years}}$$

$slope = 35$ people per year

In this example, the population in Appleton increased by a fixed amount each year. The graph of these data is a straight line. Therefore, the relationship is **linear.** When the graph of a set of data is not a straight line, the relationship is **nonlinear.**

Math Refresher

Bar Graphs

Bar graphs can be used to demonstrate change that is not continuous. These graphs can be used to indicate trends when the data cover a long period of time. A meteorologist gathered the precipitation data shown here for Summerville for April 1–15 and used a bar graph to represent the data.

Precipitation in Summerville, April 1–15			
Date	Precipitation (cm)	Date	Precipitation (cm)
April 1	0.5	April 9	0.25
April 2	1.25	April 10	0.0
April 3	0.0	April 11	1.0
April 4	0.0	April 12	0.0
April 5	0.0	April 13	0.25
April 6	0.0	April 14	0.0
April 7	0.0	April 15	6.50
April 8	1.75		

How to Make a Bar Graph

1 Use an appropriate scale and a reasonable starting point for each axis.

2 Label the axes, and plot the data.

3 Choose a title that accurately represents the data.

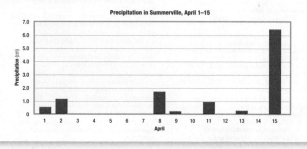

Precipitation in Summerville, April 1–15

Glossary

Pronunciation Key							
Sound	Symbol	Example	Respelling	Sound	Symbol	Example	Respelling
ă	a	pat	PAT	ŏ	ah	bottle	BAHT'l
ā	ay	pay	PAY	ō	oh	toe	TOH
âr	air	care	KAIR	ô	aw	caught	KAWT
ä	ah	father	FAH•ther	ôr	ohr	roar	ROHR
är	ar	argue	AR•gyoo	oi	oy	noisy	NOYZ•ee
ch	ch	chase	CHAYS	ŏŏ	u	book	BUK
ĕ	e	pet	PET	ōō	oo	boot	BOOT
ē (at end of a syllable)	eh	settee lessee	seh•TEE leh•SEE	ou	ow	pound	POWND
ĕr	ehr	merry	MEHR•ee	s	s	center	SEN•ter
ē	ee	beach	BEECH	sh	sh	cache	CASH
g	g	gas	GAS	ū	uh	flood	FLUHD
ĭ	i	pit	PIT	ûr	er	bird	BERD
ĭ (at end of a syllable)	ih	guitar	gih•TAR	z	z	xylophone	ZY•luh•fohn
ī	y eye (only for a complete syllable)	pie island	PY EYE•luhnd	z	z	bags	BAGZ
				zh	zh	decision	dih•SIZH•uhn
				ə	uh	around broken focus	uh•ROWND BROH•kuhn FOH•kuhs
îr	ir	hear	HIR	ar	er	winner	WIN•er
j	j	germ	JERM	th	th	thin they	THIN THAY
k	k	kick	KIK				
ng	ng	thing	THING	w	w	one	WUHN
ngk	ngk	bank	BANGK	wh	hw	whether	HWETH•er

Glossary

A

adaptation (ad·ap·TAY-shuhn) a characteristic that improves an individual's ability to survive and reproduce in a particular environment (21)
adaptación una característica que mejora la capacidad de un individuo para sobrevivir y reproducirse en un determinado ambiente

algae (AL-jee) eukaryotic organisms that convert the sun's energy into food through photosynthesis but that do not have roots, stems, or leaves (singular, alga) (99)
algas organismos eucarióticos que transforman la energía del Sol en alimento por medio de la fotosíntesis, pero que no tienen raíces, tallos ni hojas

angiosperm (AN-jee-uh-sperm) a flowering plant that produces seeds within a fruit (115)
angiosperma una planta que da flores y que produce semillas dentro de la fruta

Animalia (an-uh-MAYL-yuh) a kingdom made up of complex, multicellular organisms that lack cell walls, can usually move around, and quickly respond to their environment (61)
Animalia un reino formado por organismos pluricelulares complejos que no tienen pared celular, normalmente son capaces de moverse y reaccionan rápidamente a su ambiente

Archaea (ar-KEE-uh) a domain made up of prokaryotes, most of which are known to live in extreme environments, that are distinguished from other prokaryotes by differences in their genetics and in the makeup of their cell wall (58, 80)
Archaea un dominio compuesto por procariotes la mayoría de los cuales viven en ambientes extremos que se distinguen de otros procariotes por su genética y por la composición de su pared celular

artificial selection (ar-tuh-FISH-uhl sih-LEK-shuhn) the human practice of breeding animals or plants that have certain desired traits (18)
selección artificial la práctica humana de criar animales o cultivar plantas que tienen ciertos caracteres deseados

asexual reproduction (ay-SEK-shoo-uhl ree-pruh-DUHK-shuhn) reproduction that does not involve the union of sex cells and in which one parent produces offspring that are genetically identical to the parent (8)
reproducción asexual reproducción que no involucra la unión de células sexuales, en la que un solo progenitor produce descendencia que es genéticamente igual al progenitor

B

Bacteria (bak·TIR-ee-uh) a domain made up of prokaryotes that usually have a cell wall and that usually reproduce by cell division (58, 80)
Bacteria un dominio compuesto por procariotes que por lo general tienen pared celular y se reproducen por división celular

binary fission (BY-nuh-ree FISH-uhn) a form of asexual reproduction in single-celled organisms by which one cell divides into two cells of the same size (84)
fisión binaria una forma de reproducción asexual de los organismos unicelulares, por medio de la cual la célula se divide en dos células del mismo tamaño

C

cell (SEL) in biology, the smallest unit that can perform all life processes; cells are covered by a membrane and contain DNA and cytoplasm (6)
célula en biología, la unidad más pequeña que puede realizar todos los procesos vitales; las células están cubiertas por una membrana y tienen ADN y citoplasma

cellular respiration (SEL-yuh-luhr res-puh-RAY-shuhn) the process by which cells use oxygen to produce energy from food (123)
respiración celular el proceso por medio del cual las células utilizan oxígeno para producir energía a partir de los alimentos

chlorophyll (KLOHR-uh-fil) a green pigment that captures light energy for photosynthesis (109)
clorofila un pigmento verde que capta la energía luminosa para la fotosíntesis

consumer (kuhn-SOO-mer) an organism that eats other organisms or organic matter (141)
consumidor un organismo que se alimenta de otros organismos o de materia orgánica

D

dichotomous key (dy-KAHT-uh-muhs KEE) an aid that is used to identify organisms and that consists of the answers to a series of questions (64)
clave dicotómica una ayuda para identificar organismos, que consiste en las respuestas a una serie de preguntas

DNA (dee-en-AY) deoxyribonucleic acid, a molecule that is present in all living cells and that contains the information that determines the traits that a living thing inherits and needs to live (8)
ADN ácido desoxirribonucleico, una molécula que está presente en todas las células vivas y que contiene la información que determina los caracteres que un ser vivo hereda y necesita para vivir

domain (doh-MAYN) in a taxonomic system, one of the three broad groups that all living things fall into (58)
dominio en un sistema taxonómico, uno de los tres amplios grupos al que pertenecen todos los seres vivos

dormant (DOHR-muhnt) describes the inactive state of a seed or other plant part when conditions are unfavorable to growth (130)
aletargado término que describe el estado inactivo de una semilla u otra parte de las plantas cuando las condiciones son desfavorables para el crecimiento

E

endoskeleton (en-doh-SKEL-ih-tn) an internal skeleton made of bone and cartilage (143)
endoesqueleto un esqueleto interno hecho de hueso y cartílago

estivation (es-tuh-VAY-shuhn) a period of inactivity and lowered body temperature that some animals undergo in summer as a protection against hot weather and lack of food (157)
estivación un período de inactividad y menor temperatura corporal por el que pasan algunos animales durante el verano para protegerse del calor y la falta de alimento

Eukarya (yoo-KAIR-ee-uh) in a modern taxonomic system, a domain made up of all eukaryotes; this domain aligns with the traditional kingdoms Protista, Fungi, Piantae, and Animalia (59)
Eukarya en un sistema taxonómico moderno, un dominio compuesto por todos los eucariotes; este dominio coincide con los reinos tradicionales Protista, Fungi, Plantae y Animalia

evolution (ev-uh-LOO-shuhn) the process in which inherited characteristics within a population change over generations such that new species sometimes arise (16)
evolución el proceso por medio del cual las características heredadas dentro de una población cambian con el transcurso de las generaciones de manera tal que a veces surgen nuevas especies

exoskeleton (ek-soh-SKEL-ih-tn) a hard, external, supporting structure (143)
exoesqueleto una estructura de soporte, dura y externa

extinction (ek-STINGK-shuhn) the death of every member of a species (23, 31, 41)
extinción la muerte de todos los miembros de una especie

F

fossil (FAHS-uhl) the trace or remains of an organism that lived long ago, most commonly preserved in sedimentary rock (31, 40)
fósil los indicios o los restos de un organismo que vivió hace mucho tiempo, comúnmente preservados en las rocas sedimentarias

fossil record (FAHS-uhl REK-erd) the history of life in the geologic past as indicated by the traces or remains of living things (31, 40)
registro fósil la historia de la vida en el pasado geológico según la indican los rastros o restos de seres vivos

Fungi (FUHN-jy) a kingdom made up of nongreen, eukaryotic organisms that have no means of movement, reproduce by using spores, and get food by breaking down substances in their surroundings and absorbing the nutrients (60, 100)
Fungi un reino formado por organismos eucarióticos no verdes que no tienen capacidad de movimiento, se reproducen por esporas y obtienen alimento al descomponer sustancias de su entorno y absorber los nutrientes

G

gamete (GAM-eet) a haploid reproductive cell that unites with another haploid reproductive cell to form a zygote (97)
gameto una célula reproductiva haploide que se une con otra célula reproductiva haploide para formar un cigoto

genus (JEE-nuhs) the level of classification that comes after family and that contains similar species (56)
género el nivel de clasificación que viene después de la familia y que contiene especies similares

geologic time scale (jee-uh-LAHJ-ik TYM SKAYL) the standard method used to divide Earth's long natural history into manageable parts (42)
escala de tiempo geológico el método estándar que se usa para dividir la larga historia natural de la Tierra en partes razonables

gymnosperm (JIM-nuh-sperm) a woody, vascular seed plant whose seeds are not enclosed by an ovary or fruit (114)
gimnosperma una planta leñosa vascular que produce semillas que no están contenidas en un ovario o fruto

H

hibernation (hy-buhr-NAY-shuhn) a period of inactivity and lowered body temperature that some animals undergo in winter as a protection against cold weather and lack of food (157)
hibernación un período de inactividad y disminución de la temperatura del cuerpo que algunos animales experimentan en invierno como protección contra el tiempo frío y la escasez de comida

homeostasis (hoh-mee-oh-STAY-sis) the maintenance of a constant internal state in a changing environment (7)
homeostasis la capacidad de mantener un estado interno constante en un ambiente en cambio

host (HOHST) an organism from which a parasite takes food or shelter (88)
huésped el organismo del cual un parásito obtiene alimento y refugio

hypha (HY-fuh) a nonreproductive filament of a fungus (100)
hifa un filamento no-reproductor de un hongo

I–K

innate behavior (ih-NAYT bih-HAYV-yer) an inherited behavior that does not depend on the environment or experience (153)
conducta innata una conducta heredada que no depende del ambiente ni de la experiencia

invertebrate (in-VER-tuh-brit) an animal that does not have a backbone (143)
invertebrado un animal que no tiene columna vertebral

L

learned behavior (LERND bih-HAYV-yer) a behavior that has been learned from experience (153)
conducta aprendida una conducta que se ha aprendido por experiencia

lichen (LY-kuhn) a mass of fungal and algal cells that grow together in a symbiotic relationship and that are usually found on rocks or trees (103)
liquen una masa de células de hongos y de algas que crecen juntas en una relación simbiótica y que normalmente se encuentran en rocas o árboles

M

migration (my-GRAY-shuhn) in general, any movement of individuals or populations from one location to another; specifically, a periodic group movement that is characteristic of a given population or species (157)
migración en general, cualquier movimiento de individuos o poblaciones de un lugar a otro; específicamente, un movimiento periódico en grupo que es característico de una población o especie determinada

mutation (myoo-TAY-shuhn) a change in the nucleotide-base sequence of a gene or DNA molecule (20)
mutación un cambio en la secuencia de la base de nucleótidos de un gene o de una molécula de ADN

mycorrhiza (my-kuh-RY-zuh) a symbiotic association between fungi and plant roots (103)
micorriza una asociación simbiótica entre los hongos y las raíces de las plantas

N–O

natural selection (NACH-uhr-uhl sih-LEK-shuhn) the process by which individuals that are better adapted to their environment survive and reproduce more successfully than less-well-adapted individuals do (20)
selección natural el proceso por medio del cual los individuos que están mejor adaptados a su ambiente sobreviven y se reproducen con más éxito que los individuos menos adaptados

P–R

photosynthesis (foh-toh-SIN-thih-sis) the process by which plants, algae, and some bacteria use sunlight, carbon dioxide, and water to make food (109)
fotosíntesis el proceso por medio del cual las plantas, las algas y algunas bacterias utilizan la luz solar, el dióxido de carbono y el agua para producir alimento

pistil (PIS-tuhl) the female reproductive part of a flower that produces seeds and consists of an ovary, style, and stigma (126)
pistilo la parte reproductora femenina de una flor, la cual produce semillas y está formada por el ovario, estilo y estigma

Plantae (PLAN-tee) a kingdom made up of complex, multicellular organisms that are usually green, have cell walls made of cellulose, cannot move around, and use the sun's energy to make sugar by photosynthesis (61)
Plantae un reino formado por organismos pluricelulares complejos que normalmente son verdes, tienen una pared celular de celulosa, no tienen capacidad de movimiento y utilizan la energía del Sol para producir azúcar mediante la fotosíntesis

pollen (PAHL-uhn) the tiny granules that contain the male gametophyte of seed plants (114)
polen los gránulos diminutos que contienen el gametofito masculino en las plantas con semilla

pollination (pahl-uh-NAY-shuhn) the transfer of pollen from the male reproductive structures to the female structures of seed plants (125)
polinización la transferencia de polen de las estructuras reproductoras masculinas a las estructuras femeninas de las plantas con semillas

producer (pruh-DOO-ser) an organism that can make its own food by using energy from its surroundings (109)
productor un organismo que puede elaborar sus propios alimentos utilizando la energía de su entorno

Protista (proh-TIS-tuh) a kingdom of mostly one-celled eukaryotic organisms that are different from plants, animals, archaea, bacteria, and fungi (60, 94)
Protista un reino compuesto principalmente por organismos eucarióticos unicelulares que son diferentes de las plantas, animales, arqueas, bacterias y hongos

S

seed (SEED) a plant embryo that is enclosed in a protective coat (114)
semilla el embrión de una planta que está encerrado en una cubierta protectora

sexual reproduction (SEK-shoo-uhl ree-pruh-DUHK-shuhn) reproduction in which the sex cells from two parents unite to produce offspring that share traits from both parents (8)
reproducción sexual reproducción en la que se unen las células sexuales de los dos progenitores para producir descendencia que comparte caracteres de ambos progenitores

social behavior (SOH-shuhl bih-HAYV-yer) the interaction between animals of the same species (158)
comportamiento social la interacción entre animales de la misma especie

species (SPEE-sheez) a group of organisms that are closely related and can mate to produce fertile offspring (56)
especie un grupo de organismos que tienen un parentesco cercano y que pueden aparearse para producir descendencia fértil

spore (SPOHR) a reproductive cell or multicellular structure that is resistant to stressful environmental conditions and that can develop into an adult without fusing with another cell (97)
espora una célula reproductora o estructura pluricelular que resiste las condiciones ambientales adversas y que se puede desarrollar hasta convertirse en un adulto sin necesidad de fusionarse con otra célula

stamen (STAY-muhn) the male reproductive structure of a flower that produces pollen and consists of an anther at the tip of a filament (126)
estambre la estructura reproductora masculina de una flor, que produce polen y está formada por una antera ubicada en la punta del filamento

stimulus (STIM-yuh-luhs) anything that causes a reaction or change in an organism or any part of an organism (7, 128, 152)
estímulo cualquier cosa que causa una reacción o cambio en un organismo o cualquier parte de un organismo

T–U

territory (TEHR-ih-tohr-ee) an area that is occupied by one animal or a group of animals that do not allow other members of the species to enter (154)
territorio un área que está ocupada por un animal o por un grupo de animales que no permiten que entren otros miembros de la especie

transpiration (tran-spuh-RAY-shuhn) the process by which plants release water vapor into the air through stomata; also the release of water vapor into the air by other organisms (128)
transpiración el proceso por medio del cual las plantas liberan vapor de agua al aire por medio de los estomas; también, la liberación de vapor de agua al aire por otros organismos

tropism (TROH-piz-uhm) growth of all or part of an organism in response to an external stimulus, such as light (129)
tropismo el crecimiento de un organismo o de una parte de él en respuesta a un estímulo externo, como por ejemplo, la luz

V-Z

variation (vair·ee·AY·shuhn) the occurrence of hereditary or nonhereditary differences between different invidivuals of a population (20)

variabilidad la incidencia de diferencias hereditarias o no hereditarias entre distintos individuos de una población

vascular system (VAS·kyuh·ler SIS·tuhm) a conducting system of tissues that transport water and other materials in plants or in animals (110)

sistema vascular un sistema de transporte de los tejidos que lleva agua y otros materiales en las plantas o en los animales

vertebrate (VER·tuh·brit) an animal that has a backbone (143)

vertebrado un animal que tiene columna vertebral

virus (VY·ruhs) a nonliving, infectious particle composed of a nucleic acid and a protein coat; it can invade and destroy a cell (86)

virus una partícula infecciosa sin vida formada por un ácido nucleico y una cubierta de proteína; puede invadir una célula y destruirla

COMMON CORE

State STANDARDS FOR ENGLISH LANGUAGE ARTS
Correlations

This table shows correlations to the *Reading Standards for Literacy in Science and Technical Subjects* for grades 6–8.

⊙ **Go online at thinkcentral.com** for correlations of all *ScienceFusion* Modules to Common Core State Standards for Mathematics and to the rest of the *Common Core State Standards for English Language Arts*.

Grade 6–8 Standard Code	Citations for Module K "Introduction to Science and Technology"
READING STANDARDS FOR LITERACY IN SCIENCE AND TECHNICAL SUBJECTS	
Key Ideas and Details	
RST.6–8.1 Cite specific textual evidence to support analysis of science and technical texts.	*Student Edition* pp. 25, 75, 113 *Teacher Edition* pp. 98, 117
RST.6–8.2 Determine the central ideas or conclusions of a text; provide an accurate summary of the text distinct from prior knowledge or opinions.	*Student Edition* pp. 25, 32, 60, 75, 113, 132, 137, 149, 157, 163, 171, 189 *Teacher Edition* pp. 17, 21, 22, 35, 51, 61, 62, 98, 106, 117, 128, 130, 161, 178, 179, 206, 213, 237, 240. Also use "Synthesizing Key Topics" items in the Extend Science Concepts sections of the Teacher Edition.
RST.6–8.3 Follow precisely a multistep procedure when carrying out experiments, taking measurements, or performing technical tasks.	*Student Edition* pp. 83, 90–91 *Teacher Edition* p. 94 *Other* Use the Lab Manual, Project-Based Assessments, Video-Based Projects, and the Virtual Labs.
Craft and Structure	
RST.6–8.4 Determine the meaning of symbols, key terms, and other domain-specific words and phrases as they are used in a specific scientific or technical context relevant to *grades 6–8 texts and topics*.	*Student Edition* pp. 5, 17, 31, 43, 63, 64, 77, 93, 115, 131, 141, 153, 169, 181 *Teacher Edition* p. 111. Also use "Previewing Vocabulary" and "Reinforcing Vocabulary" items in the Explain Science Concepts sections of the Teacher Edition.

Grade 6–8 Standard Code (continued)	Citations for Module K "Introduction to Science and Technology"
RST.6–8.5 Analyze the structure an author uses to organize a text, including how the major sections contribute to the whole and to an understanding of the topic.	*Student Edition* p. 75 *Teacher Edition* pp. 51, 128, 213, 237, 240
RST.6–8.6 Analyze the author's purpose in providing an explanation, describing a procedure, or discussing an experiment in a text.	*Student Edition* pp. 25, 75 *Teacher Edition* pp. 14, 47, 98

Integration of Knowledge and Ideas

RST.6–8.7 Integrate quantitative or technical information expressed in words in a text with a version of that information expressed visually (e.g., in a flowchart, diagram, model, graph, or table).	*Student Edition* pp. 3, 35, 54, 66–67, 81, 122–123, 144, 147, 158, 159 *Teacher Edition* pp. 21, 40, 53, 54, 123, 194, 201, 206, 208, 224, 237, 240. Also use the "Graphic Organizer" items in the Teacher Edition. *Other* Use the lessons in the Digital Path.
RST.6–8.8 Distinguish among facts, reasoned judgment based on research findings, and speculation in a text.	*Student Edition* pp. 13, 25, 74–75, 113 *Teacher Edition* pp. 14, 17, 98
RST.6–8.9 Compare and contrast the information gained from experiments, simulations, video, or multimedia sources with that gained from reading a text on the same topic.	*Student Edition* pp. 113, 137, 163 *Teacher Edition* pp. 40, 79, 117 *Other* Use the Lab Manual, Project-Based Assessments, Video-Based Projects, and the lessons in the Digital Path.

Range of Reading and Level of Text Complexity

RST.6–8.10 By the end of grade 8, read and comprehend science/technical texts in the grades 6–8 text complexity band independently and proficiently.	*Student Edition* pp. 3, 22, 75, 90, 113, 132, 137, 149, 157, 163, 171, 189. Also use all lessons in the Student Edition. *Teacher Edition* pp. 47, 48, 61, 62, 117

Bibliography

This bibliography is a compilation of trade books that can supplement the materials covered in *ScienceFusion* Grades 6–8. Many of the books are recommendations of the National Science Teachers Association (NSTA) and the Children's Book Council (CBC) as outstanding science trade books for children. These books were selected because they meet the following rigorous criteria: they are of literary quality and contain substantial science content; the theories and facts are clearly distinguished; they are free of gender, ethnic, and socioeconomic bias; and they contain clear, accurate, up-to-date information. Several selections are award-winning titles, or their authors have received awards.

As with all materials you share with your class, we suggest you review the books first to ensure their appropriateness. While titles are current at time of publication, they may go out of print without notice.

Grades 6–8

Acids and Bases (Material Matters/ Express Edition) by Carol Baldwin (Heinemann-Raintree, 2005) focuses on the properties of acids and bases with photographs and facts.

Acids and Bases by Eurona Earl Tilley (Chelsea House, 2008) provides a thorough, basic understanding of acid and base chemistry, including such topics as naming compounds, writing formulas, and physical and chemical properties.

Across the Wide Ocean: The Why, How, and Where of Navigation for Humans and Animals at Sea by Karen Romano Young (Greenwillow, 2007) focuses on navigational tools, maps, and charts that researchers and explorers use to learn more about oceanography. AWARD-WINNING AUTHOR

Adventures in Sound with Max Axiom, Super Scientist (Graphic Science Series) by Emily Sohn (Capstone, 2007) provides information about sound through a fun graphic novel.

Air: A Resource Our World Depends on (Managing Our Resources) by Ian Graham (Heinemann-Raintree, 2005) examines this valuable natural resource and answers questions such as "How much does Earth's air weigh?" and "Why do plants need wind?"

The Alkaline Earth Metals: Beryllium, Magnesium, Calcium, Strontium, Barium, Radium (Understanding the Elements of the Periodic Table) by Bridget Heos (Rosen Central, 2009) describes the characteristics of these metals, including their similar physical and molecular properties.

All About Light and Sound (Mission: Science) by Connie Jankowski (Compass Point, 2010) focuses on the importance of light and sound and how without them we could not survive.

Alternative Energy: Beyond Fossil Fuels by Dana Meachen Rau (Compass Point, 2010) discusses the ways that water, wind, and sun provide a promising solution to our energy crisis and encourages readers to help the planet by conserving energy. AWARD-WINNING AUTHOR

Amazing Biome Projects You Can Build Yourself (Build it Yourself Series) by Donna Latham (Nomad, 2009) provides an overview of eight terrestrial biomes, including characteristics about climate, soil, animals, and plants.

Archaea: Salt-Lovers, Methane-Makers, Thermophiles, and Other Archaeans (A Class of Their Own) by David M. Barker (Crabtree, 2010) provides interesting facts about different types of archaeans.

The Art of Construction: Projects and Principles for Beginning Engineers and Architects by Mario Salvadori (Chicago Review, 2000) explains how tents, houses, stadiums, and bridges are built, and how to build models of such structures using materials found around the house. AWARD-WINNING AUTHOR

Astronomy: Out of This World! by Simon Basher and Dan Green (Kingfisher, 2009) takes readers on a journey of the universe and provides information about the planets, stars, galaxies, telescopes, space missions, and discoveries.

At the Sea Floor Café: Odd Ocean Critter Poems by Leslie Bulion (Peachtree, 2011) provides poetry to educate students about how ocean creatures search for food, capture prey, protect their young, and trick their predators.

Battery Science: Make Widgets That Work and Gadgets That Go by Doug Stillinger (Klutz, 2003) offers an array of activities and gadgets to get students excited about electricity.

The Biggest Explosions in the Universe by Sara Howard (BookSurge, 2009) tells the story of stars in our universe through fun text and captivating photographs.

Biology: Life as We Know It! by Simon Basher and Dan Green (Kingfisher, 2008) offers information about all aspects of life from the animals and plants to the minuscule cells, proteins, and DNA that bring them to life.

Birds of a Feather by Jane Yolen (Boyds Mills Press, 2011) offers facts and information about birds through fun poetry and beautiful photographs. AWARD-WINNING AUTHOR

Blackout!: Electricity and Circuits (Fusion) by Anna Claybourne (Heinemann-Raintree, 2005) provides an array of facts about electricity and how we rely on it for so many things in everyday life. AWARD-WINNING AUTHOR

Cell Division and Genetics by Robert Snedden (Heinemann, 2007) explains various aspects of cells and the living world, including what happens when cells divide and how characteristics are passed on from one generation to another. AWARD-WINNING AUTHOR

Chemistry: Getting a Big Reaction by Dan Green and Simon Basher (Kingfisher, 2010) acts as a guide about the chemical "characters" that fizz, react, and combine to make up everything around us.

Cool Stuff Exploded by Chris Woodford (Dorling Kindersley, 2008) focuses on today's technological marvels and tomorrow's jaw-dropping devices. OUTSTANDING SCIENCE TRADE BOOK

Disaster Deferred: How New Science Is Changing Our View of Earthquake Hazards in the Midwest by Seth Stein (Columbia University, 2010) discusses technological innovations that make earthquake prediction possible.

The Diversity of Species (Timeline: Life on Earth) by Michael Bright (Heinemann, 2008) explains how and why things on Earth have genetic and physical differences and how they have had and continue to have an impact on Earth.

Drip! Drop!: How Water Gets to Your Tap by Barbara Seuling (Holiday House, 2000) introduces students to JoJo and her dog, Willy, who explain the water cycle and introduce fun experiments about filtration, evaporation, and condensation. AWARD-WINNING AUTHOR

Eat Fresh Food: Awesome Recipes for Teen Chefs by Rozanne Gold (Bloomsbury, 2009) includes more than 80 recipes and places a strong emphasis on fresh foods throughout the book.

Eco-Tracking: On the Trail of Habitat Change (Worlds of Wonder) by Daniel Shaw (University of New Mexico, 2010) recounts success stories of young people involved in citizen science efforts and encourages others to join in to preserve nature's ecosystems.

Electric Mischief: Battery-Powered Gadgets Kids Can Build by Alan Bartholomew (Kids Can Press, 2002) offers a variety of fun projects that include making battery connections and switches and building gadgets such as electric dice and a bumper car.

Electricity (Why It Works) by Anna Claybourne (QED Publishing, 2008) provides information about electricity in an easy-to-follow manner. AWARD-WINNING AUTHOR

Electricity and Magnetism (Usborne Understand Science) by Peter Adamczyk (Usborne, 2008) explains the basics about electricity and magnetism, including information about static electricity, electric circuits, and electromagnetism.

Energy Transfers (Energy Essentials) by Nigel Saunders and Steven Chapman (Raintree, 2005) explains the different types of energy, how they can change, and how different forms of energy help us in our everyday lives.

The Everything Machine by Matt Novak (Roaring Brook, 2009) tells the silly story of a machine that does everything for a group of people until they wake up one day and discover that the machine has stopped working. AWARD-WINNING AUTHOR

Experiments with Plants and Other Living Things by Trevor Cook (PowerKids, 2009) provides fun, hands-on experiments to teach students about flowers, plants, and biology.

Exploring the Oceans: Seafloor by John Woodward (Heinemann, 2004) takes readers on a virtual tour through the bottom part of the ocean, highlighting the plants and animals that thrive in this environment.

Extreme Structures: Mega Constructions of the 21st Century (Science Frontiers) by David Jefferis (Crabtree, 2006) takes a look at how some of the coolest buildings in the world were built and what other kinds of structures are being planned for the future. AWARD-WINNING AUTHOR

Fascinating Science Projects: Electricity and Magnetism by Bobbi Searle (Aladdin, 2002) teaches the concepts of electricity and magnetism through dozens of projects and experiments and color illustrations.

Fizz, Bubble and Flash!: Element Explorations and Atom Adventures for Hands-on Science Fun! by Anita Brandolini, Ph.D. (Williamson, 2003) introduces chemistry to students in a nonintimidating way and focuses on the elements and the periodic table. PARENTS' CHOICE

Floods: Hazards of Surface and Groundwater Systems (The Hazardous Earth) by Timothy M. Kusky (Facts on File, 2008) explores the processes that control the development and flow in river and stream systems and when these processes become dangerous.

Fossils (Geology Rocks!) by Rebecca Faulkner (Raintree, 2008) educates students about rock formation and the processes and characteristics of rocks and fossils.

Friends: True Stories of Extraordinary Animal Friendships by Catherine Thimmesh (Houghton Mifflin Harcourt, 2011) depicts true stories of unlikely animal friendships, including a wild polar bear and a sled dog as well as a camel and a Vietnamese pig. AWARD-WINNING AUTHOR

The Frog Scientist (Scientists in the Field) by Pamela S. Turner (Houghton Mifflin Harcourt, 2009) follows a scientist and his protégés as they research the effects of atrazine-contaminated water on vulnerable amphibians. BOOKLIST EDITORS' CHOICE

From Steam Engines to Nuclear Fusion: Discovering Energy (Chain Reactions) by Carol Ballard (Heinemann-Raintree, 2007) tells the fascinating story of energy, from the heat produced by a simple fire to the extraordinary power contained in an atom.

Fully Charged (Everyday Science) by Steve Parker (Heinemann-Raintree, 2005) explains how electricity is generated, harnessed, and used and also the difference between electricity, including static electricity, and electronics. AWARD-WINNING AUTHOR

Galileo for Kids: His Life and Ideas by Richard Panchyk (Chicago Review, 2005) includes experiments that demonstrate scientific principles developed by the astronomer Galileo.

Genes and DNA by Richard Walker (Kingfisher, 2003) offers an abundance of information about characteristics of genes, gene function, DNA technology, and genetic engineering, as well as other fascinating topics. NSTA TRADE BOOK; OUTSTANDING SCIENCE TRADE BOOK

Hands-on Science Series: Simple Machines by Steven Souza and Joseph Shortell (Walch, 2001) investigates the concepts of work, force, power, efficiency, and mechanical advantage.

How Animals Work by David Burnie (Dorling Kindersley, 2010) provides vivid photographs and intriguing text to describe various animals and their characteristics, diets, and families. AWARD-WINNING AUTHOR

How Does an Earthquake Become a Tsunami? (How Does it Happen?) by Linda Tagliaferro (Heinemann-Raintree, 2009) describes the changes in water, waves, and tides that occur between an earthquake and a tsunami. AWARD-WINNING AUTHOR

How the Future Began: Machines by Clive Gifford (Kingfisher, 1999) acts as a guide to historical and current developments in the field of machinery, including mass production, computers, robots, microengineering, and communications technology. AWARD-WINNING AUTHOR

How Scientists Work (Simply Science) by Natalie M. Rosinsky (Compass Point, 2003) discusses the scientific method, equipment, and procedures and also describes how scientists compile information and answer questions.

How to Clean a Hippopotamus: A Look at Unusual Animal Partnerships by Steve Jenkins and Robin Page (Houghton Mifflin Harcourt, 2010) explores animal symbiosis with fun illustrations and a close-up, step-by-step view of some of nature's most fascinating animal partnerships. ALA NOTABLE BOOK

Human Spaceflight (Frontiers in Space) by Joseph A. Angelo (Facts on File, 2007) examines the history of space exploration and the evolution of space technology from the dawn of the space age to the present time.

The Hydrosphere: Agent of Change by Gregory L. Vogt, Ed.D. (Twenty-First Century, 2006) discusses the impact this 20-mile-thick sphere has had on the surface of the planet and the processes that go on there, including the ability of Earth to sustain life. AWARD-WINNING AUTHOR

In Rivers, Lakes, and Ponds (Under the Microscope) by Sabrina Crewe (Chelsea Clubhouse, 2010) educates readers about the microscopic critters that live in these various bodies of water.

A Kid's Guide to Climate Change and Global Warming: How to Take Action! by Cathryn Berger Kaye, M.A. (Free Spirit, 2009) encourages students to learn about the climate changes happening around the world and to get involved to help save our planet.

Lasers (Lucent Library of Science and Technology) by Don Nardo (Lucent, 2003) discusses the scientific discovery and development of lasers—high-intensity light—and their use in our daily lives. AWARD-WINNING AUTHOR

Leonardo's Horse by Jean Fritz (Putnam, 2001) tells the story of Leonardo da Vinci—the curious and inquisitive artist, engineer, and astronomer—who created a detailed horse sculpture for the city of Milan. ALA NOTABLE BOOK; NOTABLE SOCIAL STUDIES TRADE BOOK; NOTABLE CHILDREN'S BOOK IN THE LANGUAGE ARTS

Light: From Sun to Bulbs by Christopher Cooper (Heinemann, 2003) invites students to investigate the dazzling world of physical science and light through fun experiments. AWARD-WINNING AUTHOR

Magnetism and Electromagnets (Sci-Hi: Physical Science) by Eve Hartman (Raintree, 2008) offers colorful illustrations, photographs, quizzes, charts, graphs, and text to teach students about magnetism.

Making Good Choices About Nonrenewable Resources (Green Matters) by Paula Johanson (Rosen Central, 2009) focuses on the different types of nonrenewable natural resources, alternative resources, conservation, and making positive consumer choices.

Making Waves: Sound (Everyday Science) by Steve Parker (Heinemann-Raintree, 2005) describes what sound is, how it is formed and used, and properties associated with sound, such as pitch, speed, and volume. AWARD-WINNING AUTHOR

The Manatee Scientists: Saving Vulnerable Species (Scientists in the Field Series) by Peter Lourie (Houghton Mifflin Harcourt, 2011) discusses three species of manatees and the importance of preserving these mammals. AWARD-WINNING AUTHOR

The Man Who Named the Clouds by Julie Hannah and Joan Holub (Albert Whitman, 2006) tells the story of 18th-century English meteorologist Luke Howard and also discusses the ten classifications of clouds.

Medicine in the News (Science News Flash) by Brian R. Shmaefsky, Ph.D. (Chelsea House, 2007) focuses on medical advancements that are in the news today and the innovative tools that are used for diagnosis and treatment.

Metals and Metalloids (Periodic Table of the Elements) by Monica Halka, Ph.D., and Brian Nordstrom, Ed.D. (Facts on File, 2010), offers information about the physics, chemistry, geology, and biology of metals and metalloids.

Meteorology: Ferguson's Careers in Focus by Ferguson (Ferguson, 2011) profiles 18 different careers pertaining to the science of the atmosphere and its phenomena.

The Microscope (Great Medical Discoveries) by Adam Woog (Lucent, 2003) recounts how the microscope has had an impact on the history of medicine.

Microscopes and Telescopes: Great Inventions by Rebecca Stefoff (Marshall Cavendish Benchmark, 2007) describes the origin, history, development, and societal impact of the telescope and microscope. OUTSTANDING SCIENCE TRADE BOOK

Mighty Animal Cells by Rebecca L. Johnson (Millbrook, 2007) takes readers on a journey to discover how people and animals grow from just one single cell. AWARD-WINNING AUTHOR

Moon (Eyewitness Books) by Jacqueline Mitton (Dorling Kindersley, 2009) offers information about our planet's mysterious nearest neighbor, from the moon's waterless seas and massive craters to its effect on Earth's ocean tides and its role in solar eclipses. AWARD-WINNING AUTHOR

MP3 Players (Let's Explore Technology Communications) by Jeanne Sturm (Rourke, 2010) discusses the technological advances in music in our society.

Nanotechnologist (Cool Science Careers) by Ann Heinrichs (Cherry Lake, 2009) provides information about nanotechnologists—scientists who work with materials on a subatomic or atomic level.

Ocean: An Illustrated Atlas by Sylvia A. Earle (National Geographic, 2008) provides an overview on the ocean as a whole, each of the major ocean basins, and the future of the oceans. AWARD-WINNING AUTHOR

Oceans (Insiders) by Beverly McMillan and John A. Musick (Simon & Schuster, 2007) takes readers on a 3-D journey of the aquatic universe—exploring the formation of waves and tsunamis as well as the plant and animal species that live beneath the ocean's surface.

Organic Chemistry and Biochemistry (Facts at Your Fingertips) by Graham Bateman (Brown Bear, 2011) provides diagrams, experiments, and testing aids to teach students the basics about organic chemistry and biochemistry.

An Overcrowded World?: Our Impact on the Planet (21st Century Debates) by Rob Bowden (Heinemann, 2002) investigates how and why the world's population is growing so fast, the effects of this growth on wildlife and habitats, and the pressure on resources, and suggests ways of controlling growth.

The Pebble in My Pocket: A History of Our Earth by Meredith Hooper (Viking, 1996) follows the course of a pebble, beginning 480 million years ago, through a fiery volcano and primordial forest and along the icy bottom of a glacier and how it looks today as the result of its journey. AWARD-WINNING AUTHOR

The Periodic Table: Elements with Style! by Simon Basher and Adrian Dingle (Kingfisher, 2007) offers information about the different elements that make up the periodic table and their features and characteristics.

Phenomena: Secrets of the Senses by Donna M. Jackson (Little, Brown, 2008) focuses on the senses and how to interpret them and discusses ways that technology is changing how we experience the world around us. AWARD-WINNING AUTHOR

Pioneers of Light and Sound (Mission: Science) by Connie Jankowski (Compass Point, 2010) focuses on various scientists and their accomplishments and achievements.

Planet Animal: Saving Earth's Disappearing Animals by B. Taylor (Barron's, 2009) focuses on the planet's most endangered animals, their relationships to the environment, and steps that are being taken to try to save these animals from extinction.

Plant and Animal Science Fair Projects (Biology Science Projects Using the Scientific Method) by Yael Calhoun (Enslow, 2010) provides an array of experiments about plants and animals and describes the importance of the scientific method, forming a hypothesis, and recording data for any given project.

Plant Secrets: Plant Life Processes by Anna Claybourne (Heinemann-Raintree, 2005) includes informative text, vivid photographs, and detailed charts about characteristics of various plants. AWARD-WINNING AUTHOR

Polar Regions: Human Impacts (Our Fragile Planet) by Dana Desonie (Chelsea House, 2008) focuses on pollutants and global warming in the Arctic and Antarctic and future dangers that will occur if our planet continues on its current path.

Potato Clocks and Solar Cars: Renewable and Non-renewable Energy by Elizabeth Raum (Raintree, 2007) explores various topics, including alternative energy sources, fossil fuels, and sustainable energy.

The Power of Pressure (How Things Work) by Andrew Dunn (Thomson Learning, 1993) explains how water pressure and air work and how they are used in machines.

Protists and Fungi (Discovery Channel School Science) by Katie King and Jacqueline A. Ball (Gareth Stevens, 2003) focuses on the appearance, behavior, and characteristics of various protists and fungi, using examples of algae, mold, and mushrooms.

Protozoans, Algae and Other Protists by Steve Parker (Compass Point, 2010) introduces readers to the parts, life cycles, and reproduction of various types of protists, from microscopic protozoans to seaweedlike algae, and some of the harmful effects protists have on humans. AWARD-WINNING AUTHOR

Sally Ride: The First American Woman in Space by Tom Riddolls (Crabtree, 2010) focuses on the growth and impact of Sally Ride Science—an educational program founded by the astronaut to encourage girls to pursue hobbies and careers in science.

Science and Technology in 20th Century American Life by Christopher Cumo (Greenwood, 2008) takes readers on a history of technology from agricultural implements through modern computers, telecommunications, and skateboards.

Sedimentary Rock (Geology Rocks!) by Rebecca Faulkner (Raintree, 2008) educates students about rock formation and the processes and characteristics of sedimentary rock.

Shaping the Earth by Dorothy Hinshaw Patent (Clarion/Houghton Mifflin, 2000) combines vivid photographs with informative text to explain the forces that have created the geological features on Earth's surface. AWARD-WINNING AUTHOR

Silent Spring by Rachel Carson (Houghton Mifflin, 2002) celebrates marine biologist and environmental activist Rachel Carson's contribution to Earth through an array of essays.

Skywalkers: Mohawk Ironworkers Build the City by David Weitzman (Flash Point, 2010) focuses on the ironworkers who constructed bridges and skyscrapers in New York and Canada. AWARD-WINNING AUTHOR

Sustaining Earth's Energy Resources (Environment at Risk) by Ann Heinrichs (Marshall Cavendish, 2010) offers information on Earth's sources of nonrenewable and renewable energy, how they are used, and their disadvantages and benefits.

Team Moon: How 400,000 People Landed Apollo 11 on the Moon by Catherine Thimmesh (Houghton Mifflin, 2006) tells the story of the first moon landing and celebrates the dedication, ingenuity, and perseverance of the people who made this event happen. ALA NOTABLE BOOK; ORBIS PICTUS HONOR; NOTABLE CHILDREN'S BOOK IN THE LANGUAGE ARTS; ALA BEST BOOK FOR YOUNG ADULTS; GOLDEN KITE HONOR

The Top of the World: Climbing Mount Everest by Steve Jenkins (Houghton Mifflin, 1999) describes the conditions and terrain of Mount Everest, attempts that have been made to scale this peak, and information about the equipment and techniques of mountain climbing. ALA NOTABLE BOOK; SLJ BEST BOOK; BOSTON GLOBE–HORN BOOK AWARD; ORBIS PICTUS HONOR

Transmission of Power by Fluid Pressure: Air and Water by William Donaldson (Nabu, 2010) describes the transmission of fluid pressure as it pertains to the elements of air and water in the world of motion, forces, and energy.

Tsunami: The True Story of an April Fools' Day Disaster by Gail Langer Karwoski (Darby Creek, 2006) offers a variety of viewpoints about the wave that struck Hawaii in 1946. NOTABLE SOCIAL STUDIES TRADE BOOK

Vapor, Rain, and Snow: The Science of Clouds and Precipitation (Weatherwise) by Paul Fleisher (Lerner, 2010) answers an array of questions about water, such as "How does a cloud form?" and "Why do ice cubes shrink in the freezer?" AWARD-WINNING AUTHOR

Water Supplies in Crisis (Planet in Crisis) by Russ Parker (Rosen Central, 2009) describes a world where safe drinking water is not readily available, polluted water brings disease, and lakes are disappearing.

Weird Meat-Eating Plants (Bizarre Science) by Nathan Aaseng (Enslow, 2011) provides information about a variety of carnivorous plants, reversing the food chain's usual order. AWARD-WINNING AUTHOR

What Are Igneous Rocks? (Let's Rock!) by Molly Aloian (Crabtree, 2010) explains how granite, basalt, lava, silica, and quartz are formed after hot molten rock cools.

What's Living Inside Your Body? by Andrew Solway (Heinemann, 2004) offers information about an array of viruses, germs, and parasites that thrive inside the human body.

Why Should I Bother to Keep Fit? (What's Happening?) by Kate Knighton and Susan Meredith (Usborne, 2009) motivates students to get fit and stay fit.

The World of Microbes: Bacteria, Viruses, and Other Microorganisms (Understanding Genetics) by Janey Levy (Rosen Classroom, 2010) describes the world of microbes, a history of microbiology, and the characteristics of both harmful and beneficial bacteria.

Written in Bone: Buried Lives of Jamestown and Colonial Maryland by Sally M. Walker (Carolrhoda, 2009) describes the way that scientists used forensic anthropology to investigate colonial-era graves near Jamestown, Virginia. ALA NOTABLE BOOK; OUTSTANDING SCIENCE TRADE BOOK; NOTABLE SOCIAL STUDIES TRADE BOOK

You Blink Twelve Times a Minute and Other Freaky Facts About the Human Body by Barbara Seuling (Picture Window, 2009) provides fun and unusual facts about various ailments, medical marvels, and body parts and their functions. AWARD-WINNING AUTHOR

Correlation to
ScienceSaurus

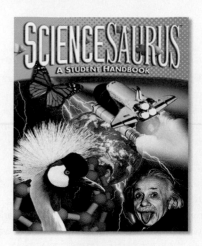

ScienceSaurus, **A Student Handbook,** is a "mini-encyclopedia" that students can use to find out more about unit topics. It contains numerous resources including concise content summaries, an almanac, many tables, charts, and graphs, history of science, and a glossary. **ScienceSaurus** is available from Houghton Mifflin Harcourt..

ScienceFusion **Page References**	**Topics**	*ScienceFusion* **Grades 6-8**
Scientific Investigation, pp. 1–19		
	Scientific Inquiry	Mod K, Unit 1, Lessons 1-3
		Mod K, Unit 2, Lessons 1, 3
	Designing Your Own Investigations	Mod K, Unit 1, Lessons 2, 4
Working in the Lab, pp. 20–72		
	Laboratory Safety	Mod K, Unit 2, Lesson 2
	Glassware and Microscopes	Mod K, Unit 2, Lesson 2
	Measurement	Mod K, Unit 2, Lesson 2
Life Science, pp. 73–164		
	Structure of Life	Mod A, Unit 1, Lessons 1-3
		Mod A, Unit 2, Lessons 1, 3
	Human Biology	Mod C, Unit 1, Lessons 1-6
		Mod C, Unit 2, Lesson 1
	Physiology and Behavior	Mod A, Unit 1, Lesson 5
		Mod B, Unit 2, Lessons 3-6
	Genes and Heredity	Mod A, Unit 2, Lessons 2-6
	Change and Diversity of Life	Mod B, Unit 1, Lessons 2-4

ScienceFusion Page References	Topics	*ScienceFusion* Grades 6-8
Life Science, pp. 73–164 (continued)		
	Ecosystems	Mod D, Unit 1, Lessons 1-4
		Mod D, Unit 2, Lessons 1-4
		Mod D, Unit 2, Lesson 5
	Classification	Mod B, Unit 1, Lesson 5
		Mod B, Unit 2, Lessons 3, 5
Earth Science, pp. 165–248		
	Geology	Mod E, Unit 4, Lesson 1
		Mod E, Unit 3, Lessons 1-3
		Mod E, Unit 4, Lessons 2-5
		Mod E, Unit 1, Lessons 2-4
		Mod E, Unit 2, Lessons 1-4
		Mod E, Unit 1, Lessons 3, 5
	Oceanography	Mod F, Unit 1, Lesson 1
		Mod F, Unit 2, Lessons 1, 3
	Meteorology	Mod F, Unit 3, Lesson 1
		Mod F, Unit 1, Lesson 2
		Mod F, Unit 4, Lesson 1, 2, 3, 6
	Astronomy	Mod G, Unit 3, Lessons 1-3
		Mod G, Unit 2, Lessons 2-6
		Mod G, Unit 1, Lessons 1-3
Physical Science, pp. 249–321		
	Matter	Mod H, Unit 1, Lessons 1-6
		Mod H, Unit 3, Lessons 1-4
		Mod H Unit 4, Lessons 1-3
		Mod H, Unit 5, Lessons 1-3

ScienceFusion Page References	Topics	ScienceFusion Grades 6-8
Physical Science, pp. 249–321 (continued)		
	Forces and Motion	Mod I, Unit 1, Lessons 1-5
		Mod I, Unit 2, Lessons 1-3
	Energy	Mod H, Unit 2, Lessons 1-4
		Mod I, Unit 3, Lessons 1-5
		Mod J, Unit 1, Lessons 1, 2
		Mod J, Unit 2, Lessons 1, 2
		Mod J, Unit 3, Lessons 1-4
Natural Resources and the Environment, pp. 322–353		
	Earth's Natural Resources	Mod D, Unit 3, Lessons 2-5
	Resource Conservation	Mod D, Unit 3, Lesson 5
	Solid Waste and Pollution	Mod D, Unit 4, Lessons 1-4 Mod F, Unit 4, Lesson 7
Science, Technology, and Society, pp. 354–373		
	Science and Technology	Mod A, Unit 2, Lesson 7
		Mod G, Unit 4, Lesson 2
		Mod I, Unit 3, Lesson 6
		Mod J, Unit 2, Lesson 3
		Mod J, Unit 3, Lesson 5
	Science and Society	Mod K, Unit 1, Lesson 4
		Mod K, Unit 3, Lesson 6

ScienceFusion Page References	Topics	*ScienceFusion* Grades 6-8
Almanac, pp. 374–438		
	Scientific Numbers	May be used with all units.
	Using Data Tables and Graphs	Mod K, Unit 2, Lesson 1
	Solving Math Problems in Science	May be used with all units.
	Classroom and Research Skills	May be used with all units.
	Test-Taking Skills	May be used with all units.
	References	May be used with all units.
Yellow Pages, pp. 439–524		
	History of Science Timeline	See People in Science features.
	Famous Scientists	See People in Science features.
	Greek and Latin Word Roots	Glossary
	Glossary of Scientific Terms	Glossary

Index

Key:
Teacher Edition page numbers follow the Student Edition page numbers and are printed in **blue** type.
Student Edition page numbers for highlighted definitions are printed in **boldface** type.
Student Edition page numbers for illustrations, maps, and charts are printed in *italics*.